REFLECTIONS OF WAR

PRAISE FOR
REFLECTIONS OF WAR

'As a career naval officer for over four decades, I have known war throughout my long career. This extraordinary work of photographic literature perfectly illuminates the tragedy and triumph of combat. It illuminates the faces of men and women confronted with their own mortality, fear, and heroism. Above all, the book captures – image by beautifully reconstructed image – the sweep of history in the Second World War. An astonishing work of art.'

Admiral James Stavridis, 16th Supreme Allied Commander of NATO and author of
The Restless Wave: A Novel of the US Navy in WWII

'One of the most important collections of World War II photographs to be found in a generation. Deleuran has restored 150 previously lost photographs and, in so doing, tells a powerful story. These evocative images leave a lasting impression ...'

Historian Dr Helen Fry, author of *The Walls Have Ears: The Greatest Intelligence Operation of World War II*

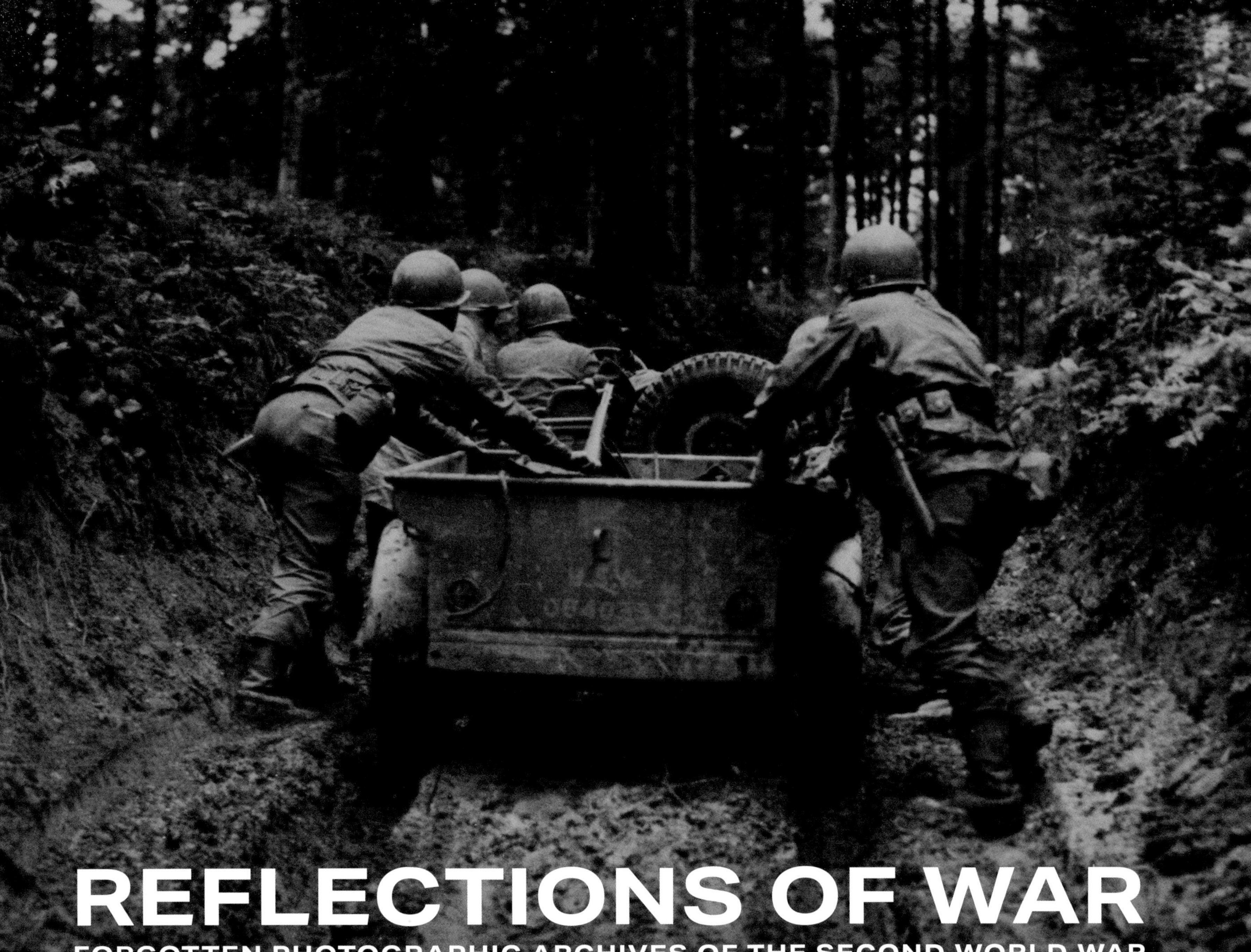

REFLECTIONS OF WAR

FORGOTTEN PHOTOGRAPHIC ARCHIVES OF THE SECOND WORLD WAR

PETER DELEURAN

Our shared destructive past holds the blueprints for avoiding the loss of our shared peaceful future.

First published 2025

The History Press
97 St George's Place, Cheltenham,
Gloucestershire, GL50 3QB
www.thehistorypress.co.uk

British Library Cataloguing in Publication Data.
A catalogue record for this book is available from the British Library.

ISBN 978 1 80399 898 5

Typesetting and origination by The History Press
Printed in Turkey by IMAK

EU Authorised Representative: Easy Access System Europe
Mustamäe tee 50, 10621 Tallinn, Estonia
gpst.request@easproject.com

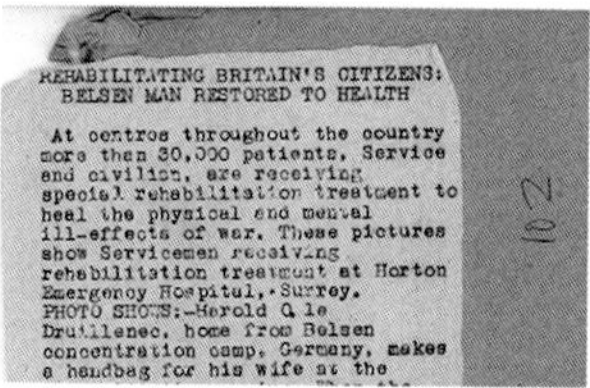
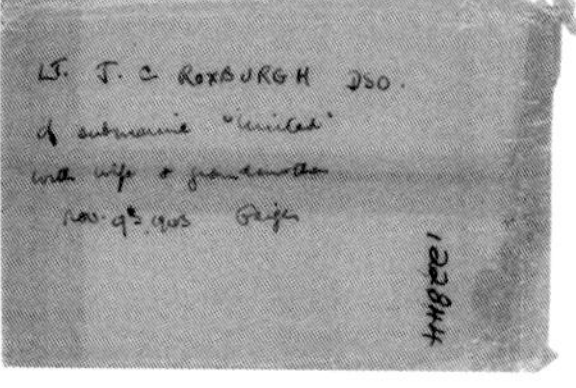
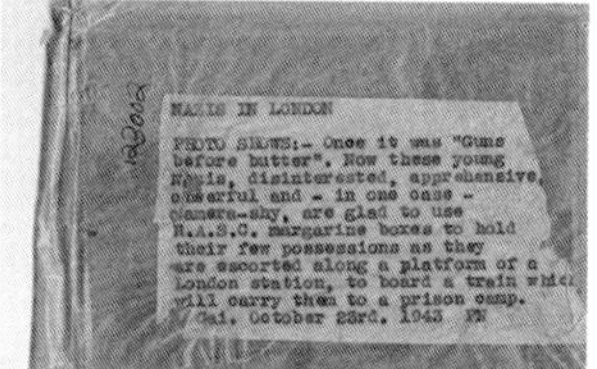
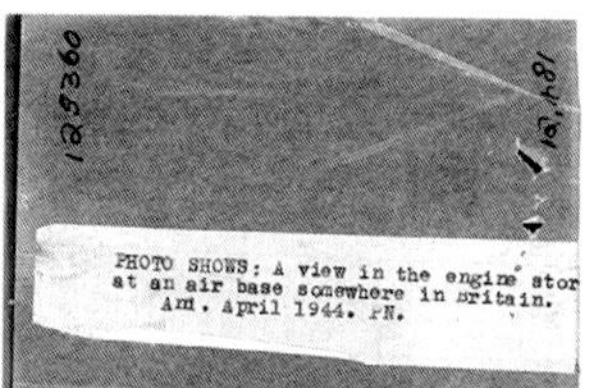
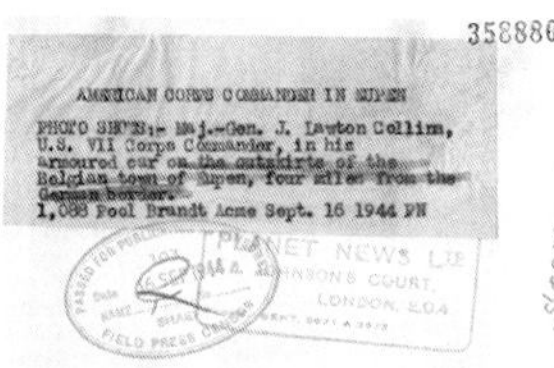
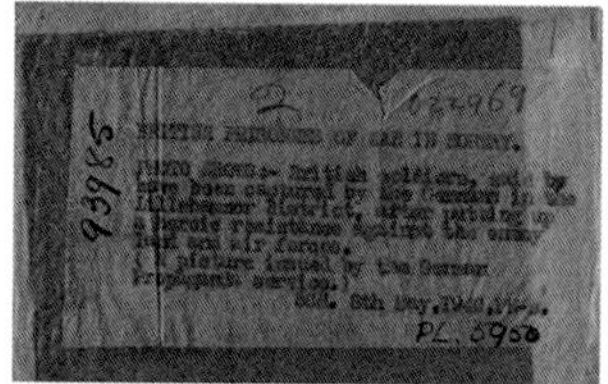
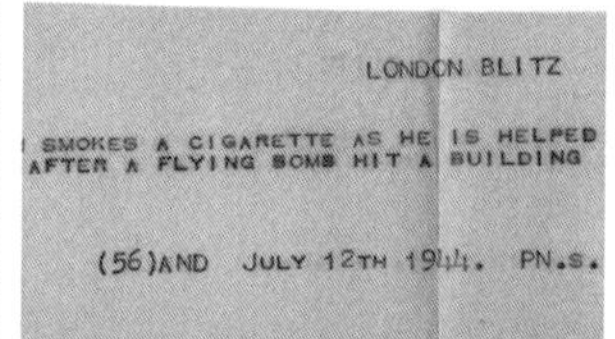
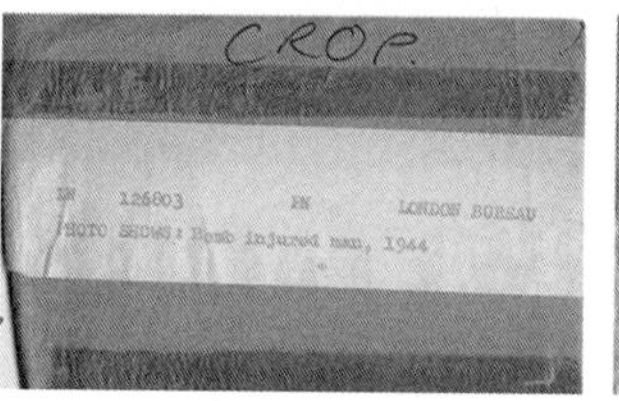
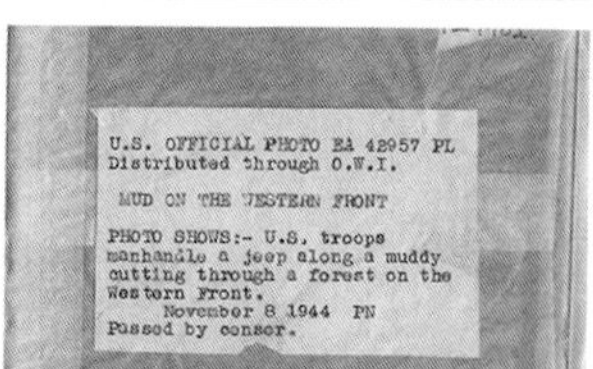
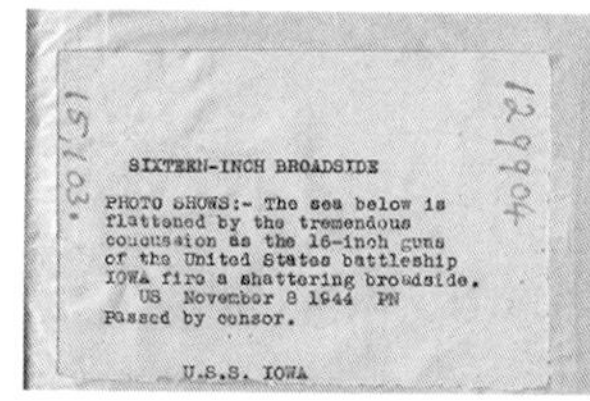
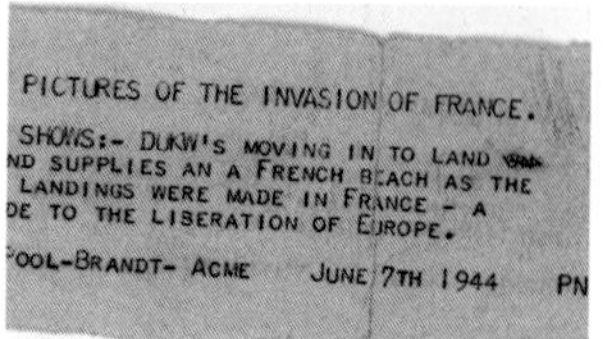
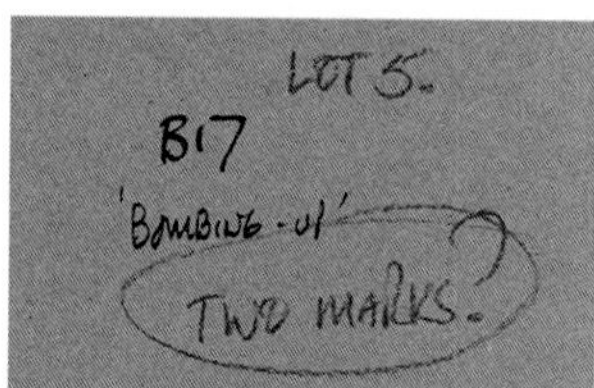
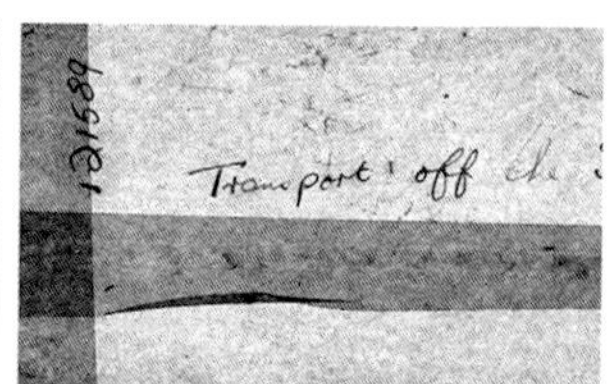
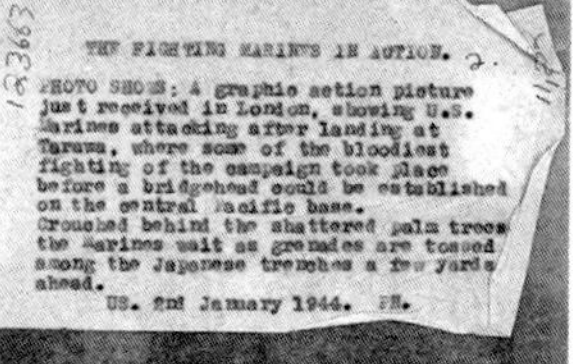
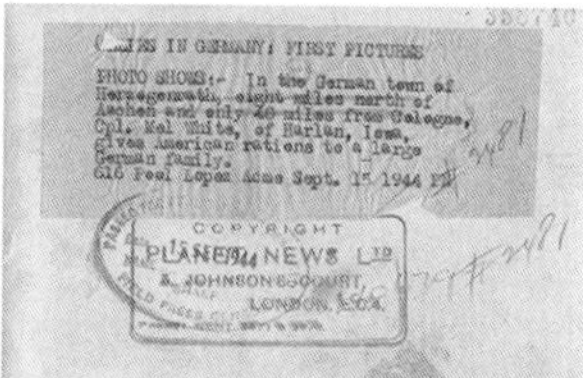

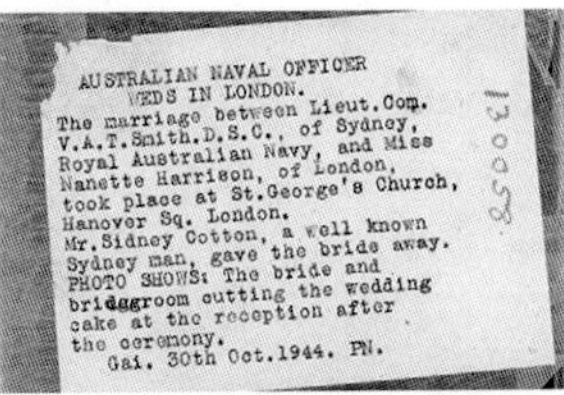
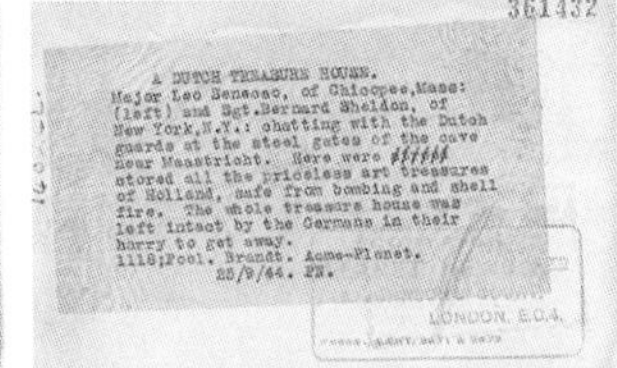
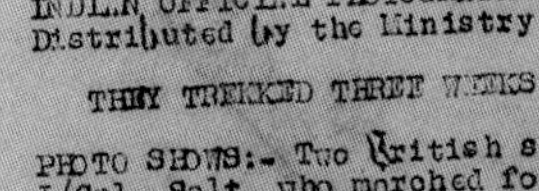
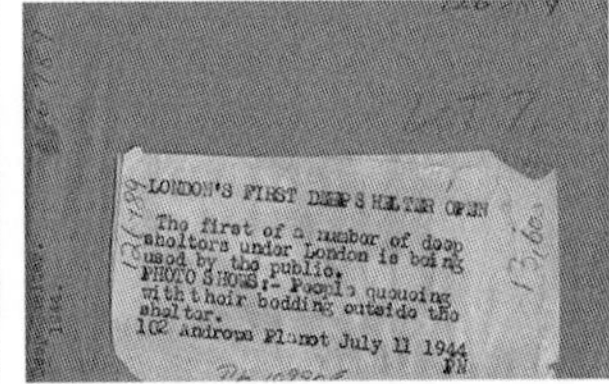
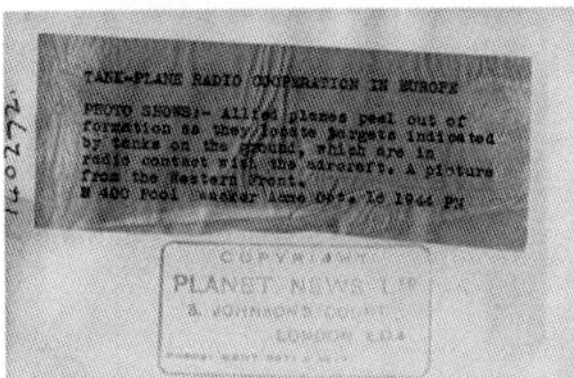
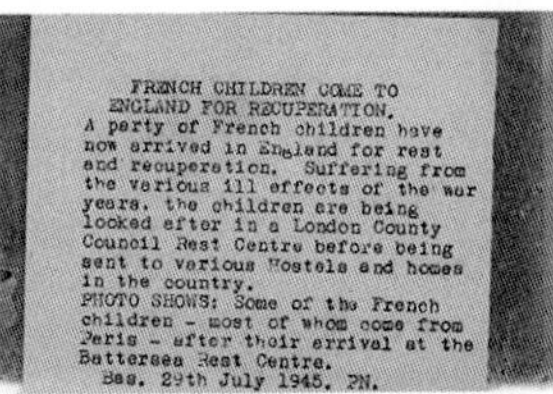
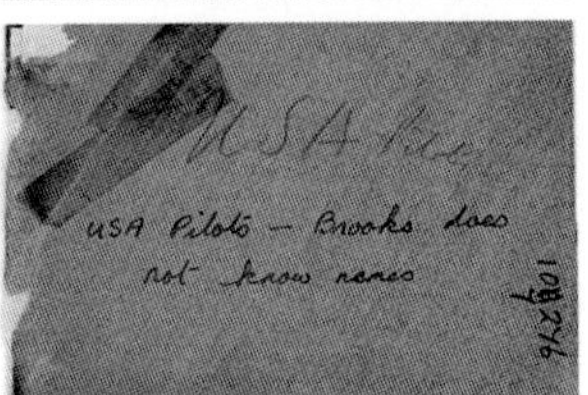
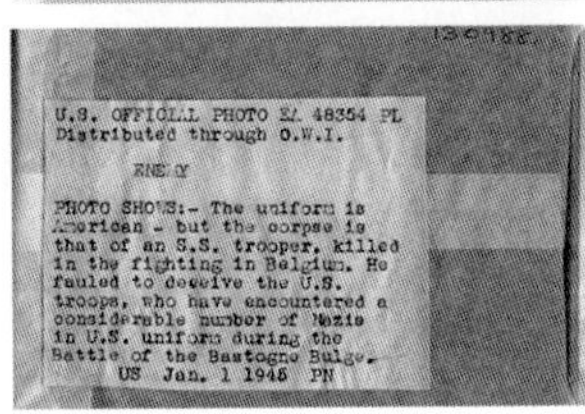
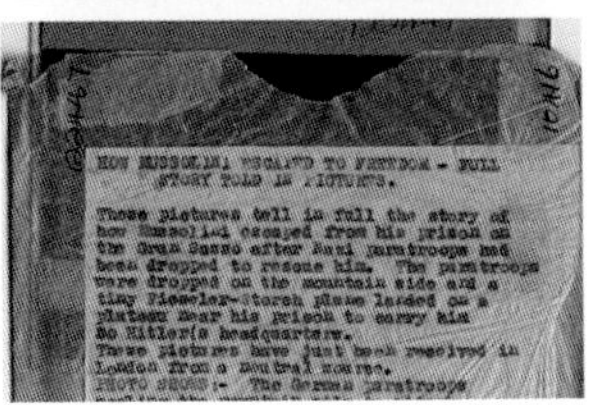
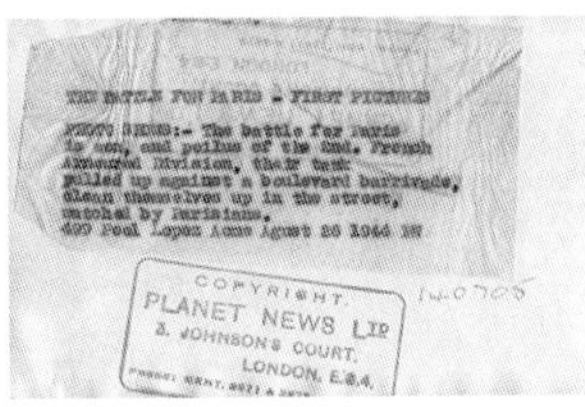
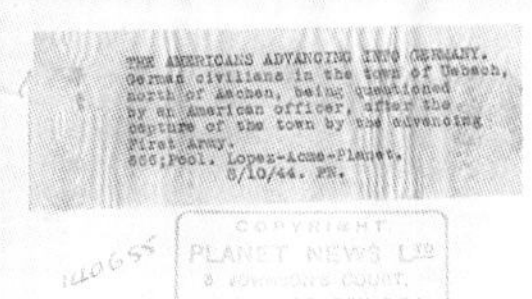
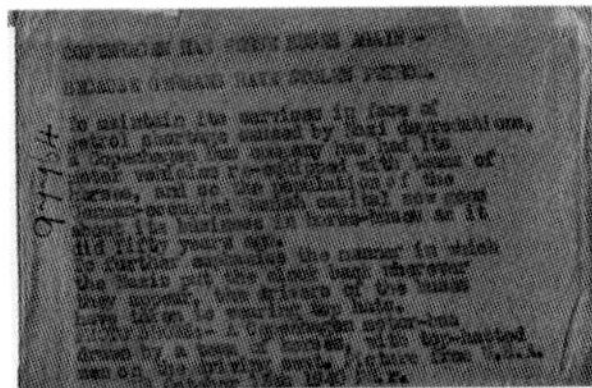
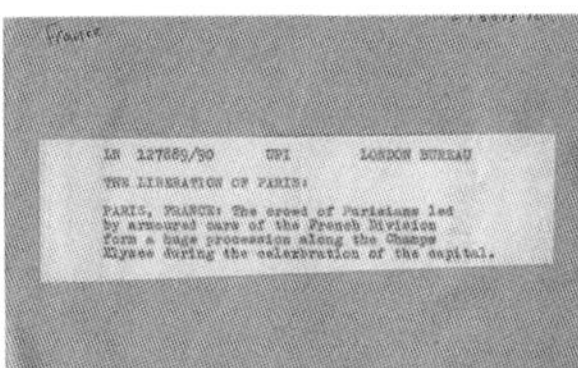
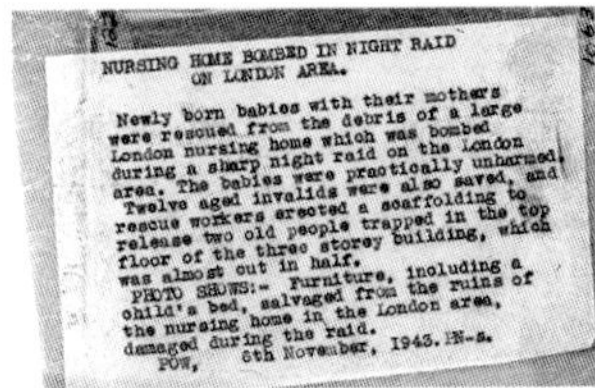
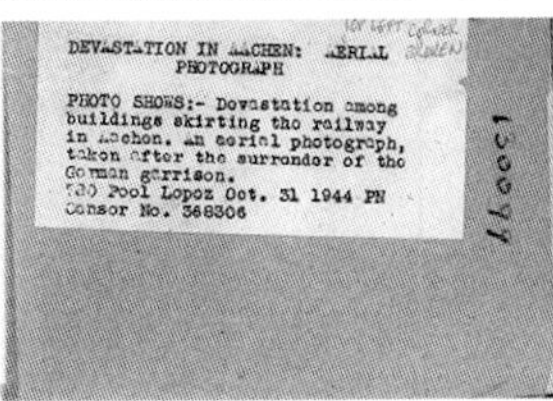

CONTENTS

◀ A collage of sleeves from the original negatives.

FOREWORD

During the course of what seemed to be just an ordinary busy week at Topfoto in 2020, the phone rang and time seemed to stand still for a moment. Peter Deleuran called me with an extraordinary offer and a missing piece of our archive, which is to say a missing piece of the true stories safeguarded in our archive in visual form. Peter Deleuran's discovery, talent for storytelling and obsession with history has made a perfect connection between his devoted scholarship and the treasures of the Topfoto archive. It has been our pleasure to work with Peter as he brought the images he found back to life, for all to explore through the medium of this wonderful book. These intensely real photographs honour the courage of the soldiers, and honour the photographers who were there to witness history so that we might learn from their moment of truth – a truth captured in acetate or glass – here for us all, for as long as civilisation lasts.

Each photo in this book has a unique **TOPFOTO CODE** that corresponds to an identical number in our archives. If you are a journalist, a writer, a scholar or maybe an enthusiast who would like a high-resolution poster printed from the original negative, you can simply go to TopFoto.co.uk and type in the code. Just choose the photo and you will be presented with a variety of options depending on your request. Our online archive holds more than 4 million photos – just dive in and start exploring!

Flora Smith
Managing Partner
TopFoto.co.uk

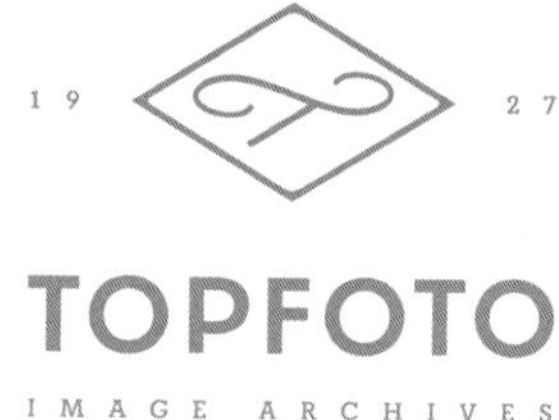

INTRODUCTION

I have always had a passion for old things. Dusty libraries or dirty barns, it didn't matter what, when, or where. It was ever the exhilaration of the hunt for the next hidden treasure and the revelation of some illusory lost truth that propelled me forward. An almost childish 'Indiana Jones'-like obsession with the need to uncover every little secret of any object and expose its history to the world – to place it into a museum for all to see – just like my hero.

In June 2020, having spent half a lifetime finding, buying, researching, and selling old things, I had a stroke of luck. While making a deal with a seller for some vintage watches, I was offered access to a cache of old photos. At first glance, it all looked in a sorry state, but that old feeling of treasure hunt made me curious and after a little while I finally acquired the collection. It was a complete mess, but I slowly began to see the importance of what I had acquired.

In total, the collection counted almost 300 Second World War press release glass negatives and developed photos, most of them with their original typewritten caption sleeves. After some research, I discovered that around 200 of them had belonged to the Planet News press photo agency.

Established in 1927, Planet News was a London-based agency that supplied Britain, and the world, with news and photographs, until they merged with the United Press Association (UPI), forming UPI London in 1958. In the 1970s, the esteemed independent British picture library TopFoto bought the picture library of UPI and all the rights contained within it.

Three months after my acquisition, I got in touch with TopFoto's Managing Partner, Flora Smith, and explained what I had discovered. After some internal investigation, she found that, while TopFoto owned the rights to these photos, they did not have any copies of the actual images. In fact, they had never seen many of them. These have never seen the light of day since the Second World War. Until now.

Mrs Smith and I made a deal. I would scan and restore the photos so that they could be reunited with the archive where they rightfully belonged. Preserved and protected as a part of history, for all to see. In return, I received the generous gesture of being able to use the photos to publish the book I had envisioned since acquiring them.

An immense amount of work has gone into this. Thousands of hours of exciting research, and, at times, long and tedious hours of digitally repairing and restoring extremely damaged high-resolution scans. I have attempted to show what they truly looked like at the time: to bring back their raw honesty, sincerity, simplicity, brutality, and at times heart-wrenching beauty.

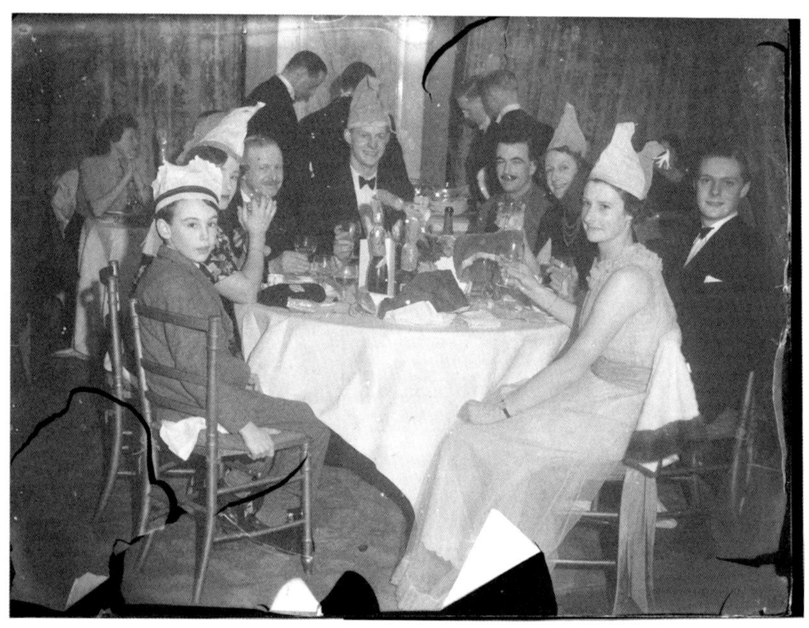
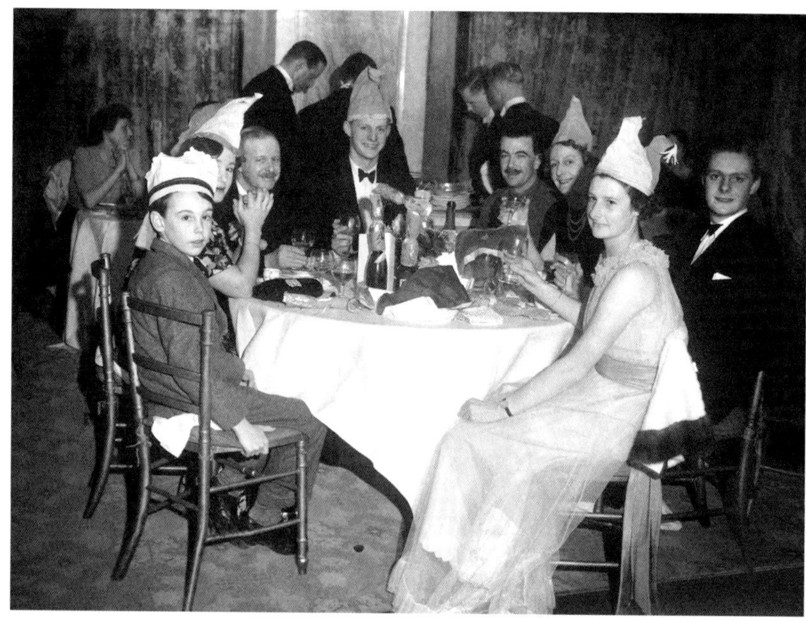
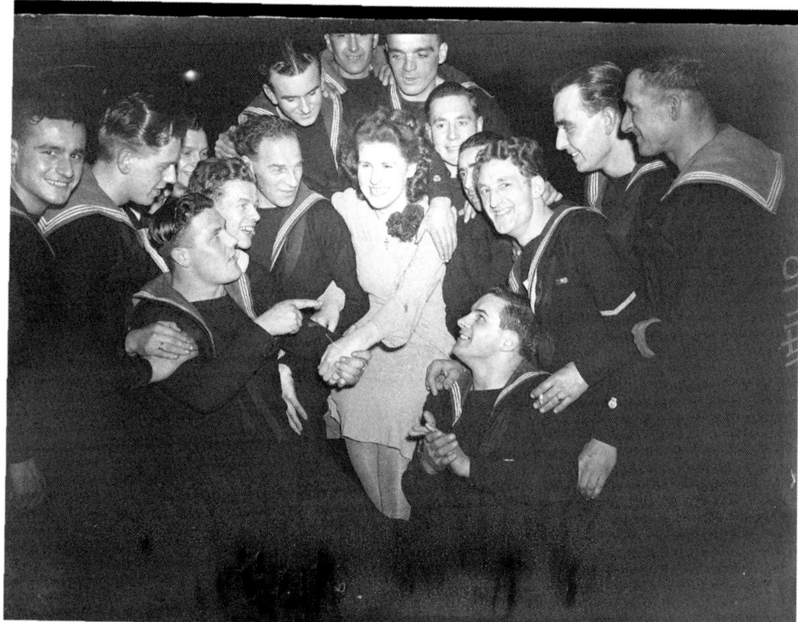
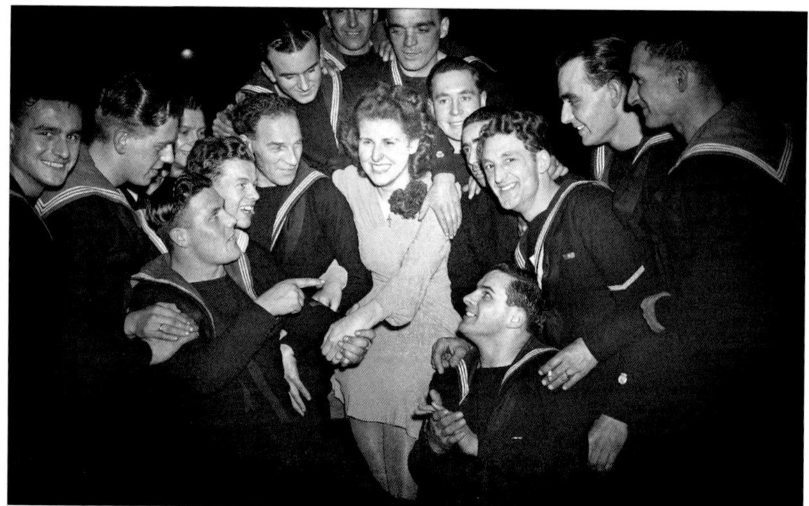

A selection of before and after examples to indicate the restoration work carried out on these images.

Alone, some of these images might seem trivial or even mundane, but together they tell a quite nuanced story of what life was really like during these years for both soldiers and civilians. Little individually wrapped time capsules from one of the most important periods of the modern era.

Some have been given more space than others, as in these cases the research has led deeper. Some have little or no background at all, and are therefore naturally more sparsely described. The need to limit certain parts to fit the length of the book also had a part to play.

Many of the original sleeves and the official typewritten information connected to the photos, names, places, times, etc. were wrong or misspelled. Much of the research has also led to sources, more often than not, stating very conflicting facts as to how an incident occurred, or who or what it involved. I have tried as much as possible to use information that seemed most credible from the most credible sources. That means, invariably, having had to choose one 'fact' over another, or sometimes simply omitting certain incidents as too many of the available sources were in disagreement.

That is the crux of 'history'. It is never clear-cut, and is generally written by the victor. Two people will remember the same incident very differently, and often with sources from this period, there might have been an interest in covering up certain details or putting a different spin on it.

2025 marks the eightieth anniversary of the end of the Second World War; however, the issues that led to its beginning seem to still be festering in our world today. Dark ideologies and convictions are very much alive in the hearts and minds of men and women, politicians and voters, unable to comprehend where ignorance like this leads. Deaf and blind to the voices and images of the past, they keep on marching self-righteously backwards into this darkness, seemingly oblivious to the destruction it brought before and inevitably will bring once again. The concept of Historic Recurrence is completely lost on them.

My humble but sincere hope is that this book in some small way will contribute to shining a light on our past and make anyone who reads it reflect upon it and remember what happened. History repeats itself. Do not let it. Change the narrative – alter the course. It begins with a thought. It begins with an active decision towards change. It begins with you. The responsibility lies with each and every one of us. Our shared destructive past holds the blueprints for avoiding the loss of our shared peaceful future.

I hope that the reader will enjoy the book as much as I have enjoyed putting it together. It truly is a collaboration between a staggering number of people, over the course of more than eighty years, that has finally culminated in the book you see before you. The people that were there, the photographers that caught the moments, the journalists that explained the events, and finally the people that made this all happen. It is a reflection upon the Second World War, experienced through this photo cache, forgotten in time. I am but a very small part of this, though this small part I have been allowed to play makes me immensely proud. I hope I have not done any of these people a disservice.

Sit back, relax and immerse yourself in their stories.

If any facts in the book are inaccurate, it is entirely my fault. If you encounter any such errors, please contact The History Press and we will venture to remedy this.

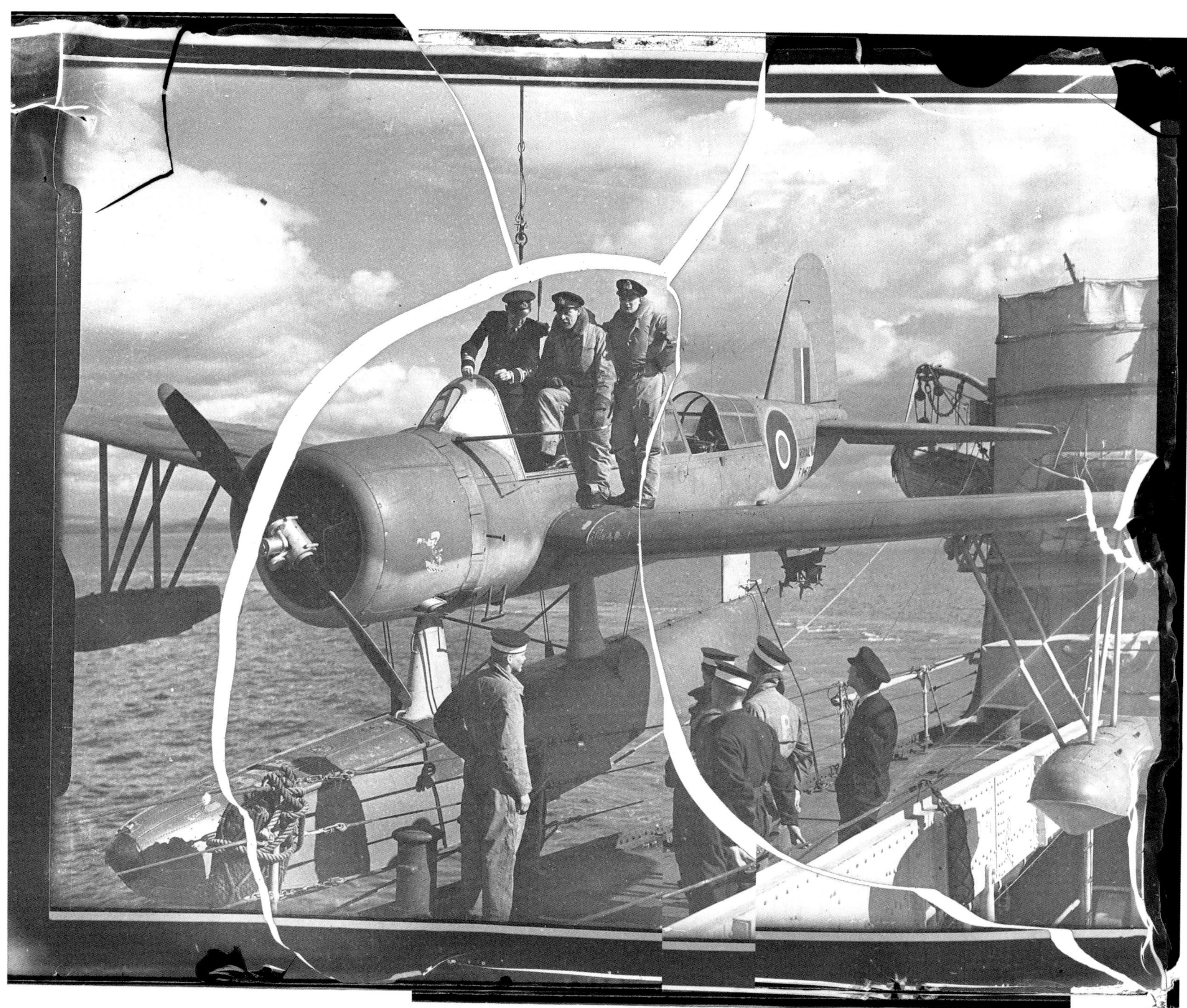

I would like to thank the entire team at The History Press for spotting some potential in my original draft, and to my editor Amy Rigg for her hard work and commitment to the book. Thank you also to TopFoto's Flora Smith and John Balean for all the help and advice through the years. Lastly, thank you to Peter Trolle Jakobsen, Lise Deleuran, Steen Kølle-Jørgensen, Mats Olzon and to other family members and friends for listening to my incessant talk about the project. Most of all, thank you to Johanna Olzon – the love and light of my life. Without your support this would have never happened.

For clarity when reading this book, the data from the original negatives comprises the basic captions throughout the book, and the deeper text that follows is my own research.

Peter Deleuran
2024

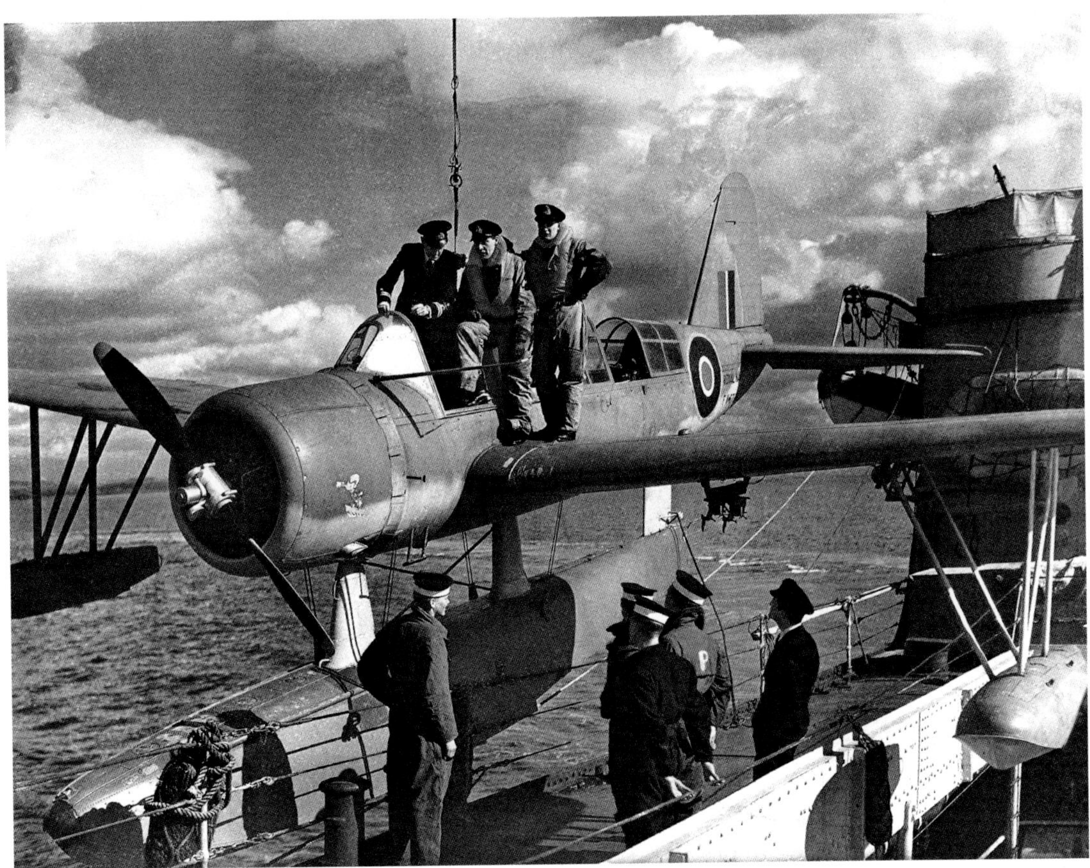

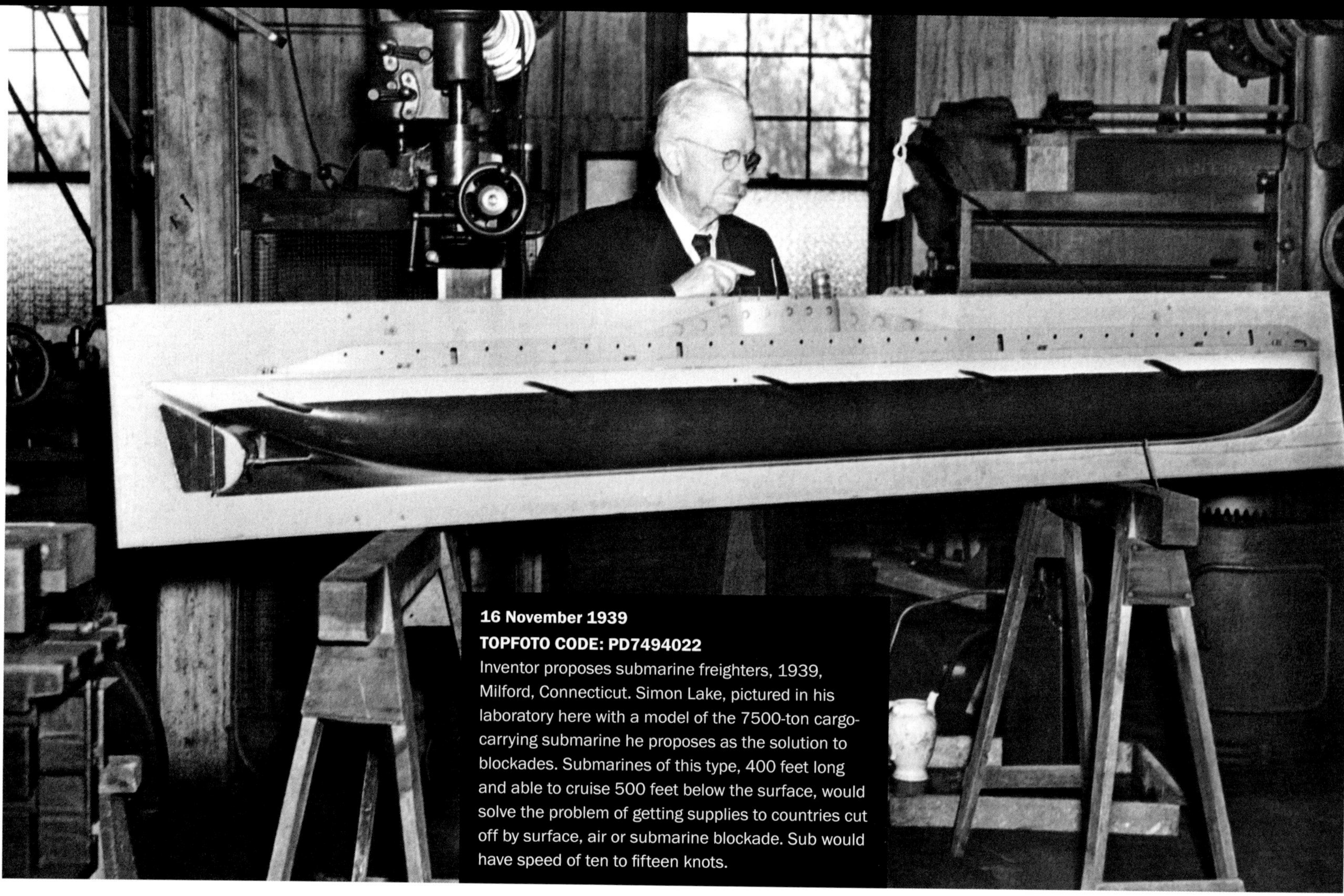

16 November 1939
TOPFOTO CODE: PD7494022
Inventor proposes submarine freighters, 1939, Milford, Connecticut. Simon Lake, pictured in his laboratory here with a model of the 7500-ton cargo-carrying submarine he proposes as the solution to blockades. Submarines of this type, 400 feet long and able to cruise 500 feet below the surface, would solve the problem of getting supplies to countries cut off by surface, air or submarine blockade. Sub would have speed of ten to fifteen knots.

The idea for, and the use of, rudimentary submarines goes all the way back to a time before Christ, although the first fully operational submarine wasn't built until 1620 by the Dutch engineer Cornelis van Drebbel. Simon Lake (pictured) and his rival John Philip Holland, were in fierce competition to build the very first US Navy submarine. Ultimately, Holland's USS *Holland* SS-1 prevailed and was commissioned on 12 October 1900. Simon Lake, though, still held more than 200 naval design patents. While some of his early inventions were not accepted by the US Navy, he built fifty-five subs for them during the First World War, and supplied a large number for many other nations.

He passed away on 23 June 1945, and the US Navy later honoured him by naming a submarine tender class after him that was in service from the mid-1960s to the late '90s.

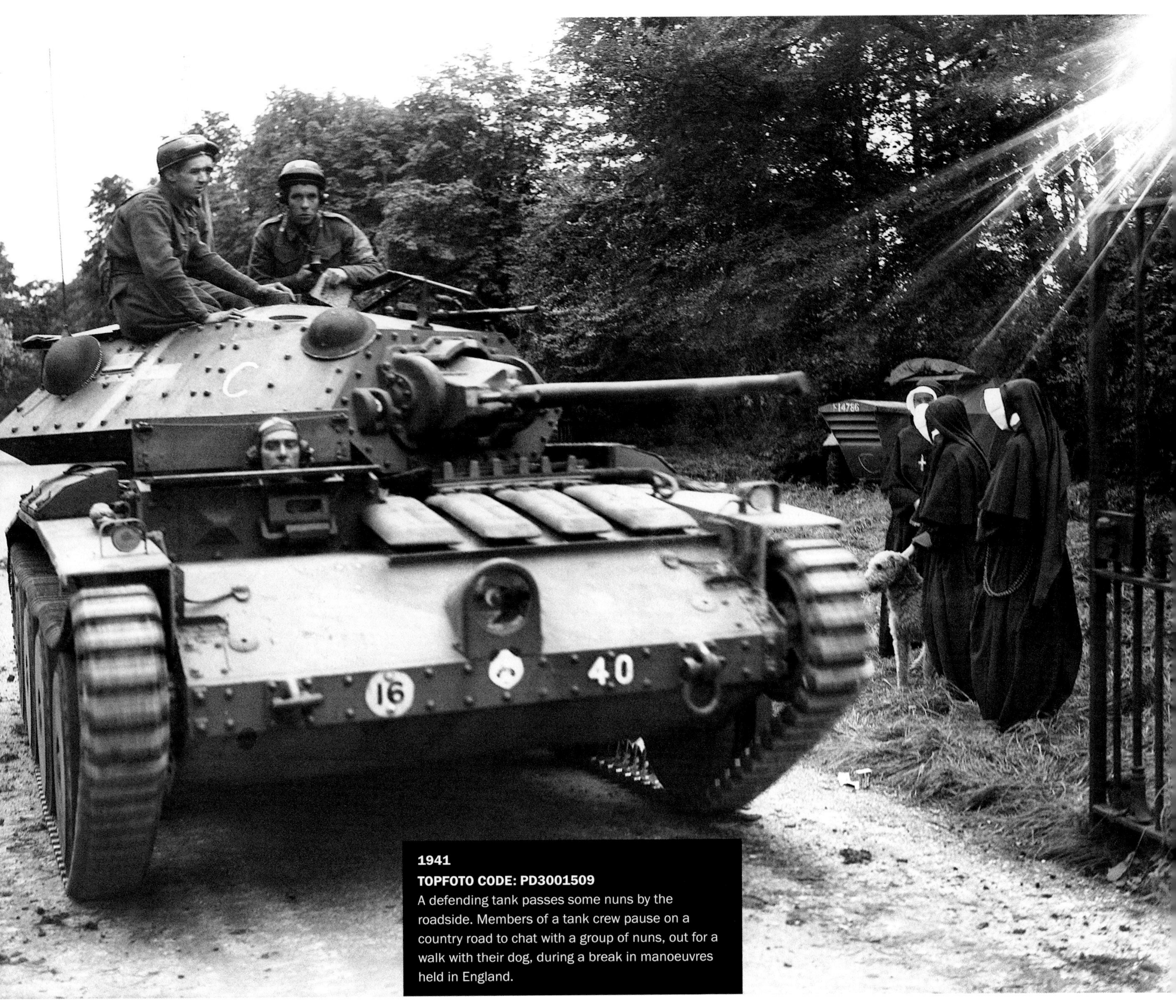

1941

TOPFOTO CODE: PD3001509

A defending tank passes some nuns by the roadside. Members of a tank crew pause on a country road to chat with a group of nuns, out for a walk with their dog, during a break in manoeuvres held in England.

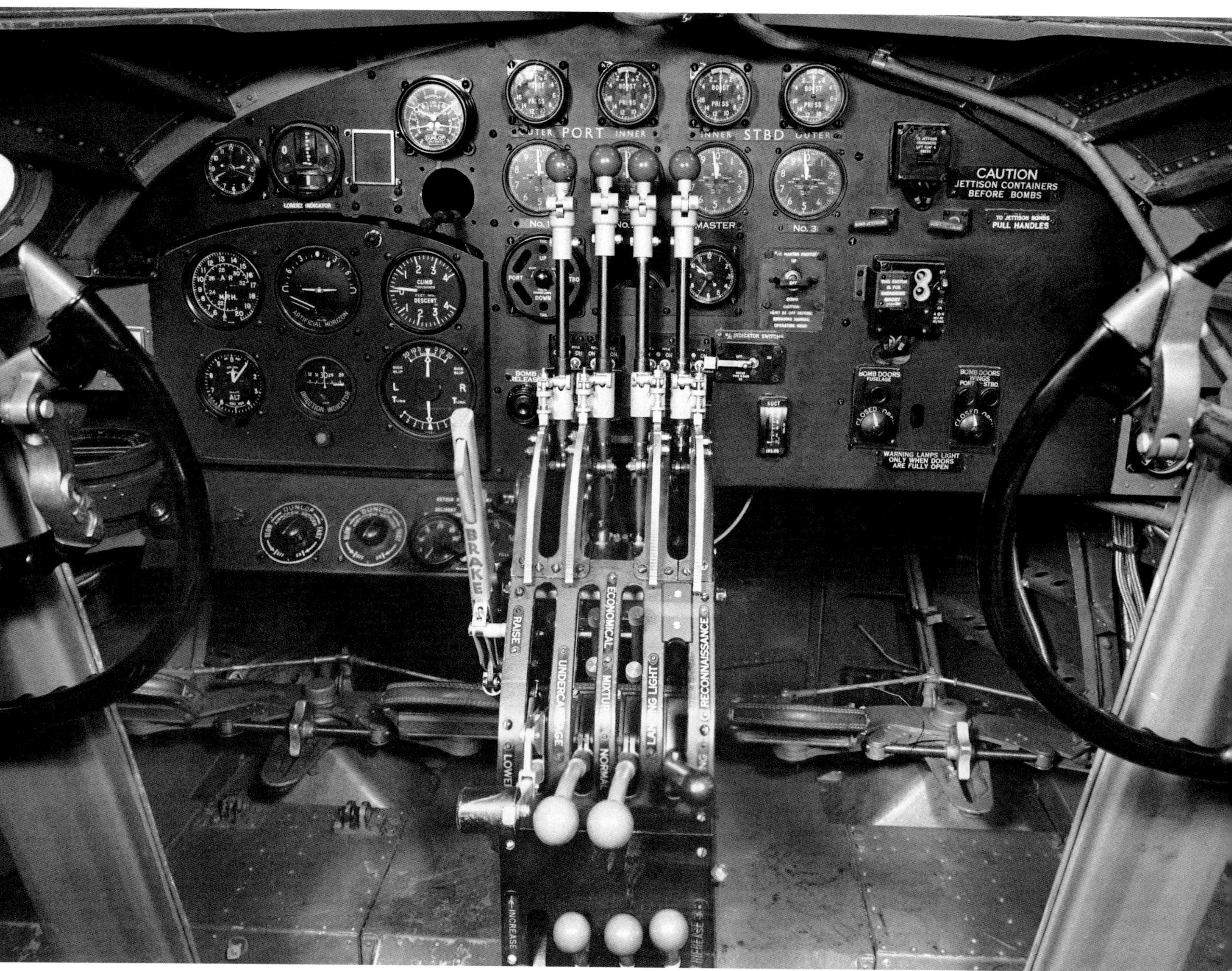

PORT
STBD
OUTER INNER INNER OUTER
No. 1
No. 3
MASTER
CAUTION
JETTISON CONTAINERS
BEFORE BOMBS
TO JETTISON BOMBS
PULL HANDLES
BOMB DOORS
FUSELAGE
BOMB DOORS
WINGS
PORT STBD
CLOSED OPEN
CLOSED OPEN
WARNING LAMPS LIGHT
ONLY WHEN DOORS
ARE FULLY OPEN
INDICATOR SWITCH
SUCT
BOMB
RELEASE
BRAKE
RAISE
LOWER
UNDERCARRIAGE
ECONOMICAL
NORMAL
MIXTURE
LANDING LIGHT
RECONNAISSANCE
INCREASE
CLIMB
DESCENT
ARTIFICIAL HORIZON
DIRECTION INDICATOR
M.P.H.
ALT
LORENZ INDICATOR
DUNLOP
UP
DOWN
PORT
STBD
TAIL

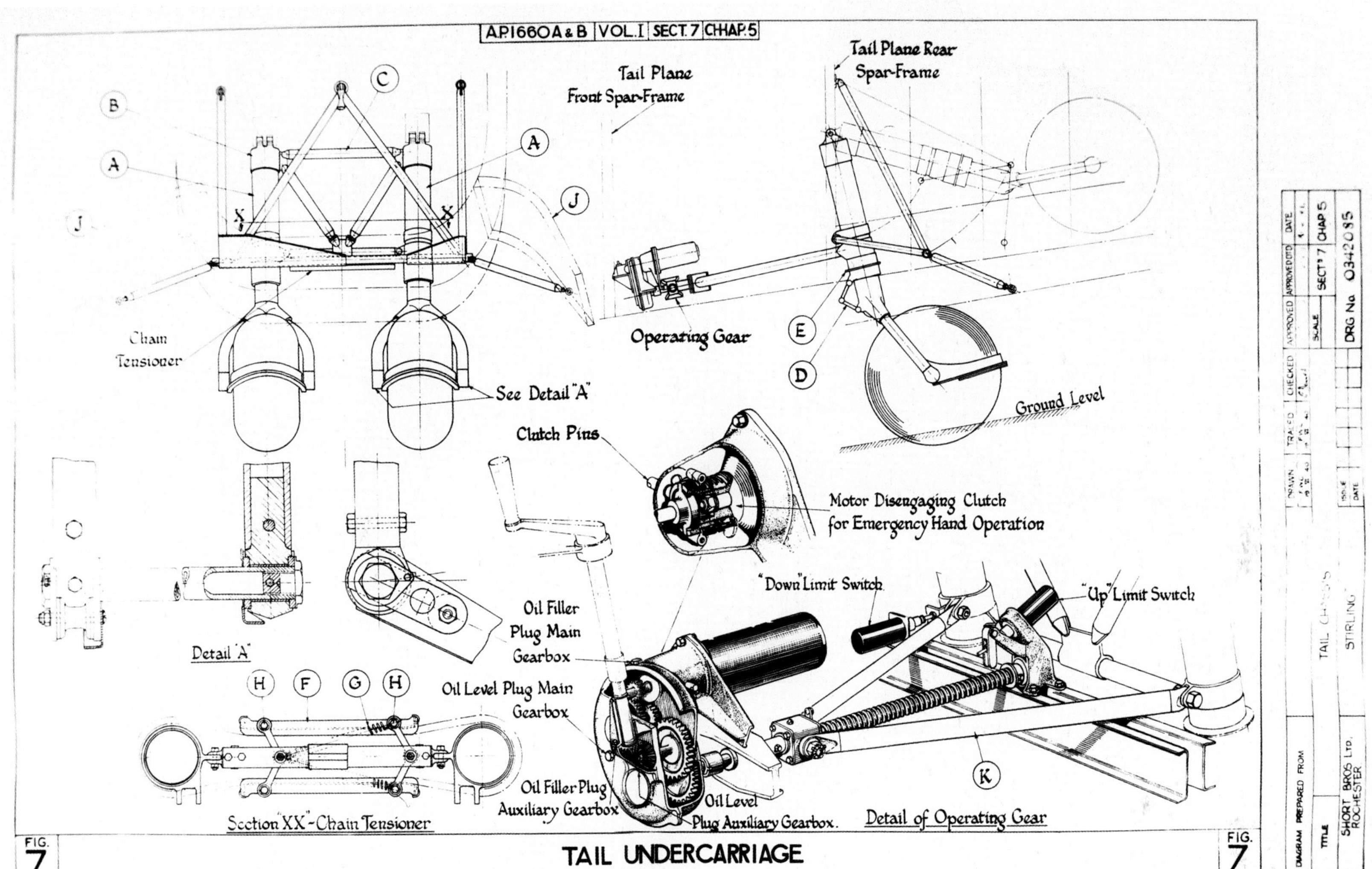

The Short Stirling bomber, at 87ft 3in (26.59m) long, was by no measures short. The name originated from Short Brothers, the Belfast-based aerospace company that designed the plane. It was the first four-engine bomber to be used by the RAF during the Second World War, and while initially praised, it was outperformed by the later Handley Page Halifax and the Avro Lancaster. Some 2,371 Short Stirling bombers were built, and post-war a few continued to serve within the civilian airline industry.

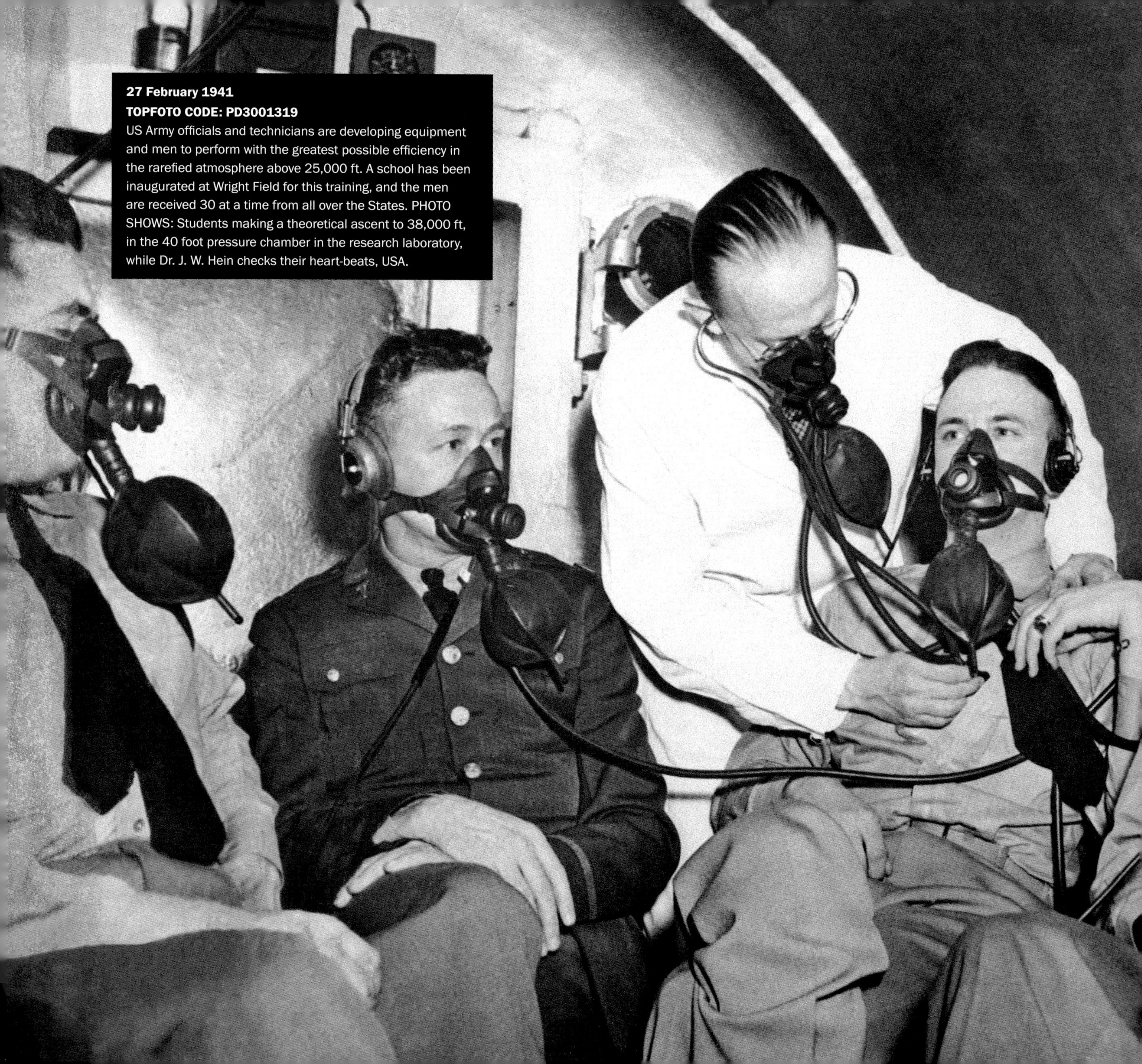

27 February 1941
TOPFOTO CODE: PD3001319
US Army officials and technicians are developing equipment and men to perform with the greatest possible efficiency in the rarefied atmosphere above 25,000 ft. A school has been inaugurated at Wright Field for this training, and the men are received 30 at a time from all over the States. PHOTO SHOWS: Students making a theoretical ascent to 38,000 ft, in the 40 foot pressure chamber in the research laboratory, while Dr. J. W. Hein checks their heart-beats, USA.

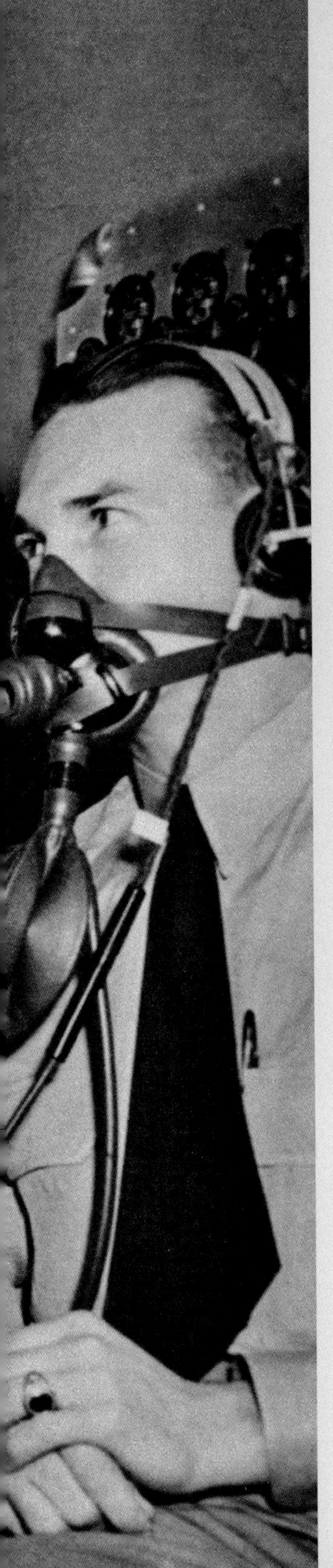

The Germans began using the Focke-Wulf Fw 190 in August 1941, and it immediately gave the British a lot of trouble, outperforming the RAF's Spitfire Mk V in almost every aspect. Casualties were increasing to a point where the RAF began planning Operation Air Thief, a commando raid on a Luftwaffe airfield in France to capture one of these planes and reveal its secrets.

Operation Air Thief was as simple as it was daring. The plan was to transport the two-man team, Commando Captain Philip Pinckney of 'E' Troop and his friend the test pilot F/O Jeffrey Quill, to the French shore on a Navy gunboat. Using a folding canoe, they would get themselves as close to the airfield as possible, and lay in wait until the following night when they would attempt a stealth intrusion into the closed compound. Here they would wait for a German pilot to start a machine, overpower him, and get Quill into the cockpit, while Pinckney provided cover. Once Quill was away, Pinckney would backtrack their steps and return to England by boat.

Quill, especially, had very little faith in their ability to succeed, and luckily for him the plan was never initiated. On the same day as Operation Air Thief was put forward for approval, a Luftwaffe pilot named Armin Faber made a grave mistake that was to radically change the fortunes of the RAF.

On 23 June 1942, Oberleutnant Armin Faber was sent on a combat mission with the 7th Staffel to attack a group of Allied bombers returning from a mission. His Fw 190 was engaged by a Spitfire flown by Sergeant Trejtnar from 310 Squadron RAF. A fierce dogfight ensued over Exeter, ending with Faber shooting down Trejtnar, who fortunately managed to bail out. Afterwards, however, Faber had become disoriented and mistook the Bristol Channel for the English Channel, thus heading north instead of south. Believing RAF Pembrey airfield was the French airfield of Morlaix, he excitedly waggled his wings in victory and landed his precious Fw 190 in south Wales. He was immediately captured, and remained a POW until he was repatriated just before the war ended.

The plane that had caused the RAF so many headaches had literally landed in their laps, and it became a major inspiration for the Spitfire Mk IX.

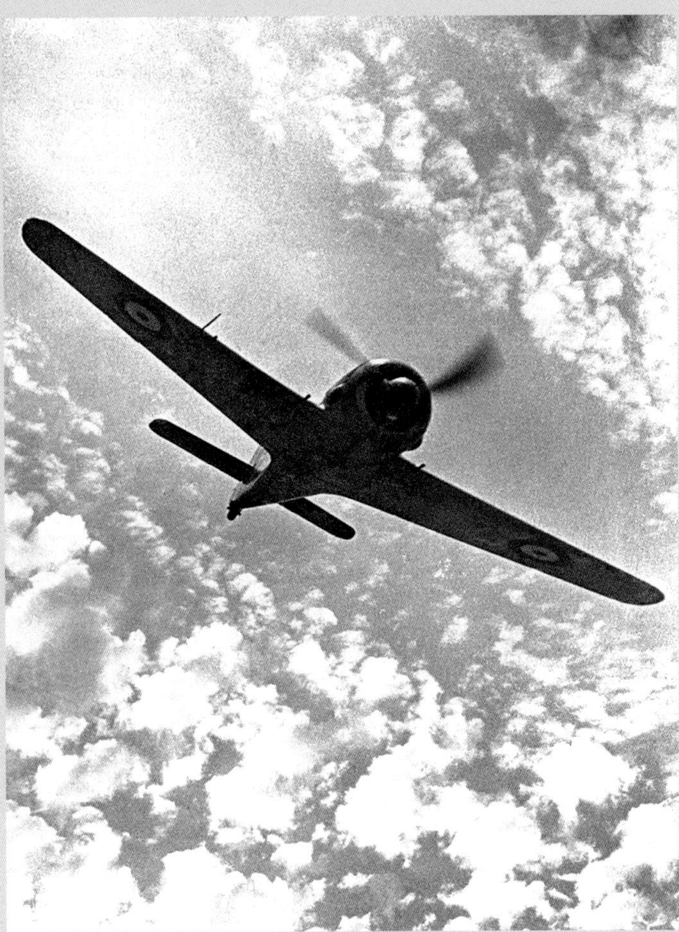

1942
TOPFOTO CODE: PD7494023
A Focke Wulf 190, one of the Luftwaffe's newest single-seat fighters, was captured intact when it was forced down in England owing to lack of fuel. Now, with R.A.F. markings, it is undergoing exhaustive flying tests and examinations by technical experts. (BRITISH OFFICIAL PHOTOGRAPH CH6410 Air Ministry photo. Crown copyright reserved.)

The day that Faber landed his plane on British soil, the concentration camp initiated part of Nazi Germany's euthanasia operation. Some 566 Polish psychiatric patients were gassed to death in Birkenau's Bunker 1 that day.

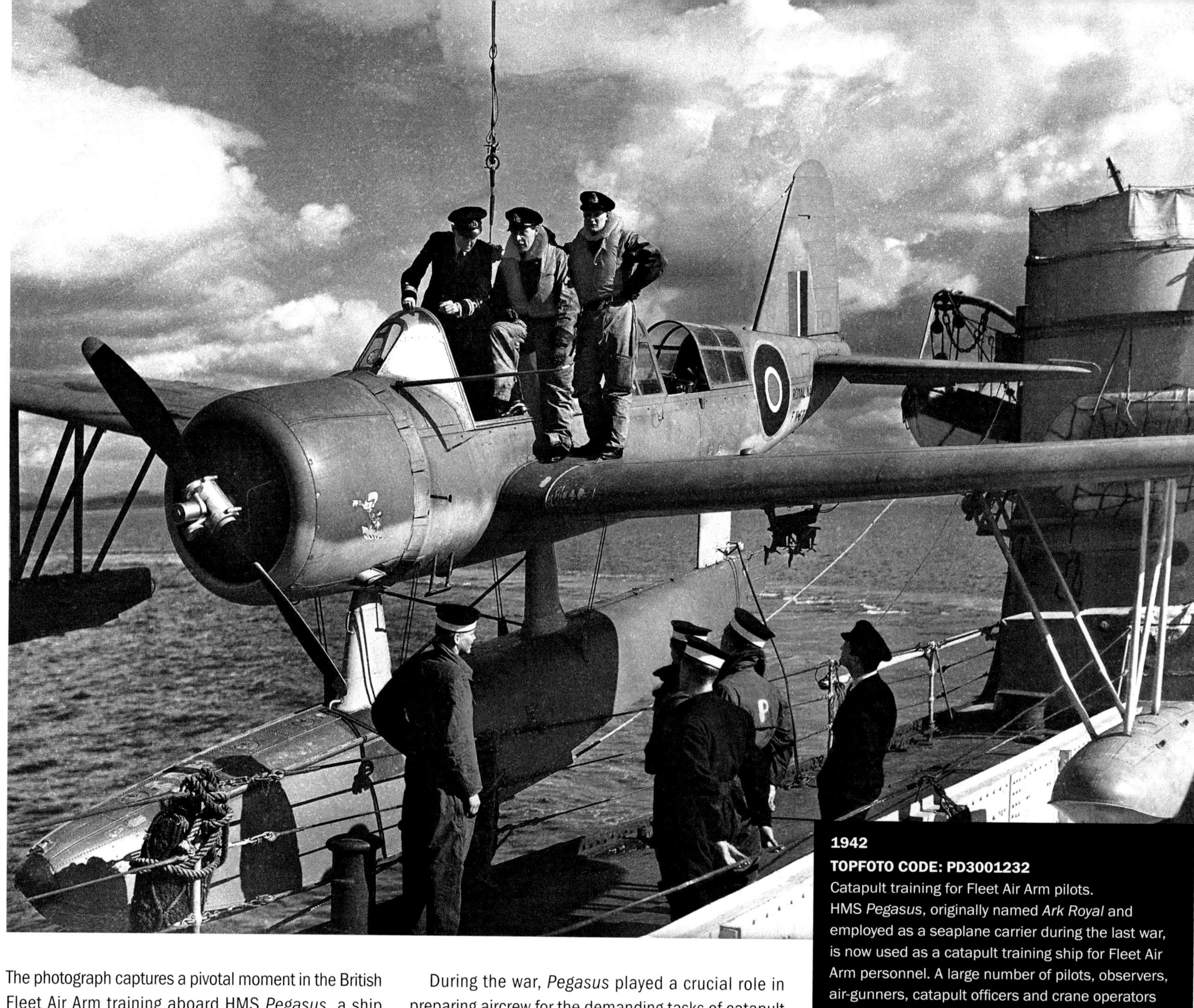

1942

TOPFOTO CODE: PD3001232

Catapult training for Fleet Air Arm pilots. HMS *Pegasus*, originally named *Ark Royal* and employed as a seaplane carrier during the last war, is now used as a catapult training ship for Fleet Air Arm personnel. A large number of pilots, observers, air-gunners, catapult officers and crane operators are trained in the 'Pegasus' every year, after which they are drafted to battleships and cruisers carrying catapult-operated aircraft. PHOTO SHOWS:- An instructor with a pilot and observer in a 'Kingfisher' float plane, while a party of officer cadets watch from the deck of the 'Pegasus'.

The photograph captures a pivotal moment in the British Fleet Air Arm training aboard HMS *Pegasus*, a ship steeped in naval aviation history. Originally commissioned as HMS *Ark Royal* during the First World War, it was renamed *Pegasus* in 1934 and repurposed in the Second World War as a training vessel. The plane is a Vought OS2U Kingfisher: 1,519 were built, of which the UK got 100.

During the war, *Pegasus* played a crucial role in preparing aircrew for the demanding tasks of catapult launching from battleships and cruisers. These training exercises were important, as catapult-launched aircraft were often used for reconnaissance and spotting duties in the absence of aircraft carriers.

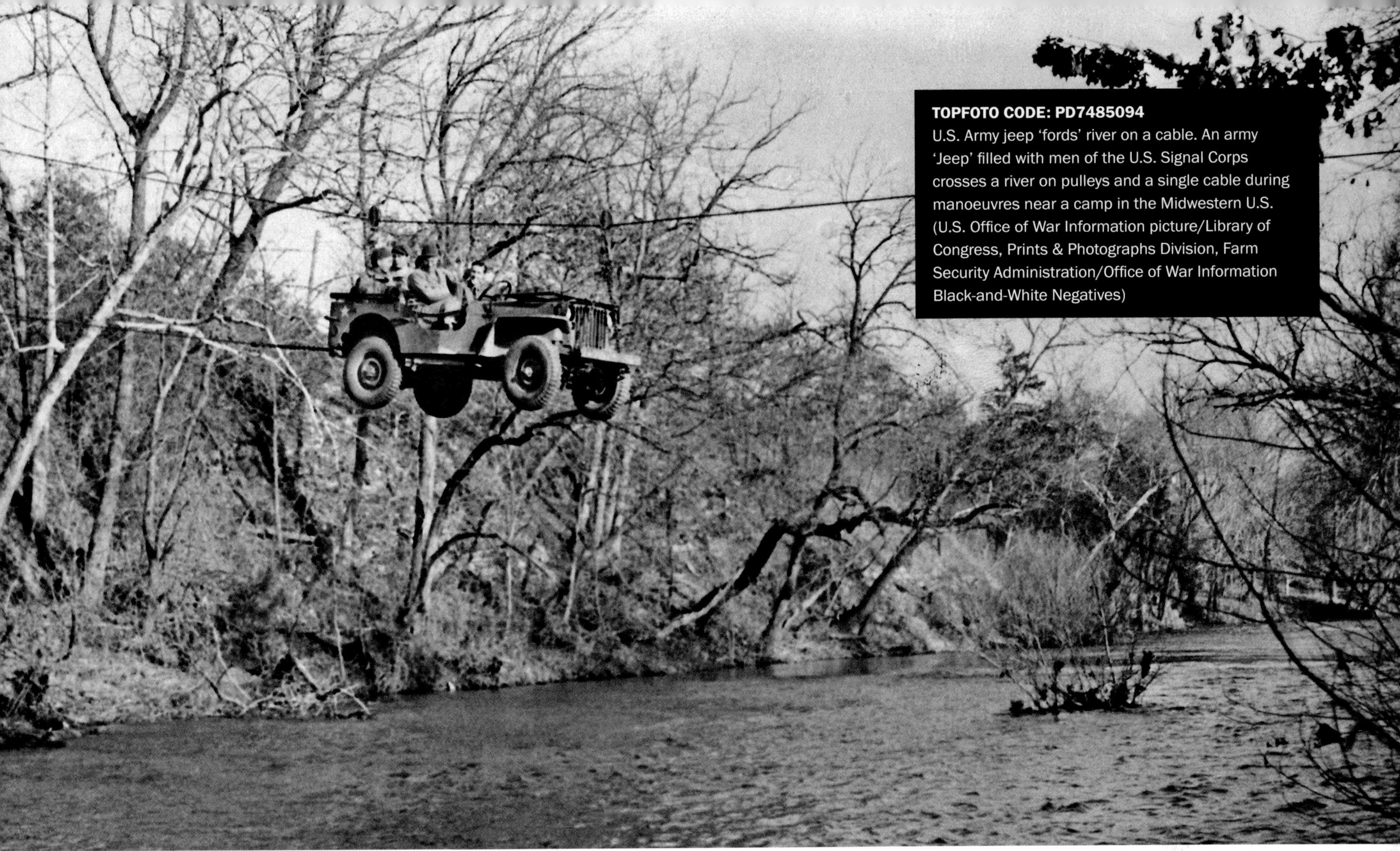

Today almost everyone is familiar with the iconic Jeep. It has become synonymous with off-roading, country living and, in more recent years, tricked-out rides and urban cruisers. The latter usage is far from the utilitarian and modest origins of a brand that wasn't even a brand to begin with.

In 1940, with the war blazing in Europe, the US Army began searching for a car manufacturer that could produce a reconnaissance vehicle with military specifications. The list of demands was long and included stipulations regarding shape, height, weight, load capacity, four-wheel drive, blackout light options and much more. They contacted 135 manufacturers but had only three replies, from Bantam Car Company, Willys-Overland and Ford.

Each company endeavoured to build their own version but ultimately Willys was awarded the coveted Army production contract. The initial stages had, however, seen blueprints changing hands between the three companies and the striking design similarities made it easier when the US War Department realised that Willys would not be able to supply the number of vehicles they needed. A non-exclusive licence was granted and Ford was chosen to supplement the production. Of the first 16,000 Willys MB cars built in 1941 (each costing $738.74), only around thirty exist today.

Disagreements about the origin of the name 'Jeep' persist, but the overall consensus seems to be that the term 'GP', an abbreviation for 'General Purpose', evolved into the word Jeep. Willys-Overland applied for the trademark in 1943 and a long and arduous legal battle ensued. It would take an additional seven years until they finally obtained it.

Today, vintage Jeeps have a fastidious following and the scrutiny of which parts originated from what manufacturer and model seems a big part of the allure.

(Notice the rather stale pun used in the negative caption – how a Jeep 'fords' a river.)

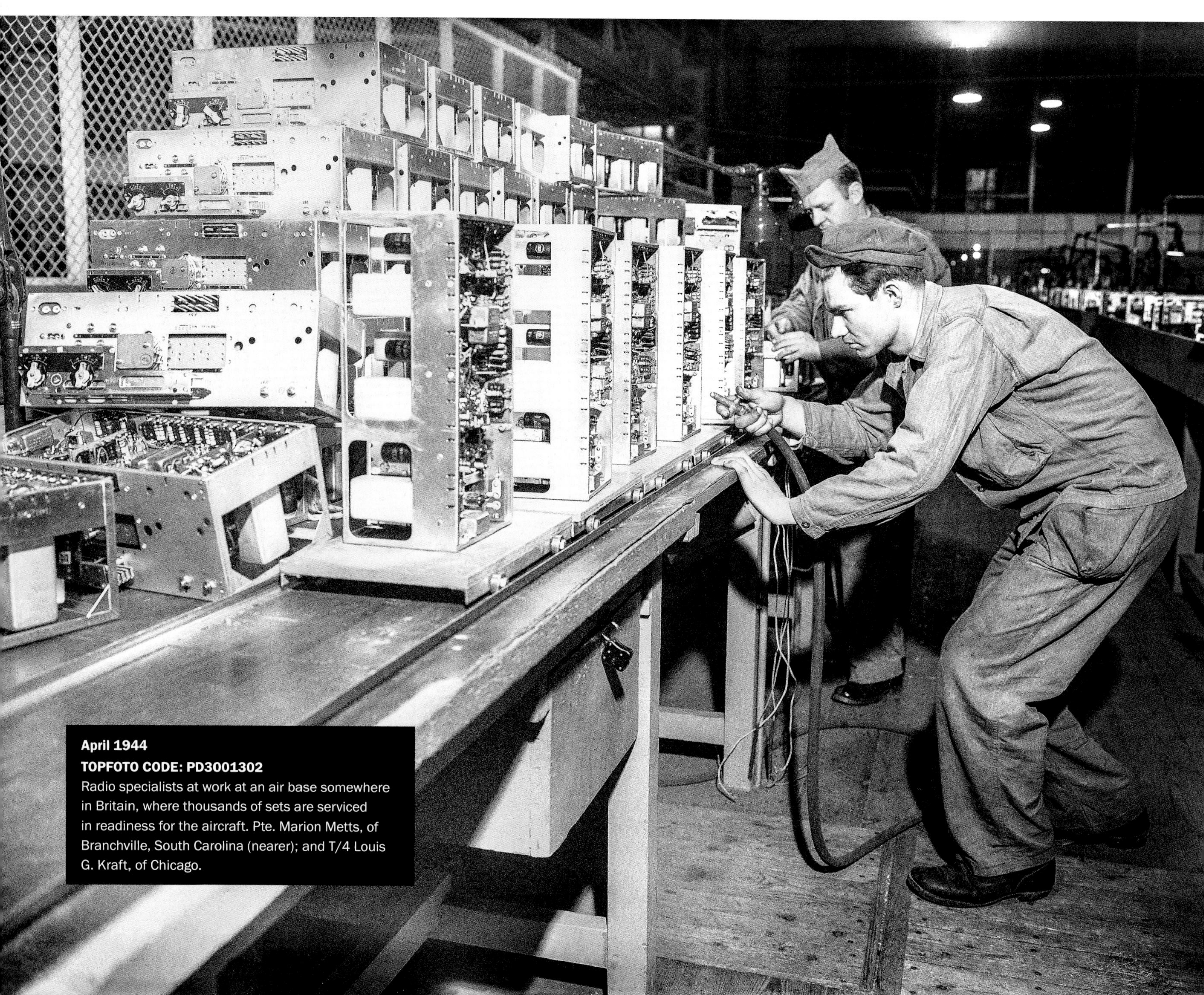

April 1944
TOPFOTO CODE: PD3001302
Radio specialists at work at an air base somewhere in Britain, where thousands of sets are serviced in readiness for the aircraft. Pte. Marion Metts, of Branchville, South Carolina (nearer); and T/4 Louis G. Kraft, of Chicago.

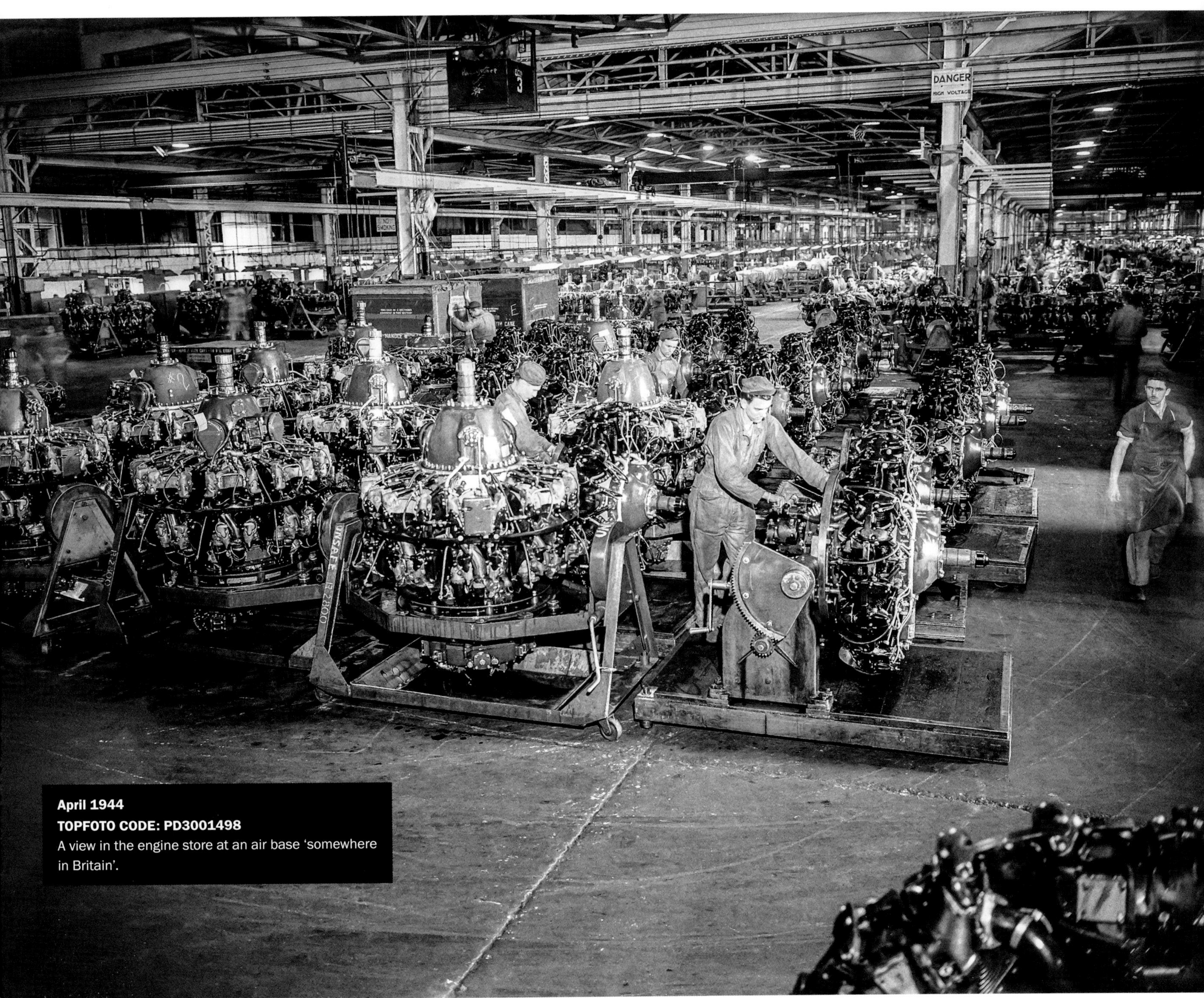

April 1944
TOPFOTO CODE: PD3001498
A view in the engine store at an air base 'somewhere in Britain'.

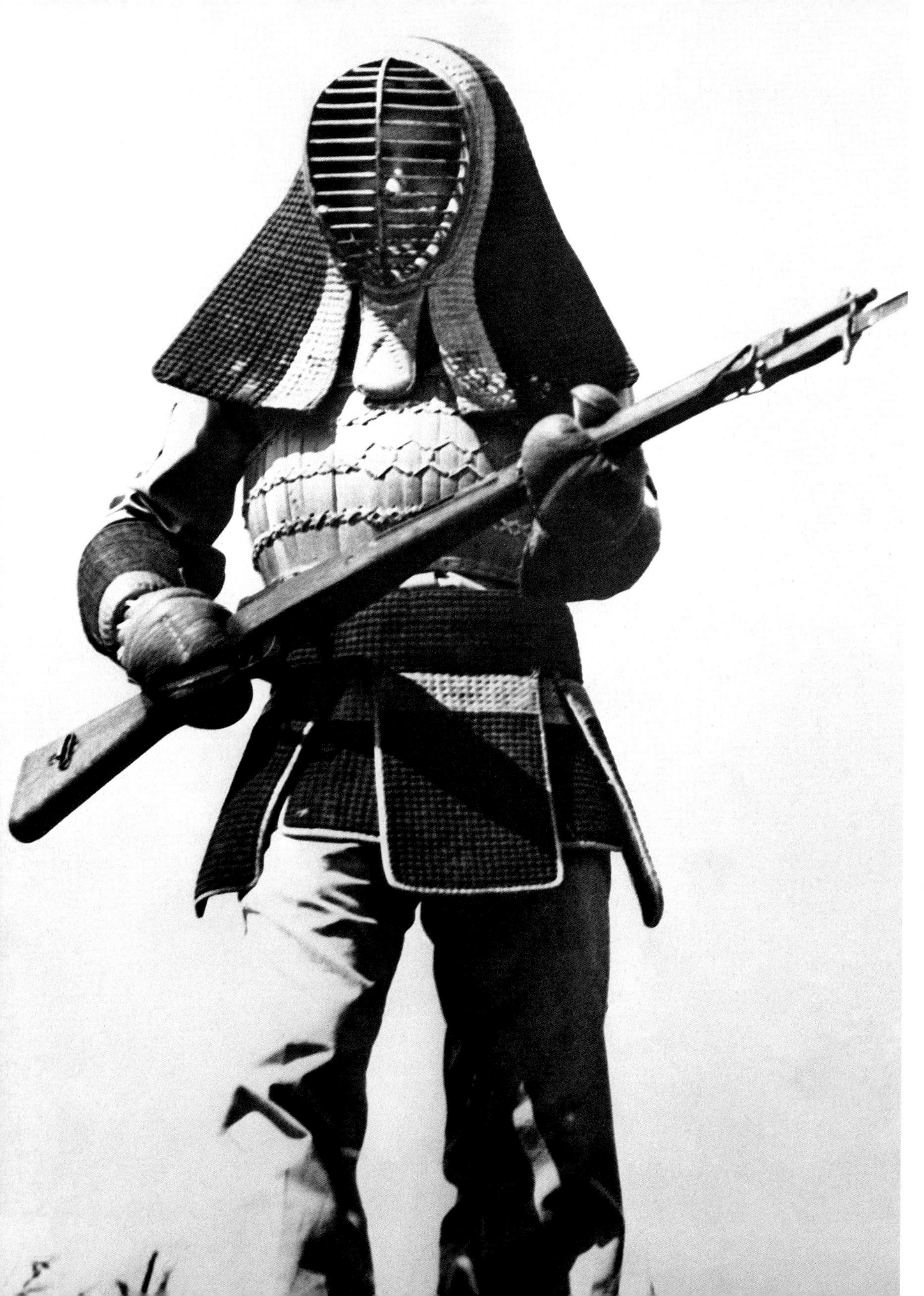

6th May 1944
TOPFOTO CODE: PD3001506
John Jones Jr. of East Springfield, Ohio, USA, demonstrates a Japanese bayonet-fighting suit worn at practice. Looking like medieval armour, it was captured at Kwajalein Island by troops of the U.S. Seventh Division. Sgt. Jones is holding a Japanese .38 Arisaka rifle; for bayonet practice the Japanese use a wooden replica of the same size.

The Kwajalein Atoll in the Marshall Islands was part of the US Army's path on the road through the Pacific towards Japan. On 31 January 1944, US forces launched a twin assault on Kwajalein in the north and Roi-Namur in the south. The estimated forces of the US were 46,670 against a mere 4,300 Japanese troops on Kwajalein and 3,500 on Roi-Namur. The battle lasted just four days, and though intense, the Japanese were completely outnumbered. Out of the original combined Japanese forces of 7,800 men, only 253 survived. It was an important victory for the US in the wake of the heavy losses sustained in the Battle of Tarawa.

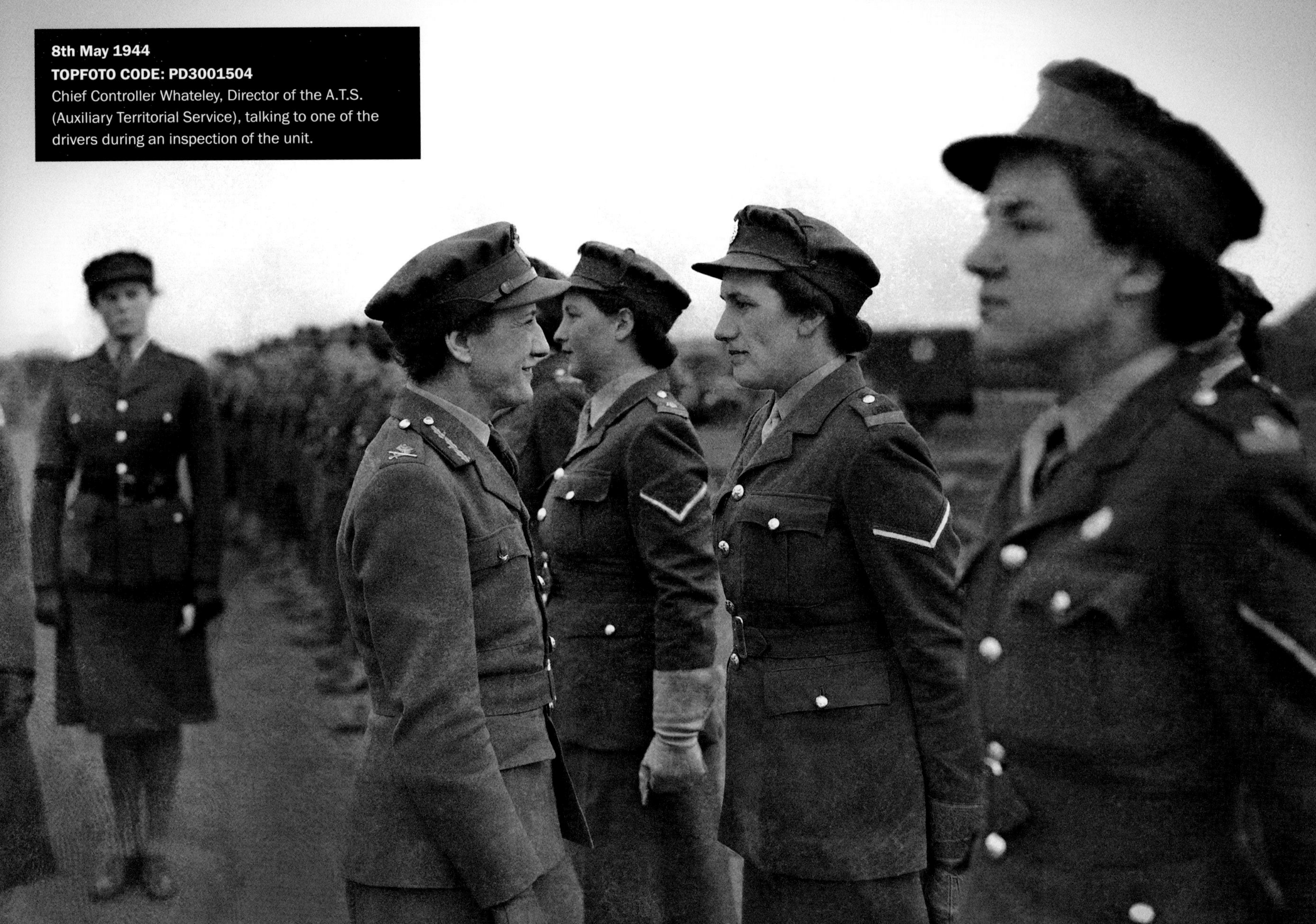

The British Auxiliary Territorial Service (ATS) was created in 1938 as the women's branch of the British Army. It allowed women to actively contribute to the war effort beyond their contemporary, traditional domestic chores.

More than 250,000 women served in the ATS during the Second World War, working as radar operators, anti-aircraft gun crews and military police, among other jobs. Although they were not allowed to fire weapons, it was still a pivotal point in modern history as women were allowed to be directly involved in combat-related tasks.

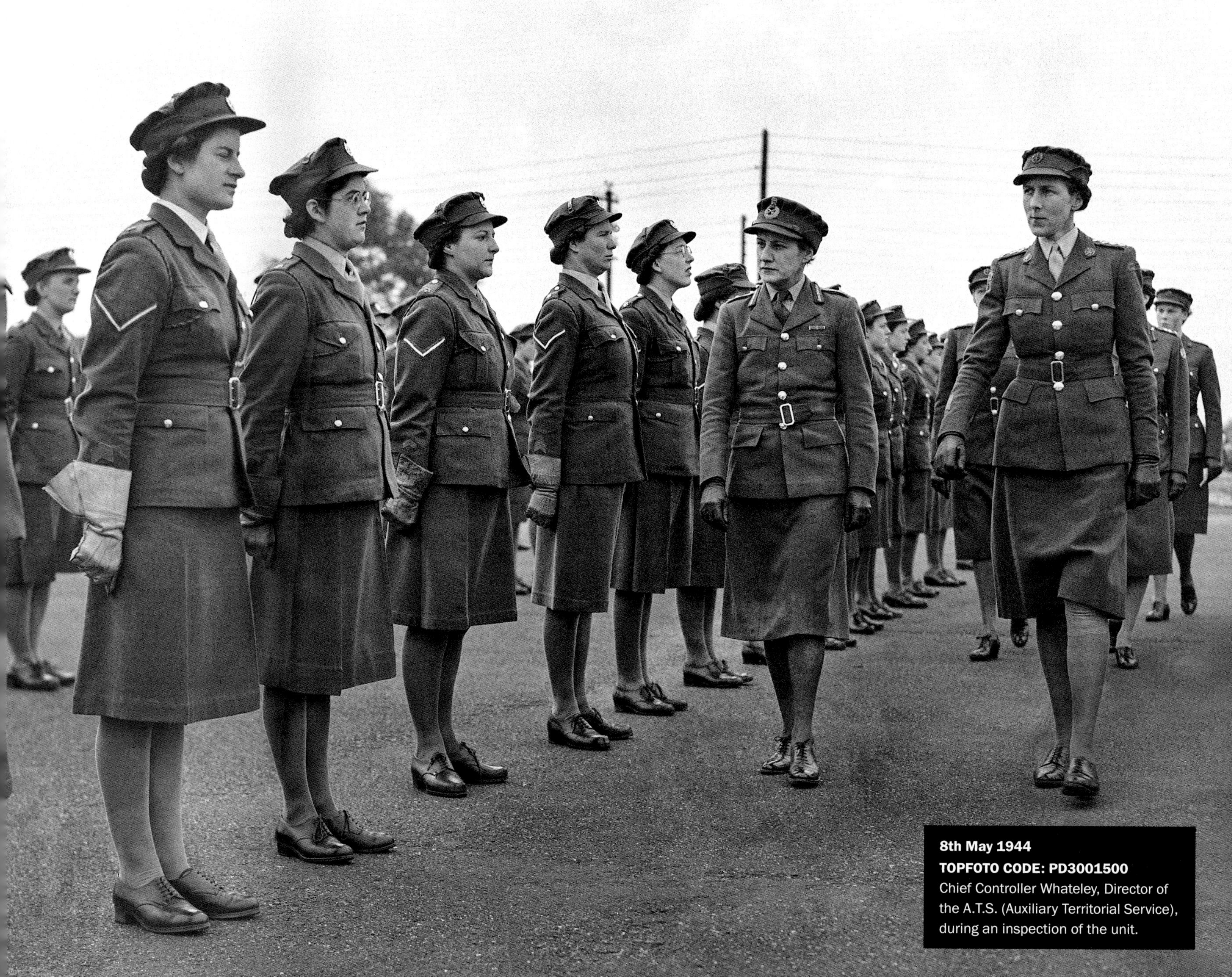

8th May 1944
TOPFOTO CODE: PD3001500
Chief Controller Whateley, Director of
the A.T.S. (Auxiliary Territorial Service),
during an inspection of the unit.

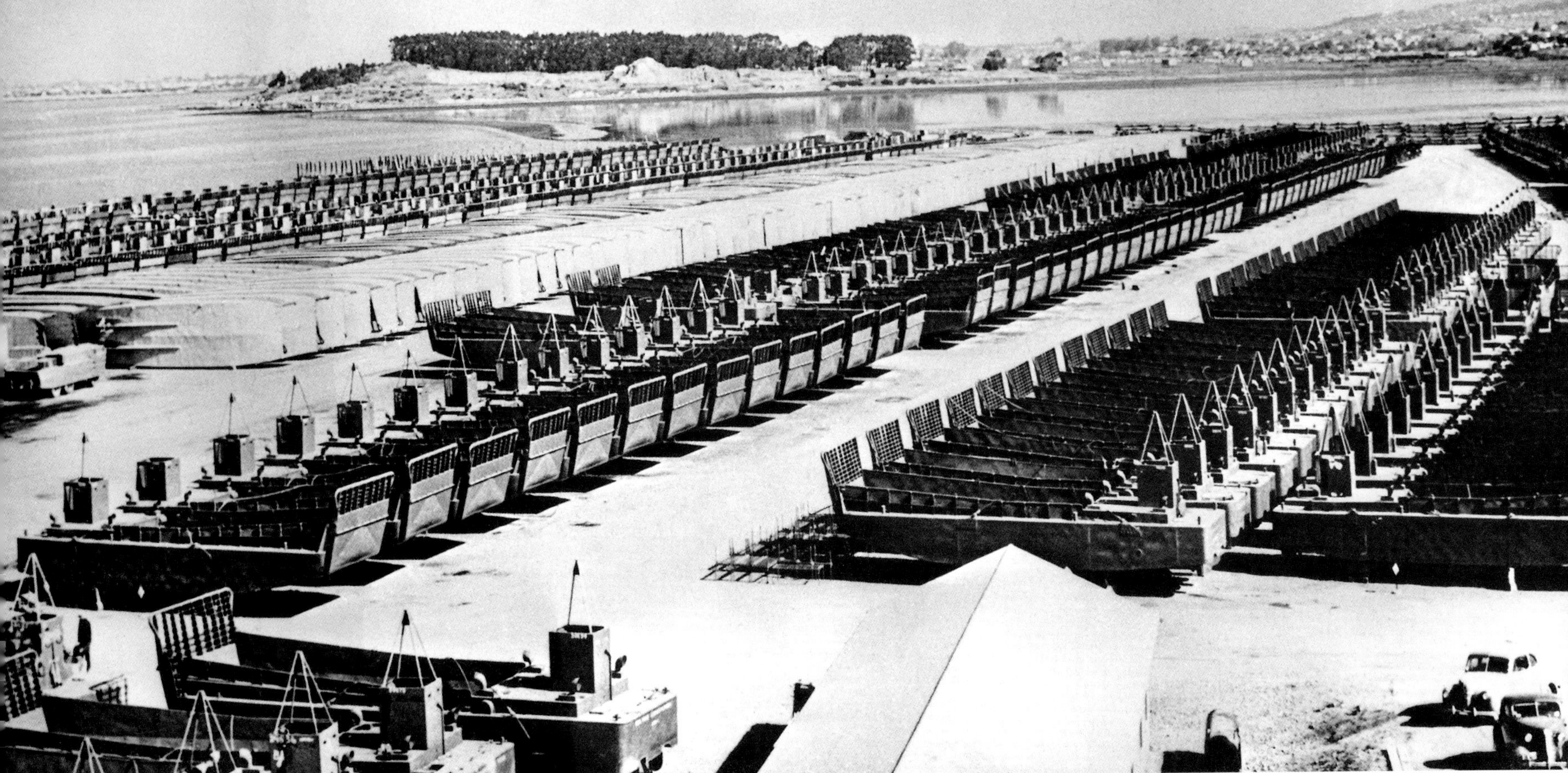

6th September 1944
TOPFOTO CODE: PD7485096
Long rows of American landing barges, lined up at a U.S. West Coast port, foretell of future Allied amphibious operations against the Japanese in the Pacific. The attack pattern being followed by the U.S. forces to wrestle Pacific island bases from the enemy has been: pre-landing air and sea bombardment followed by waves of assault troops who landed in barges of this type, covered by the off-shore fire of U.S. Navy warships. The high, protective bow wall of the craft lets down to form a ramp, facilitating speedy troop landings. APPROVED BY APPROPRIATE U.S. AUTHORITY. Released to morning papers 9/6/44. (U.S Office of War Information picture/Library of Congress, Prints & Photographs Division, Farm Security Administration/Office of War Information Black-and-White Negatives)

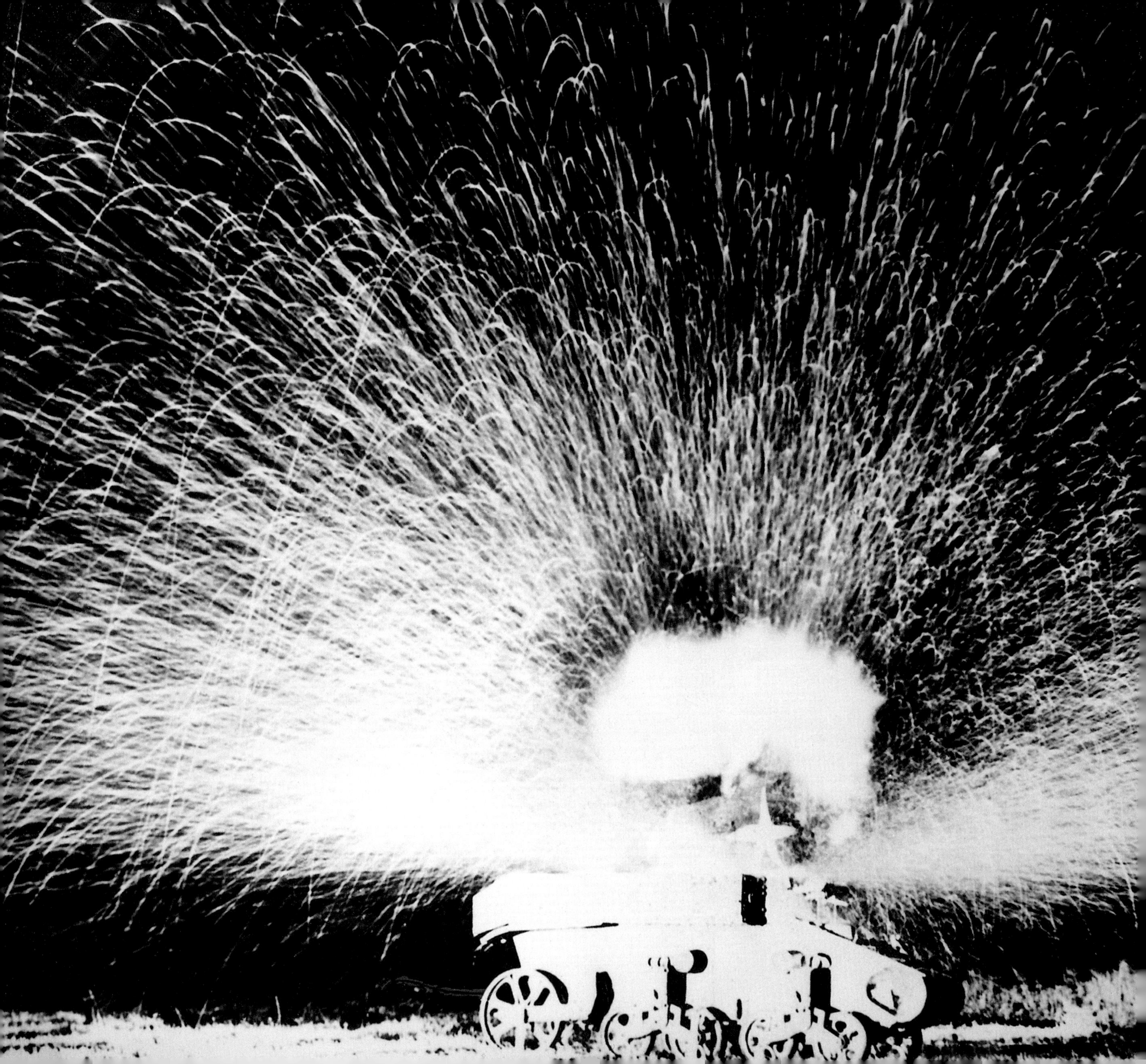

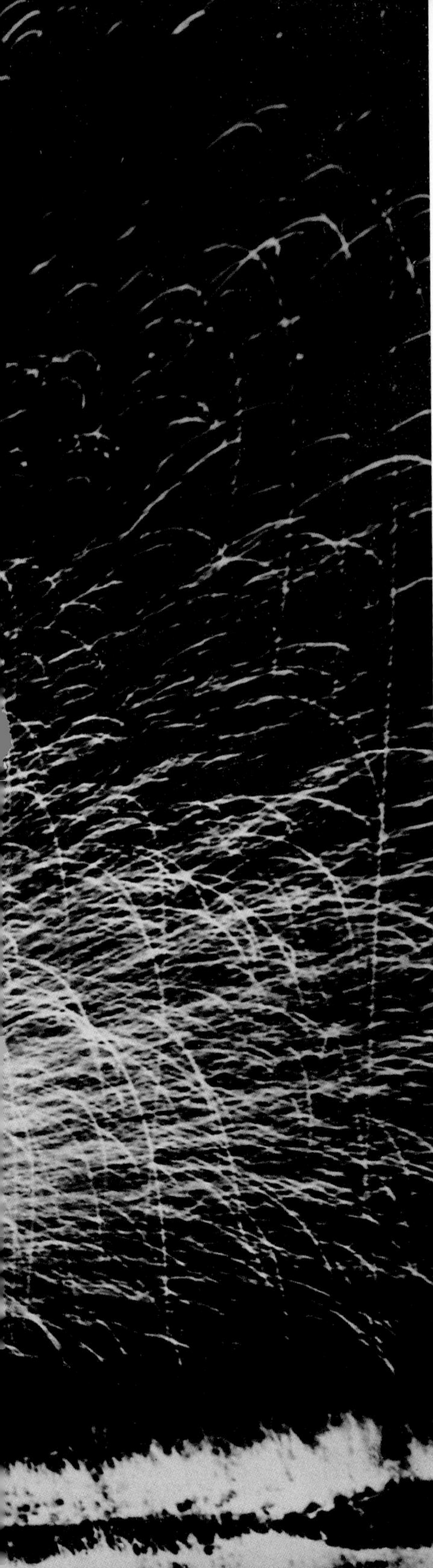

Bizarrely, the name Bazooka comes from the inventive mind of a 1930s American radio comedian by the name of Bob Burns. Burns served in the US Marine Corps during the First World War but had been a jazz musician prior to enlisting. Before the war, he had created a wind instrument from a pipe and named it 'Bazooka', allegedly derived from the Dutch word Bazuin, meaning trumpet.

During the First World War he created another version of his Bazooka made out of a stovepipe and a whisky funnel, with which he would entertain the troops during downtime. A newspaper article mentioned his strange instrument and when the M1 rocket launcher was tested in 1942, observers noticed the striking similarity with Burns' strange instrument. From then on the M1 was simply known as the Bazooka.

The Bazooka equalled the playing field for American infantrymen encountering tanks and hard fortifications in the field. The advantage was short-lived though, as the Germans captured several M1s during skirmishes in North Africa in 1943. They quickly made their own version, which they dubbed the Panzerschreck – literally meaning 'tank fright', and for good reason. While the American Bazooka was a modest 57mm calibre, the Panzerschreck was a terrifying 88mm calibre. This was, in comparison, 13mm larger than the main armament of the US Sherman tanks used by the Allies during the Second World War.

The Bazooka has evolved much since then and is still in active use today by scores of nations in a multitude of variations.

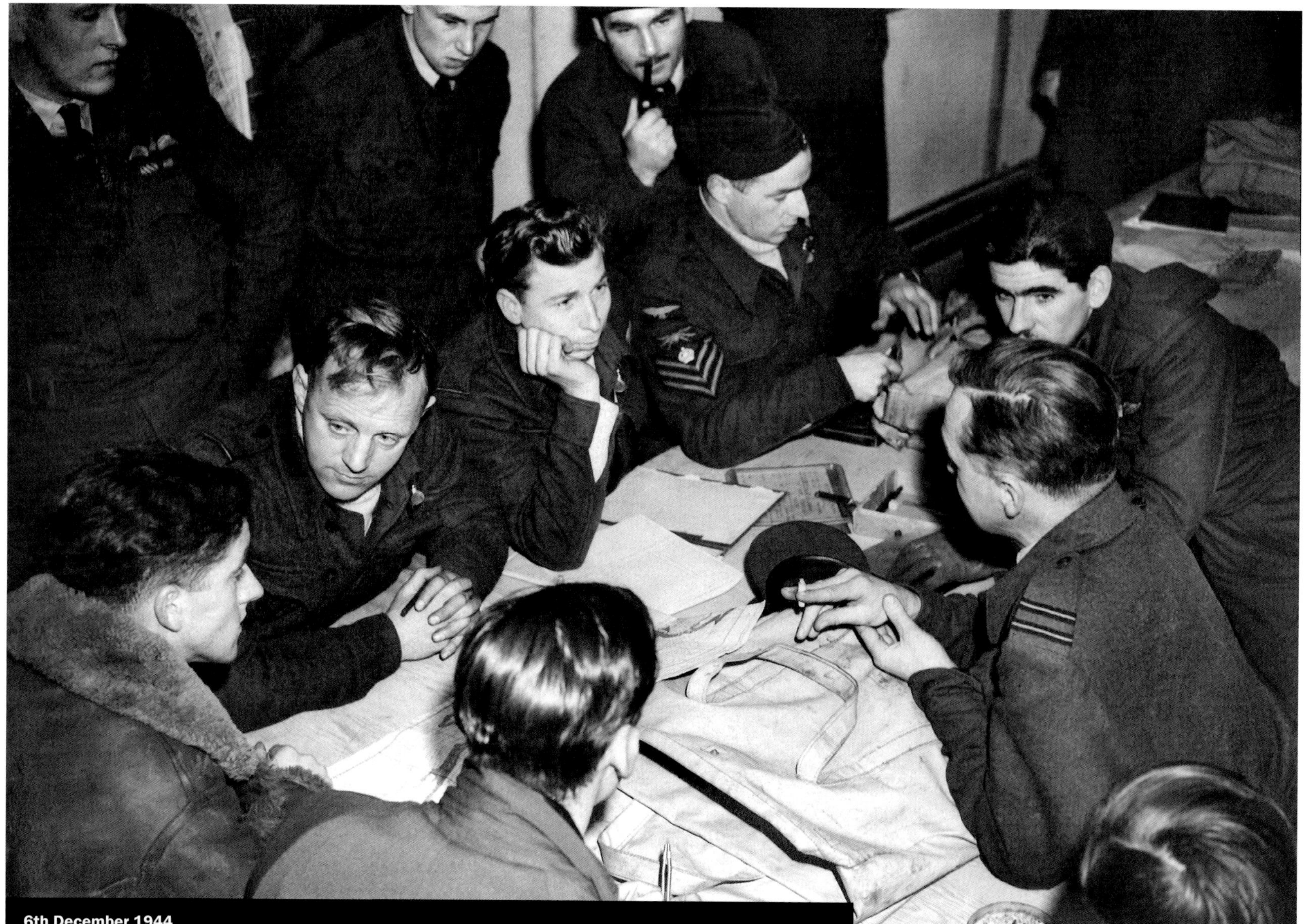

6th December 1944

TOPFOTO CODE: PD3001191

Incessant attacks by Coastal Command forced the Germans to run their North Sea convoys under cover of darkness, and now the Shipfinder Force of Coastal Command has made night almost as hazardous as day for Nazi vessels. Flares of immense candle-power are dropped by Wellington bombers, silhouetting the targets for other Wellingtons or Beaufighter strike forces, which attack in powerful formations. Shipfinder Force has made more than 100 attacks since D-Day, and while the nature of the new tactics makes observation of results difficult, it is known that many direct hits have been scored on enemy shipping. PHOTO SHOWS:- After being briefed for a night attack on German shipping, a Coastal Command Shipfinder Force crew makes final arrangements before setting out in search of the enemy. (Gaiger Planet Dec, 6 1944 PN Censor No. 376622)

Coastal Command played a vital role in the protection of the Allied ships. Primarily defensive in nature, it collectively clocked more than 1 million hours flying a staggering 240,000 operations. By the end of the war, it had sunk 366 German transport vessels and 212 submarines – aside from rescuing more than 10,000 people.

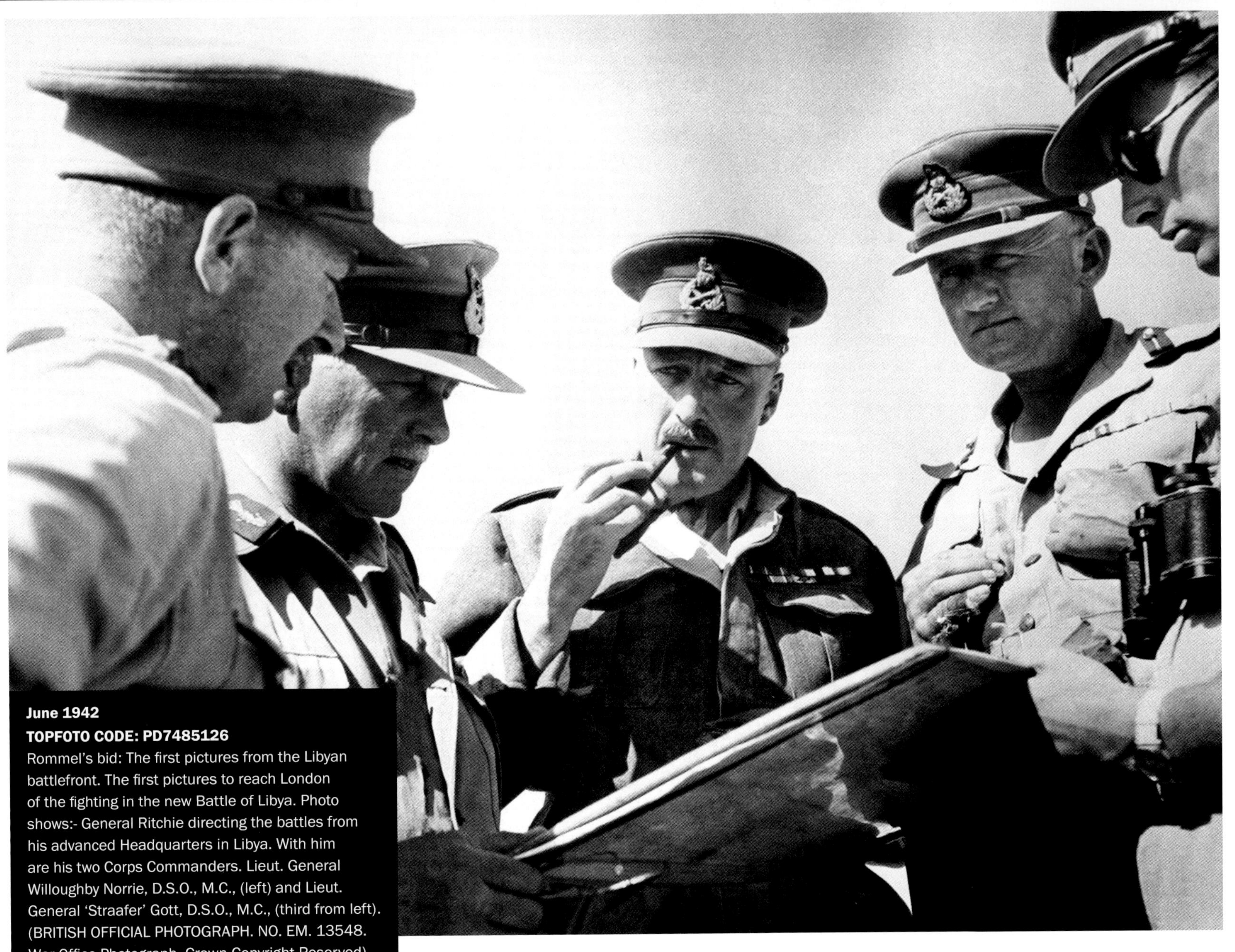

June 1942
TOPFOTO CODE: PD7485126
Rommel's bid: The first pictures from the Libyan battlefront. The first pictures to reach London of the fighting in the new Battle of Libya. Photo shows:- General Ritchie directing the battles from his advanced Headquarters in Libya. With him are his two Corps Commanders. Lieut. General Willoughby Norrie, D.S.O., M.C., (left) and Lieut. General 'Straafer' Gott, D.S.O., M.C., (third from left). (BRITISH OFFICIAL PHOTOGRAPH. NO. EM. 13548. War Office Photograph, Crown Copyright Reserved)

The Western Desert Campaign

The Western Desert Campaign (or simply the Desert War) was one of three major campaigns of the overall North African Campaign during the Second World War. It was fought in the harsh North African desert landscapes of Egypt and Libya, as well as Morocco, Algeria and Tunisia. It ran from 10 June 1940 to 13 May 1943, beginning when Italy officially entered the war after nearly a year on the sidelines. Germany had, since September 1939, encouraged Benito Mussolini to participate, but Il Duce had feared a full-scale war, in part due to Italy's poor supply of raw materials.

On 10 June, Italy declared war on France and Great Britain, and a formal alliance with Nazi Germany was established. Adolf Hitler's alleged response to Italy's sudden engagement was, with a wry and terse reflection, that they had been too cowardly to take part in the fighting but were now in a mighty hurry to take part in the spoils. Hitler did, however, accept the Italians' outrageous demands for territories in the Mediterranean, Africa, and the British-controlled Middle East – without comment.

Italy already had control over Libya and Abyssinia, and Mussolini saw the opportunity to incorporate a large part of north-east Africa under Italian rule by taking control of Sudan as well as Egypt, both of which were in British hands. As part of this fascist plan for territorial expansion, Mussolini led the Italian invasion of Egypt in direct opposition to the British Commonwealth and the Free French Forces.

For centuries Britain had deep-seated colonial interests in North Africa and Egypt, specifically because of the oil supplies flowing from the Middle East. The easy access to British-controlled India and the Far East, via the strategically important Suez Canal, was also put at immediate risk. On 8 September 1940, a feeble and poorly trained army attacked Egypt. Italy made small gains, but despite Mussolini's urges to keep advancing, Marshal Rodolfo Graziani halted near Sidi Barrani in scattered camps. Prior to the invasion, Graziani already had serious doubts about his forces' ability to engage and defeat the Allied forces, and rightly so as not long after the British launched Operation Compass to drive them out.

The Italian Tenth Army vastly outnumbered the Western Desert Force (WDF) in every aspect, with 150,000 infantry soldiers against a mere 36,000 British; 1,600 guns against 120; 600 tanks against 275; and 331 aircraft against the RAF's 142. Still, after a swift two-month battle, the combined British forces had suffered the death of only 500 men with 1,300 wounded, against a staggering 5,500 Italians killed, 10,000 wounded, and 138,000 Italians and Libyans captured. The RAF lost twenty-six aircraft, while Italy sustained the catastrophic losses of 420 tanks and 845 guns.

By the end of the operation in February 1941, the WDF, mainly due to wear and tear on equipment, was forced to stop their pursuit of the enemy at El Agheila, but nevertheless had destroyed and forced the surrender of the remnants of the Italian Tenth Army.

Operation Compass was a gigantic success that ultimately left Hitler at a crossroads: would he support his most important ally or leave him to his own devices? Hitler decided to send in General Erwin Rommel and the German Afrika Korps. Rommel came to Tripoli along with 16,000 men and 100 tanks. This turned the tables considerably, as large parts of the WDF had been redirected by Churchill to aid Greece in its own fight against the Italian dictator.

The British were forced to retreat from the Greek mainland to Crete and from here, under heavy attacks by German Stukas and paratroopers, they had to further evacuate 15,000 men, while 18,000 were taken prisoner. Germany now controlled a large part of the Mediterranean and the supply routes, while the British, having lost substantial troops in the Balkans, had left the forces in North Africa at a huge disadvantage.

Having pushed and pursued the Italians back to the most western part of Libya, Rommel's counter-offensive, Operation Sonnenblume, now drove the British right back into Egypt. His audacious, bold and aggressive strategies had taken the British, and Commander in Chief General Archibald Wavell, completely by surprise. (For more information about the battle in North Africa read about Operation Torch on page 119.)

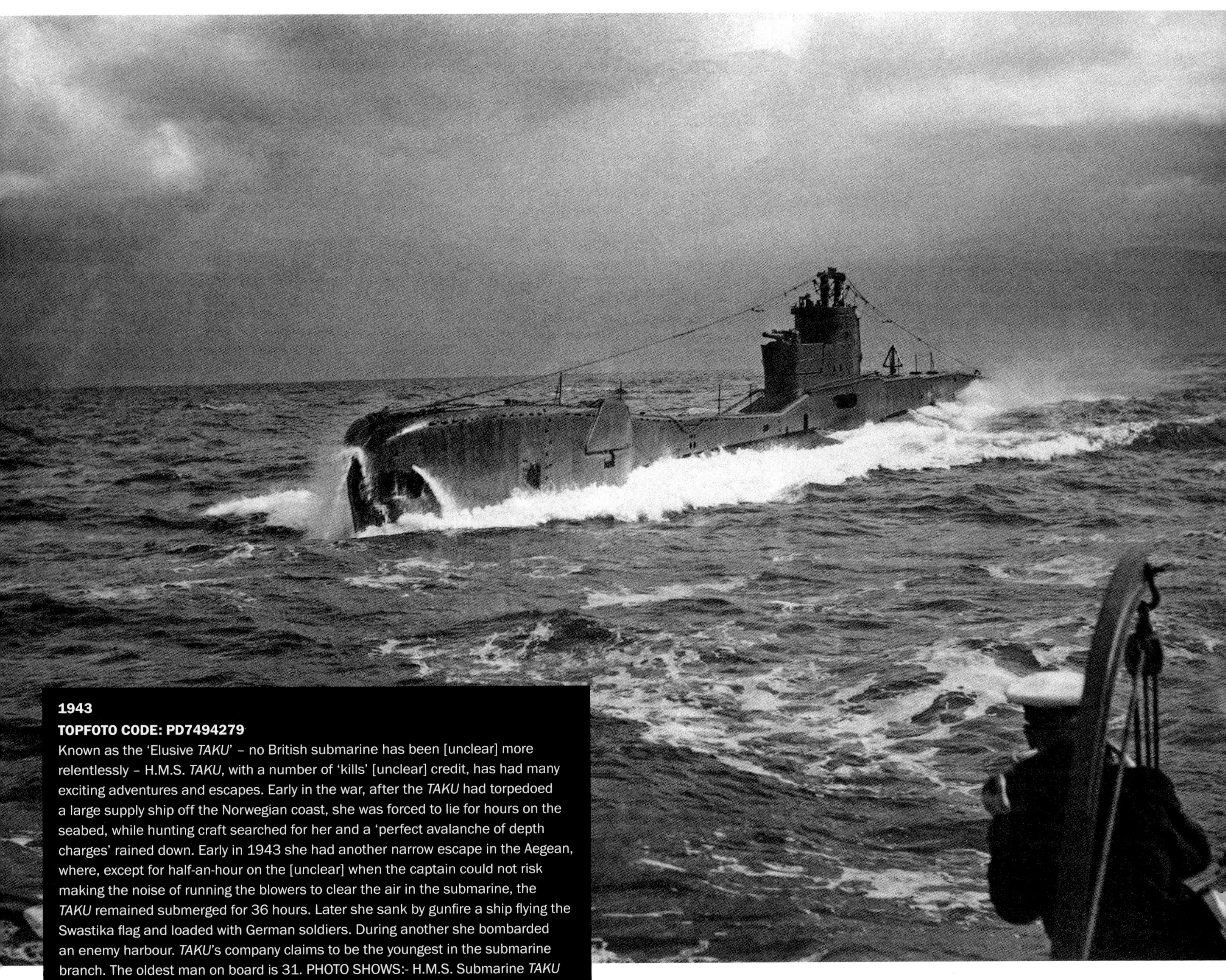

1943

TOPFOTO CODE: PD7494279

Known as the 'Elusive *TAKU*' – no British submarine has been [unclear] more relentlessly – H.M.S. *TAKU*, with a number of 'kills' [unclear] credit, has had many exciting adventures and escapes. Early in the war, after the *TAKU* had torpedoed a large supply ship off the Norwegian coast, she was forced to lie for hours on the seabed, while hunting craft searched for her and a 'perfect avalanche of depth charges' rained down. Early in 1943 she had another narrow escape in the Aegean, where, except for half-an-hour on the [unclear] when the captain could not risk making the noise of running the blowers to clear the air in the submarine, the *TAKU* remained submerged for 36 hours. Later she sank by gunfire a ship flying the Swastika flag and loaded with German soldiers. During another she bombarded an enemy harbour. *TAKU*'s company claims to be the youngest in the submarine branch. The oldest man on board is 31. PHOTO SHOWS:- H.M.S. Submarine *TAKU* on patrol.

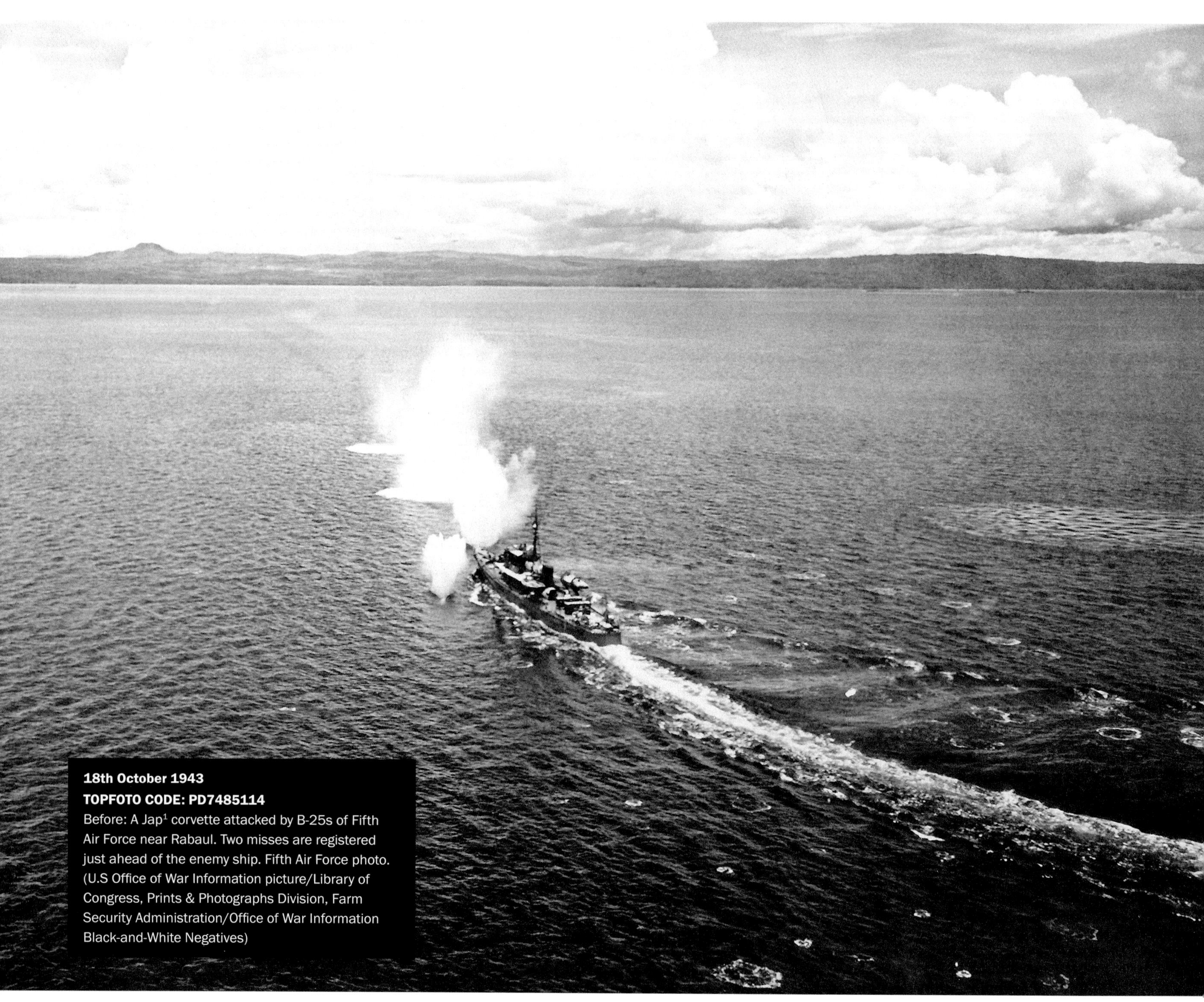

18th October 1943

TOPFOTO CODE: PD7485114

Before: A Jap[1] corvette attacked by B-25s of Fifth
Air Force near Rabaul. Two misses are registered
just ahead of the enemy ship. Fifth Air Force photo.
(U.S Office of War Information picture/Library of
Congress, Prints & Photographs Division, Farm
Security Administration/Office of War Information
Black-and-White Negatives)

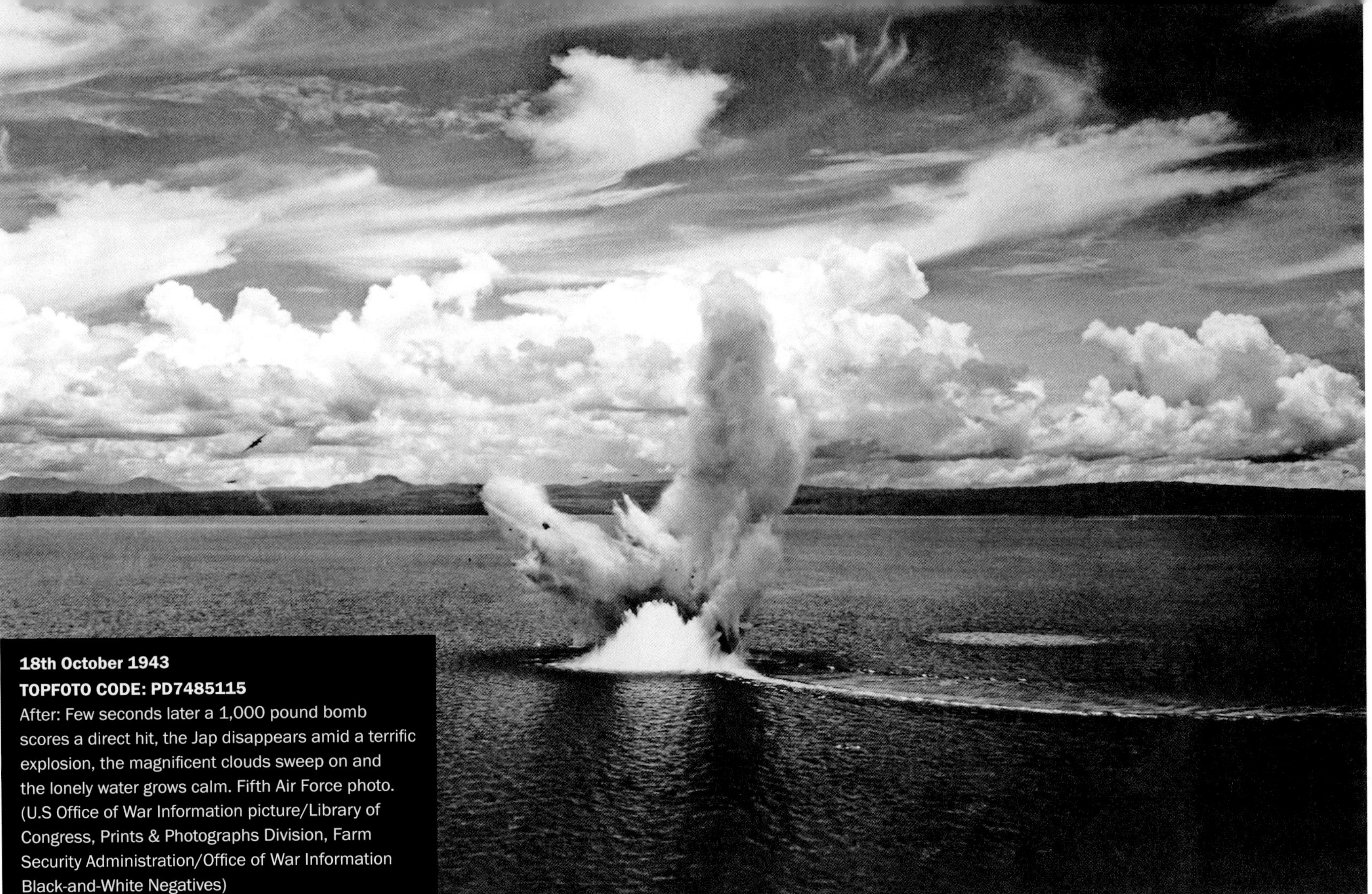

Following the success in Guadalcanal (read more on page 39) at the beginning of 1943, the Allied forces began their advance through the Solomon Islands, aiming at Rabaul. It was an important and heavily fortified naval and air base that had been held by the Japanese since 1942 (with over 100,000 men), that enabled them to control much of the Pacific sea lanes and block the Allied advancement into the Philippines.

Operation Cartwheel, with the aim of neutralising Rabaul, was a complex plan consisting of several subordinate operations. Combined land and sea attacks under General Douglas MacArthur and Admiral William Halsey would eventually isolate a number of islands, cut them off from their main forces and render them inert. The hope was that, by employing a bypass strategy rather than a frontal attack, they would avoid large numbers of casualties.

On 12 October 1943, 349 aircraft initiated the bombing campaign, in what became known as the 'Neutralisation of Rabaul'. The before and after photos here show the follow-up raid on 18 October, where fifty B-25 Mitchell medium bombers from the US Fifth Air Force attacked the harbour, the airfield, and the ships at Rabaul. Systematic bombing continued until early 1944.

The outcome of the battles at Rabaul was disastrous for the Japanese, who lost hundreds of planes, several warships, and invaluable skilled manpower. The isolation strategy was an overwhelming success, effectively turning Rabaul into a prison island – without ever having to actually capture its prisoners.

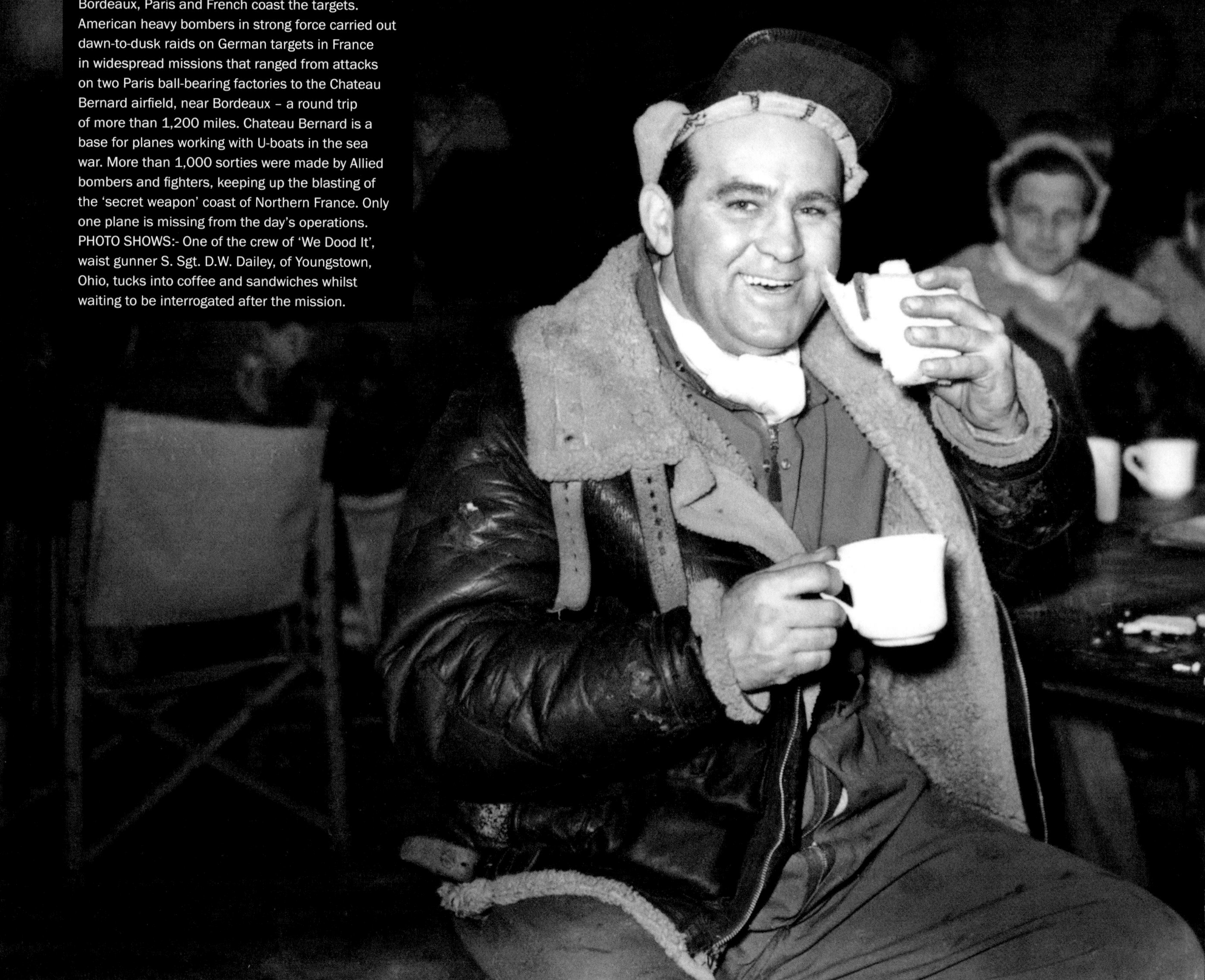
Bordeaux, Paris and French coast the targets. American heavy bombers in strong force carried out dawn-to-dusk raids on German targets in France in widespread missions that ranged from attacks on two Paris ball-bearing factories to the Chateau Bernard airfield, near Bordeaux – a round trip of more than 1,200 miles. Chateau Bernard is a base for planes working with U-boats in the sea war. More than 1,000 sorties were made by Allied bombers and fighters, keeping up the blasting of the 'secret weapon' coast of Northern France. Only one plane is missing from the day's operations. PHOTO SHOWS:- One of the crew of 'We Dood It', waist gunner S. Sgt. D.W. Dailey, of Youngstown, Ohio, tucks into coffee and sandwiches whilst waiting to be interrogated after the mission.

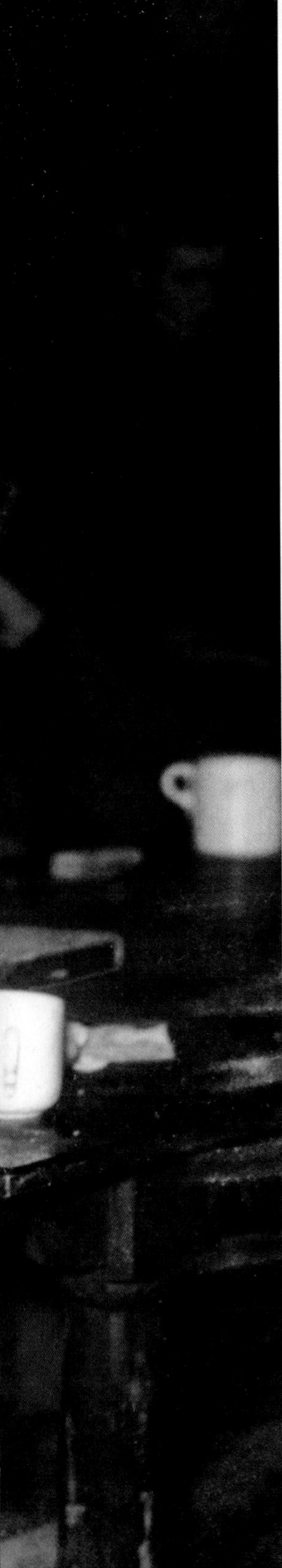

Initially, the US Army Air Force stated that a total of twenty-five missions flown was required to complete a tour of duty for anyone serving in a heavy bomber. It was an estimate based on what could be expected by the men, determined by the very heavy physical and mental strain placed upon them. It seemed a near-impossible task, but nevertheless gave everyone an idea – or at least the illusion – of having a finishing line in sight. This number was later raised to thirty-five missions. This was part of the inspiration for the Army Air Force veteran Joseph Heller's book *Catch 22*, spawning the idea of a paradox from which there is no escape.

Combat losses were extremely high for the bomber crews. Statistically, across the duration of the whole war, a staggering 51 per cent of aircrews were KIA (Killed In Action), 12 per cent were killed in non-operational incidents and a further 13 per cent ended up as POWs. Only 24 per cent survived the war unscathed – a one in four chance of survival. Furthermore, gunners and waist gunners in particular, were the most likely of all positions in the plane to end up KIA, mainly due to their exposed positions in the open gunner windows.

While German flak (Fliegerabwehrkanone, or aircraft defence cannon) was feared by all aircrew, the biggest threat to bombers was the enemy fighters. It was not until late in 1943 that the B-17s were accompanied by long-range fighter escorts, so the only protection available up until then were the gunners such as our man S/Sgt Dailey.

During the period from 7 September 1943 to 18 April 1944, Dailey flew twenty-six combat missions as a flexible (waist) gunner and was awarded the Good Conduct Medal on 15 January 1944. On 11 March, he was promoted to staff sergeant.

On 30 January 1944 (one month after the photo was taken), 'We Dood It' went on its last flight. During the 384th BG mission #56, it was attacked by several of the Luftwaffe's feared Fw 190 fighters (read more about this on page 17). Bursting into flames, the crew still managed to continue and drop their bombs on the target before finally crashing in Minden, Germany.

Three of the ten crew members managed to bail out, but the other seven were killed instantly.

Luckily for Dailey, on that very day, he was assigned as a gunner on a different plane named 'Patches II/Spotted Cow' that never took off. S/Sgt Dailey's last duty date was on 18 April 1944. After completing his tour and twenty-six missions, he returned safely to the US. Remarkably, he was never once injured.

Of the 1½ million tons of bombs dropped over Germany during the war, 640,000 tons – or more than one third – were dropped from B-17s. Some 12,731 B-17s were built, with 4,754 lost during the war. About fifty are preserved today.

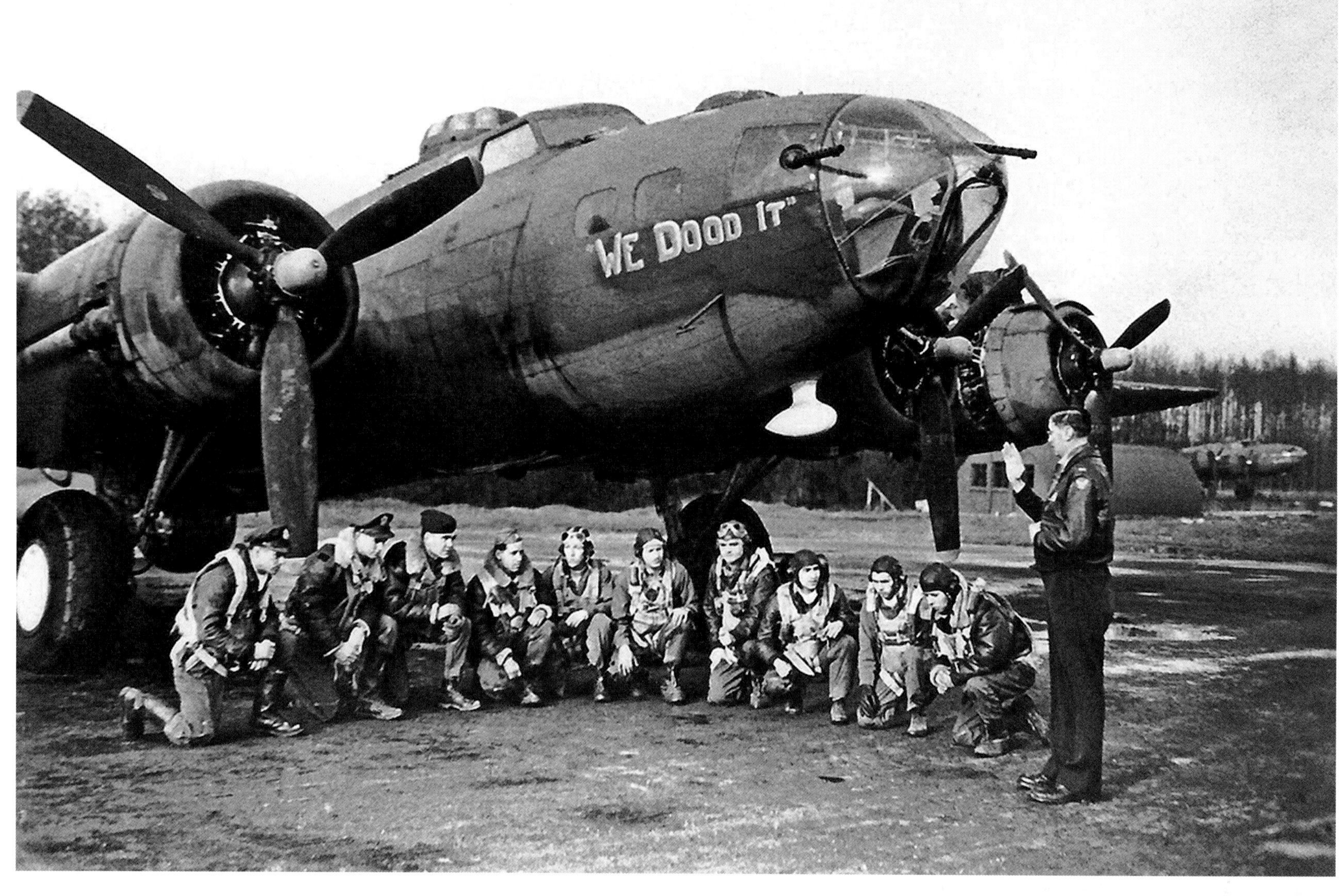

Photo of 'We Dood It', with Father Billy, blessing the men and the machine before the mission. (Courtesy of https://384thbombgroup.com)

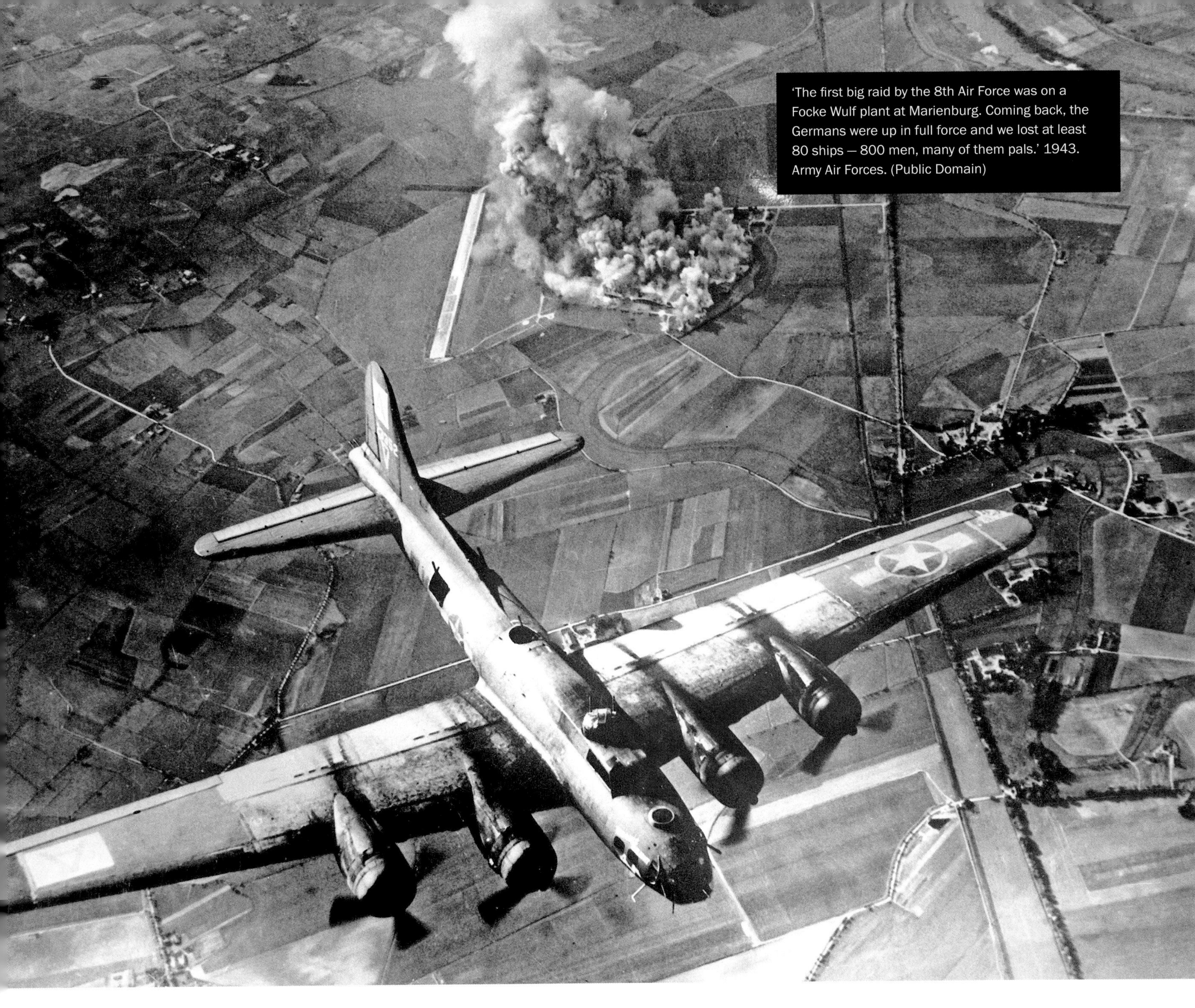

'The first big raid by the 8th Air Force was on a
Focke Wulf plant at Marienburg. Coming back, the
Germans were up in full force and we lost at least
80 ships — 800 men, many of them pals.' 1943.
Army Air Forces. (Public Domain)

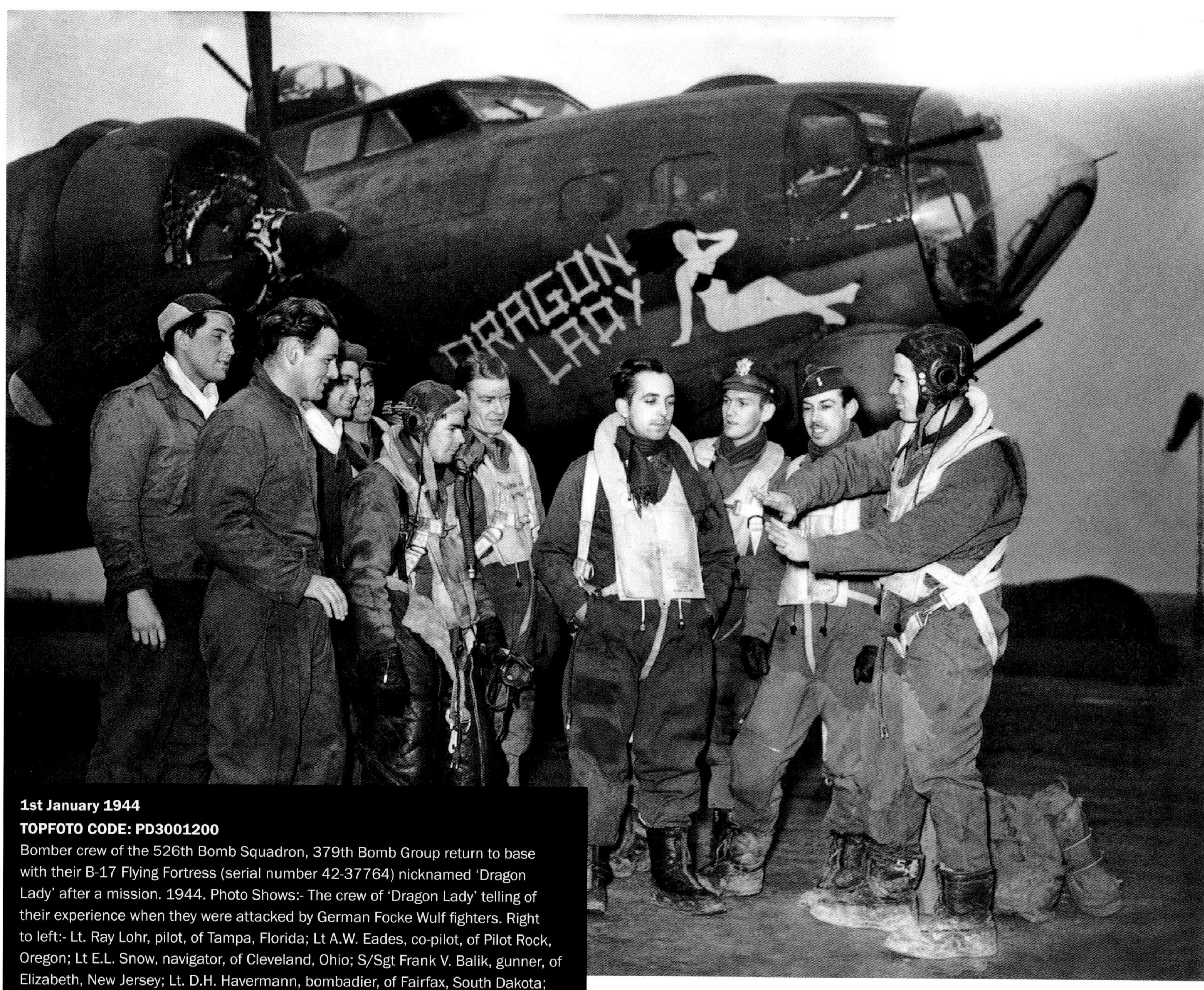

1st January 1944

TOPFOTO CODE: PD3001200

Bomber crew of the 526th Bomb Squadron, 379th Bomb Group return to base with their B-17 Flying Fortress (serial number 42-37764) nicknamed 'Dragon Lady' after a mission. 1944. Photo Shows:- The crew of 'Dragon Lady' telling of their experience when they were attacked by German Focke Wulf fighters. Right to left:- Lt. Ray Lohr, pilot, of Tampa, Florida; Lt A.W. Eades, co-pilot, of Pilot Rock, Oregon; Lt E.L. Snow, navigator, of Cleveland, Ohio; S/Sgt Frank V. Balik, gunner, of Elizabeth, New Jersey; Lt. D.H. Havermann, bombadier, of Fairfax, South Dakota; S/Sgt. Z.Y. Cambell, turret gunner, of Leakesville, Miss., S/Sgt V.V. Dalberto, tailgunner, of Berwick, Pennsylvania; S/Sgt. W.E. Cronin, ball turret gunner, of Worcester, Mass. T/Sgt B.A. Curran, radio, of Omaha, Nebraska; and S/Sgt. S.H Kirkpatrick, waistgunner of Philadelphia.

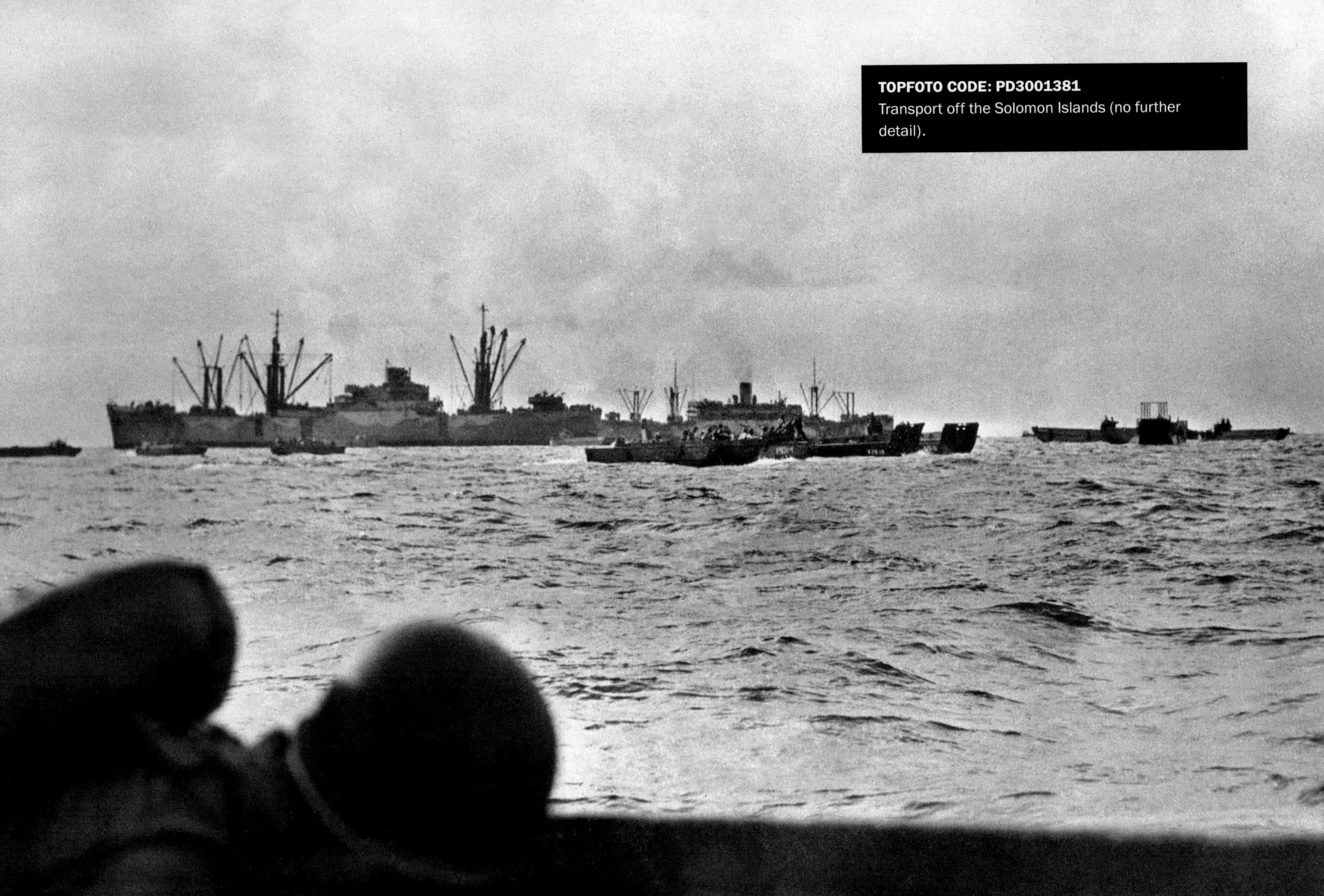

The Solomon Islands campaign was a massive undertaking fought between primarily US and Japanese forces in the Pacific. Following the devastating attack on Pearl Harbor in 1941 and the Americans' subsequent entry into the Second World War, the Japanese attempted to create a bulwark against the US, with the occupation of a number of islands in the Pacific.

In August 1942, US forces began their first major offensive against the Empire of Japan on the island of Guadalcanal in the Solomon Islands. Guadalcanal was strategically extremely important for the Americans, as the Japanese presence there disrupted the supply lines between the US and Australia and enabled them to control the sea routes.

Hard battles were fought at land, sea, and air, though the land battles in particular proved to be brutal. Both sides suffered tremendous losses of men, ships and aircraft. The attrition in weaponry was fairly equal but Japanese casualties were almost three to one, with the loss of nearly 20,000 men against approximately 7,000 US troops.

The eventual Allied victory came at a heavy cost, but nevertheless provided a much-needed boost in morale and was an important step towards defeating Japan.

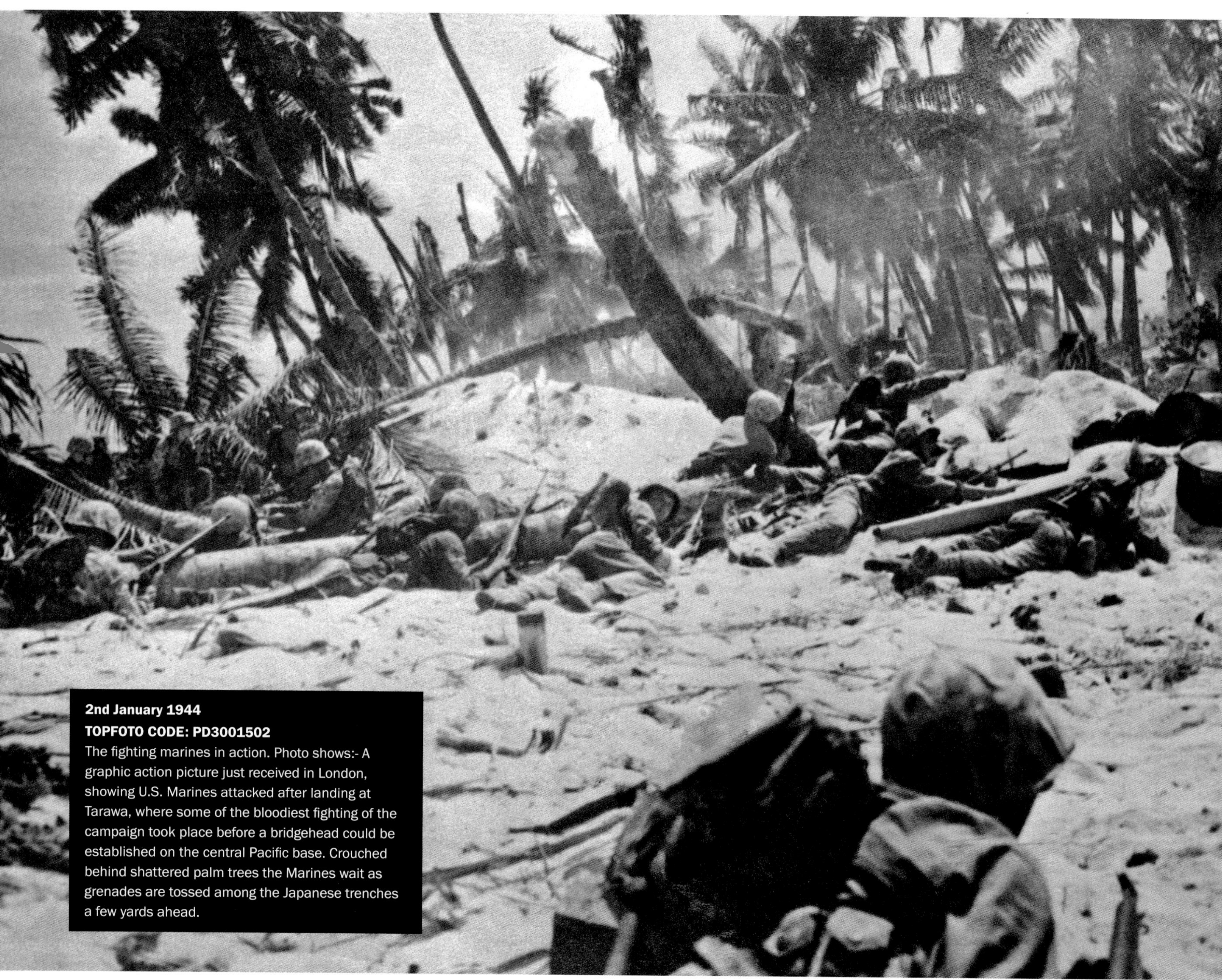

2nd January 1944
TOPFOTO CODE: PD3001502
The fighting marines in action. Photo shows:- A
graphic action picture just received in London,
showing U.S. Marines attacked after landing at
Tarawa, where some of the bloodiest fighting of the
campaign took place before a bridgehead could be
established on the central Pacific base. Crouched
behind shattered palm trees the Marines wait as
grenades are tossed among the Japanese trenches
a few yards ahead.

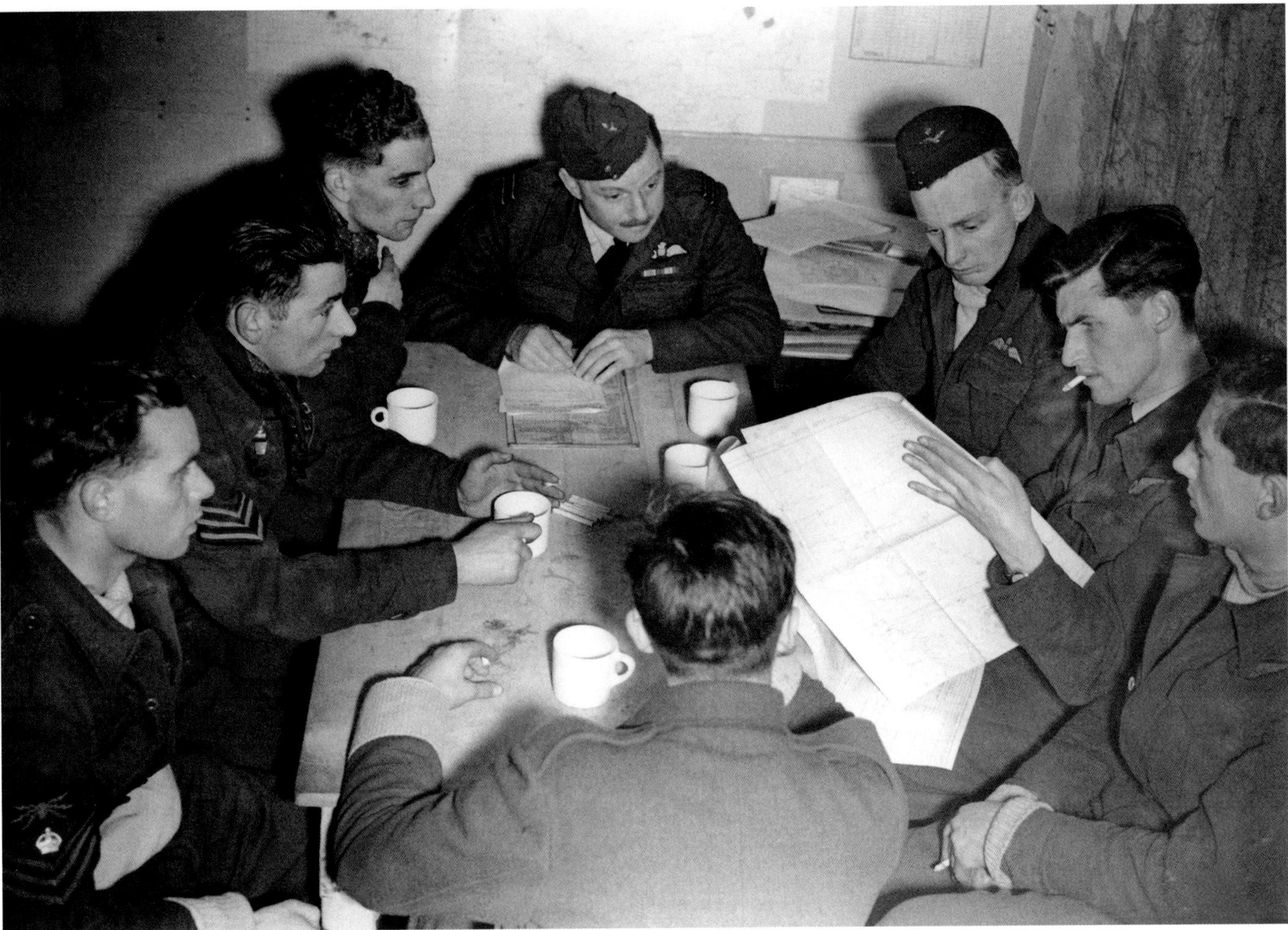

From November 1943 until March 1944, RAF Bomber Command led a campaign known as the Battle of Berlin, a relentless bombing of mainly the German capital. Air Marshal Sir Arthur 'Bomber' Harris had calculated that British losses would be around 400–500 aircraft, but he believed that the Germans would lose the war as a result.

Though significant damage was inflicted on German infrastructure, industry and workers, the campaign was an abject failure. The costs were much too high – even for wartime projections – and far exceeded what the RAF considered to be the maximum sustainable operational loss rate. A total of 492 aircraft were lost, with their crew killed or captured, and nearly twice that number of aircraft were damaged. Bomber Command accumulated 7 per cent of its total losses of the Second World War during these months, with 2,690 dead and 1,000 ending up as prisoners of war.

It is a sad fact that in the present day, no one seems to have learned the lesson that history has taught us. A brief look at the news reveals similar issues in the conflict between Israel and Palestine, as well as the war in Ukraine. The hazardous willingness to gamble and sustain such great losses in order to possibly achieve a win recalls a much earlier conflict in history, the Battle of Asculum in 279 BC. Pyrrhus of Epirus' battle against the Romans was at the cost of such heavy casualties that, while he won the battle, he lost the war as his forces were all but annihilated, spawning the phrase 'Pyrrhic victory'.

While the true intention of Harris' bombing campaign was to subjugate the German civilian population and force a surrender by its government (much like the Germans intended with the London Blitz), in practice during a conflict this has often had the opposite effect. The adversity seems to just make the inflicted population dig deeper and spiral down into pursuits of vengeance and basic retaliation. It elevates the level of patriotism rather than subdues it, and generally renders diplomatic solutions harder to achieve.

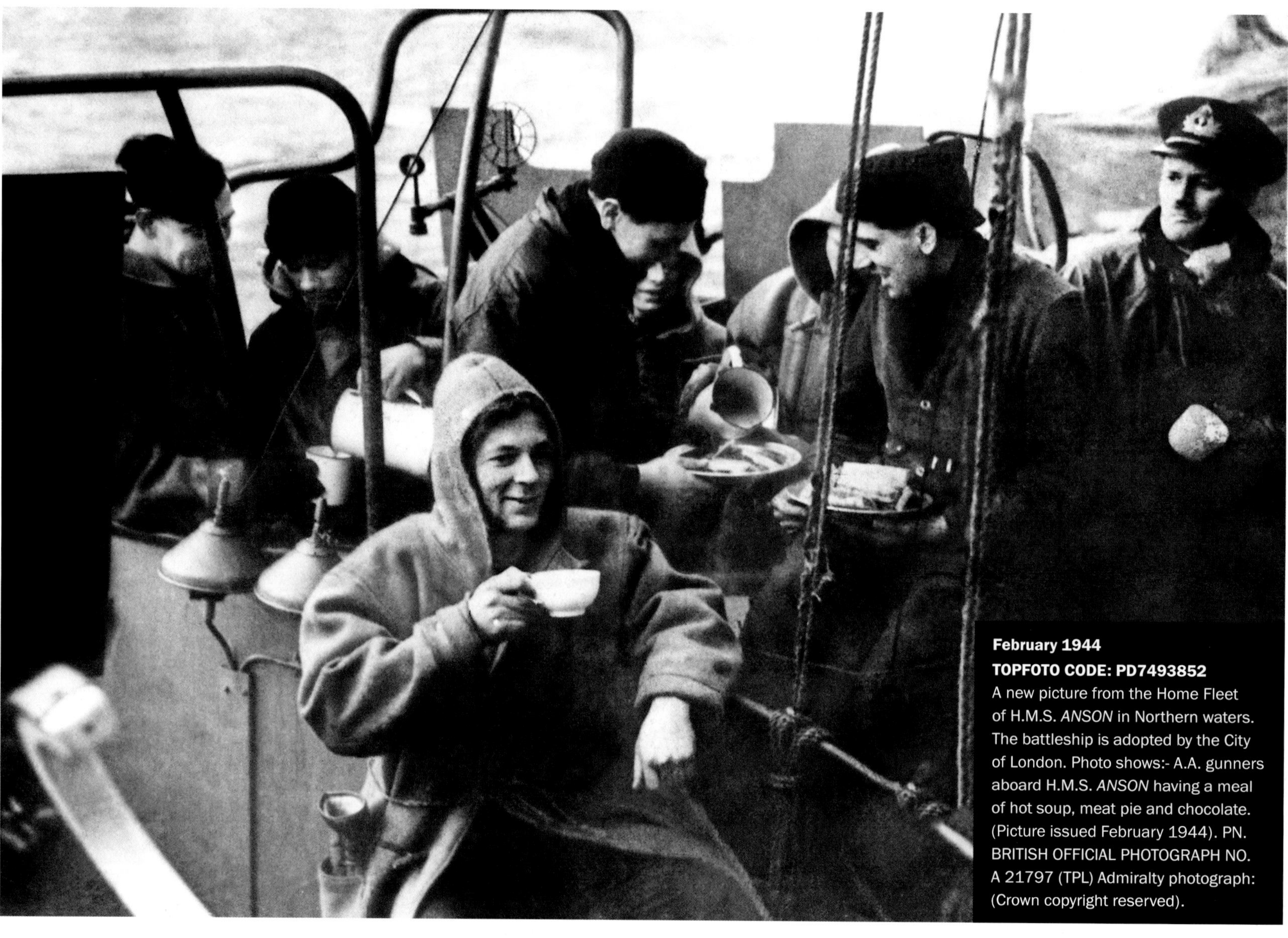

HMS *Anson* was one of five top-of-the-line battleships used by the British during the Second World War. Part of the King George V class, and with a length of 744ft and 11.5in, it was finished on 22 June 1942.

Active in service until 1949, the battleship participated in numerous operations, among them Operation Tungsten to take out the German battleship *Tirpitz* (in the same month as the photo was taken).

Due to the number of ships already lost during the Second World War, and the rising demand for convoy escorts in the Atlantic, the British government came up with the idea for Warship Week. It was a national savings campaign, where cities, towns, and villages would raise enough funds to pay for a vessel. In turn, the city would then 'adopt' the vessel and its crew, and as the caption text shows, HMS *Anson* was adopted by London. This was done following a Warship Week campaign in March 1942. *Anson* was eventually sold for scrap in December 1957.

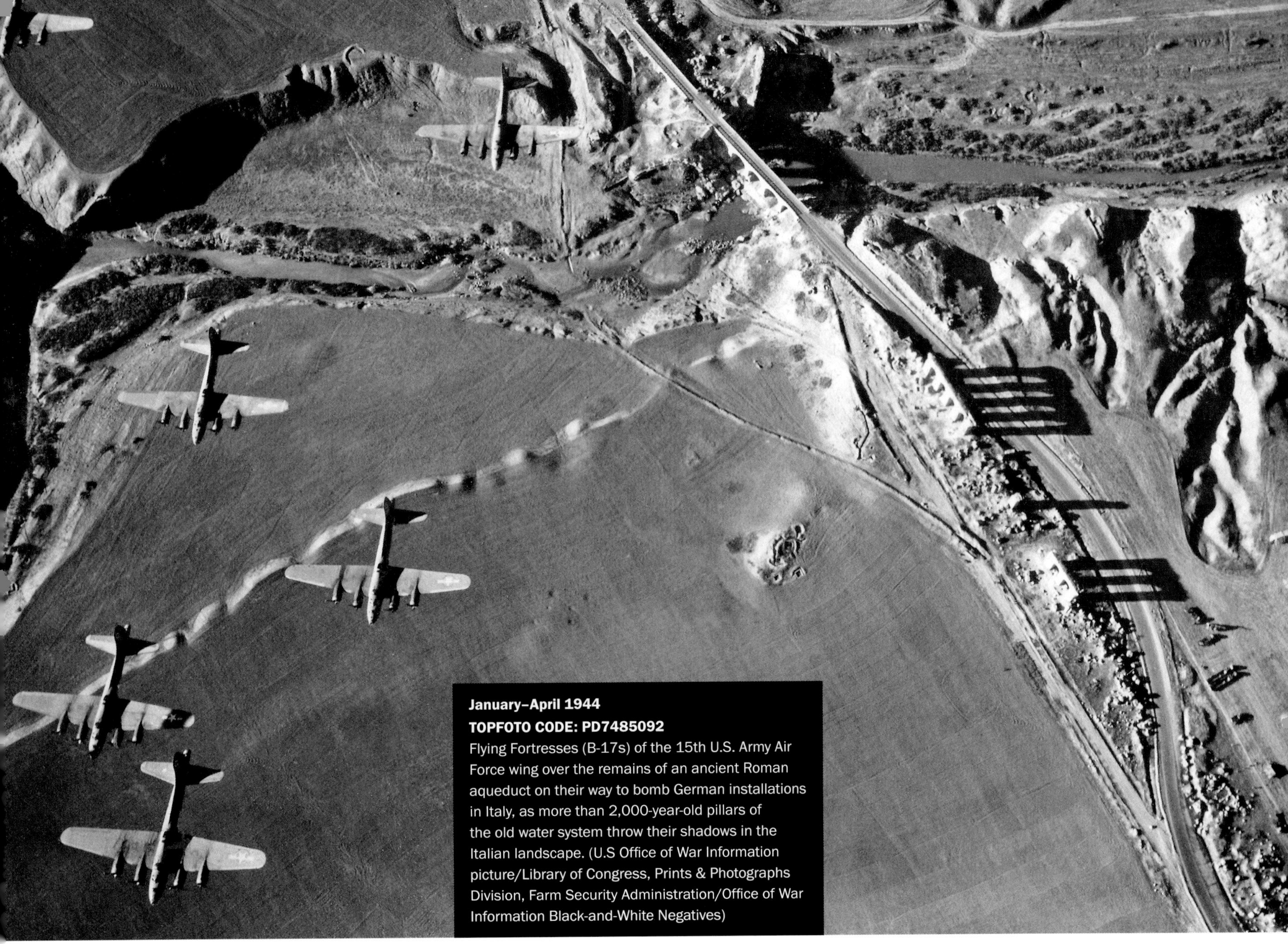

The B-17 bombers in the photo are part of the 347th Bomb Squadron, 99th Bombardment Group of the 15th Air Force. Some sources indicate this photo was taken on 6 January 1944, while others state that it was taken on 16 April.

The 99th Bomb Group was active from 28 January 1942. It had previously been in the 12th Air Force and was reassigned to the 15th in November 1943. The group participated in strategic bombings on most occupied European countries during the following two years until it was inactivated on 8 November 1945. While in service it earned two DUCs (Distinguished Unit Citation, later renamed PUC, Presidential Unit Citation) for heroism in action.

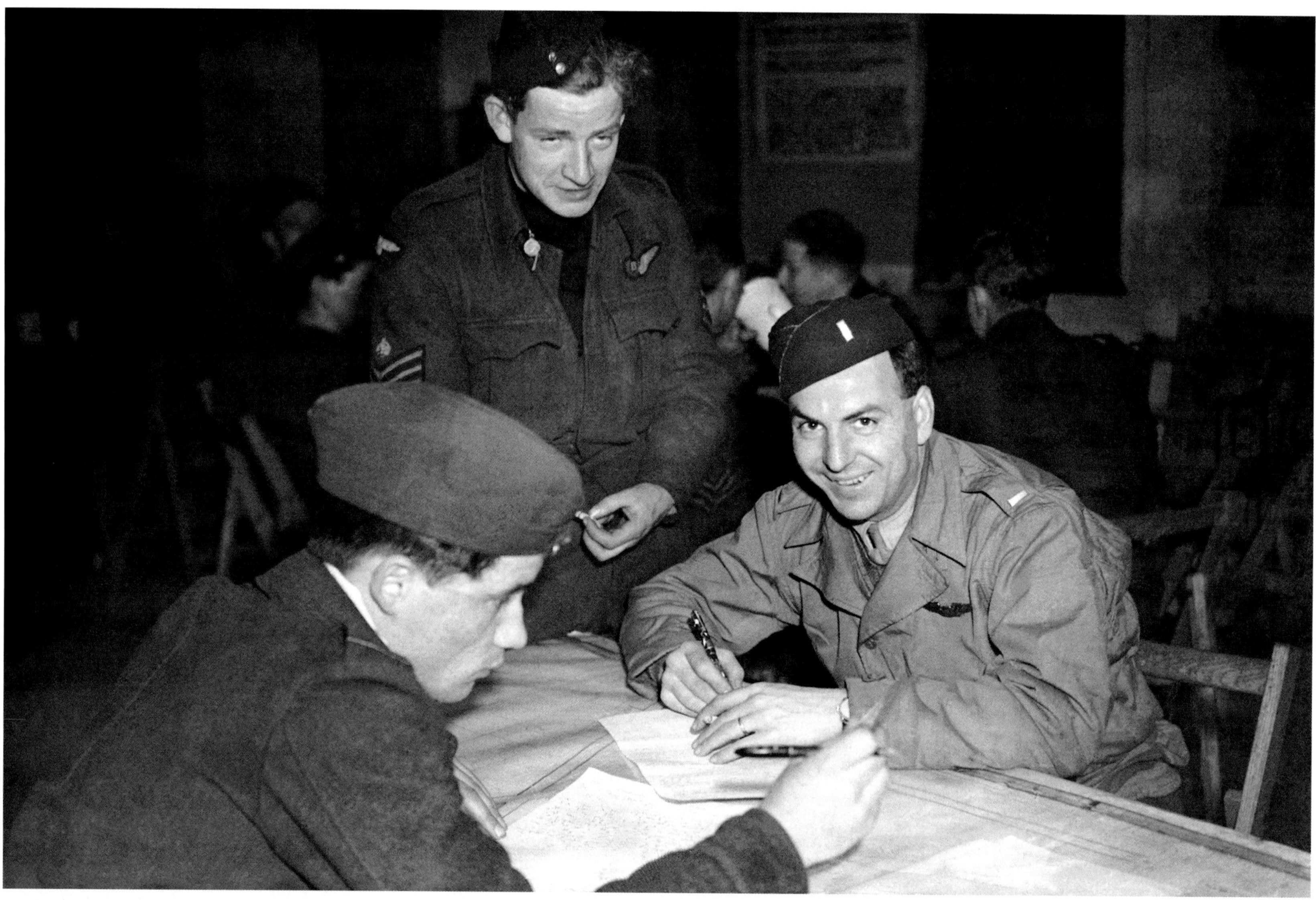

An RAF campaign report from these attacks on 22 and 23 April 1944 indicates that there were three targets – Düsseldorf, Brunswick and the Laon railway yards in northern France. A total of 596 aircraft flew to attack Düsseldorf – 323 Lancasters, 254 Halifaxes, and 19 Mosquitos – which dropped a total of 2,150 tons of bombs.

A total of 238 Lancasters and seventeen Mosquitos of No. 5 Group and ten Lancasters of No. 1 Group flew to Brunswick, and a further 181 aircraft were dispatched to Laon. A number of other aircraft flew diversion raids, intruder patrols and leaflet flights. The total sorties were 1,116, during which forty-two aircraft were lost.

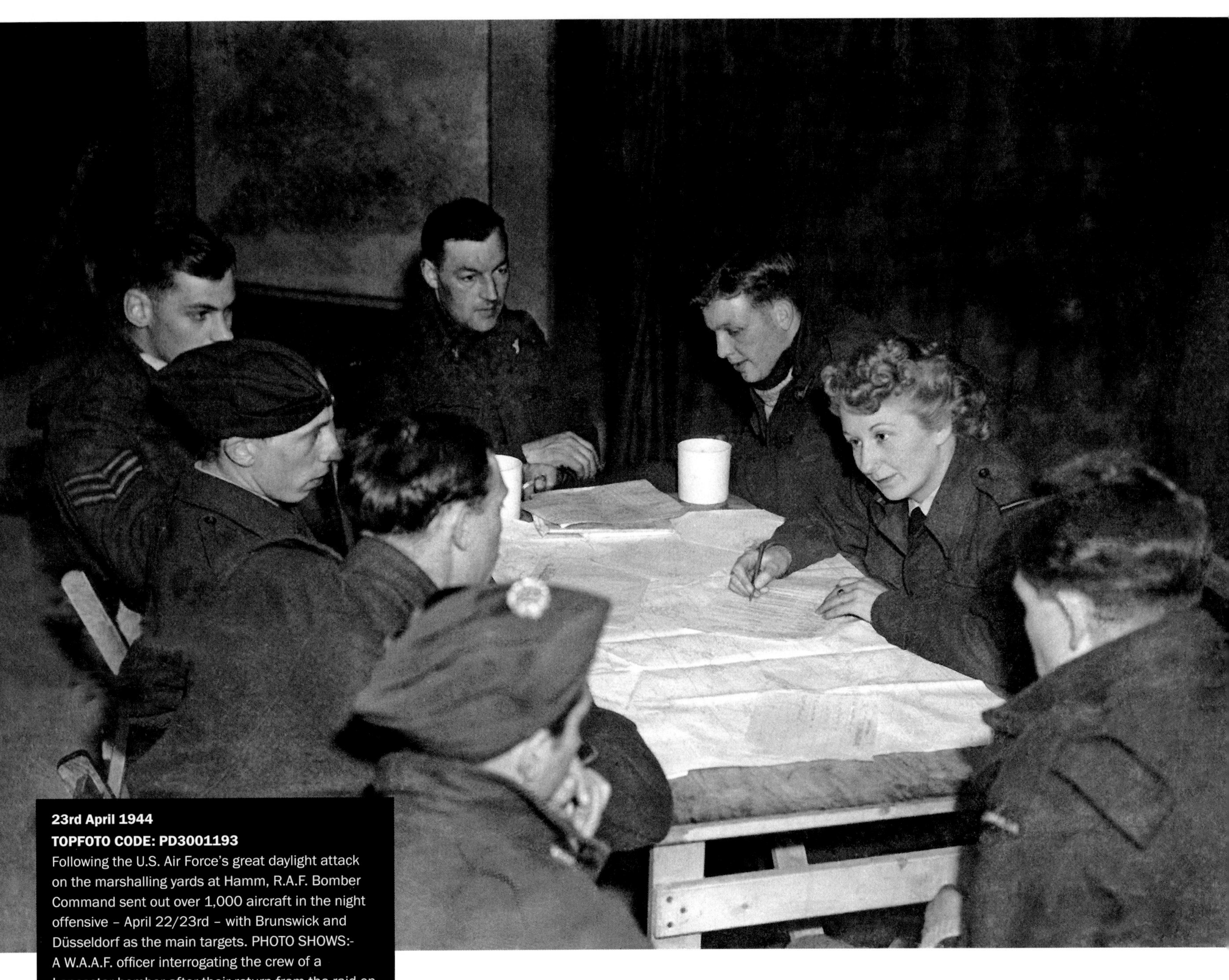

23rd April 1944
TOPFOTO CODE: PD3001193
Following the U.S. Air Force's great daylight attack on the marshalling yards at Hamm, R.A.F. Bomber Command sent out over 1,000 aircraft in the night offensive – April 22/23rd – with Brunswick and Düsseldorf as the main targets. PHOTO SHOWS:- A W.A.A.F. officer interrogating the crew of a Lancaster bomber after their return from the raid on Düsseldorf.

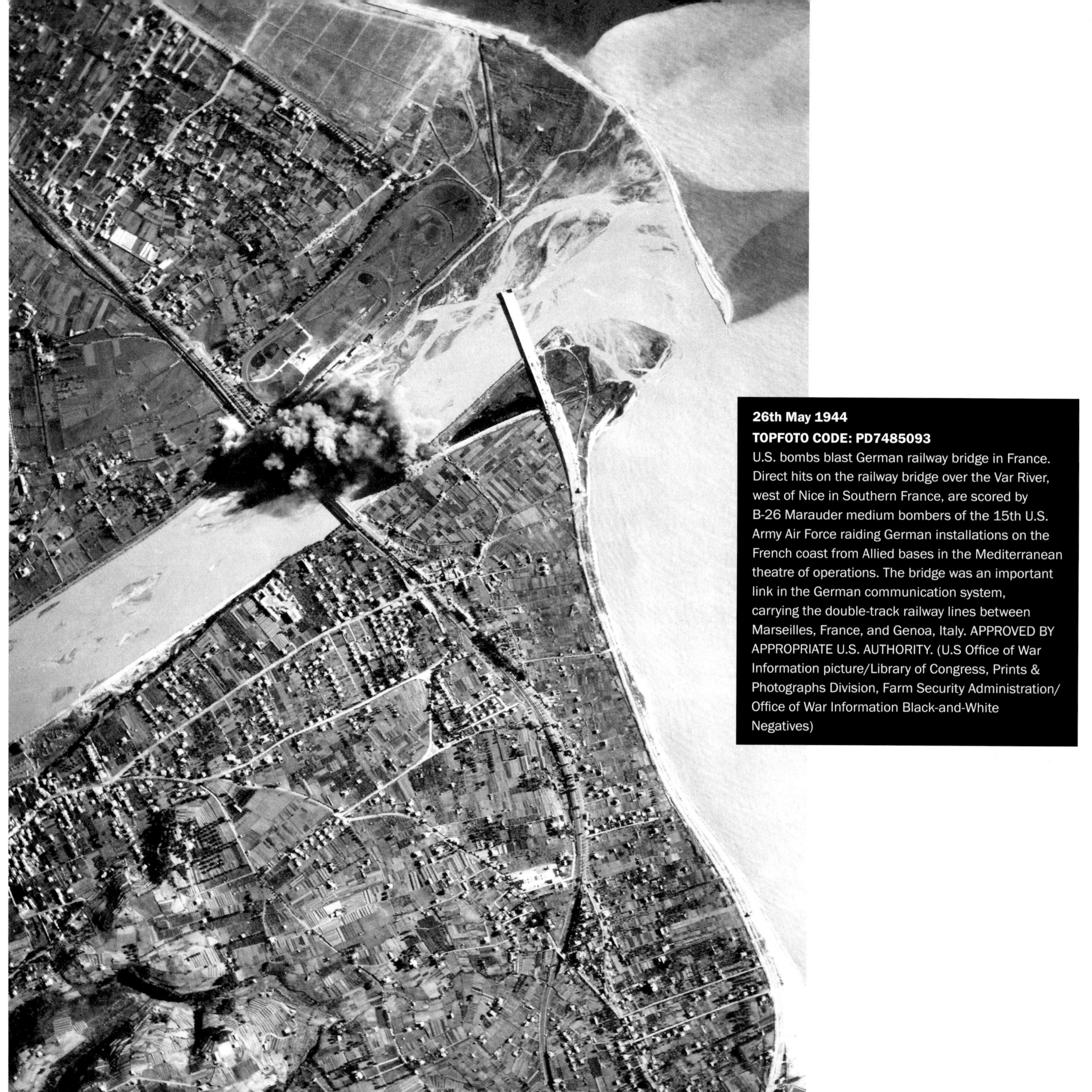

26th May 1944
TOPFOTO CODE: PD7485093
U.S. bombs blast German railway bridge in France.
Direct hits on the railway bridge over the Var River,
west of Nice in Southern France, are scored by
B-26 Marauder medium bombers of the 15th U.S.
Army Air Force raiding German installations on the
French coast from Allied bases in the Mediterranean
theatre of operations. The bridge was an important
link in the German communication system,
carrying the double-track railway lines between
Marseilles, France, and Genoa, Italy. APPROVED BY
APPROPRIATE U.S. AUTHORITY. (U.S Office of War
Information picture/Library of Congress, Prints &
Photographs Division, Farm Security Administration/
Office of War Information Black-and-White
Negatives)

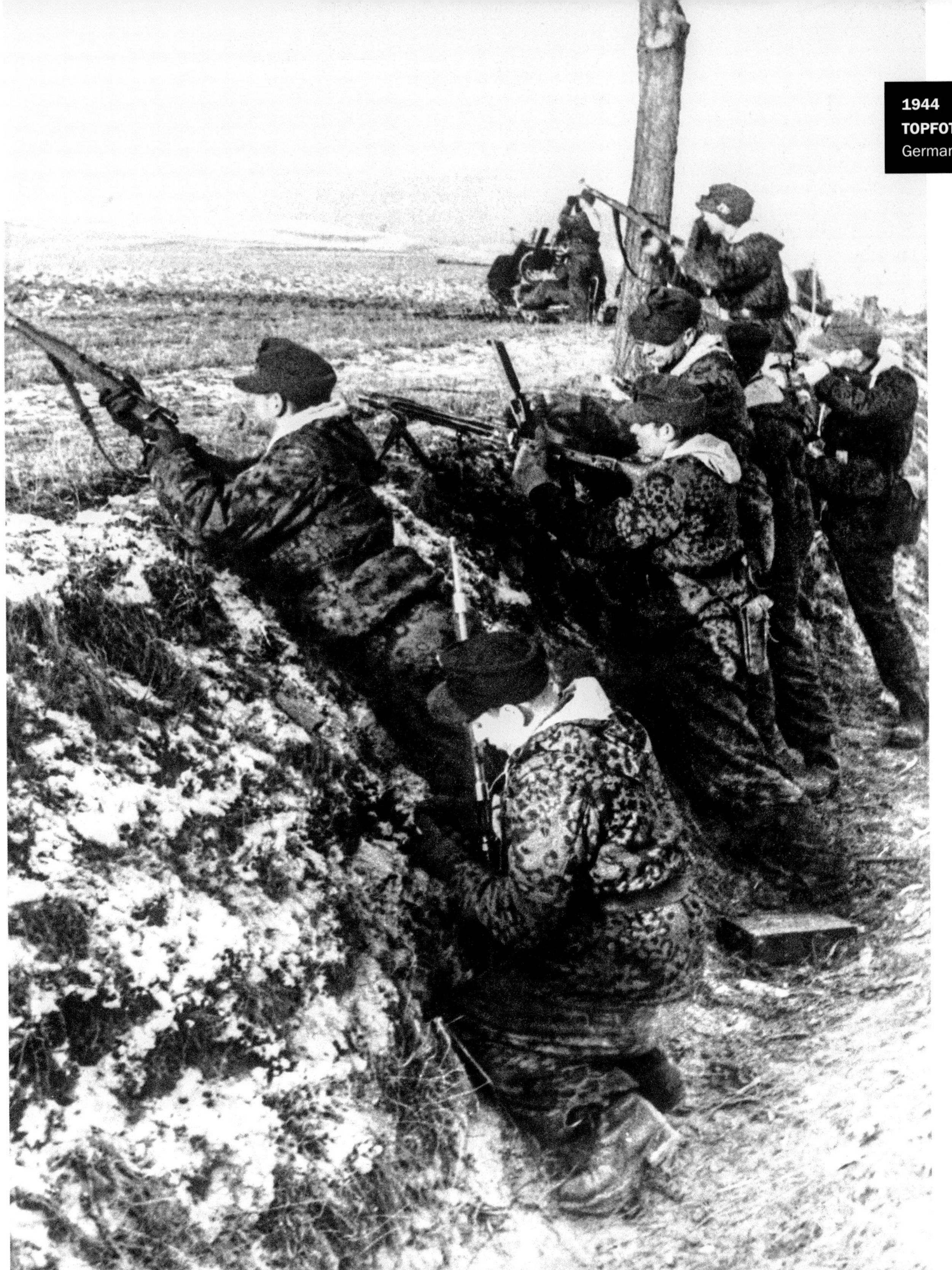

1944
TOPFOTO CODE: PD3001495
German troops in action in Hungary.

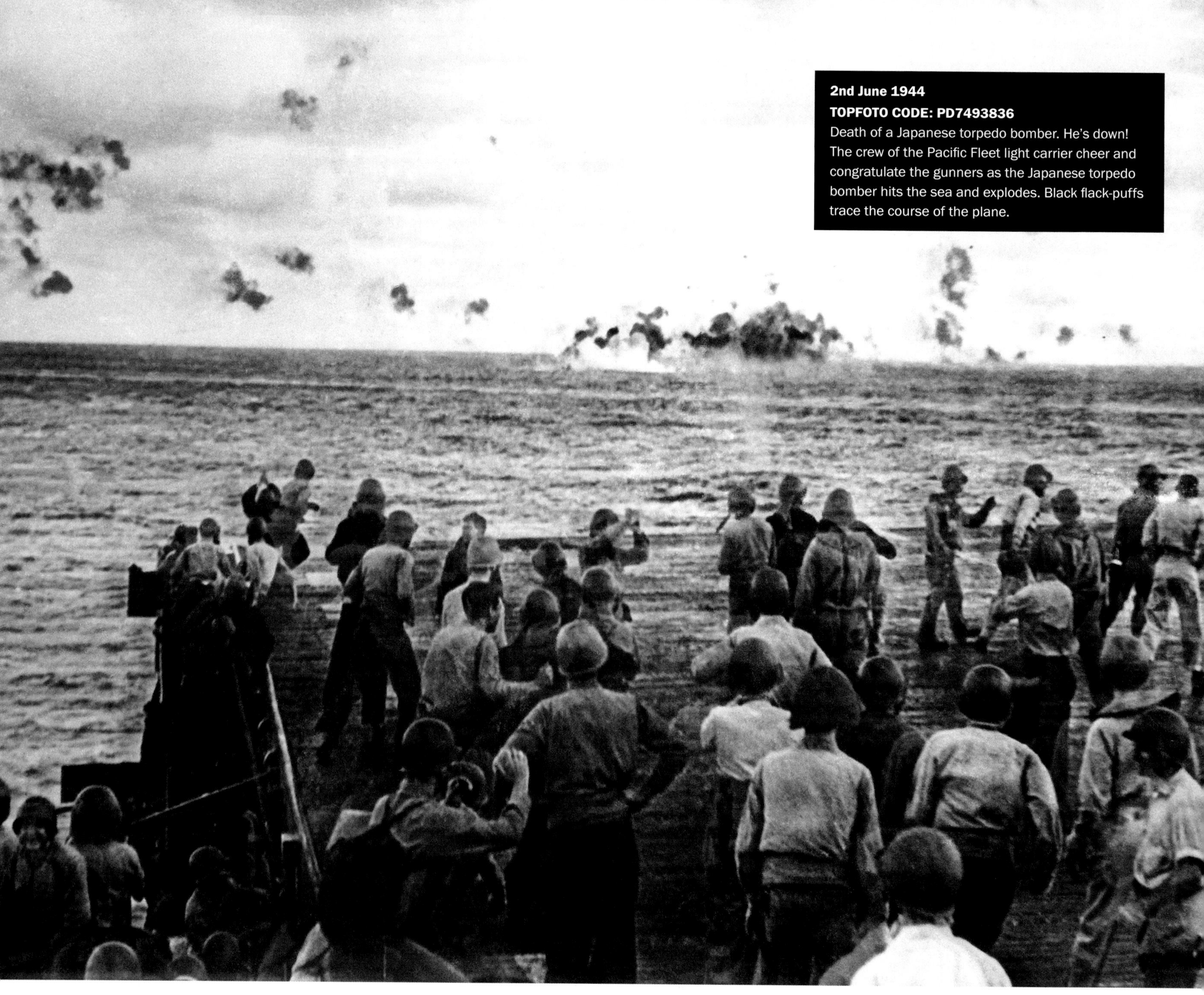

2nd June 1944
TOPFOTO CODE: PD7493836
Death of a Japanese torpedo bomber. He's down!
The crew of the Pacific Fleet light carrier cheer and
congratulate the gunners as the Japanese torpedo
bomber hits the sea and explodes. Black flack-puffs
trace the course of the plane.

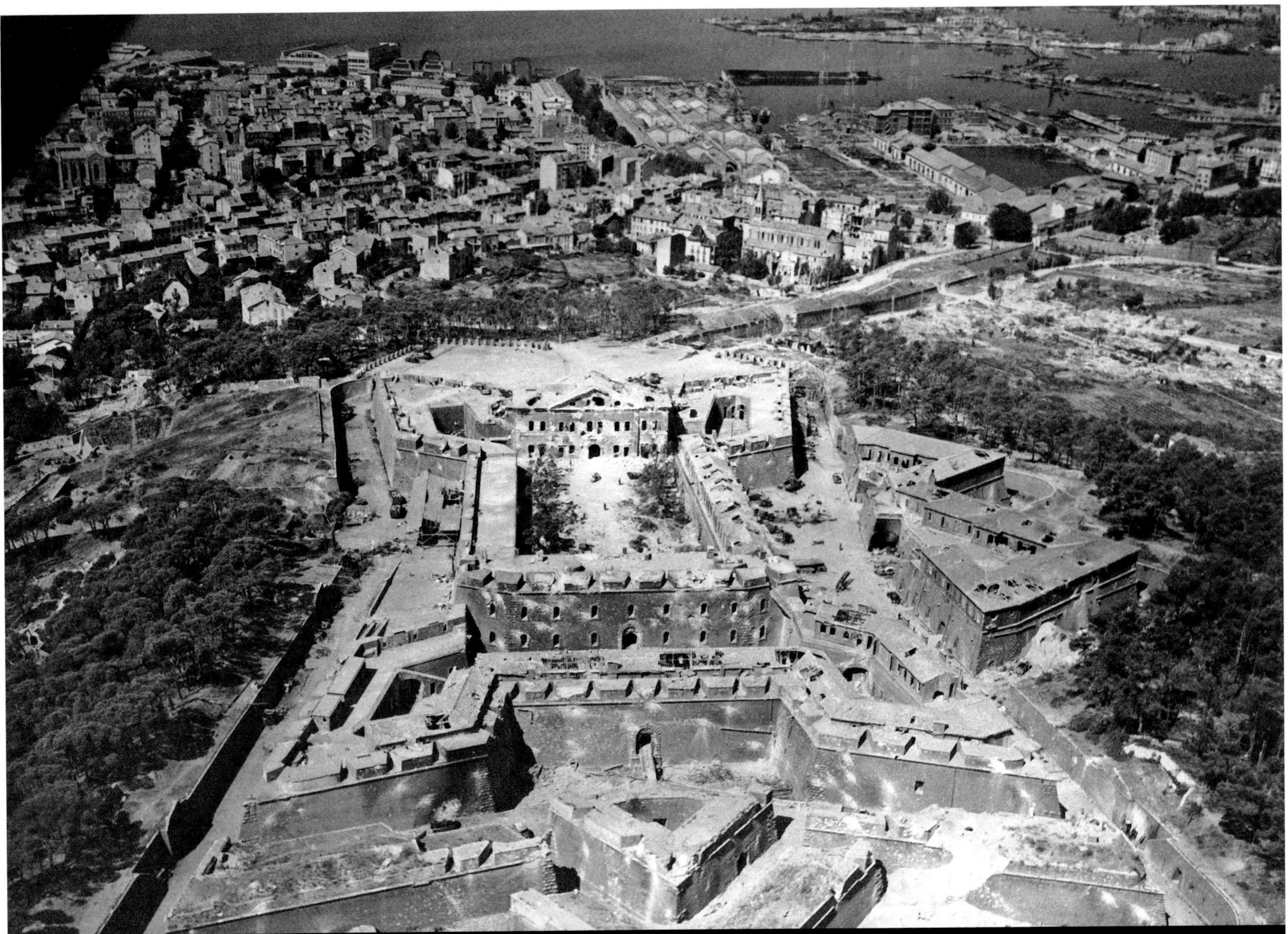

9th September 1944

TOPFOTO CODE: PD7485101, INDEX NUMBER: 32484-FF

9/9/44 Toulon fort silenced by Allied Seventh Army. Blasted by bombs and shell-fire, this enemy-held fort in Toulon was forced to surrender to the Allied Seventh Army which liberated the French port city on Aug. 27th, 1944. Once the headquarters for the French Mediterranean fleet, the city has port facilities (background) which provide the Allies with additional means of supplying their swiftly-advancing troops. Early in September, 1944, the forces led by U.S. Lieutenant General Alexander M. Patch, Jr., were advancing up the Saone Valley towards a junction with Allied forces in the north. SERVICED BY NEW YORK TO LIST A. APPROVED BY APPROPRIATE U.S. AUTHORITY. (U.S. Office of War Information picture/Library of Congress, Prints & Photographs Division, Farm Security Administration/Office of War Information Black-and-White Negatives)

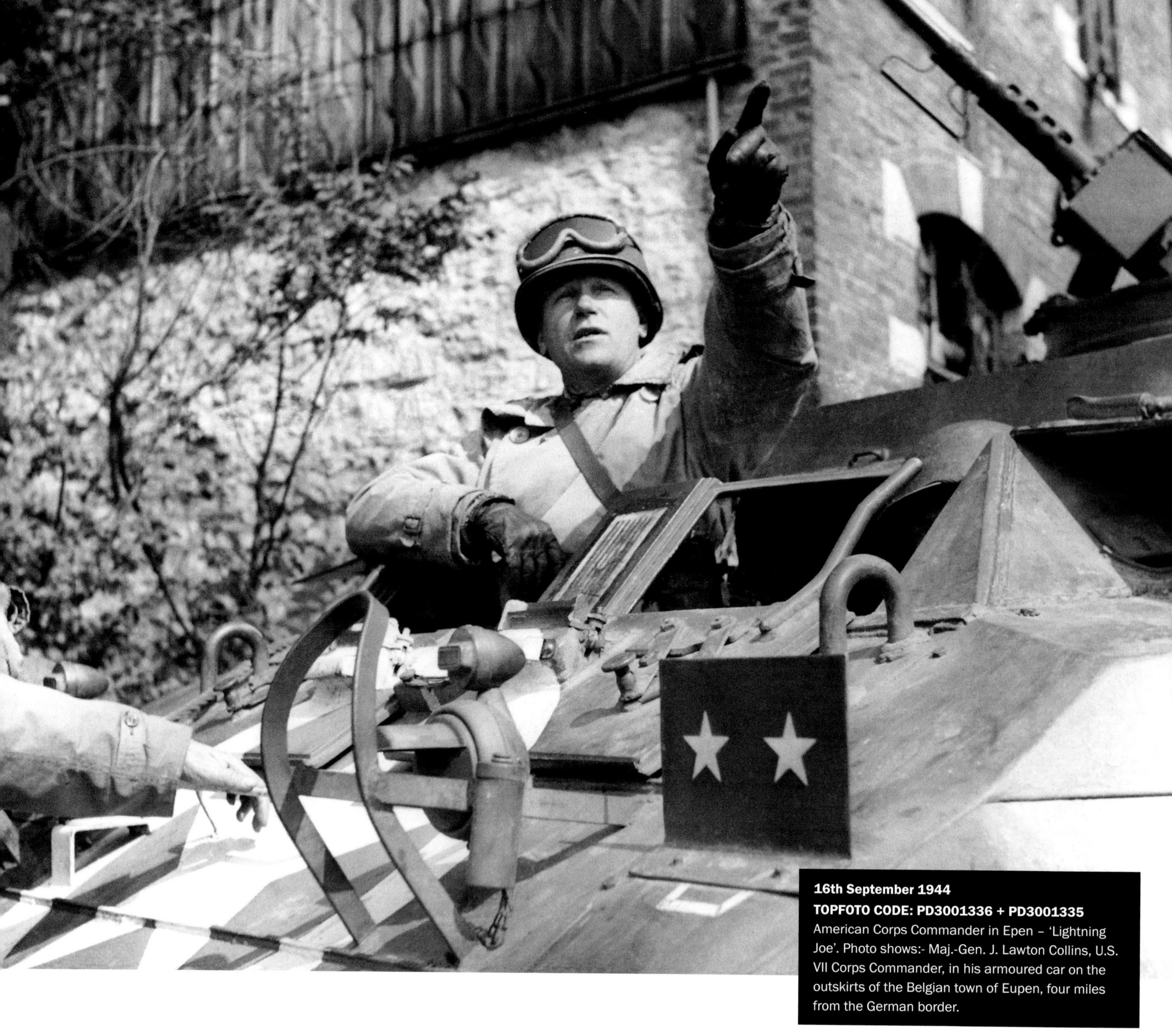

16th September 1944
TOPFOTO CODE: PD3001336 + PD3001335
American Corps Commander in Epen – 'Lightning Joe'. Photo shows:- Maj.-Gen. J. Lawton Collins, U.S. VII Corps Commander, in his armoured car on the outskirts of the Belgian town of Eupen, four miles from the German border.

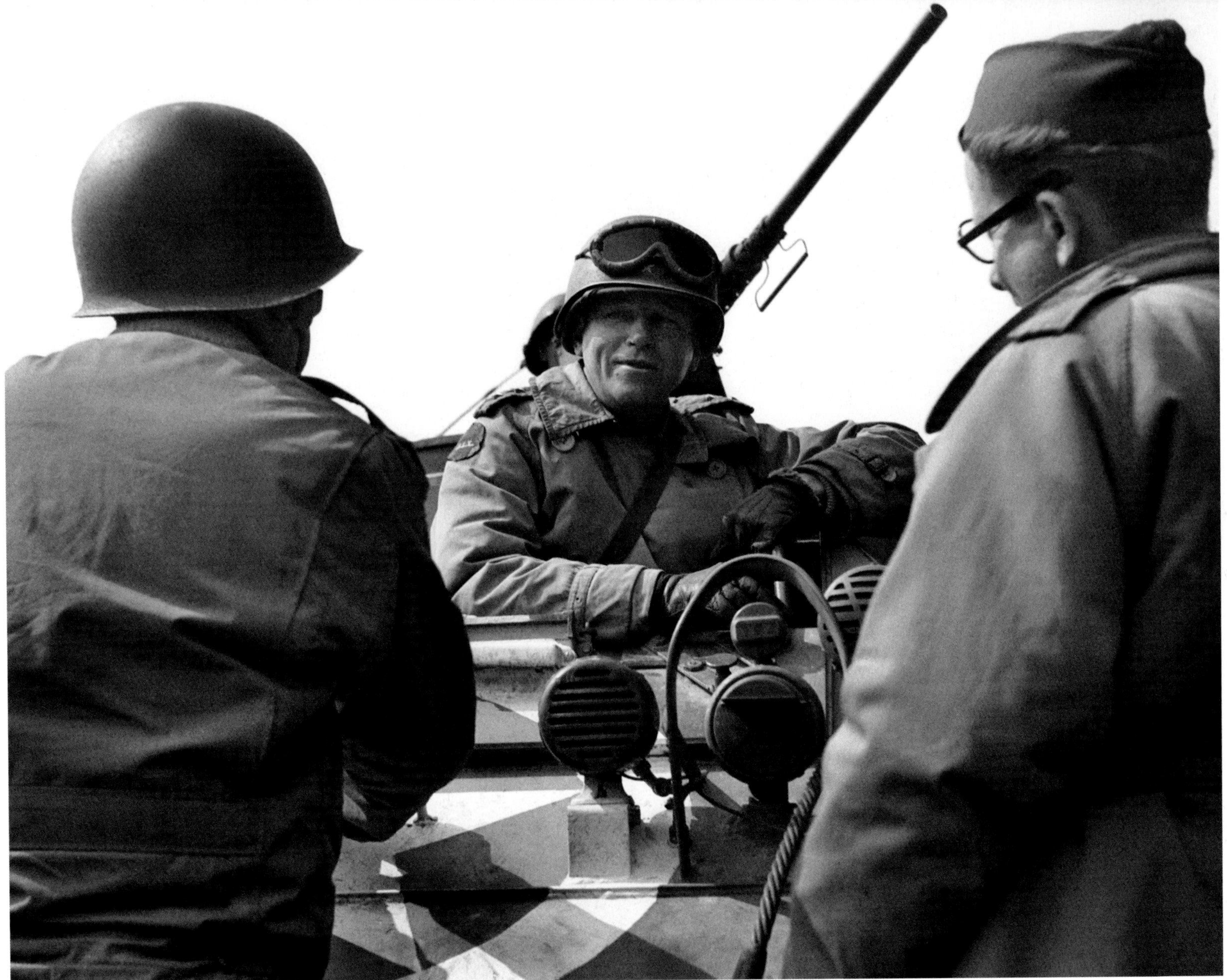

Major General Joseph 'Lightning Joe' Lawton Collins came from a large Irish family, and several of his family members also held high-ranking positions in the US Army.

A West Point graduate, he was one of just a few senior US commanders to serve in both the Pacific and the European Theatres. Following a series of rapid promotions at the beginning of the Second World War, he became the Chief of Staff for the Hawaiian Department and was later given command of the 25th Infantry Division. The division participated in the tough Guadalcanal Campaign and was given the nickname 'Tropic Lightning', from where Collins' moniker 'Lightning Joe' was derived.

He was awarded the Silver Star, the Legion of Merit, and the Distinguished Service Medal (DSM) for his service here. The DSM was one of just three he was awarded in the duration.

He was transferred to the European Theatre to lead the VII Corps during the Normandy landings, which he did up until VE Day. At only 47, he became the youngest US Corps commander during the Second World War. The importance of the VII Corps, and the leadership of Collins, cannot be overstated in the successful conquest of German-occupied Europe.

➤

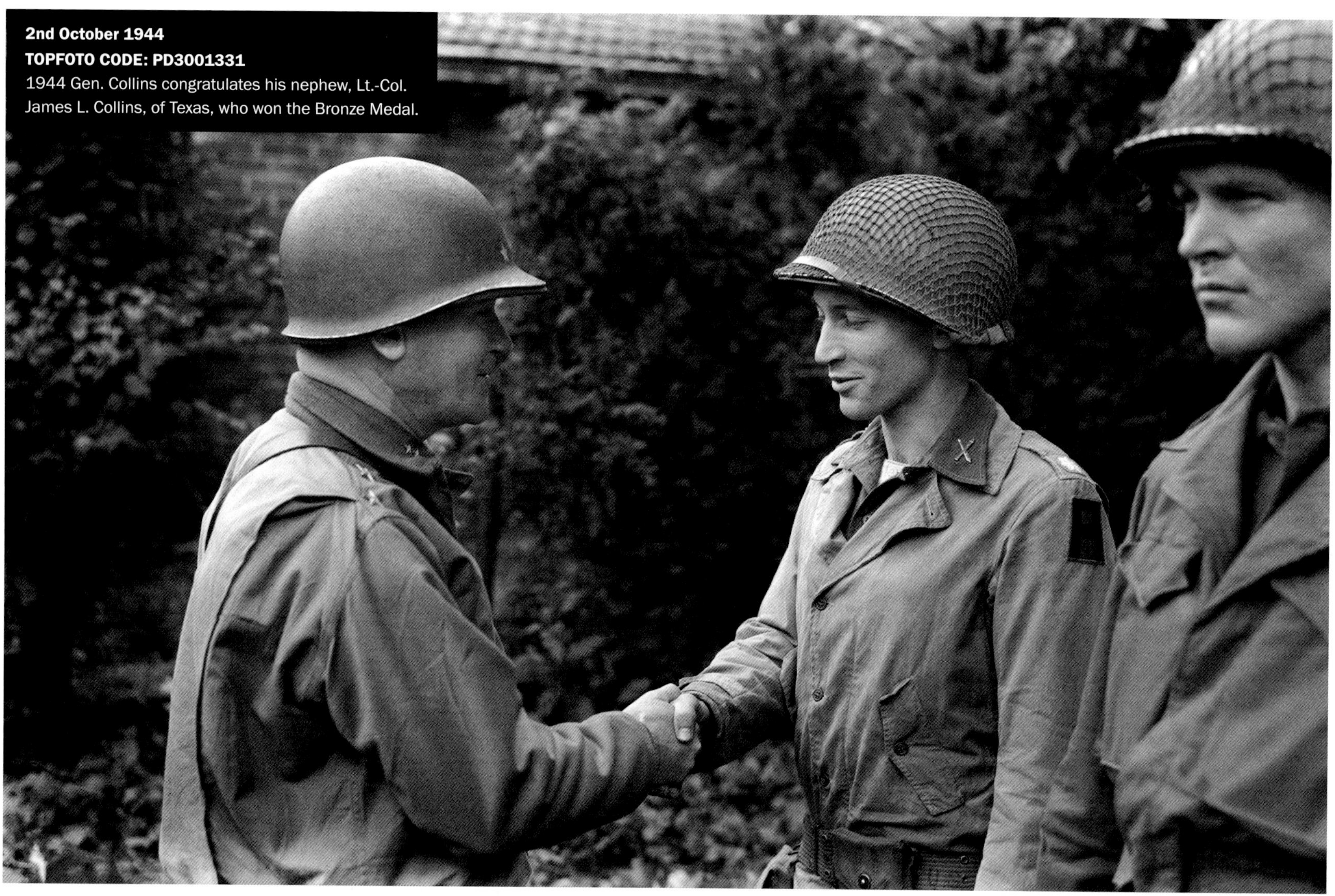

They participated in D-Day, Operation Cobra, the Falaise Pocket, the Liberation of Paris (see page 139), the Battle of Hürtgen Forest, and the Battle of the Bulge, just to name a few. They had 337 combat days under Lightning Joe's watchful gaze and destroyed fourteen German divisions along their nearly 1,200-mile path through Europe.

Collins made full major general in 1948 and later became the Chief of Staff for the US Army during the entirety of the Korean War. He worked for NATO and served as a special representative during the Vietnam War.

In the above photo, Lightning Joe is pictured congratulating his nephew, later Brigadier General James L. Collins Jr, with his Bronze Medal (Junior, not to be confused with Lightning Joe's brother J. Lawton Collins Senior, also a major general). Collins Jr had a younger brother named Michael Collins, who was an astronaut and participated in the legendary Apollo 11 mission in 1969. Michael flew the Columbia module around the moon while his two colleagues Buzz Aldrin and Neil Armstrong became the first men to walk on the surface.

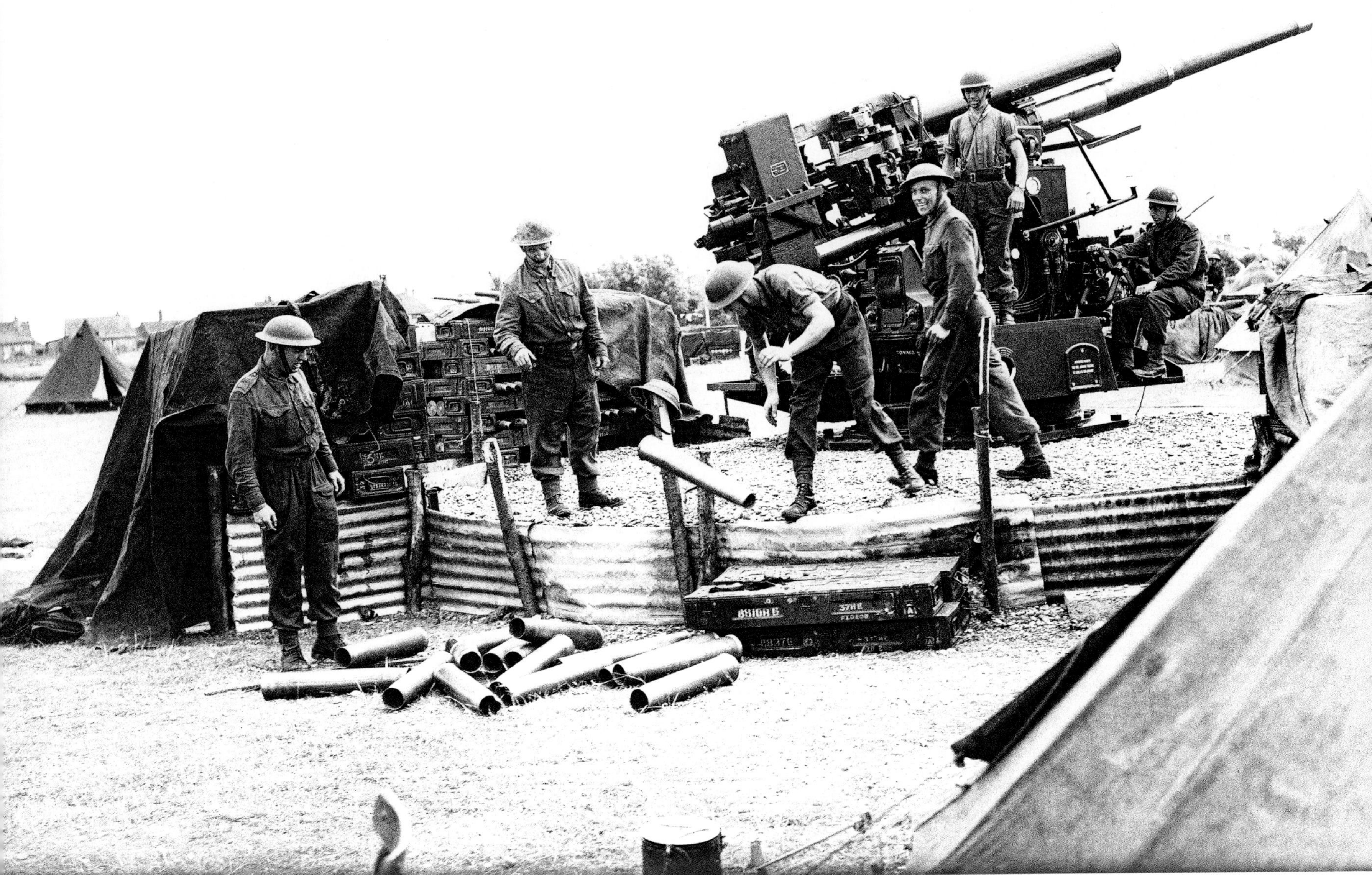

1944
TOPFOTO CODE: PD3001199
Anti-aircraft gunners at Rye, South-East
coast of England.

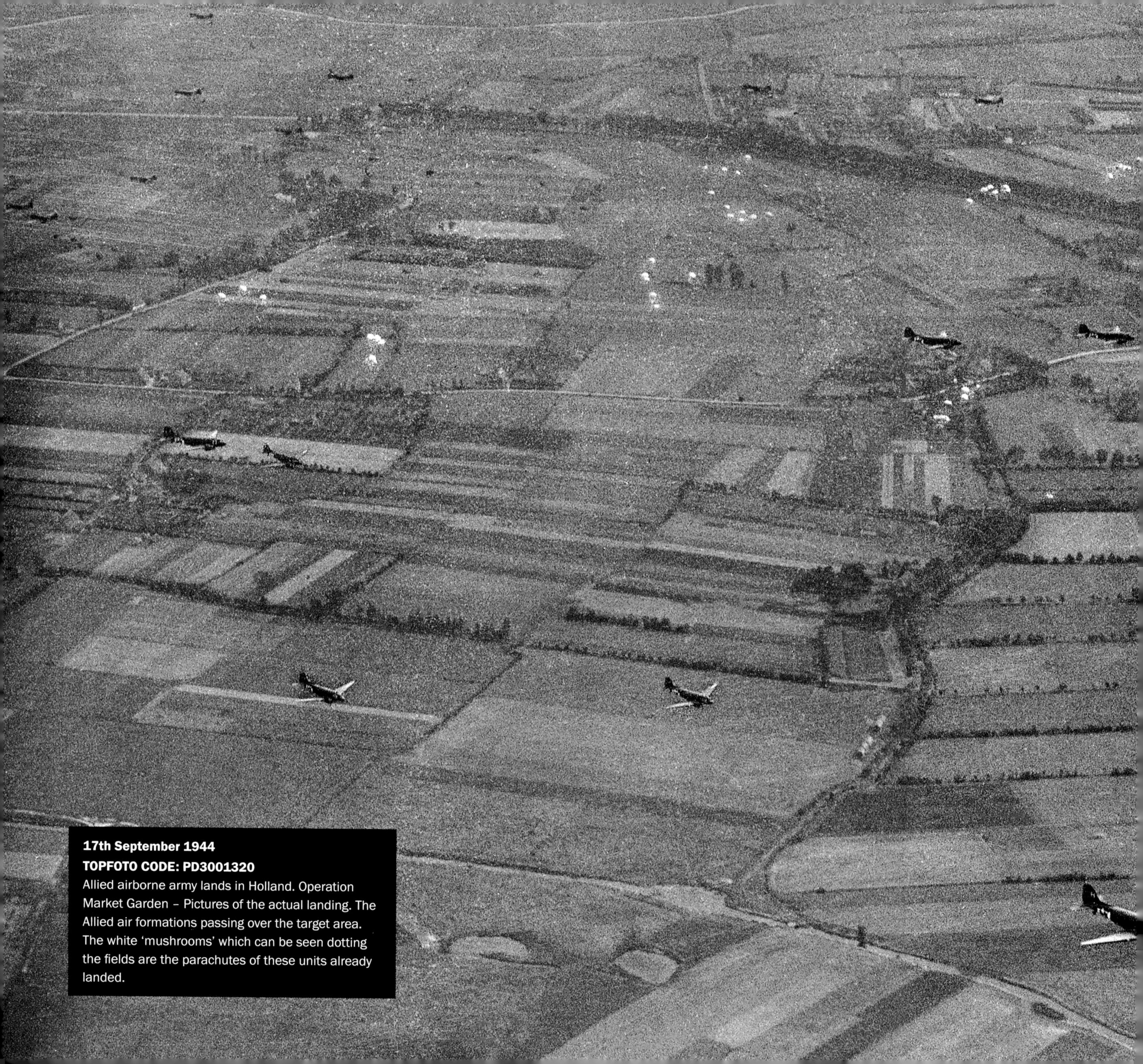

17th September 1944
TOPFOTO CODE: PD3001320
Allied airborne army lands in Holland. Operation
Market Garden – Pictures of the actual landing. The
Allied air formations passing over the target area.
The white 'mushrooms' which can be seen dotting
the fields are the parachutes of these units already
landed.

Operation Market Garden

In September 1944, the Allied forces stood at a crucial crossroads. There was a prevailing sense of euphoria, due to the successful progression of the Normandy landings; however, the momentum from D-Day was slipping away. The logistical system was strained, and the field armies were exhausted.

There was a clear division, both politically and militarily, on how to progress and end the war. Some, like Dwight D. Eisenhower, argued for the broad front/last push approach, believing the Germans were at the end of the line. Others, like Bernard 'Monty' Law Montgomery, argued for a more narrow front approach, thinking there was still some distance to go.

The disagreement between the leaders did not help matters. Just a few weeks prior to the execution of the operation, Eisenhower had been made Supreme Allied Commander of the forces in Europe, much to the dismay of the extremely ambitious Montgomery. Furthermore, there was the economic issue of the immense investment that had been made into the Allied Airborne Army.

These extremely skilled and highly trained elite soldiers had been largely inactive since the initial drops in Normandy. All six divisions had been withdrawn for re-forming in England, and while eighteen missions had subsequently been prepared, all had been cancelled due to the ground forces' rapid and unexpected advancement into the planned drop zones.

The expenditure on this now huge and idle army had to be justified. Out of this situation, Operation Market Garden was born. It was the brainchild of Montgomery and had strong support from both Churchill and US President Roosevelt. Originally, an old plan code-named Operation Comet, based on a swift attack, was reworked into a new and far more elaborate two-part operation.

Part one: Market – an airborne assault, to seize key bridges in Holland.

Part two: Garden – a ground attack, moving north from Belgium, through Holland, and over the seized bridges, creating a salient.

Combined, these two attacks would yield a 103km bulge into German-occupied territory, providing a bridgehead over the River Rhine and ultimately giving the Allies a direct invasion route into northern Germany. With open supply routes and an opportunity to strike into the Ruhr area, the beating heart of the German industrial war machine, the hope was to end the war before Christmas 1944. It was the largest airborne operation in history – yet the planning was done in less than a week. In comparison, the planning of the landings in Sicily took several months and Operation Overlord (Normandy/D-Day landings) took years.

The belief was that, with the Germans seemingly on the run, the sooner they could initiate the offensive, the sooner the war would be won. The ambitious plan was to drop around 34,000 men into enemy territory on the first day of the operation, 17 September 1944. These troops came from three British and American airborne divisions, one Polish airborne brigade, and one glider division. A total of 14,589 troops were flown in and landed in gliders, while 20,011 were dropped by parachute. Additionally, about 1,700 vehicles and 250 heavy artillery pieces were also flown in by glider.

The land troops were to cover 103km in two days; ambitious, even for Montgomery. A significant issue was that the plan relied upon taking all the bridges. If even one objective failed, it would unravel the carpet. Another issue was that all the airborne forces tasked with taking the most important bridges were dropped so far from them that it ruined the element of surprise and stifled their mobility.

Speed was of the essence for the plan to work, so in effect the plan was doomed from the start. The willingness to take the risk and end the war, based on the seemingly defeatist attitude of the Germans, was the hubris of the Allied forces. Montgomery's personal thirst for glory, as well as his innate desire to reach Berlin before his arch rival Patton, led him to ignore multiple warning signs.

The initial landings on 17 September were successful. An estimated 89 per cent of the 82nd Airborne landed close to their landing zones, and nearly all objectives near Eindhoven and Nijmegen were taken. A further 84 per cent of the gliders also landed within 1,000m of their Landing Zones (LZs). The 101st Airborne was successful in the early stages, taking four out of the five bridges they had been assigned, but from then on, things started to unravel.

Although the Germans had expected an airborne attack, they had been taken by surprise. The momentum gained by this surprise was quickly lost though, and the local commander, Field Marshal Walter Model, who was an expert in defensive warfare, swiftly organised a counterattack.

The Germans were able to gather their forces and concentrate them in the area, including armoured units and other heavy equipment, which the Allies had not anticipated. The Dutch resistance had warned the Allies of the strength of the German forces in the area, but their warnings were ignored.

As the airborne troops landed and attempted to seize the key bridges, they were met with fierce resistance. The Germans had fortified the bridges, and the Allied troops were unable to capture them quickly. This delayed the ground forces' advance, which was the second part of the operation, and gave the Germans time to mobilise more troops.

The most critical part of the operation was the capture of the bridges at Arnhem and Nijmegen. The British 1st Airborne Division, under the command of Major General Roy Urquhart, was tasked with capturing the bridge at Arnhem. The division was dropped about 8 miles from their target, and as they made their way to the bridge, they encountered German resistance.

The British troops fought bravely, but they were unable to hold the bridge. The Germans destroyed it, preventing the Allied forces from crossing the Rhine. The division was cut off and surrounded, and after nine days of heavy fighting they were forced to surrender.

The capture of the bridge at Nijmegen was equally challenging. The 82nd Airborne Division, under the command of Brigadier General James M. Gavin, was given the task. The division faced heavy resistance from the Germans, who had fortified the bridge and were using it as a supply route.

After several days of intense fighting, the Allied forces were able to capture the bridge, but at a significant cost. The division suffered heavy casualties, and many of its men were captured or wounded.

Operation Market Garden has inspired numerous films and books; most significant of all is probably the 1977 movie *A Bridge Too Far*, directed by Richard Attenborough. The movie depicts the events leading up to and during the operation and is based on the book of the same name by Cornelius Ryan. The movie accurately portrays the challenges faced by the Allied forces, including the strength of the German defences and the difficulty of capturing the key bridges. It also depicts the disagreements between the Allied leaders and the frustration felt by the troops on the ground.

Operation Market Garden was a significant setback for the Allied forces. The operation failed to achieve its objectives and resulted in heavy casualties. The loss of the airborne troops was particularly devastating, as many of them were the best-trained soldiers in the Allied forces. The failure of the operation had several consequences. It delayed the Allied advance into Germany and allowed the Germans to regroup and strengthen their defences. It also led to a loss of confidence in Montgomery's leadership and raised questions about the effectiveness of the Allied airborne forces.

Despite the operation's failure, it remains an important part of wartime history. It was a bold and ambitious plan that demonstrated the bravery and courage of the Allied forces. The operation also highlighted the challenges of co-ordinating large-scale military operations and the importance of proper planning and preparation.

There is still to this day a huge Anglo-American disagreement between historians. Some fiercely argue the 'what-if' scenarios, with various degrees of hypothetical Allied success, believing that intelligence gathering was insufficient, and laying the blame on Montgomery. Others put the blame on Eisenhower/SHAEF (Supreme Headquarters Allied Expeditionary Force) and the operational deficiencies.

Many argued that it was not so much a plan that went bad as simply a bad plan. However, one thing is certain: the Allied commanders grossly underestimated the enemy and ignored an overwhelming amount of intelligence – chiefly the relocation of the German 2nd SS Panzer Corps to a position close to one of the key bridges in Arnhem.

Market Garden is still widely regarded as the biggest Allied failure of the war.

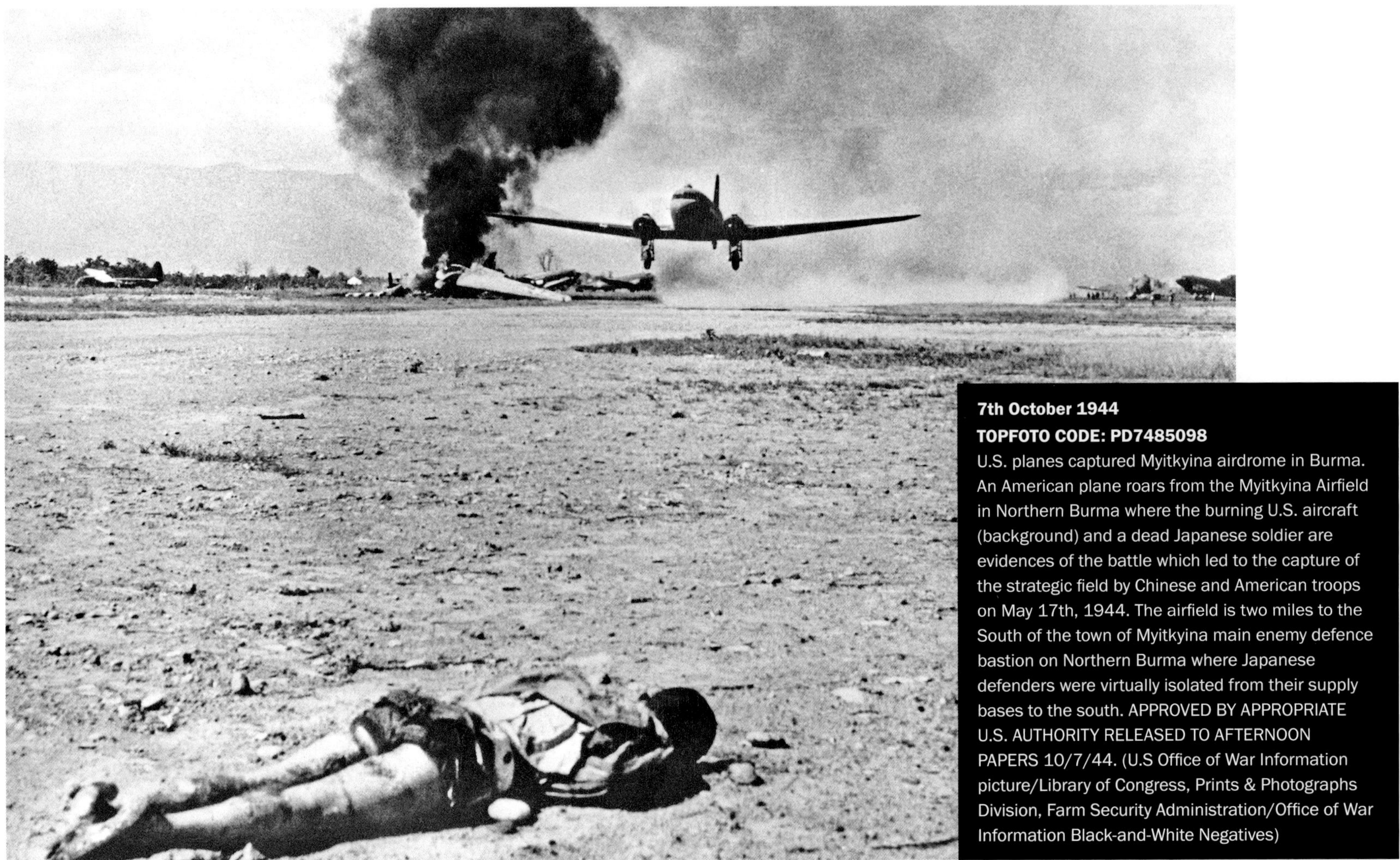

In 1944, political and military alliances were very different than they are today. In 1944 Burma (now Myanmar) was occupied by Imperial Japan, and geographically the city of Myitkyina represented an obstacle for the American and British forces, who needed to establish a supply line to their Chinese allies who had been at war with the Japanese since 1937 (the beginning of the Second Sino-Japanese War). The plan was to capture the city and the airfield and open up a land route from India to China known as the Ledo Road.

The mission was led by US General Joseph Stilwell, employing American and Chinese troops as well as an American jungle warfare unit, specialised in operating behind enemy lines. They were known as Merrill's Marauders. A film of the same name was released in 1962, which attempted to truly show what it had really been like in the unforgiving jungle and mountain terrains surrounding Myitkyina.

While the fighting was hard, the environment was brutal. Combined with low supplies of food and a gruelling 1,000-mile march, the 2,750 original Marauders had been reduced to around half by the time they finally attacked the airfield. Malnourished, disease-ridden and exhausted, they fell upon the unsuspecting Japanese and the battle was over quickly. However, the ensuing battle for the city took an additional three months and by then only 200 of the tough jungle unit were alive.

The battle of Myitkyina was the making and the breaking of the Marauders, who were disbanded a week later. Just two of the original force walked out of the jungle without being wounded or medically evacuated. Additionally, sources estimate that around 4,500 Chinese soldiers were also killed and wounded during the siege of Myitkyina.

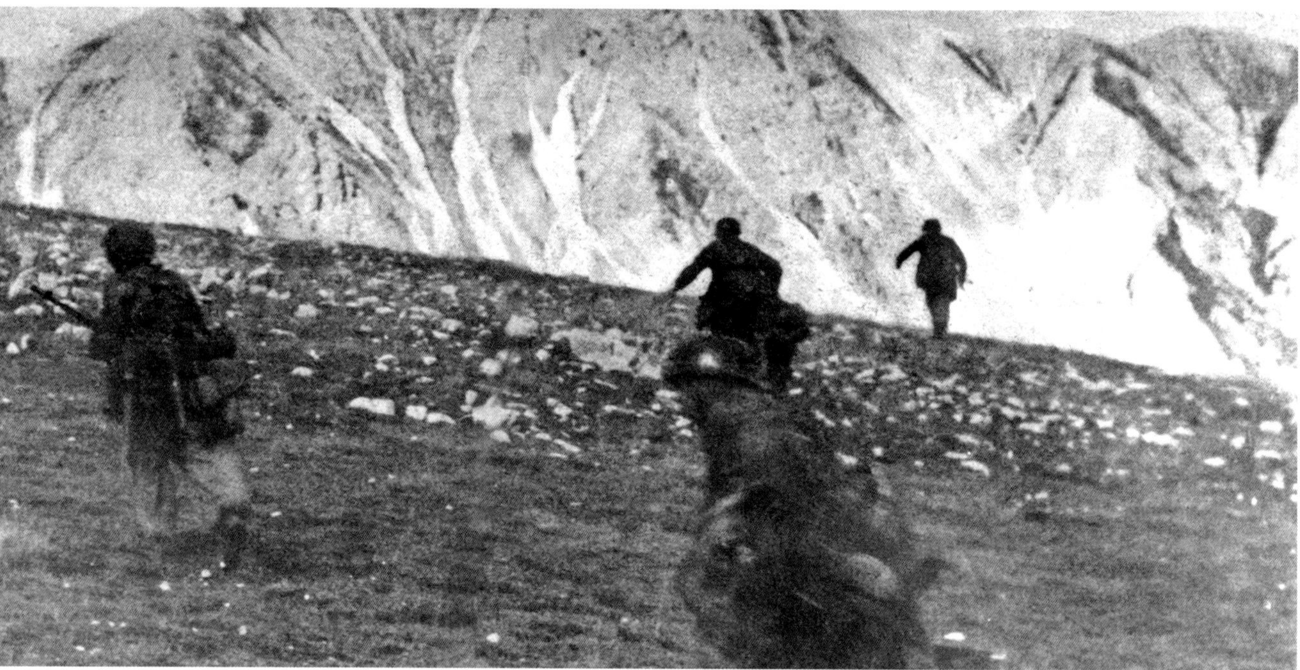

How Mussolini escaped to freedom. This picture tells the story of how Mussolini escaped from his prison on the Gran Sasso after Nazi paratroops had been dropped to rescue him. The paratroops were dropped on the mountain side and a tiny Fieseler Storch plane landed on a plateau near his prison to carry him to Hitler's headquarters. These pictures have just been received in London from a neutral source. Photo shows:- The German paratroops scaling the mountainside to attack Mussolini's prison on the Gran Sasso.

The Italian dictator Benito Mussolini, and his Fascist party PNF, had ruled Italy since 1922. Though Italy and Germany had fought each other during the First World War, Mussolini and Hitler shared radical political views and eventually they came together with Japan and signed the Tripartite Pact in September 1940.

By 1943, events were not quite turning out the way Mussolini had planned. Italy had lost its hold in North Africa, suffering huge casualties, and the Allied invasion of Sicily meant foreign boots were on Italian soil, gaining ground. An Allied bombing raid on Rome on 19 July 1943 killed 1,500 citizens in the San Lorenzo district and was the straw that broke the camel's back. The leaders of Mussolini's own Fascist party had a vote of no confidence and the Italian king, Victor Emmanuel III, had Il Duce booted out and arrested. This marked the fall of the Fascist regime in Italy after twenty-one years. No protests erupted of any kind.

The newly appointed Prime Minister, Pietro Badoglio, dissolved the Fascist party just two days later and on 3 September he threw in the towel and a cessation of hostilities was agreed with the Allies. Anarchy ensued.

Meanwhile, Mussolini was moved from prison to prison, guarded by a sizeable amount of troops. This came from the plausible fear that the Germans would want to break him out and keep the support of Fascist Italy in the war. Hitler was only too eager to oblige, and once again relied upon the infamous Otto Skorzeny to aid his friend in his escape. (Read more about Skorzeny on page 63.)

Having been politically active within the extreme right wing since the age of 14, Skorzeny joined the Austrian Nazi party early in 1931, and soon after became a member of the Nazi SA (Sturmabteilung) as well as the SS (Schutzstaffel). In 1938, during the November Pogroms (Kristallnacht), he was responsible for co-ordinating the destruction of two synagogues in Vienna and the subsequent violent and brutal attacks on its Jewish citizens.

Though the Italians did everything they could to keep the whereabouts of Mussolini a secret, it did not take the Germans long to locate him in the Hotel Campo Imperatore on the Gran Sasso, in the Apennine Mountains.

Skorzeny took off for the mountains along with a group of ninety SS paratroopers, while a simultaneous operation on the ground pacified a valley railway leading to the hotel. After landing close to the hotel, the paratroopers swiftly overburdened the 200 guards, assisted by a command 'not to engage' by an Italian general the Germans had shrewdly brought along as a hostage. The getaway plane, a Fieseler Storch, swept Mussolini and Skorzeny away. By the next day, Mussolini had joined Hitler in his secret headquarters, the Wolfsschanze (Wolf's Lair), in present-day Poland.

Later accounts have questioned the 'heroic' efforts of Skorzeny and put most of the credit for the rescue on the paratroopers as a whole, claiming that Skorzeny was simply made somewhat of a poster boy for Nazi propaganda. Mussolini was put in place as the leader of a northern Italian puppet state by Hitler but was eventually executed by a firing squad of Italian communist partisans after they intercepted him trying to escape to Switzerland with his mistress on 28 April 1945.

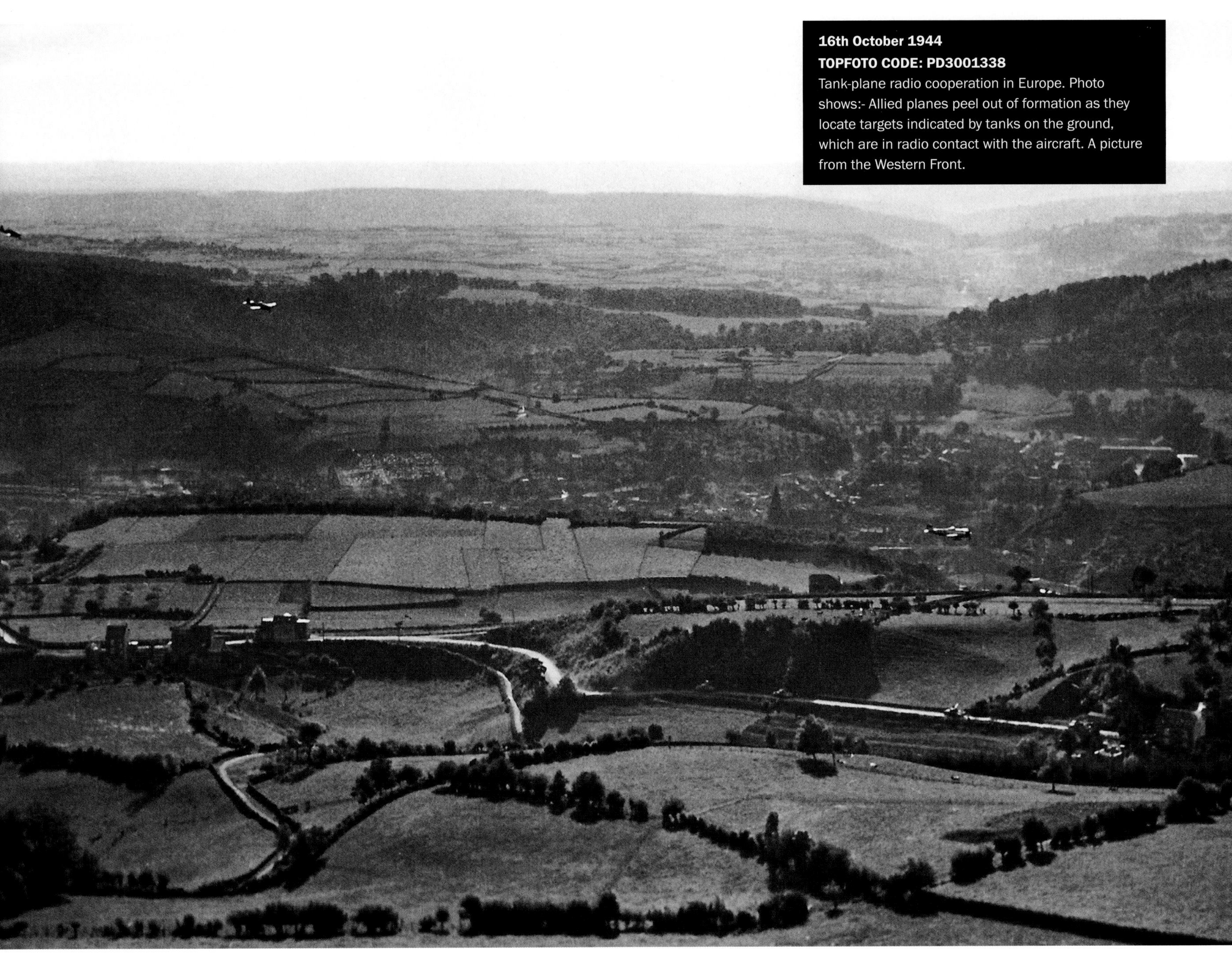

16th October 1944
TOPFOTO CODE: PD3001338
Tank-plane radio cooperation in Europe. Photo shows:- Allied planes peel out of formation as they locate targets indicated by tanks on the ground, which are in radio contact with the aircraft. A picture from the Western Front.

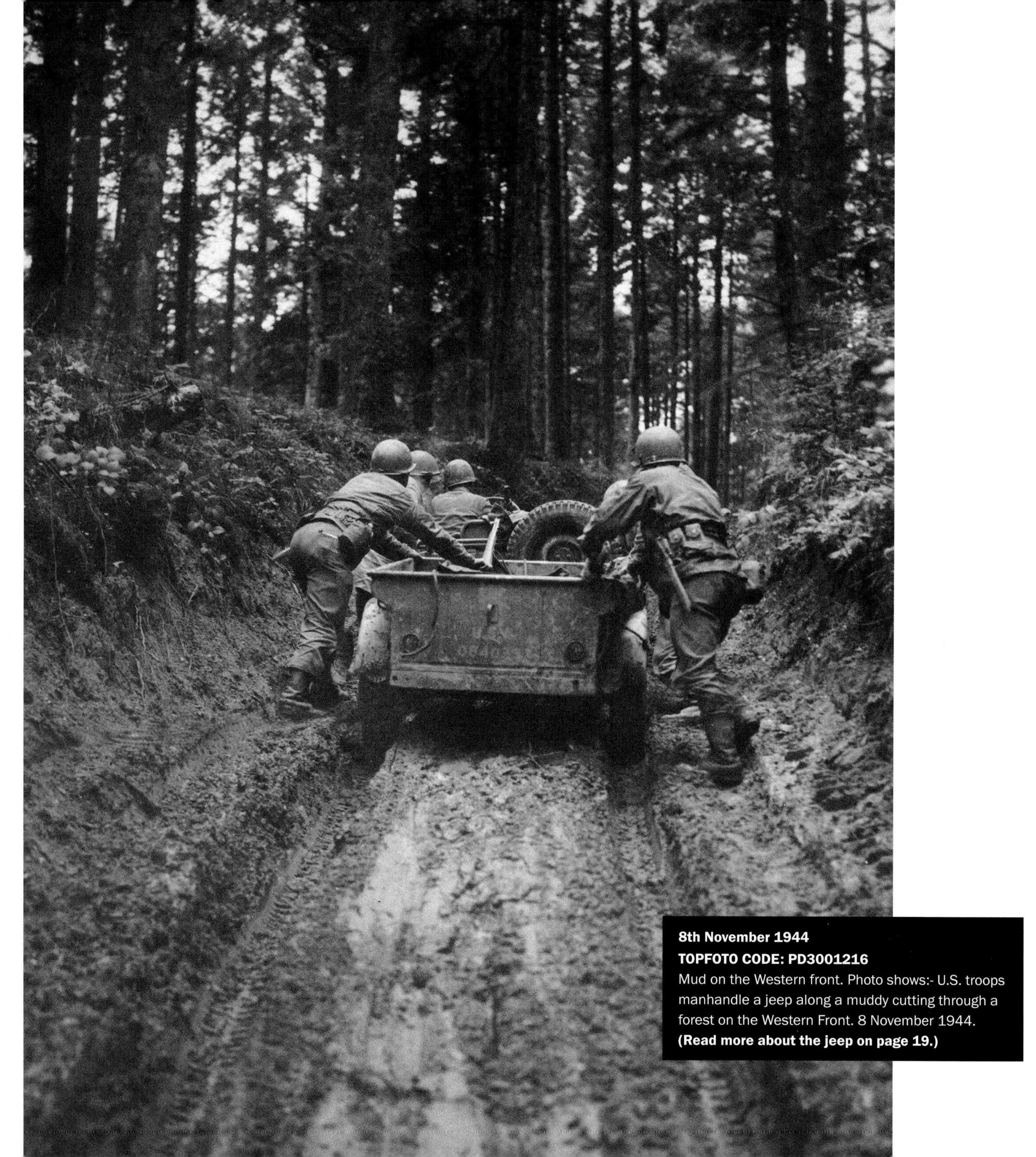

8th November 1944
TOPFOTO CODE: PD3001216
Mud on the Western front. Photo shows:- U.S. troops manhandle a jeep along a muddy cutting through a forest on the Western Front. 8 November 1944.
(Read more about the jeep on page 19.)

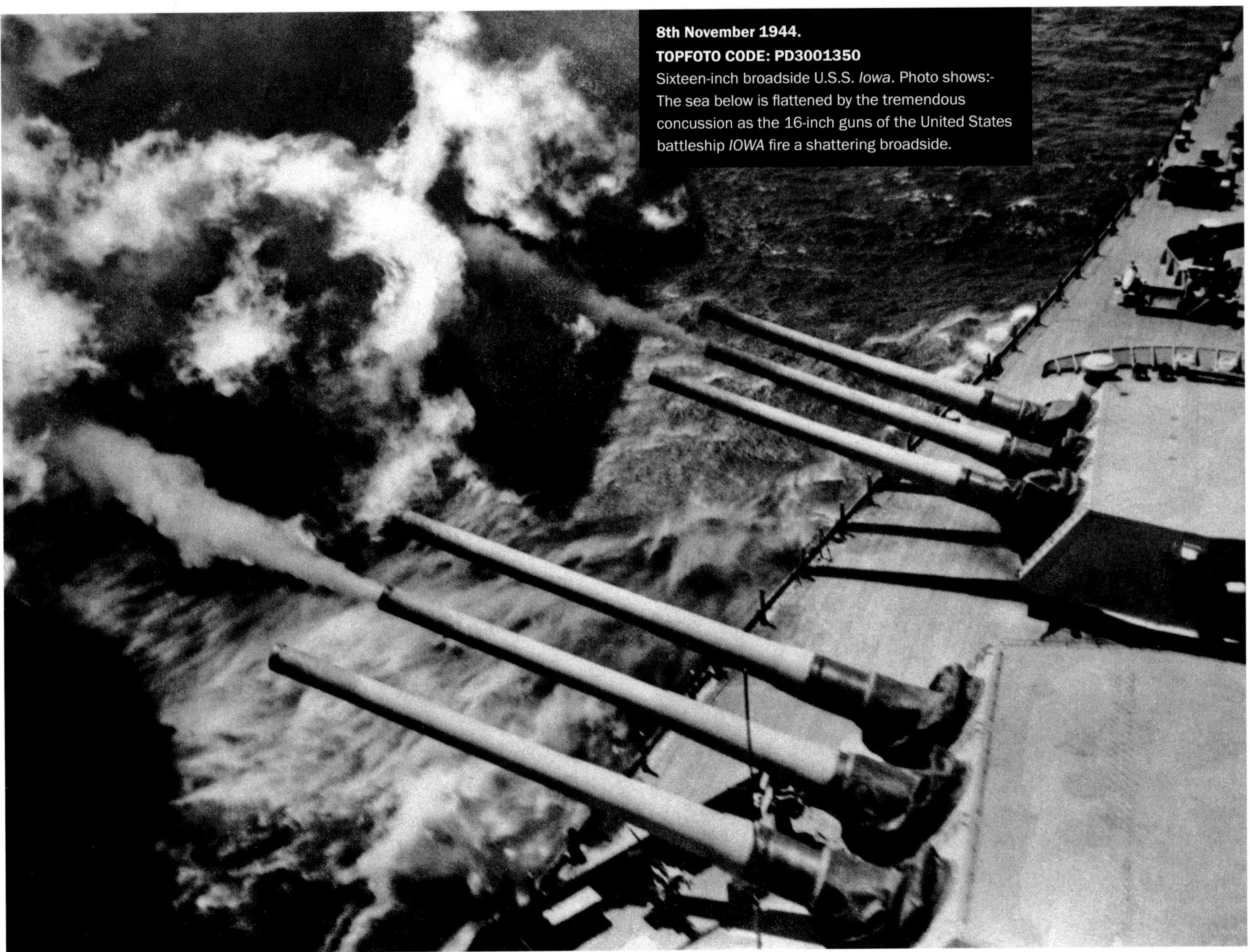

One of the primary services performed by USS *Iowa* during the Second World War was to safely transport US President Franklin D. Roosevelt and other important military personnel to the secret Tehran Conference in November 1943, to meet with Winston Churchill and Joseph Stalin. It also performed dutifully in the Pacific Theatre and was used during the preparations for the landing on Kwajalein in January and February 1944. (Read more about Kwajalein on page 22; the Stalingrad Sword on page 123; and the Tehran Conference on page 125.)

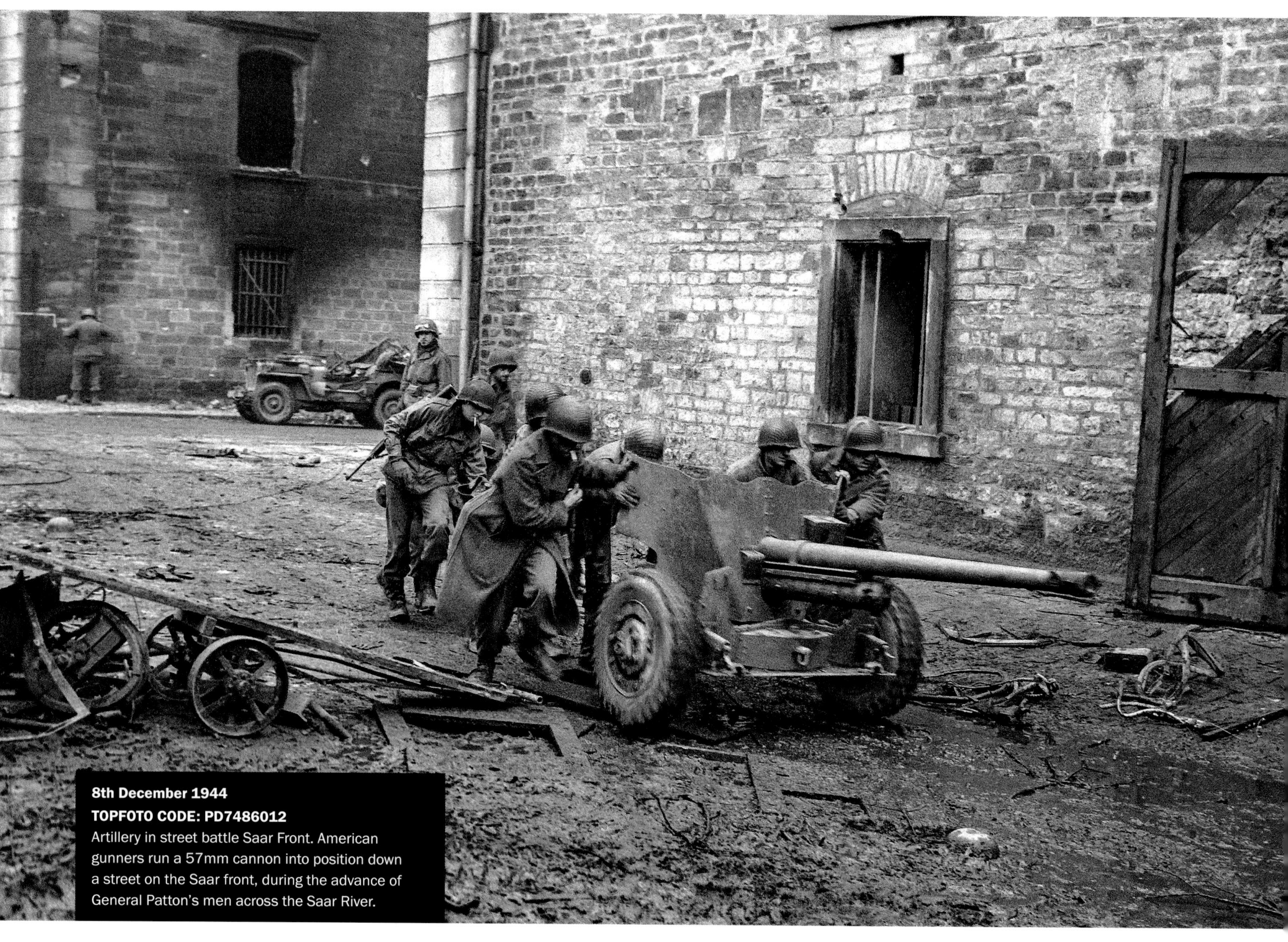

8th December 1944

TOPFOTO CODE: PD7486012

Artillery in street battle Saar Front. American gunners run a 57mm cannon into position down a street on the Saar front, during the advance of General Patton's men across the Saar River.

Operation Greif and Otto Skorzeny

On 22 October 1944, Hitler and his personal favourite, Waffen-SS commando Otto Skorzeny, had a clandestine meeting in the Führer's top-secret Wolfsschanze hideout. Here Hitler unveiled a plan, conceived by himself, that controversially went against the Hague Convention of 1907. Skorzeny had been successful in Operation Panzerfaust (kidnapping the son of Hungary's Regent) as well as the daring Gran Sasso Raid when he liberated Mussolini from captivity (read more on page 58). The Allies and the press dubbed him 'the most dangerous man in Europe'.

The mission, known as Operation Greif, was the second of two major special missions conducted by the German military during the Battle of the Bulge. (Operation Stösser was the other – read more on page 101.)

A so-called 'false flag' operation executed by German elite special forces, the mission was to capture one or more of the bridges crossing the River Meuse before the Allied forces could destroy them. Hitler asked Skorzeny to create the Panzer Brigade 150; in addition to capturing the bridges, this brigade was to wear American and British uniforms and use Allied-marked vehicles to create confusion, generate false orders, and generally disrupt communications behind the line.

At first, Skorzeny was reluctant. He knew that the chances of failure were high, and that if captured in these uniforms he and his men would be killed as spies. Duty, however, prevailed and Skorzeny was given six weeks to assemble this new brigade. He asked for 3,300 men and received a total of 2,500 from all corners of the armed forces. The Heer (Army), Luftwaffe (Air Force), the Kriegsmarine (Navy), and even the Waffen-SS contributed – which in itself made the whole assembly unique.

A request was sent out to recruit all soldiers with proficiency in English as well as American dialect and slang. Requests were also sent out for a large amount of US-issued uniforms, vehicles, and weapons. Problems occurred when vast quantities of both Polish and Russian uniforms ended up in the unit, as no one really knew what US-issue clothing specifically looked like. Language abilities were also problematic as only about 300 of the 2,500 men spoke a modicum of English.

Acquiring enough original hardware proved equally difficult, so they simply resorted to painting and disguising German tanks and vehicles to somewhat look the part. Many variations of vehicles had been produced throughout the war and even specialists could find it difficult to tell friend from foe at a glance.

Needing a way to distinguish 'real from fake' enemies, a somewhat ingenious system was invented. It involved covert paint insignia, specific tank gun positions, and differently coloured scarves and torchlight signals. Additionally, captured US dog tags from fallen soldiers and POWs were used and papers were forged to lend credibility to the identity of the insurgents.

The brigade was divided into three groups, each with a primary objective to take a specific bridge over the Meuse. Massive traffic congestion at the start of the mission made this quite difficult, and it was decided that, rather than splitting up, they would instead fight as one force. The bulk of the brigade's 2,500 men ultimately made little difference to the covert nature of the operation and failed to assume control of any of the bridges – thus going into action quite conventionally and rather unsuccessfully. One small unit within the brigade known as Einheit Stielau (consisting of just forty-four men who had the best English) was, however, successful and responsible for causing the majority of the confusion and disruption that Hitler had desired.

Many incidents occurred, some of which would have been quite amusing had it not been for the deadly seriousness of the situation. Blasting around in US jeeps, wearing GI uniforms, the Germans attempted to wreak havoc wherever they went. They changed signposts, misdirected traffic, and spread false stories all along the line. In one instance, they managed to direct an entire American regiment (around 1,500 men) in the wrong direction. Skorzeny also let a fake document be intercepted by the Allies, purporting to outline the mission. The letter divulged an elaborate and highly detailed plan to capture none other than the Allied Supreme Commander Eisenhower himself. As Skorzeny's reputation preceded him, this was taken very seriously, resulting in Ike spending the most of Christmas 1944 in solitary confinement for his own safety. In the end, he furiously marched out of his office and allegedly declared that if anyone wanted to kill him they could have at it.

Field Marshal Bernard 'Monty' Montgomery, the hero of the Desert War, was arrested by his own men and detained for hours as rumours had been circulated that Skorzeny had planted a Montgomery doppelganger behind enemy lines. He was questioned until he could prove that he was in fact 'the Real Monty'.

While these disruptions were a somewhat small nuisance in the grand scheme of things, the Germans had still succeeded in tying up most of the senior members of staff for days – men who were desperately needed at the front for command. Large portions of valuable manpower were likewise indisposed, unable to participate in the fighting, mostly due to misdirection or through being too occupied in trying to distinguish enemy from ally. Several US soldiers were wounded or killed by their own as a direct result of mistaken identity.

The Allies finally caught on and eventually most of the Germans in Einheit Stielau were identified and captured. Out of the forty-four men in the unit, seventeen are known to have been executed and only eight are known to have returned to their ranks. Three German officers, Pernass, Billing, and Schmidt, were captured

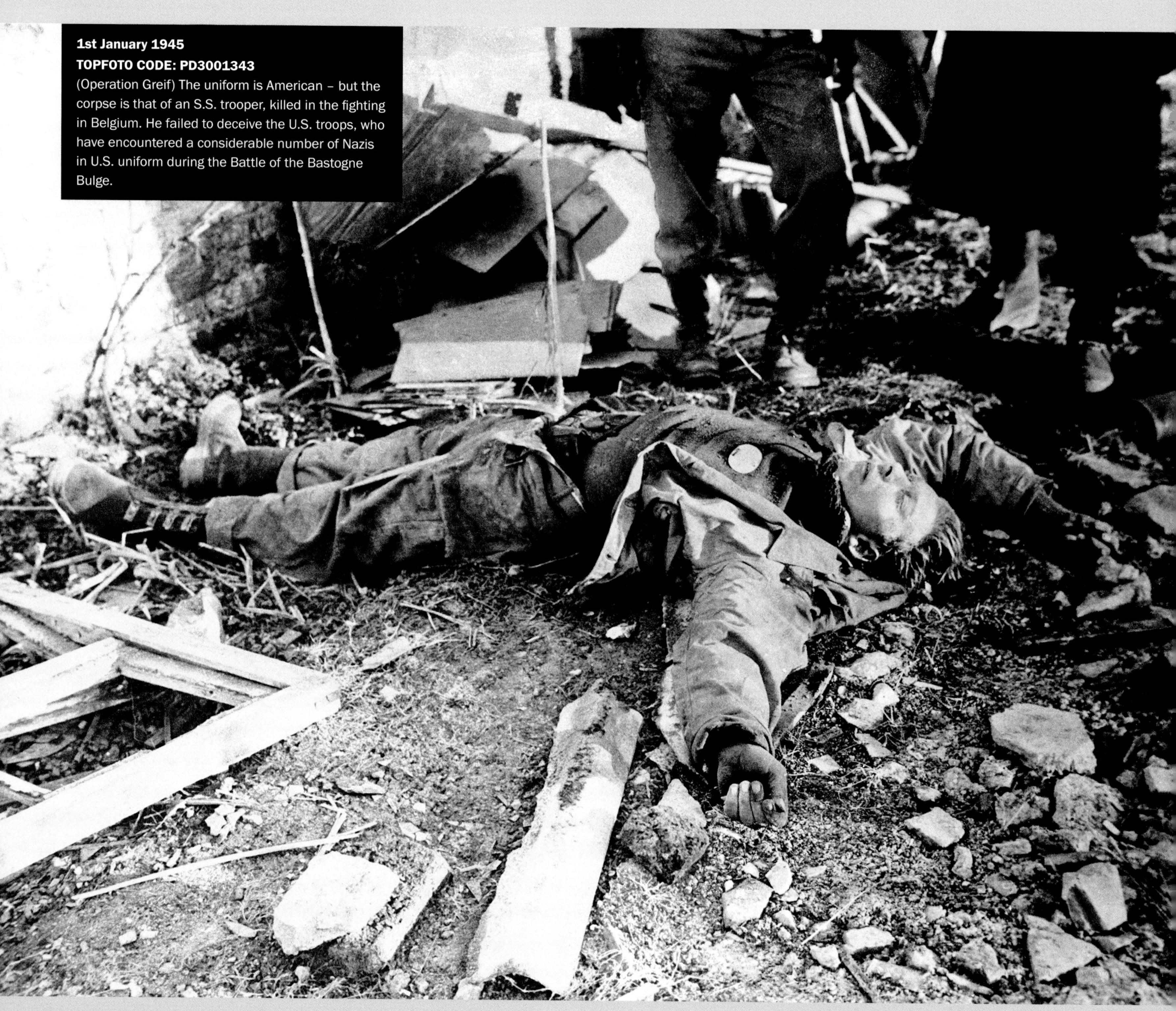

1st January 1945
TOPFOTO CODE: PD3001343
(Operation Greif) The uniform is American – but the
corpse is that of an S.S. trooper, killed in the fighting
in Belgium. He failed to deceive the U.S. troops, who
have encountered a considerable number of Nazis
in U.S. uniform during the Battle of the Bastogne
Bulge.

on 17 December 1944 after failing to provide the correct password at a roadblock. Collectively they had in their possession £1,000 (£54,000 in today's money) and $900 ($17,500 in today's money) in notes, fake identity papers, German pay books, two British Sten guns, two Colt pistols, two German sub-machine guns, and six US hand grenades. They were swiftly court martialled and shot on 23 December 1944 on the clear instructions of Dwight D. Eisenhower.

Ultimately, both Operation Greif and Operation Stösser failed and indicated the impending downfall of Hitler's Third Reich. Both missions had been desperate final attempts, just as the overall Ardennes counteroffensive had been. The early image of the Nazi war machine, completely mechanised, with its advanced technology, superior equipment, and almost superhuman soldiers, had cracked and revealed a very different picture.

The Ardennes offensive had been costly for both sides, but Germany had little left. Its last reserves were depleted, the Luftwaffe annihilated, and the army was on the run. The vice was closing from east and west, and Nazi Germany's inevitable defeat was on the horizon.

After the war ended, Skorzeny and nine other officers of the Panzer Brigade 150 were charged as war criminals at the 1947 Dachau Trials. They were tried for 'Entering into combat disguised therewith and treacherously firing upon and killing members of the armed forces of the United States' and for 'participation in wrongfully obtaining U.S. uniforms and Red Cross parcels consigned to American prisoners of war from a prisoner-of-war camp'.[2] All ten were acquitted on a technicality, as Skorzeny had been well instructed by his German legal counsel. For them to have been found guilty, the court would have had to prove that they had given direct orders to the men to enter into combat wearing US uniforms. If that could not be proven, and no admissions were made, it would be deemed as a legitimate ruse of war.

After the trials, Skorzeny was held in an internment camp, but in 1948 he managed to escape. He fled from Germany to France until he settled in Spain, where he was protected by Generalissimo Francisco Franco's authoritarian regime. Five years later, he was hired as a military advisor to Egypt's President Gamal Nasser, a known CIA asset, and enlisted a host of his 'old friends' from the Waffen-SS to train the Egyptian Army. He was an advisor for the Argentine President Juan Peron as well as a bodyguard for his wife, Eva Peron (with whom he is claimed to have had an affair).

The tabloids continued to add to the already bizarre summary, with tales of him working for Mossad (Israel's intelligence agency), performing special interrogations and assassination operations. There were stories of Cuban communist dictator Fidel Castro consulting him for his memoirs, sources connecting him to the death of Nikola Tesla, rumours of him running armies in Congo and India – and even claims of him being close to finding the Holy Grail in France.

Although formally 'denazified' in 1952 (in absentia) by the West German government, it is alleged that he was a main instigator of the famous Odessa Organisation, which helped hundreds of Nazi war criminals flee Europe. It was proven that he continued to both initiate and advise several neo-Nazi groups in various countries.

In the 1960s, further charges were raised against him for numerous atrocities performed during the war, but these were eventually dropped due to a lack of evidence. Popular culture has often used his person, directly or indirectly, as a foundation for the creation of supervillain characters, most famously the inspiration for the antagonist Auric Goldfinger in Ian Fleming's James Bond book *Goldfinger*. Fleming himself served as a high-ranking British naval intelligence officer during the Second World War and would have been well aware of Skorzeny's exploits and characteristics.

Skorzeny eventually died of lung cancer in Madrid in 1975, just four months before the death of Francisco Franco. He continues to be a widely discussed personality, and evidence attesting to his many vile actions continues to emerge.

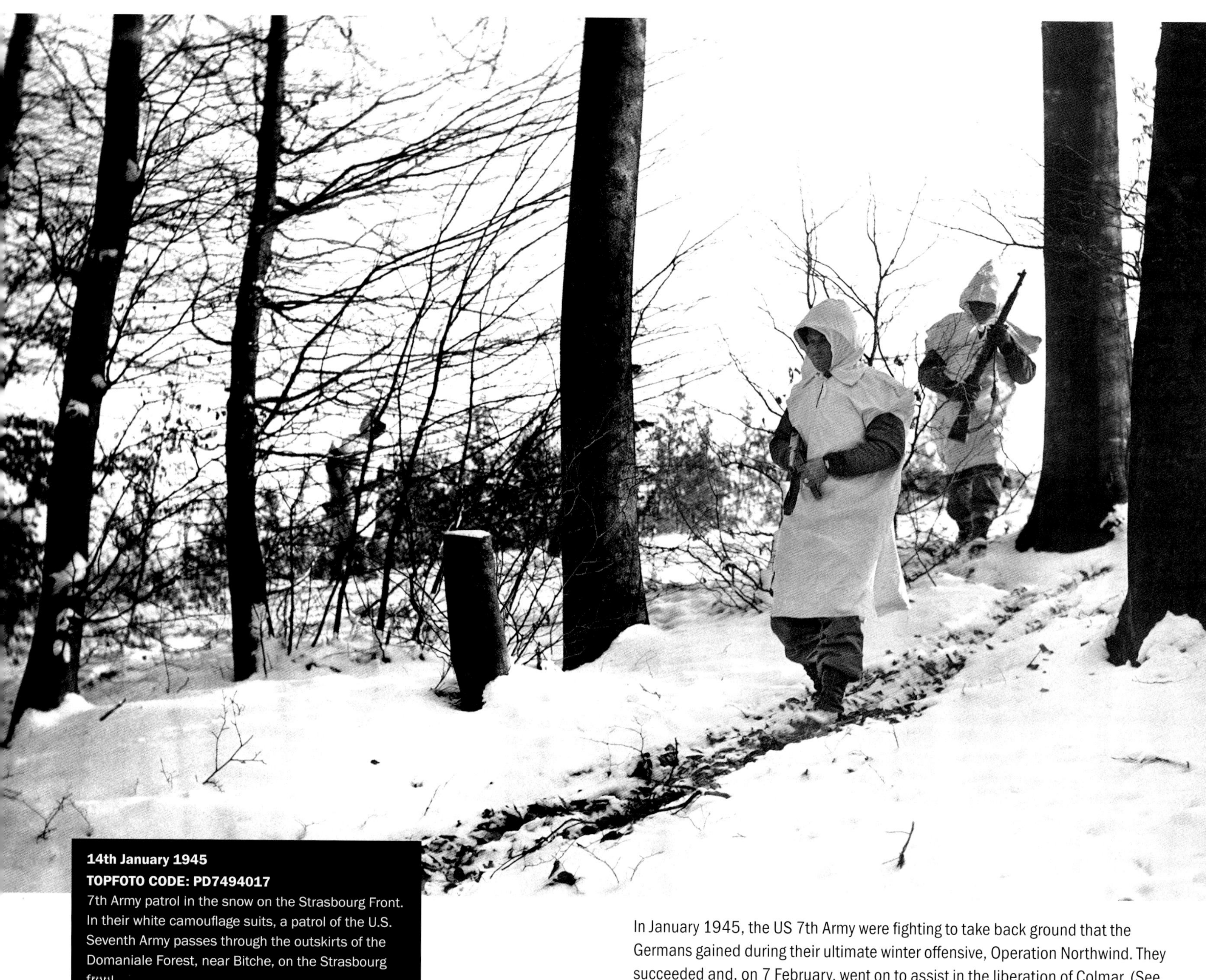

In January 1945, the US 7th Army were fighting to take back ground that the Germans gained during their ultimate winter offensive, Operation Northwind. They succeeded and, on 7 February, went on to assist in the liberation of Colmar. (See more about Colmar on page 149.)

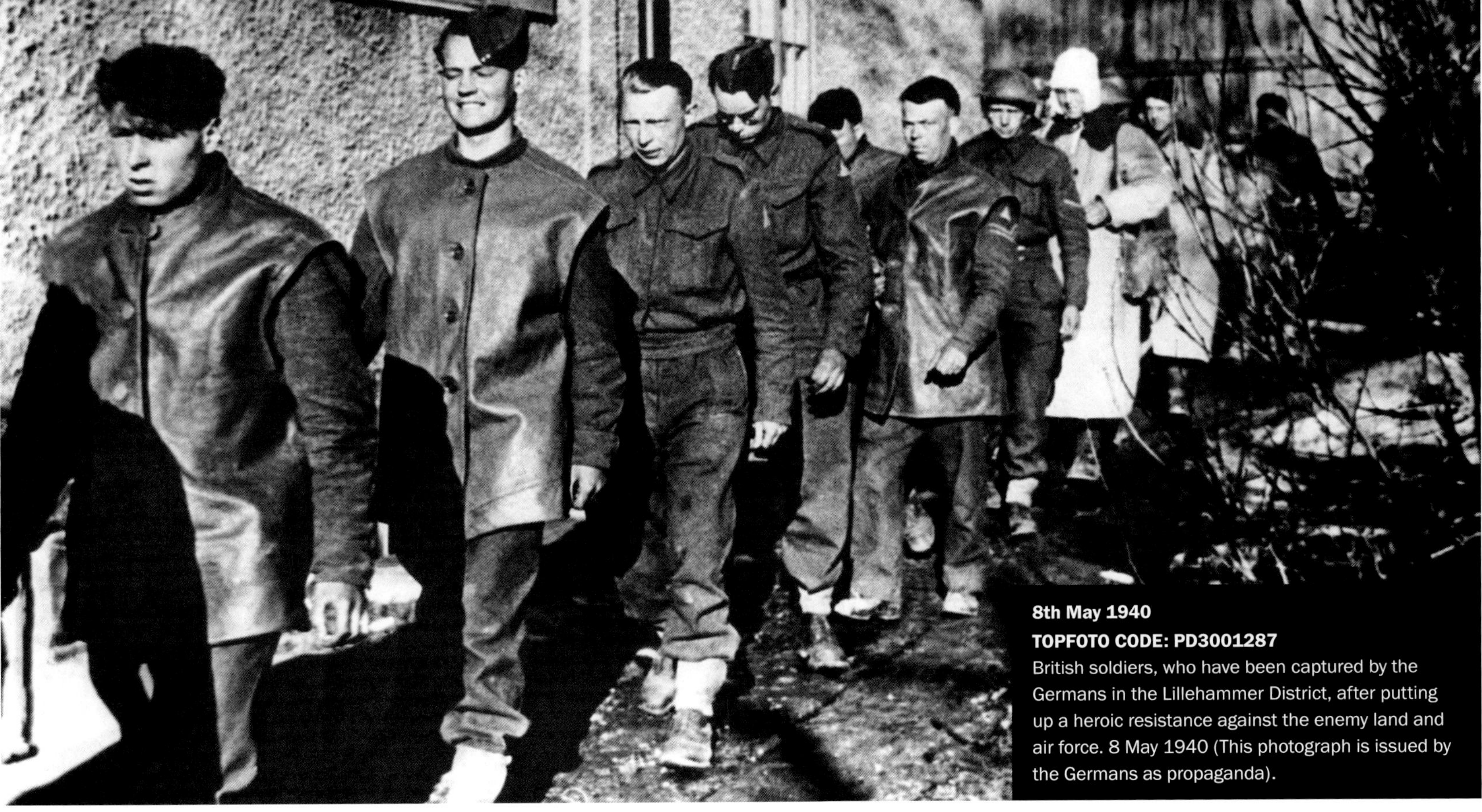

8th May 1940
TOPFOTO CODE: PD3001287
British soldiers, who have been captured by the Germans in the Lillehammer District, after putting up a heroic resistance against the enemy land and air force. 8 May 1940 (This photograph is issued by the Germans as propaganda).

On 9 April 1940 the Germans began Operation Weserübung – the invasion of Norway and Denmark. Officially, Germany told the people they were there to defend Scandinavian neutrality from 'Allied aggression', but in reality it was about the control of Narvik and its ice-free port, as well as the control of the access to the northern Atlantic and the Baltic Sea. Holding Narvik assured a winter delivery route for the extremely vital iron ore coming from neutral Sweden, feeding the Nazi war machine. From 1933 to 1943 a staggering estimated average of 43 per cent of Germany's iron ore came from Sweden, mainly from the northern mining towns of Gällivare and Kiruna. Arguments could be made that if Germany had been cut off from this supply the Second World War would have ended a lot sooner.

Germany had little interest in Denmark, but it represented a stepping stone to Norway and possessed the important Aalborg airport, which would serve as a pit stop for the German Luftwaffe flying north or south. The invasion was a pre-emptive strike and Denmark capitulated within hours. Norway, however, put up a fight.

The British had been planning too. Anticipating the German occupation, they had been preparing to mine strategic channels in Norway and had also cooked up their own plan to invade Norway and Sweden in an attempt to disrupt the German supply. Code-named Plan R4, it never happened as the Germans beat them to the punch by a day.

The Norwegian military and a 38,000-strong army, consisting of British, French and Polish forces, continued to fight the Germans but ultimately lost the battle for Norway. The Allied forces withdrew and on 10 June 1940 the Norwegian forces capitulated.

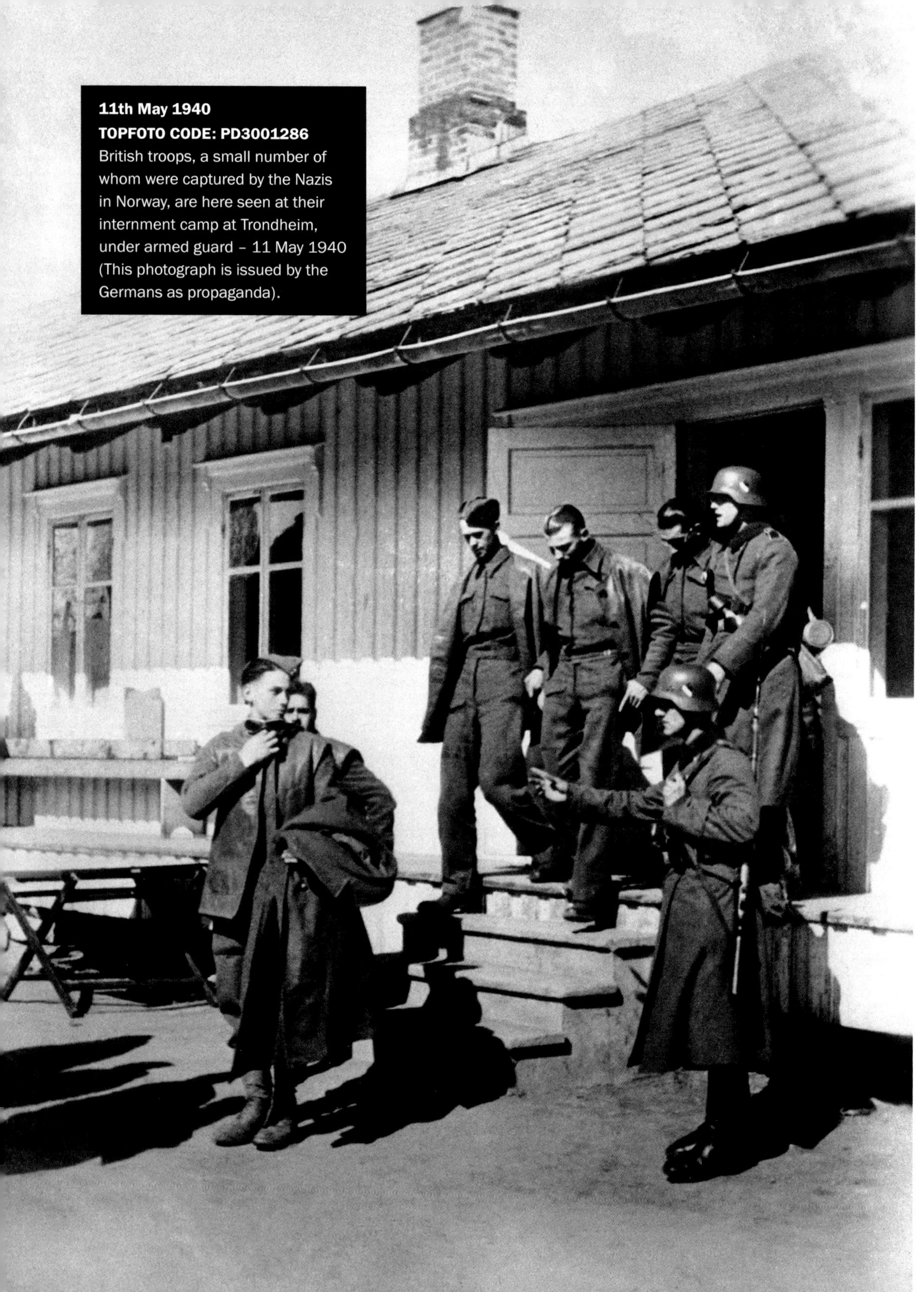

POWs in Norway and the Rinnan Gang

This photo (right) was captured in front of the Hotel Phoenix in Trondheim, Norway. The Phoenix served as the headquarters for the German SiPo (Sicherheitspolizei, Security Police) during part of the Nazi occupation of Norway. (Read more about this on pages 67 and 73.) According to a Norwegian newspaper article from 2003, a secret tunnel from the Hotel Phoenix led to Misjonshotellet across the street. This was confirmed by a local engineer that saw it himself during the war.

Here resided SS-Obersturmbannführer Gerhard Flesch, the commander of both SiPo and the SD (Sicherheitsdienst, the intelligence agency within the SS) in Bergen and Trondheim. In the basements of Misjonshotellet the Germans had conveniently set up prison cells and rooms for questioning, and this is where Flesch allegedly conducted his savage interrogations and committed several murders.

In June 1940, the Norwegian Henry Rinnan met the leader of the Gestapo in Trondheim, Gerhard Stübs, who enlisted him and gave him the designation 'agent number 1' and the code name 'Lola'. Rinnan also lodged at the Hotel Phoenix and became the leader of the Rinnan Gang (Rinnanbanden), a unit designated by the Germans as Sonderabteilung Lola (Special Unit Lola).

The Rinnan Gang consisted of a group of about fifty nationalistic and disillusioned Norwegians turned traitors, whose primary mission was to infiltrate and expose members of the Norwegian resistance movement. Working closely with both Stübs and Gerhard Flesch (and with almost no interference), the group exposed around an estimated 1,000 people and assisted in the vicious and brutal torture of hundreds, resulting in the death of at least eighty people. Further into the war, Rinnan received a rank within the SS and transitioned from peddling information to actively engaging in his own interrogations and torture of his suspects, using an array of clubs, whips, heated poker irons and cigarettes. Several sources state that Henry

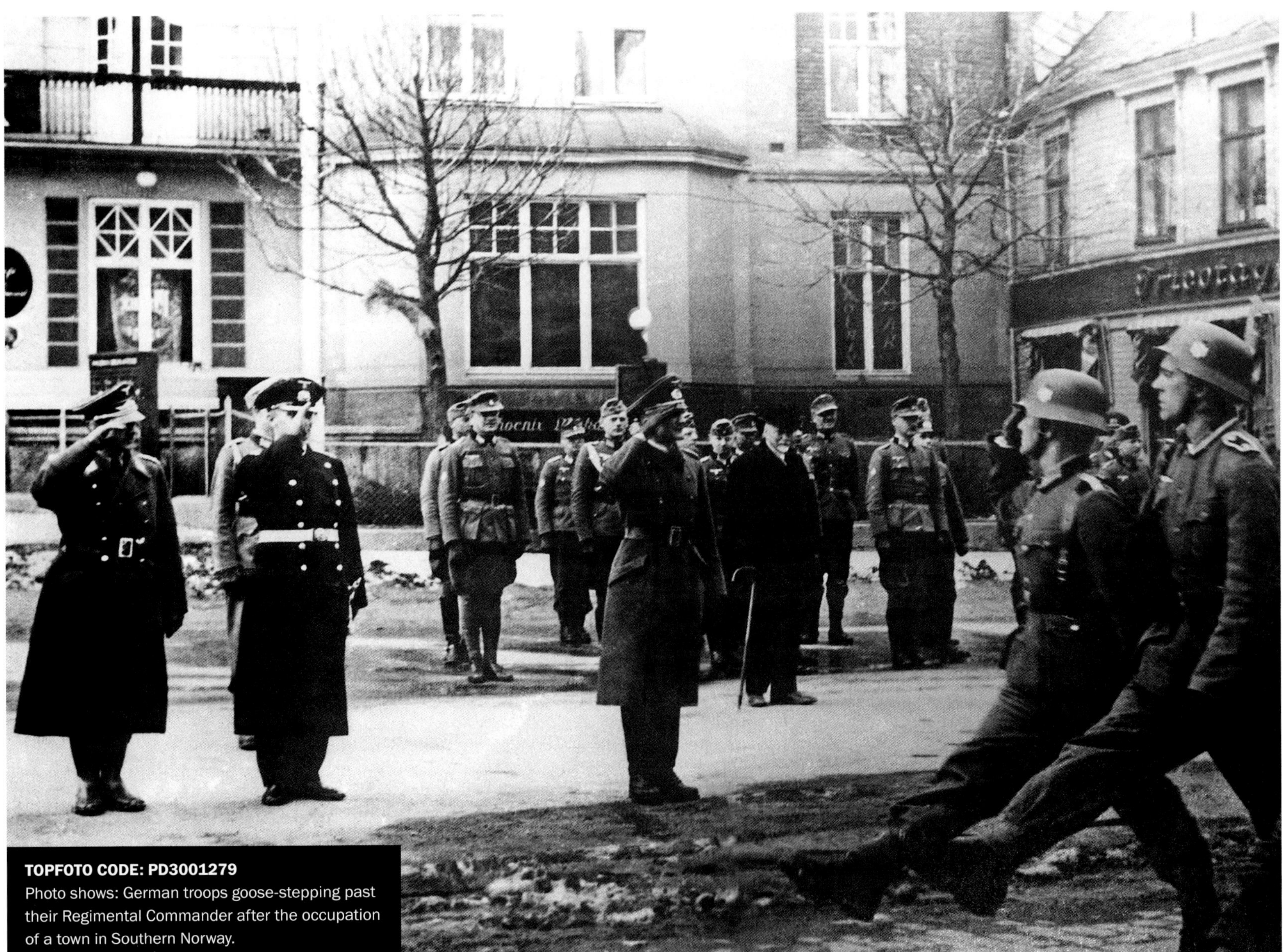

Rinnan was by far the most useful non-German that Heinrich Himmler (leader of the SS) ever had access to in northern Europe.

Rinnan was captured after the war and sentenced to death for personally committing thirteen murders. Eleven of his accomplices were likewise executed.

Rinnan was killed by a firing squad on 1 February 1947, never once showing the slightest sign of remorse. For his vile and reprehensible actions Gerhard Flesch was also sentenced to death and was executed on 28 February 1948. Before the rifles fired, he allegedly shouted 'Heil Hitler'.

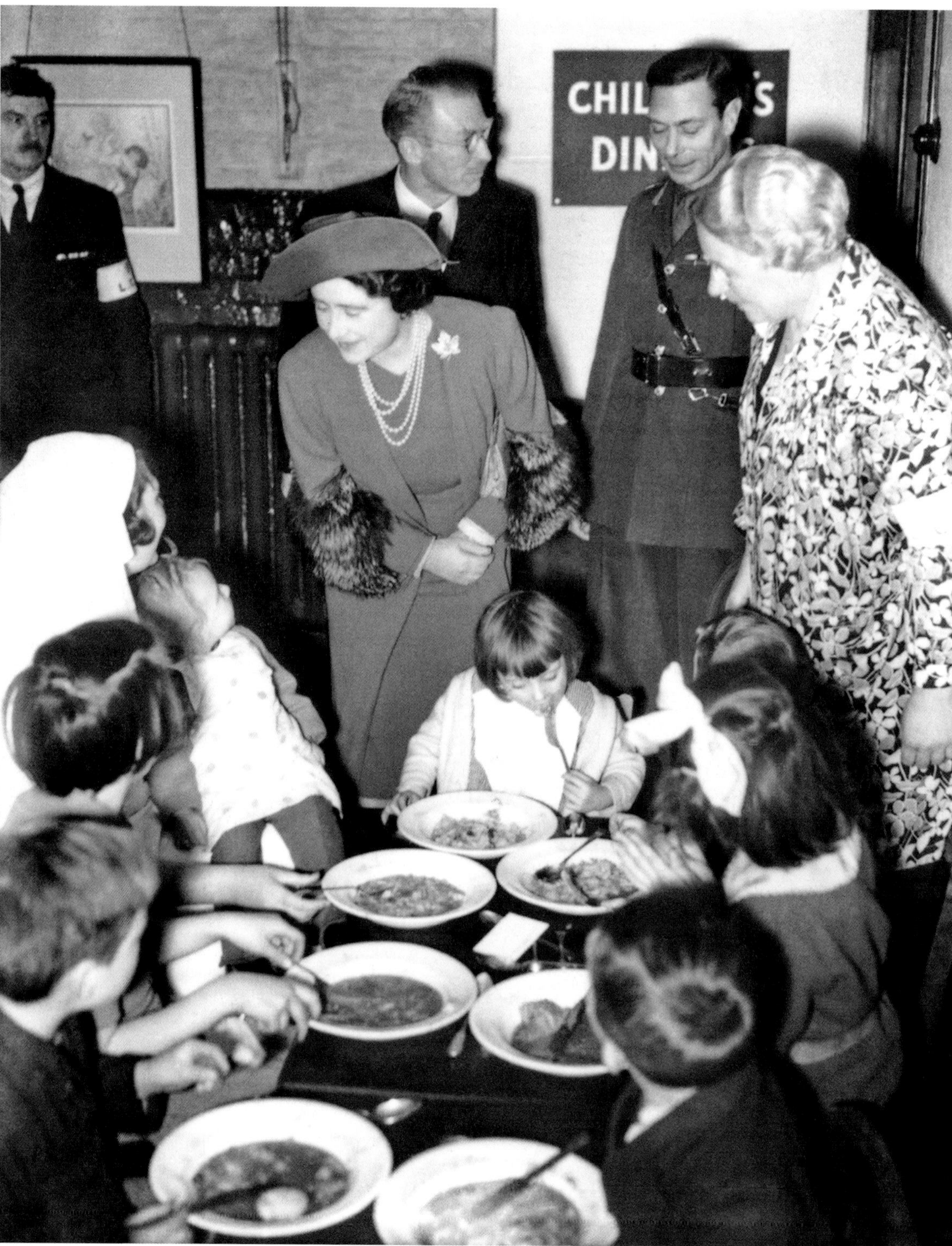

14th November 1940
TOPFOTO CODE: PD3001212
The King and Queen accompanied by Sir Edward Evans made a tour of inspection of air raid shelters and canteens in the London area. Photo shows: the Queen with the King, chatting to children enjoying their dinners at a London feeding canteen during the tour.

The systematic bombing of London by the Germans began on 7 September 1940. Though not specifically targeted, five bombs hit Buckingham Palace, injuring several workmen. (The palace was in fact hit no fewer than nine times during the war.)

Rather than leaving London, King George VI and Queen Elizabeth chose to stay at the palace and share the burden with their people. In response, and to show their concern, they went to visit parts of London that had been impacted hard and the young Princess Elizabeth went on the BBC's radio programme *Children's Hour* and spoke publicly to the children. Elizabeth later went on to join the ATS at the age of 18. (Read more about the ATS on page 23.)

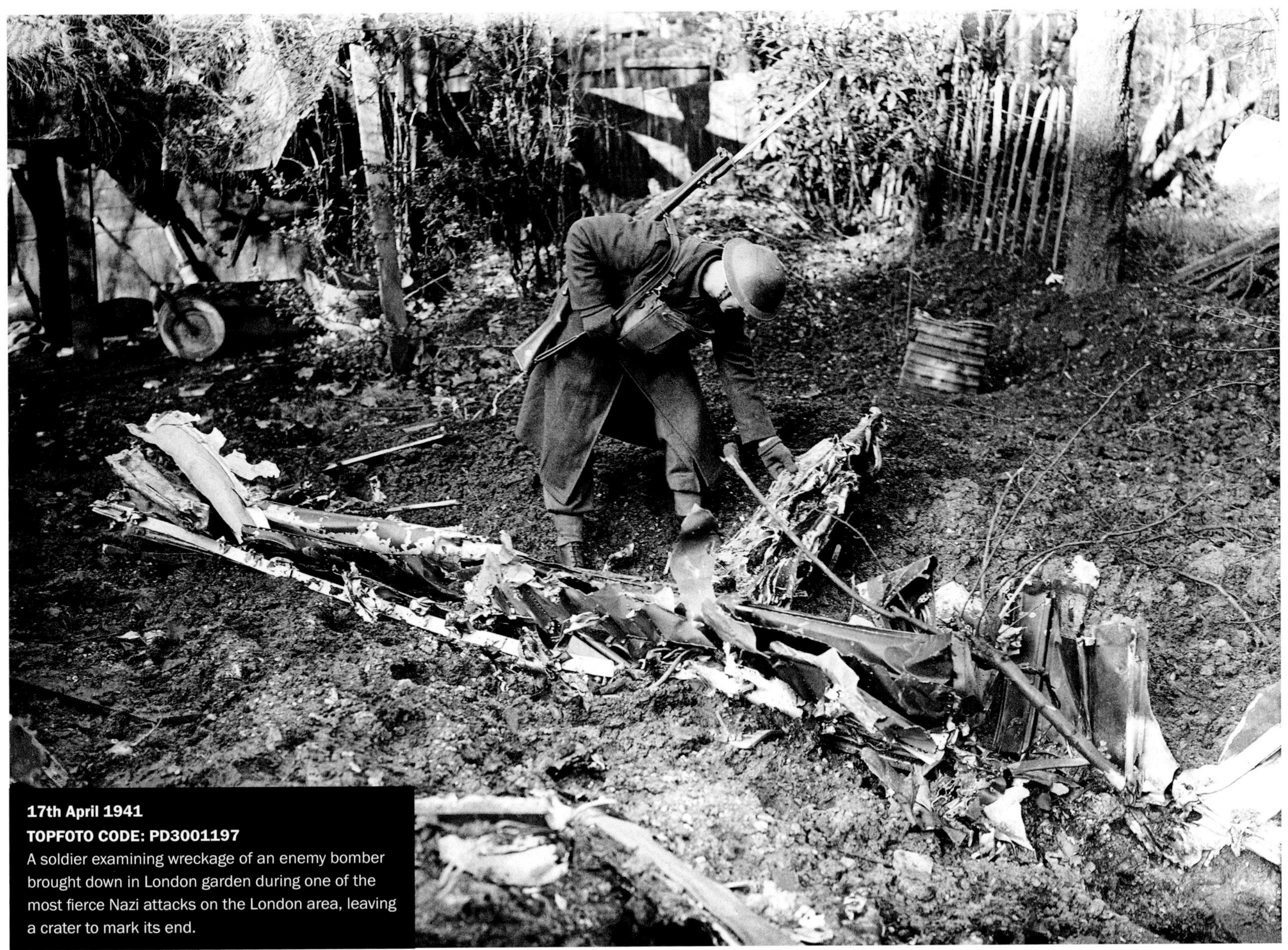

The Blitz was a relentless bombing campaign by Nazi Germany against Great Britain, lasting from September 1940 to May 1941. The Luftwaffe had lost the Battle of Britain and Reich Marshal Hermann Göring ordered his bombers to target not just military sites but also civilian areas, aiming to crush the morale of the British population and force their government to surrender. London was hit hard, enduring attacks for a full fifty-six out of fifty-seven nights, though other cities across the country also suffered. The Blitz began in earnest on 7 September 1940, when German bombers unleashed hell on London. It was a day that would become known as 'Black Saturday'.

Though the Blitz failed to achieve its objective of forcing Britain into submission, it came at a heavy cost. Reportedly, 43,500 civilians lost their lives and countless others were hurt.

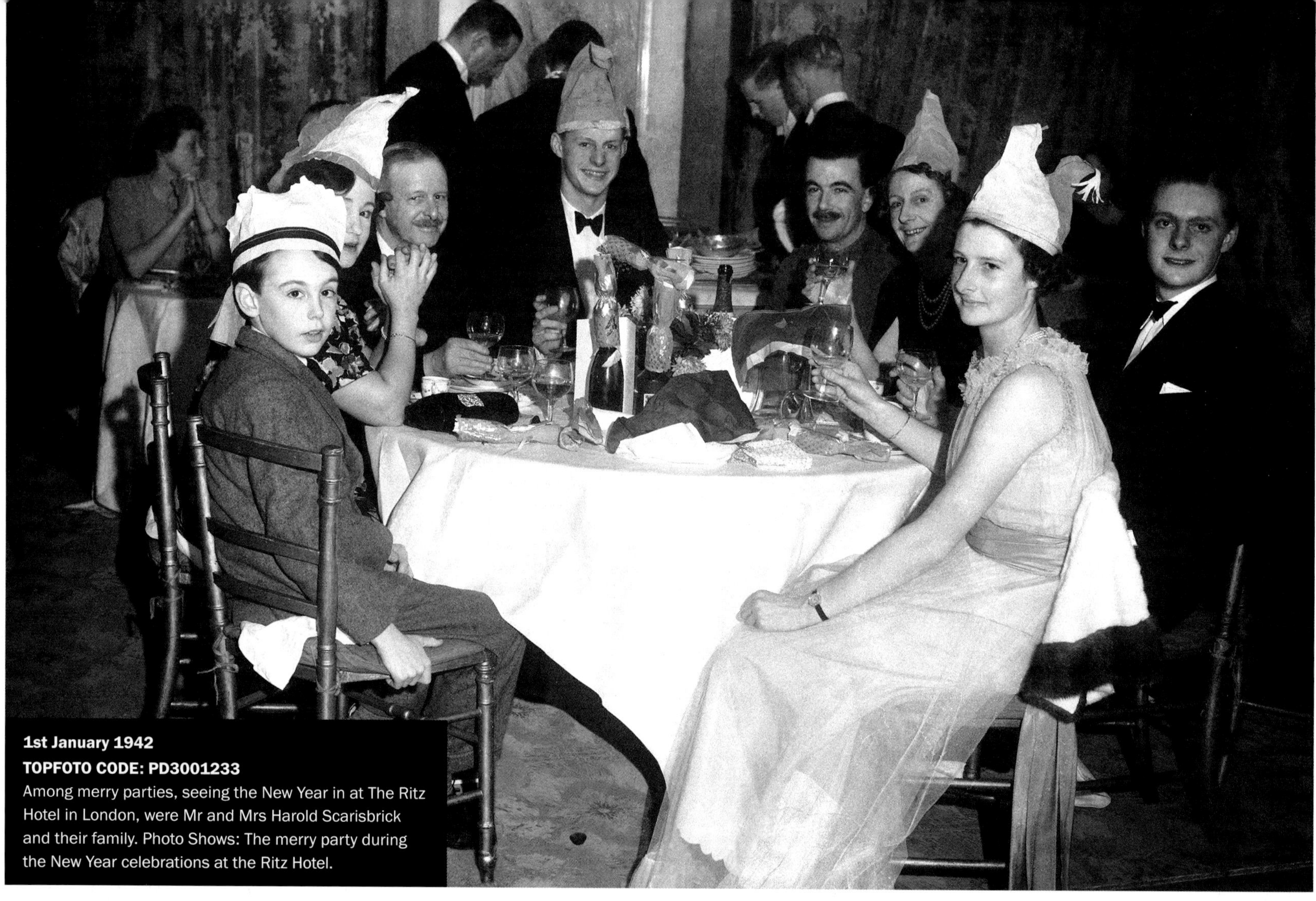

In its 118-year history, the Ritz in London has only ever closed its doors during the Covid pandemic. It was damaged no fewer than nine times during the bombing raids of the Second World War, yet the restaurant in the hotel only briefly closed twice. This is a momentous testament to the incredible tenacity that was shown by the employees and the patrons of the hotel during the war years. While the world was ablaze, the Ritz became a hub for royals, famous people, and the social elite – as well as the playground for con men, communists and spies. A place where clandestine meetings took place at any level of the social hierarchy.

Churchill and Eisenhower famously met in the Antoinette Suite to discuss operations in 1942, while two years prior the entire royal Albanian family moved in and took up a whole floor for themselves.

The world was at war, but for those who had the means, these grand hotels became bastions of safety. Here the whims of the upper crust could quietly continue, while outside the blitzkrieg was raging. The physical threshold of the hotel somehow manifested the point of immediate ascension into privilege, and in passing that step you became part of the untouchable few – those whom not even bombs could kill.

The Scarisbrick family are portrayed here as a message for the public: keep calm and carry on. The stiff upper lip and the virtues and graces of beloved England were being maintained, as evidenced by the rich doing as they pleased as always.

As a comparison, spending New Year at the Ritz London in 2024 will now set you back £1,950 per adult. That is just for the food and entertainment and does not include a room or additional services. If the Scarisbrick family had gone there that year the bill would have been £15,600. Bon appétit!

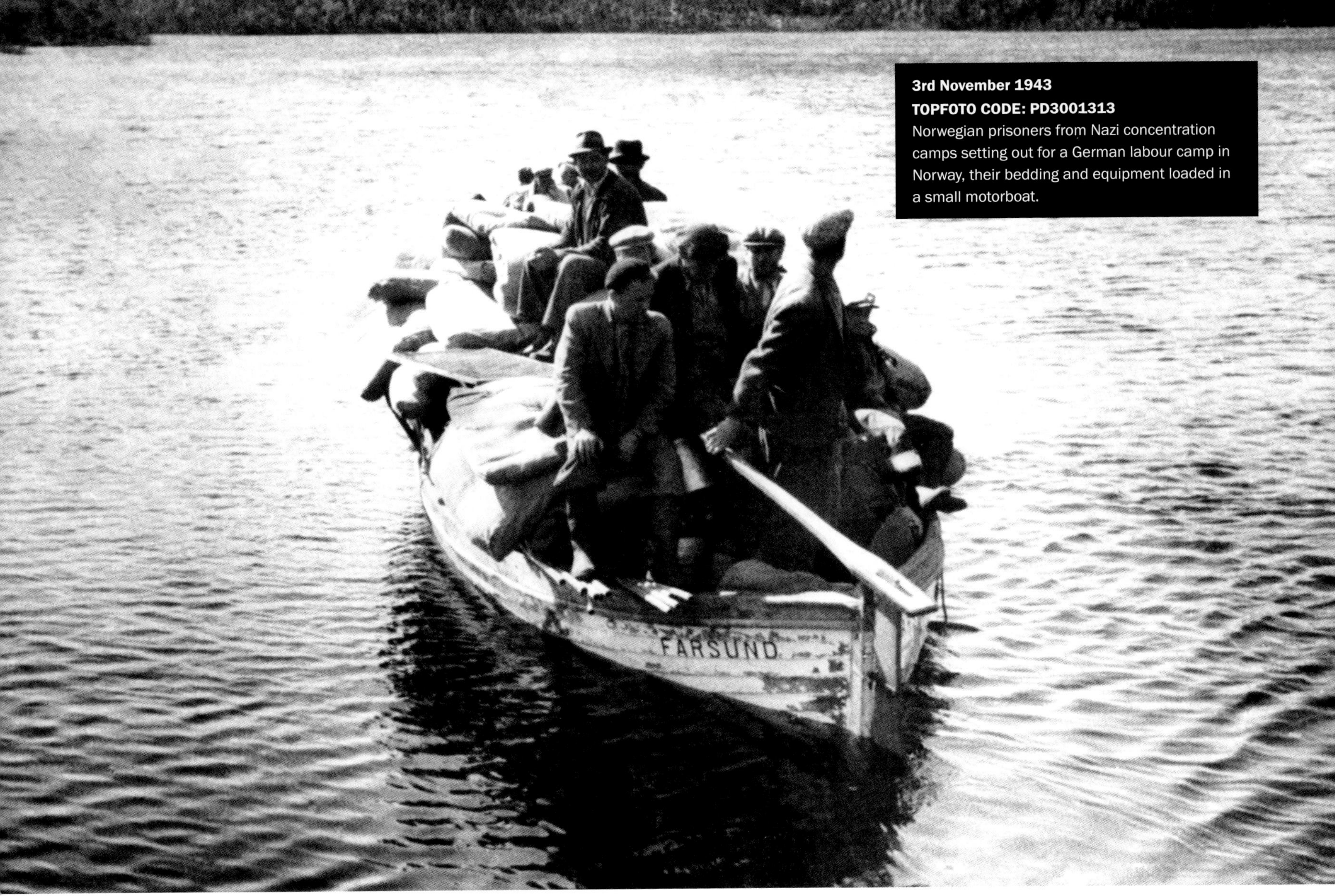

3rd November 1943
TOPFOTO CODE: PD3001313
Norwegian prisoners from Nazi concentration camps setting out for a German labour camp in Norway, their bedding and equipment loaded in a small motorboat.

Forced Labour in Norway

On 10 June 1940 the Norwegian forces capitulated to Nazi Germany. In the span of the occupation, some 40,000 Norwegians were imprisoned. Norway had around 620 prison camps, which held anyone from POWs and Jews to political prisoners and forced labourers of widely different ethnic origins. It is estimated that Norway held a total of 130,000 forced labourers, all treated very harshly – especially if foreign.

The labourers were used for a number of different projects, but mainly for the construction of infrastructure. Some of the larger projects were the Norland Railway (Nordlandsbanen), and Hitler's Atlantic Wall, stretching from the northern coast of Norway to the French coast, using a massive system of coastal fortifications, bunkers, and artillery placements.

The railway line saw the use of more than 20,000 Russians, under the watchful eye of the feared German engineering group Organisation Todt (OT). The mortality rates were high. Between 2,000 and 3,000 of these labourers died due to the unforgiving weather conditions, poor nutrition, gruelling work, or downright execution.

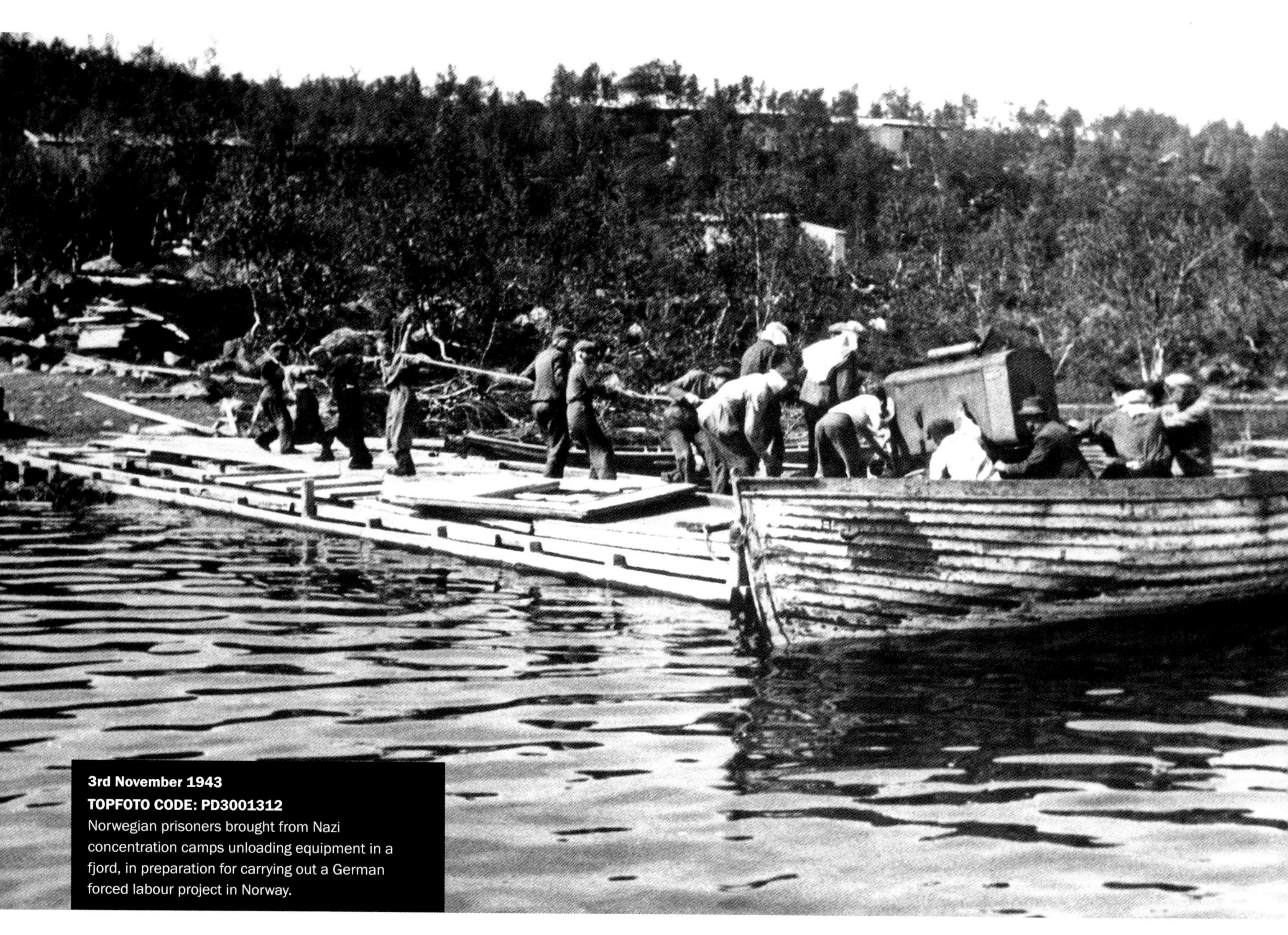

3rd November 1943
TOPFOTO CODE: PD3001312
Norwegian prisoners brought from Nazi
concentration camps unloading equipment in a
fjord, in preparation for carrying out a German
forced labour project in Norway.

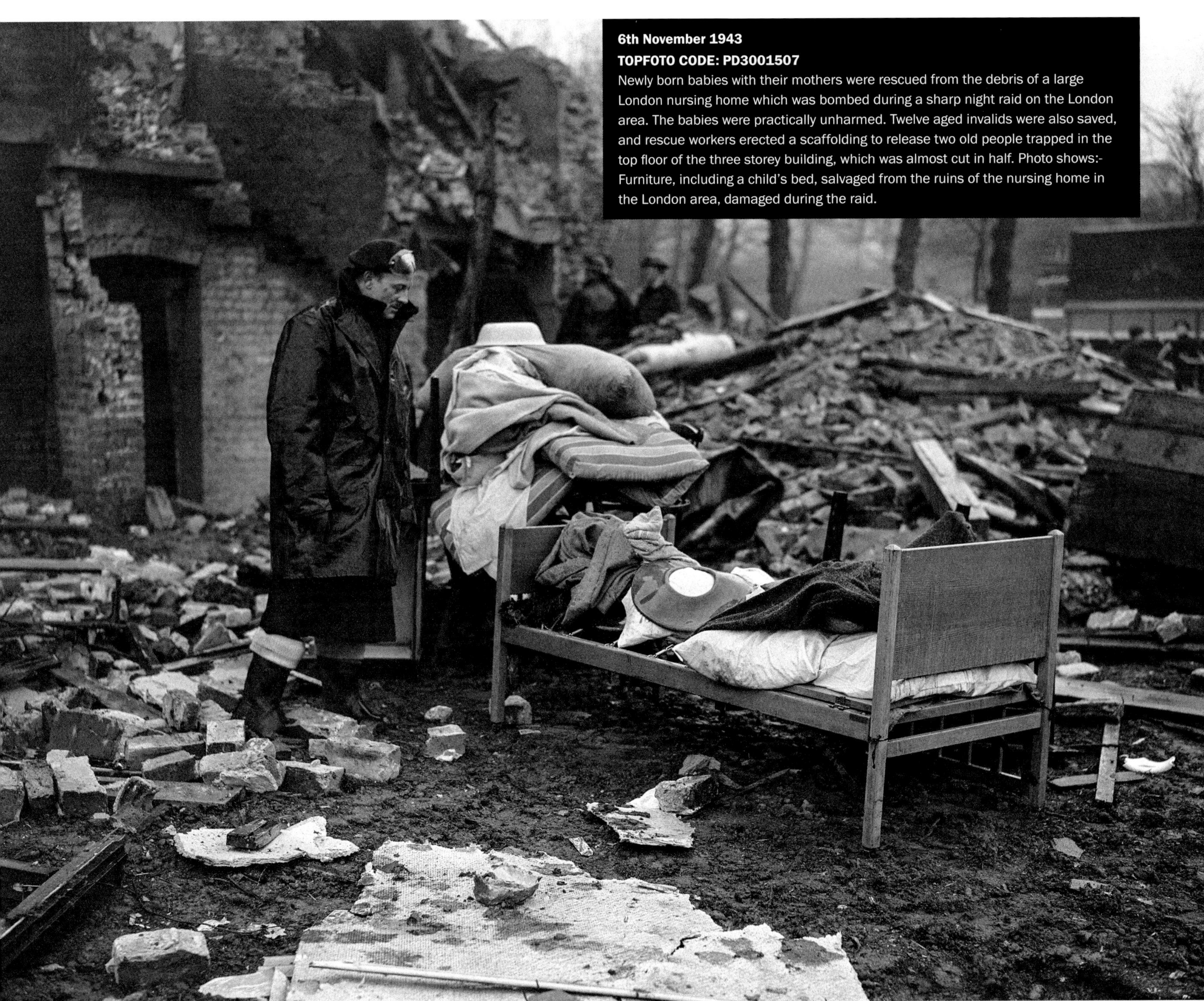

6th November 1943
TOPFOTO CODE: PD3001507
Newly born babies with their mothers were rescued from the debris of a large London nursing home which was bombed during a sharp night raid on the London area. The babies were practically unharmed. Twelve aged invalids were also saved, and rescue workers erected a scaffolding to release two old people trapped in the top floor of the three storey building, which was almost cut in half. Photo shows:- Furniture, including a child's bed, salvaged from the ruins of the nursing home in the London area, damaged during the raid.

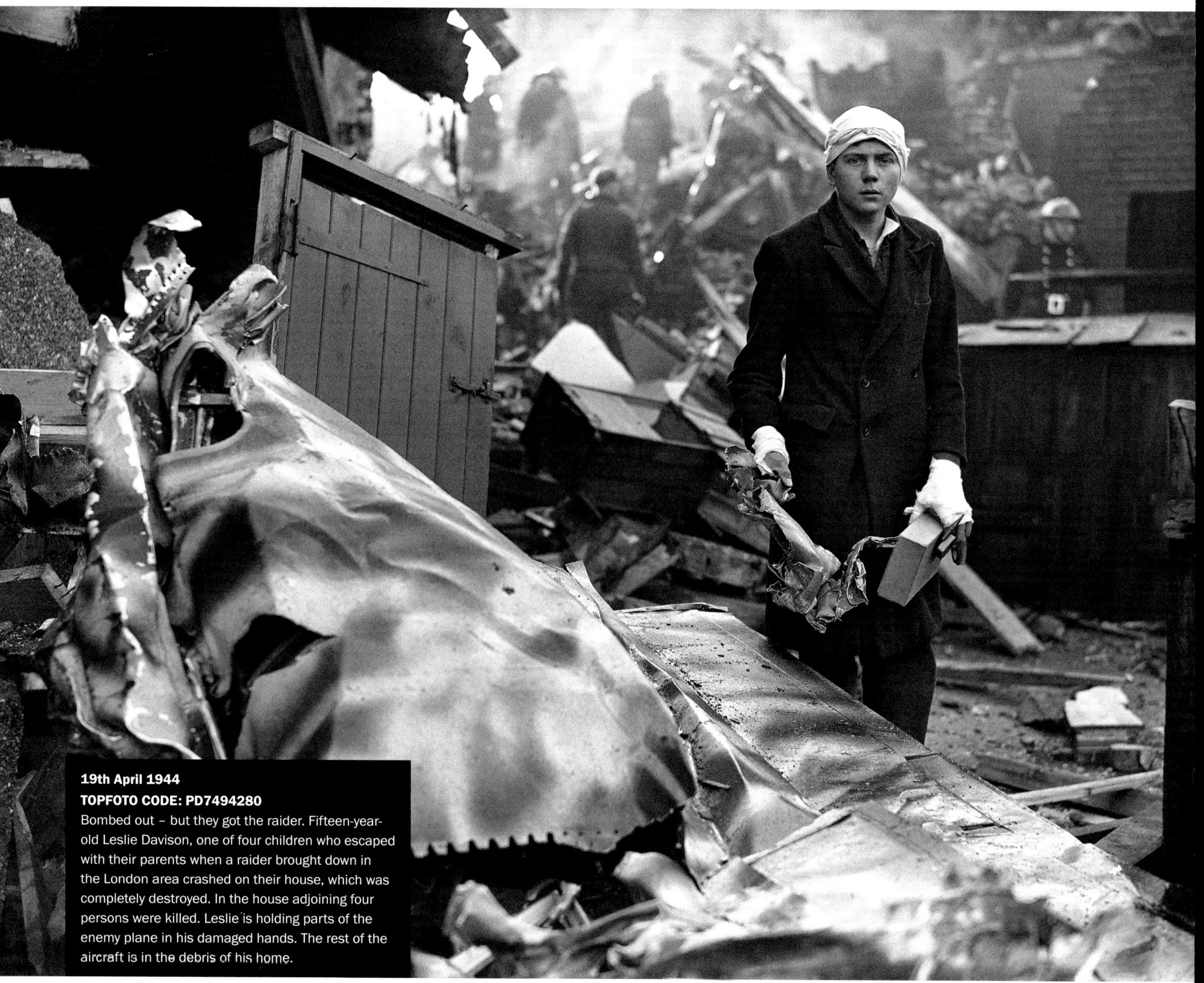

19th April 1944
TOPFOTO CODE: PD7494280
Bombed out – but they got the raider. Fifteen-year-old Leslie Davison, one of four children who escaped with their parents when a raider brought down in the London area crashed on their house, which was completely destroyed. In the house adjoining four persons were killed. Leslie is holding parts of the enemy plane in his damaged hands. The rest of the aircraft is in the debris of his home.

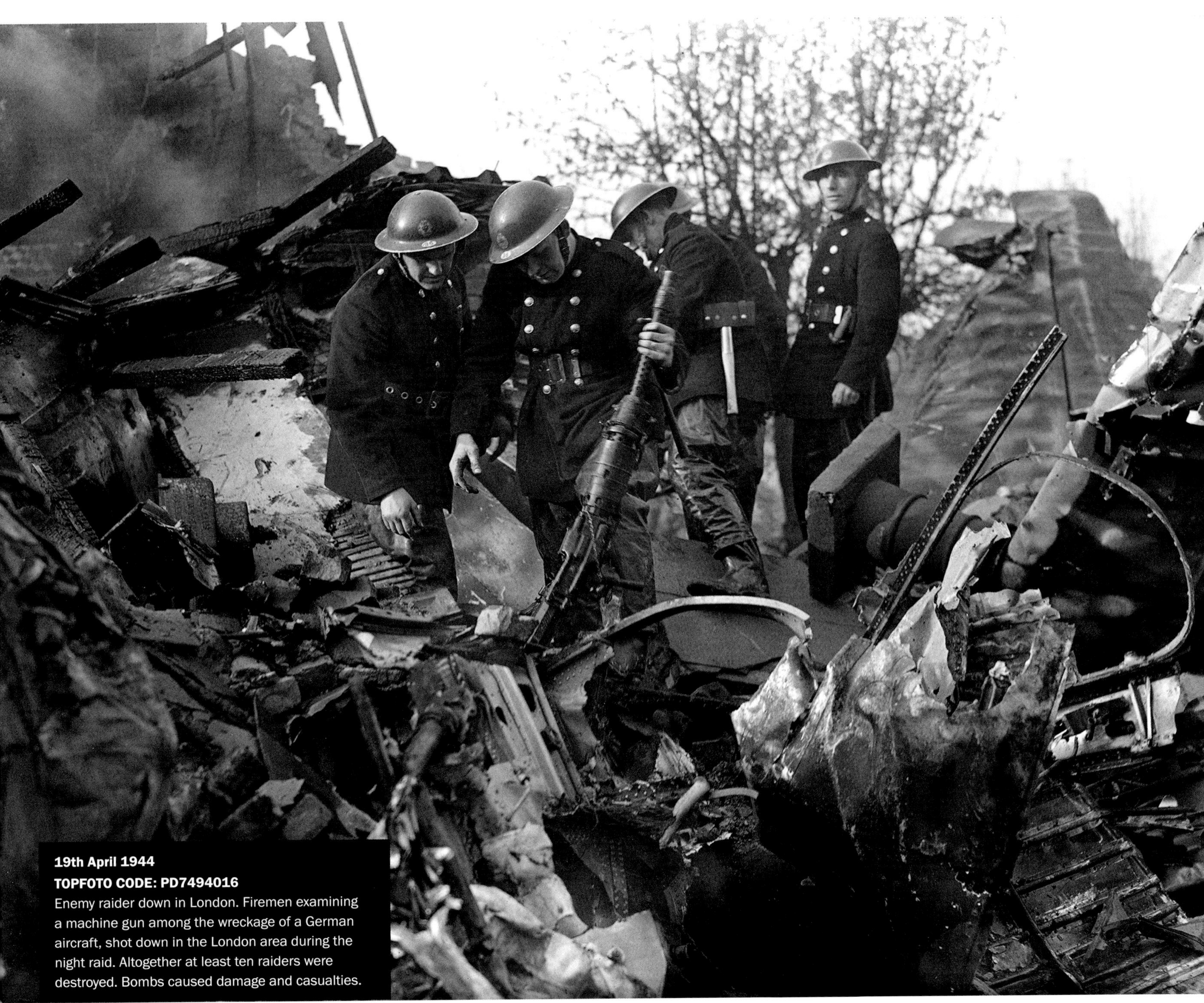

19th April 1944
TOPFOTO CODE: PD7494016
Enemy raider down in London. Firemen examining a machine gun among the wreckage of a German aircraft, shot down in the London area during the night raid. Altogether at least ten raiders were destroyed. Bombs caused damage and casualties.

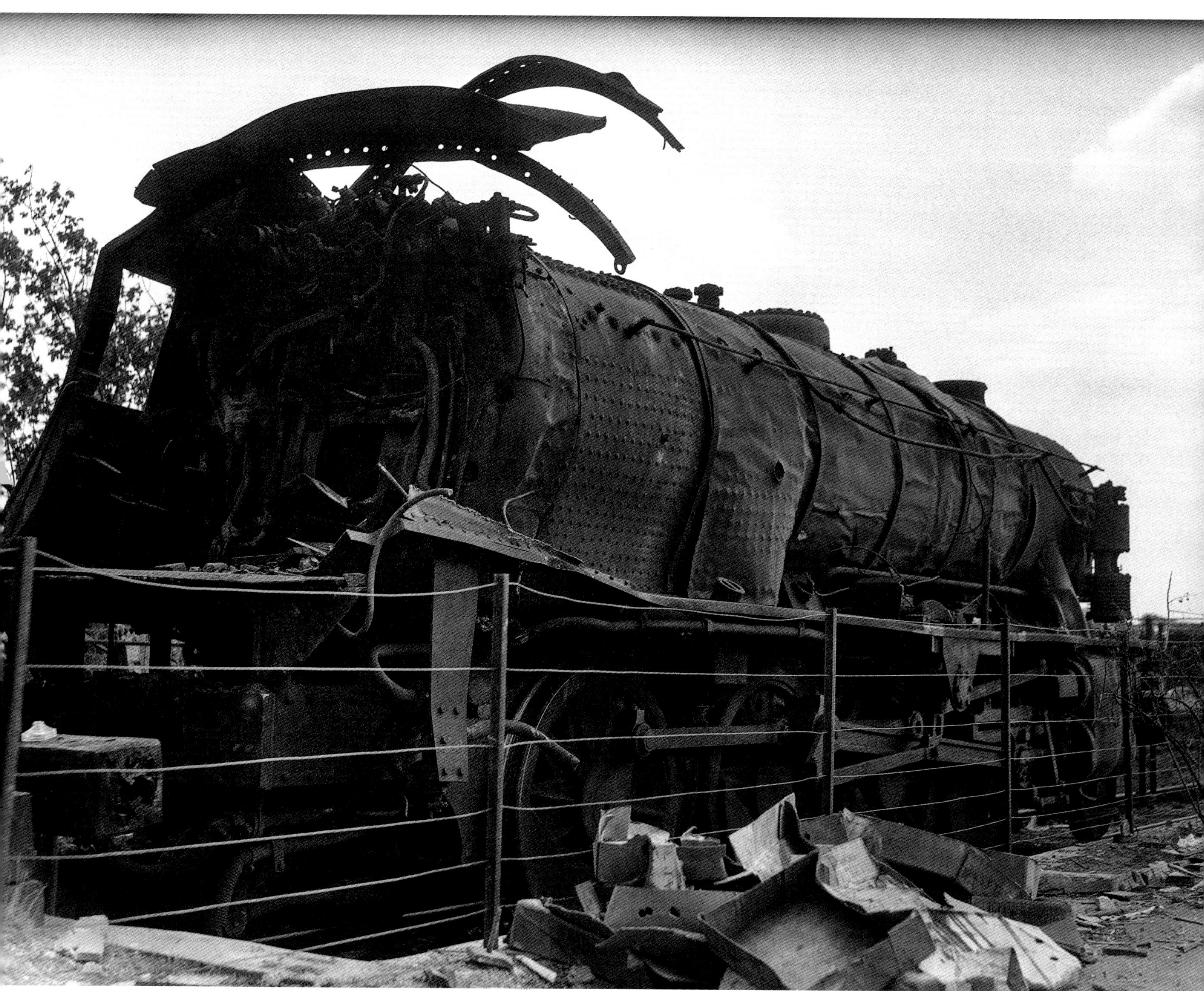

In the early hours of 2 June 1944, a train loaded with 400 tons (881,000lb) of heavy ammunition was pulling into Soham Station when its driver, Benjamin Gimbert, suddenly saw flames coming from one of the wagons containing bombs. He brought the train to a halt and beckoned to the railway fireman, James Nightall, to detach it from the rest of the train. Gimbert subsequently managed to separate the rest of the train from the inferno by about 140 yards before the bombs exploded. Reportedly just that one single wagon contained a staggering 22,000lb of explosives.

Nightall and a signalman died, but Gimbert survived. Several other people were injured though, along with various degrees of damage to around 800 of the houses and buildings in the town. However, had it not been for the heroic response of the two men, the town would have been completely obliterated. They both received the George Cross for their heroic efforts – Nightall posthumously. It has never been fully determined what caused the fire, but new evidence still surfaces eighty years on.

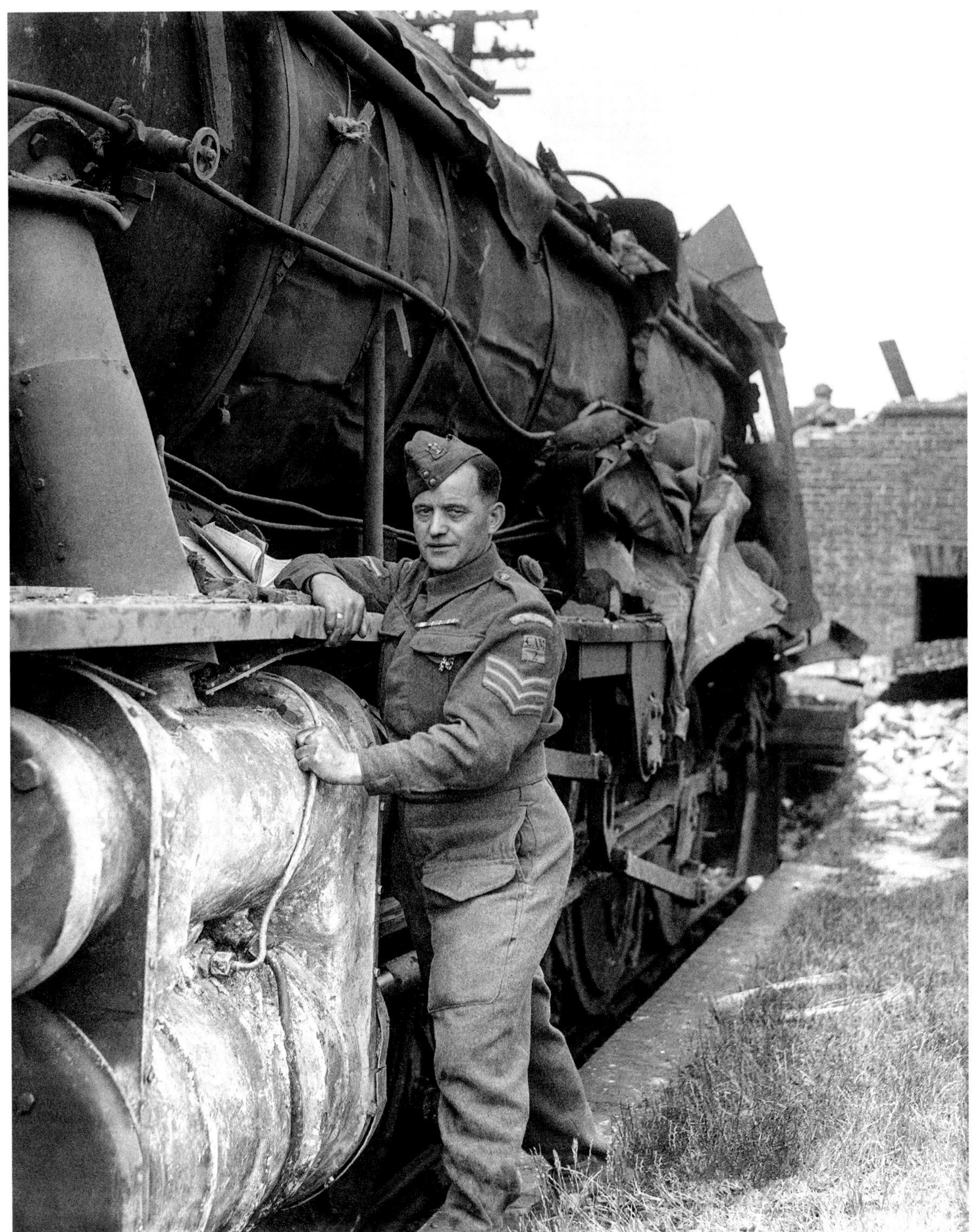

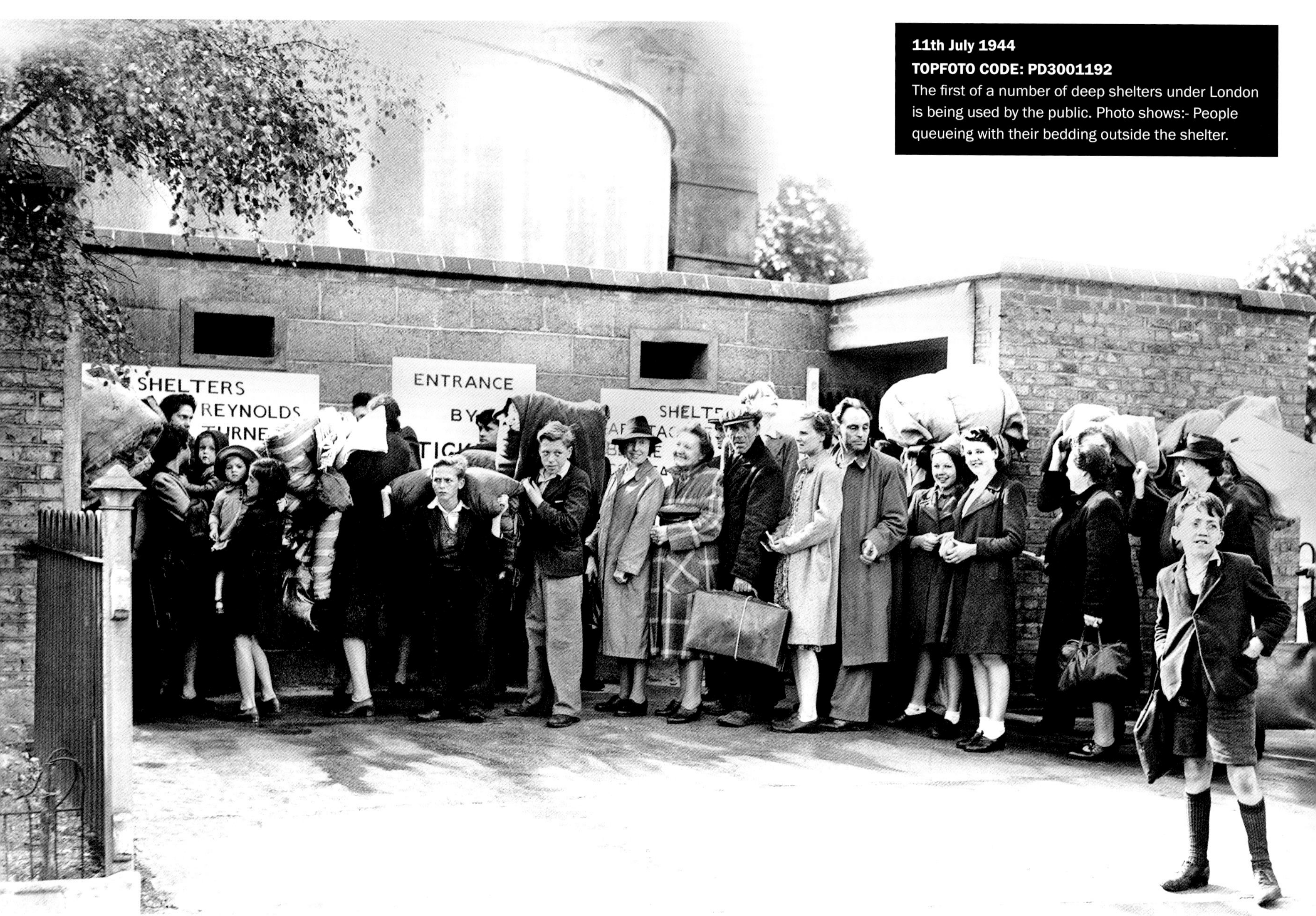

11th July 1944
TOPFOTO CODE: PD3001192
The first of a number of deep shelters under London is being used by the public. Photo shows:- People queueing with their bedding outside the shelter.

When the Germans initiated the Blitz on Britain in September 1940 many thousands sought immediate shelter in the Tube stations of the London Underground. The British government seized the opportunity and contracted London Transport to build a total of ten deep-level shelters. Eight were completed in 1942, but by then the German attacks had reduced significantly and the spaces were, therefore, repurposed for use by the military.

After the Normandy landings on 6 June 1944, the Germans renewed their attacks with flying bombs and rockets, which led to the official opening of the deep shelters to be used by civilians. (Read more about the V1 and V2 on page 82.) As seen partially in the centre of the photo, admission was by ticket. Post-war, the shelters have been used for anything from sheltering some of the first West Indian immigrants, to cheap accommodation for festival-goers, archival storage and even hydroponic farming.

"August von der Heydte is a great example of how any war and its participants cannot merely be observed retrospectively with any clear-cut and simple dualistic distinction of good and evil. Rather, they are a kaleidoscopic grid of convictions, actions and attitudes combined, providing a slightly more nuanced and wholesome understanding of the complexity of mankind."

Operation Stösser (page 103)

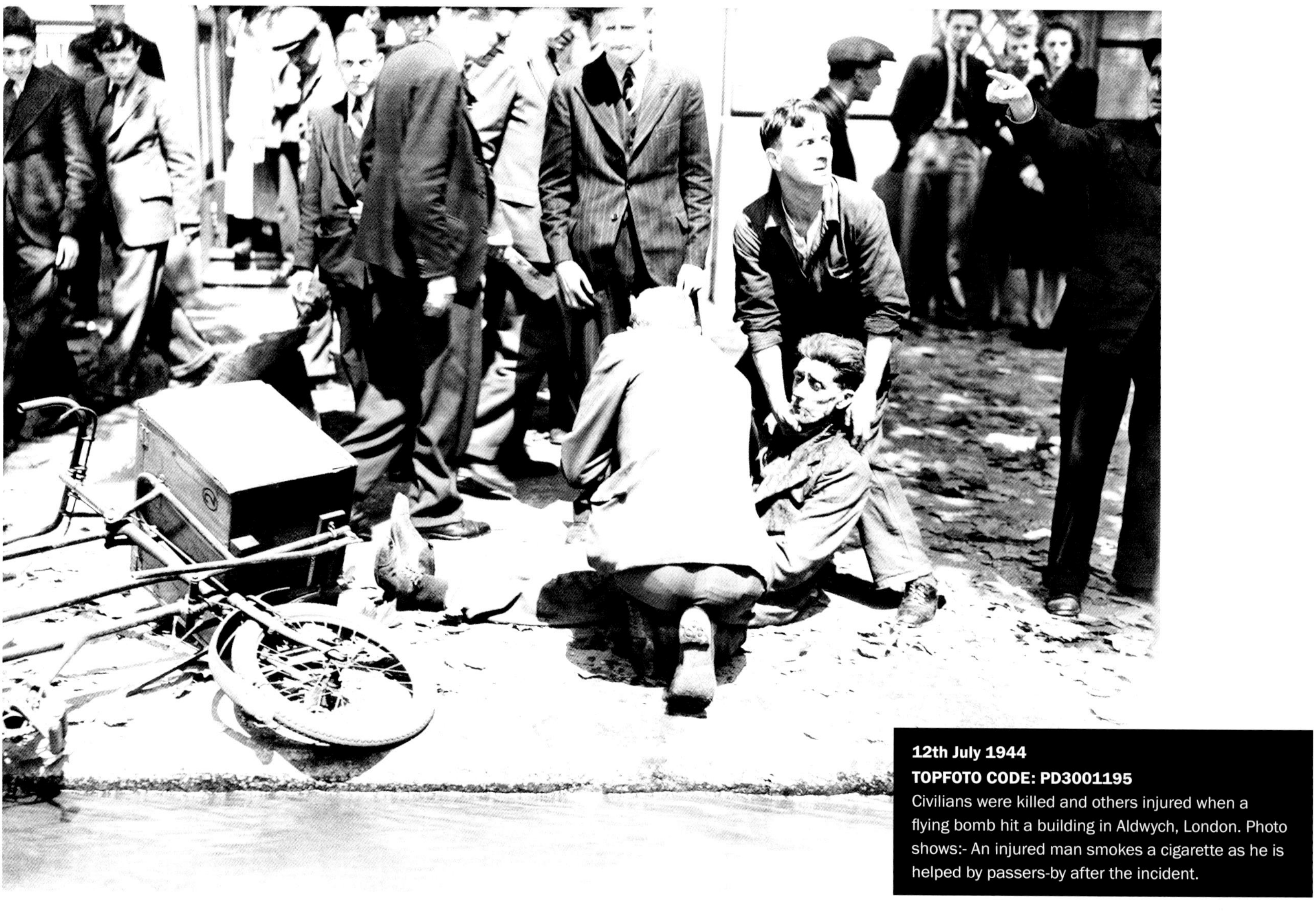

12th July 1944
TOPFOTO CODE: PD3001195
Civilians were killed and others injured when a flying bomb hit a building in Aldwych, London. Photo shows:- An injured man smokes a cigarette as he is helped by passers-by after the incident.

London Civilians Killed by Flying Bomb

The V1 bombs were a type of long-range artillery, constructed by Nazi Germany primarily as a retaliation weapon (the letter 'V' stands for Vergeltungswaffen, meaning retaliatory or reprisal weapon) to terrorise the British population. The Germans began work on launch sites in northern France in late 1943, and just a week after the D-Day landings on 6 June 1944 the first of what was to become one of the most feared weapons of the Second World War was fired against London. The lethal, winged, pulse jet-engined bomb made a terrifying noise. It would cut out and pop and there would be a sudden deadly period of silence before the devastating impact.

More than 9,000 of these bombs were launched towards Britain, mainly aimed at London, killing more than 6,000 civilians and injuring nearly 18,000. The UK National Archives state that V1 bombs combined with the even more feared V2 rockets were responsible for the death of around 43,000 people and the displacement of more than 2 million.

The two photos show the horrific and devastating effect of these weapons.

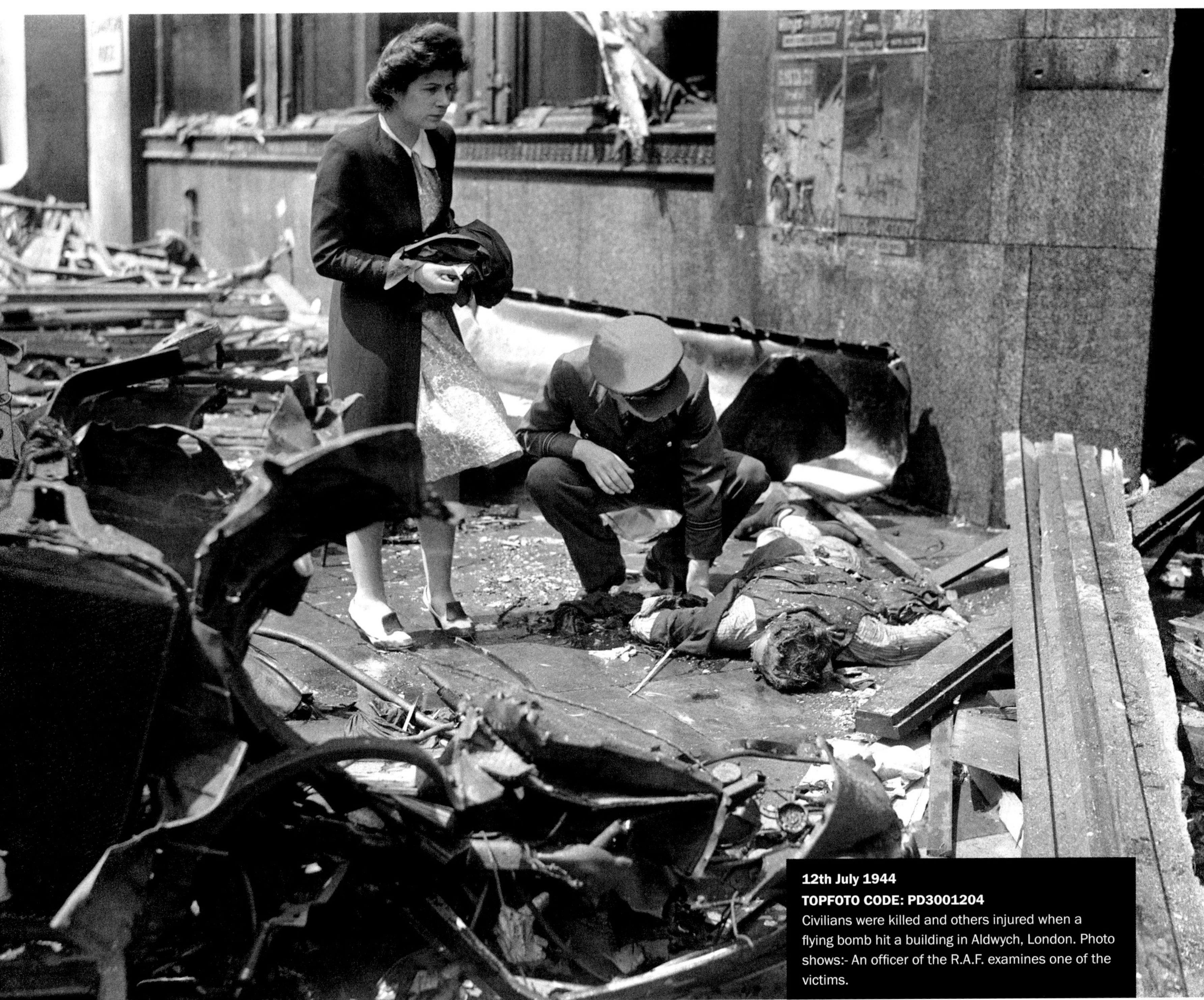

12th July 1944
TOPFOTO CODE: PD3001204
Civilians were killed and others injured when a flying bomb hit a building in Aldwych, London. Photo shows:- An officer of the R.A.F. examines one of the victims.

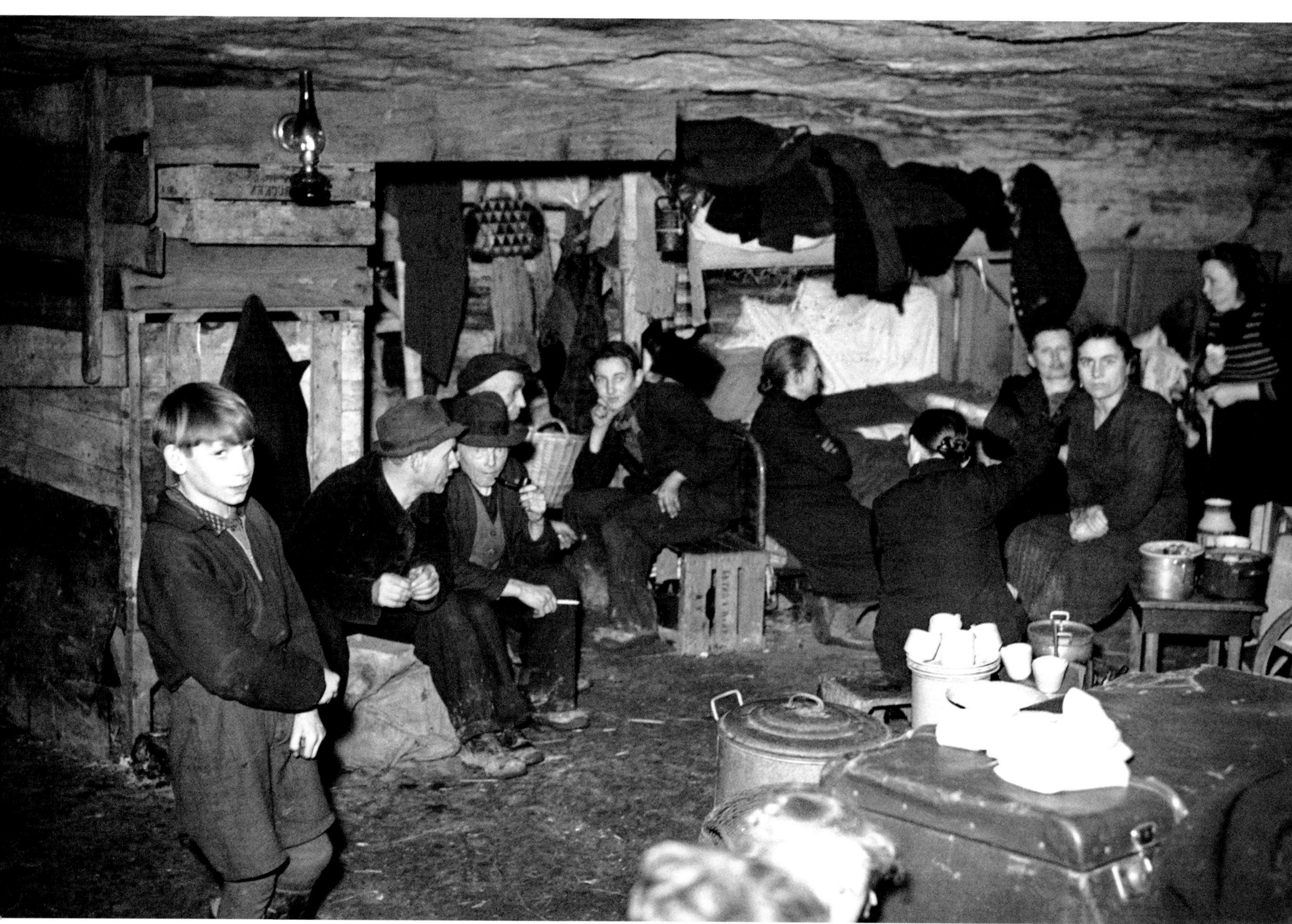

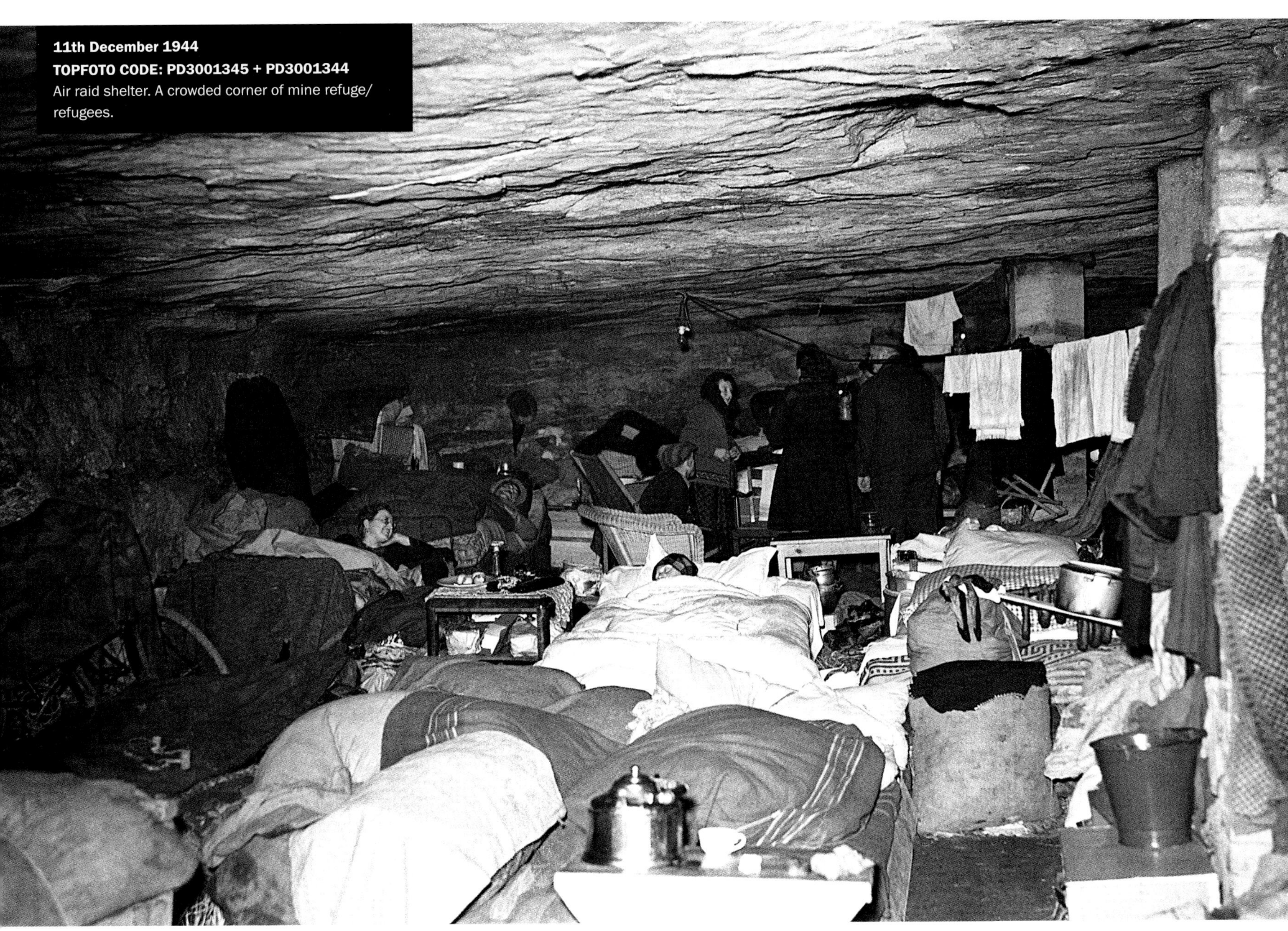

11th December 1944
TOPFOTO CODE: PD3001345 + PD3001344
Air raid shelter. A crowded corner of mine refuge/
refugees.

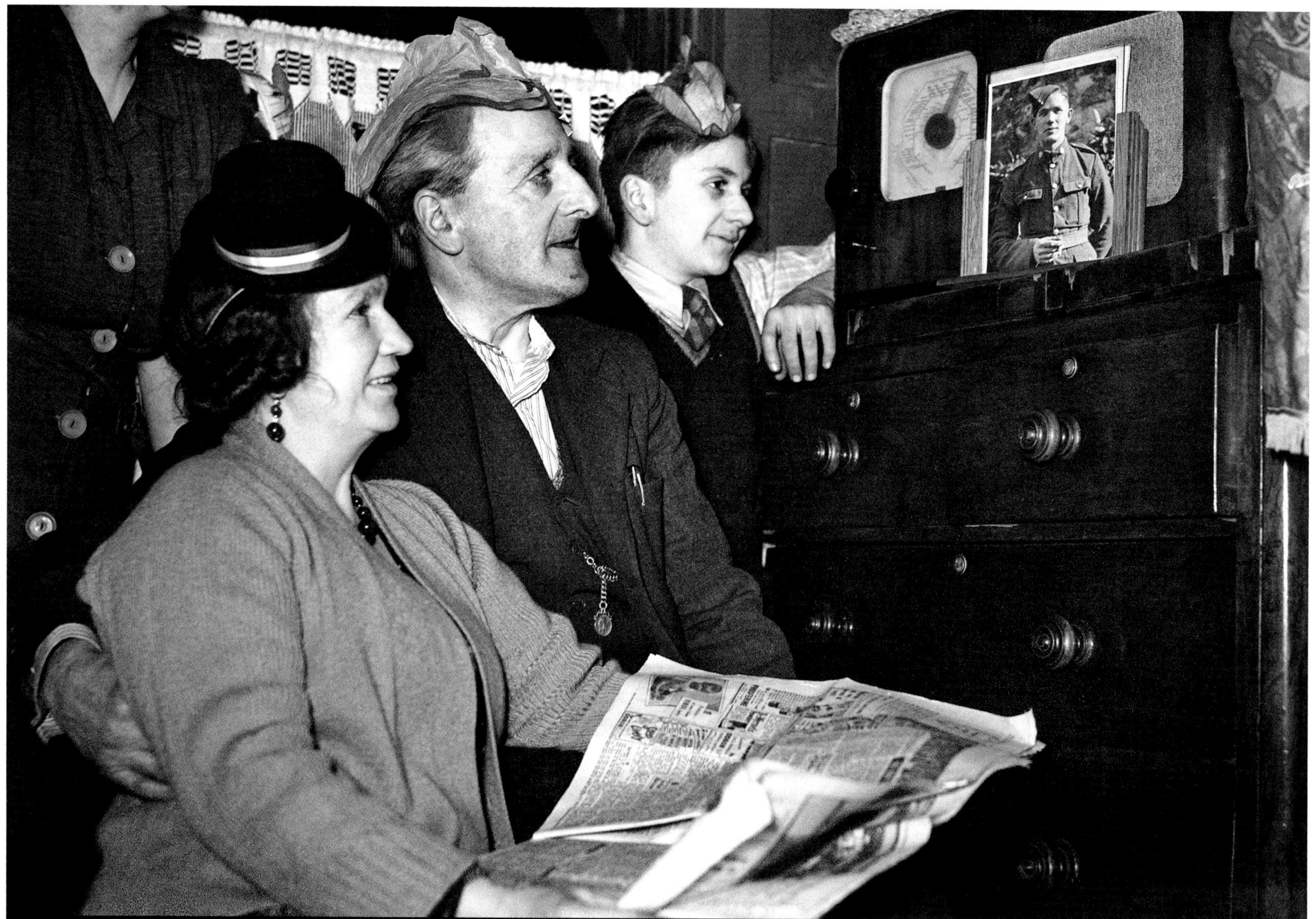

25th December 1944
TOPFOTO CODE: PD7493845
Corporal Robert Bruce Pass, aged 26, was the British Tommy who broadcast over the radio just prior to His Majesty's speech on Christmas Day in the 'Journey Home' programme. Corporal Pass, who is attached to a British Commando unit, has been through every campaign in Europe during the present war, from Dunkirk, with the 8th Army in the Middle East, and now fighting on German soil. He hopes to come home on leave to see his family in the New Year. PHOTO SHOWS: Corporal Pass's Father, Mother, and Brother Arthur, aged 15, listening in to the radio at his home at Brixton, London. A photograph of Corporal Pass stands in front of the radio. (PASS died 22 of April 1945).

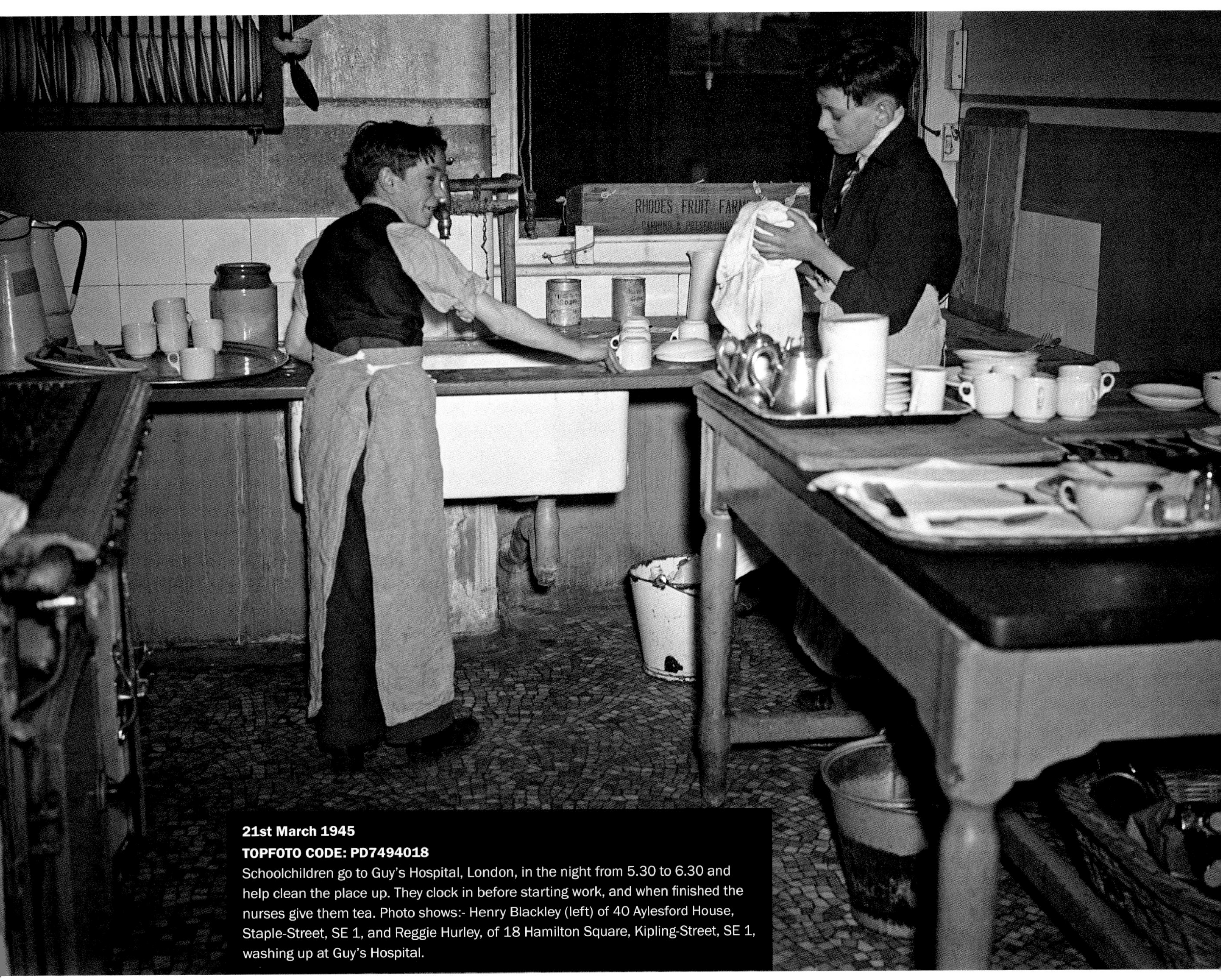

21st March 1945
TOPFOTO CODE: PD7494018
Schoolchildren go to Guy's Hospital, London, in the night from 5.30 to 6.30 and help clean the place up. They clock in before starting work, and when finished the nurses give them tea. Photo shows:- Henry Blackley (left) of 40 Aylesford House, Staple-Street, SE 1, and Reggie Hurley, of 18 Hamilton Square, Kipling-Street, SE 1, washing up at Guy's Hospital.

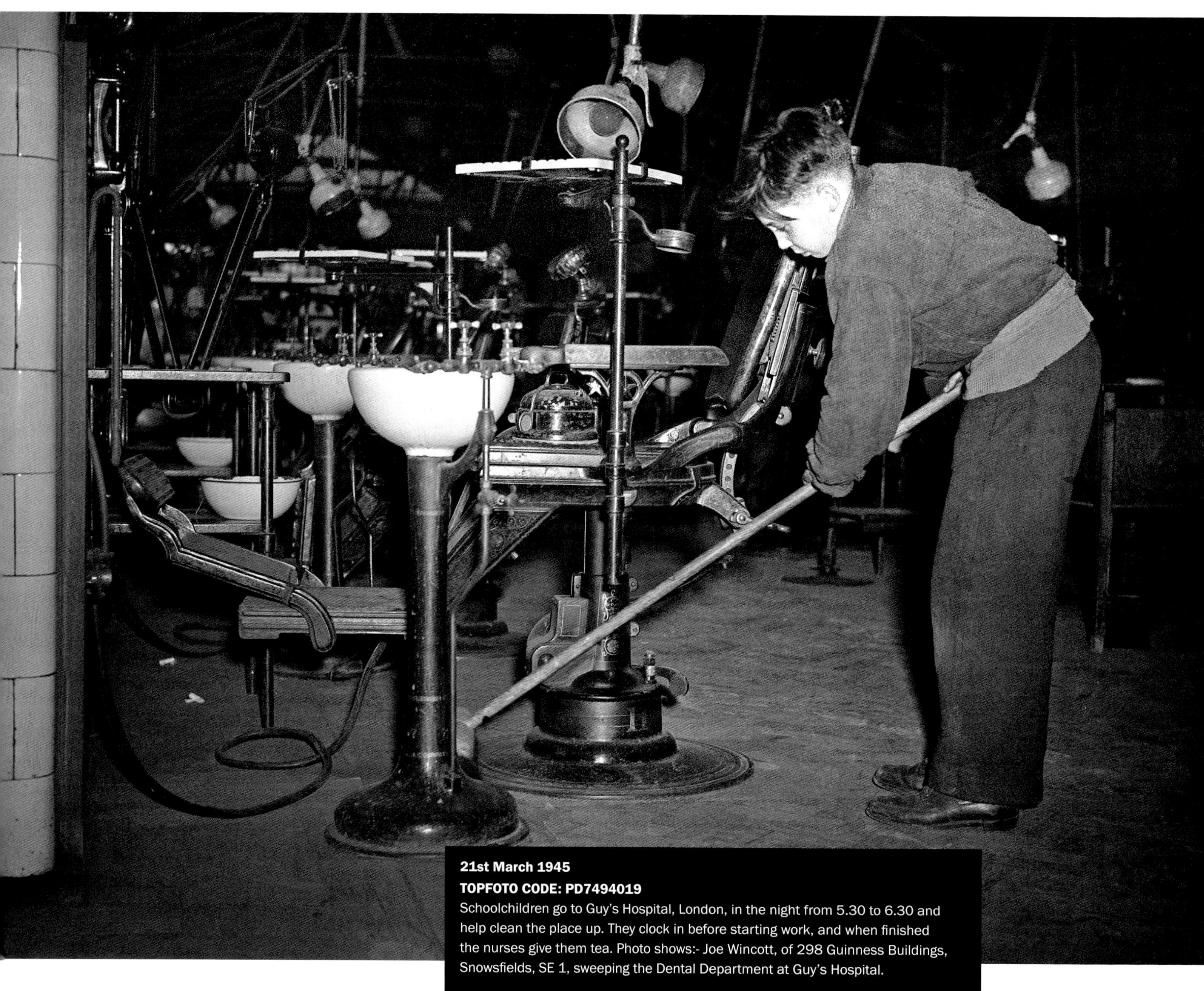

21st March 1945
TOPFOTO CODE: PD7494019
Schoolchildren go to Guy's Hospital, London, in the night from 5.30 to 6.30 and
help clean the place up. They clock in before starting work, and when finished
the nurses give them tea. Photo shows:- Joe Wincott, of 298 Guinness Buildings,
Snowsfields, SE 1, sweeping the Dental Department at Guy's Hospital.

4 MEDICAL AND HUMANITARIAN EFFORT

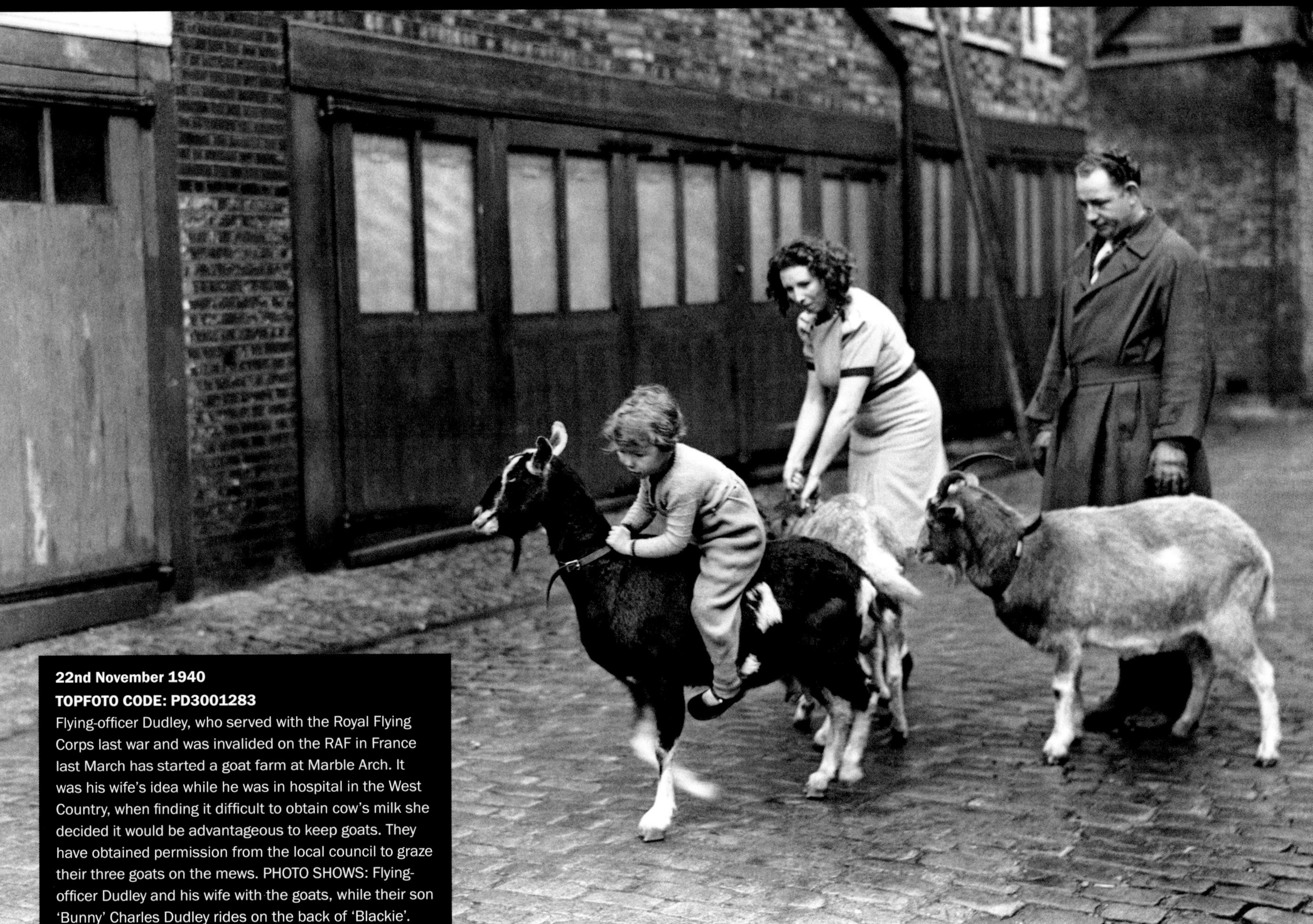

22nd November 1940

TOPFOTO CODE: PD3001283

Flying-officer Dudley, who served with the Royal Flying Corps last war and was invalided on the RAF in France last March has started a goat farm at Marble Arch. It was his wife's idea while he was in hospital in the West Country, when finding it difficult to obtain cow's milk she decided it would be advantageous to keep goats. They have obtained permission from the local council to graze their three goats on the mews. PHOTO SHOWS: Flying-officer Dudley and his wife with the goats, while their son 'Bunny' Charles Dudley rides on the back of 'Blackie'.

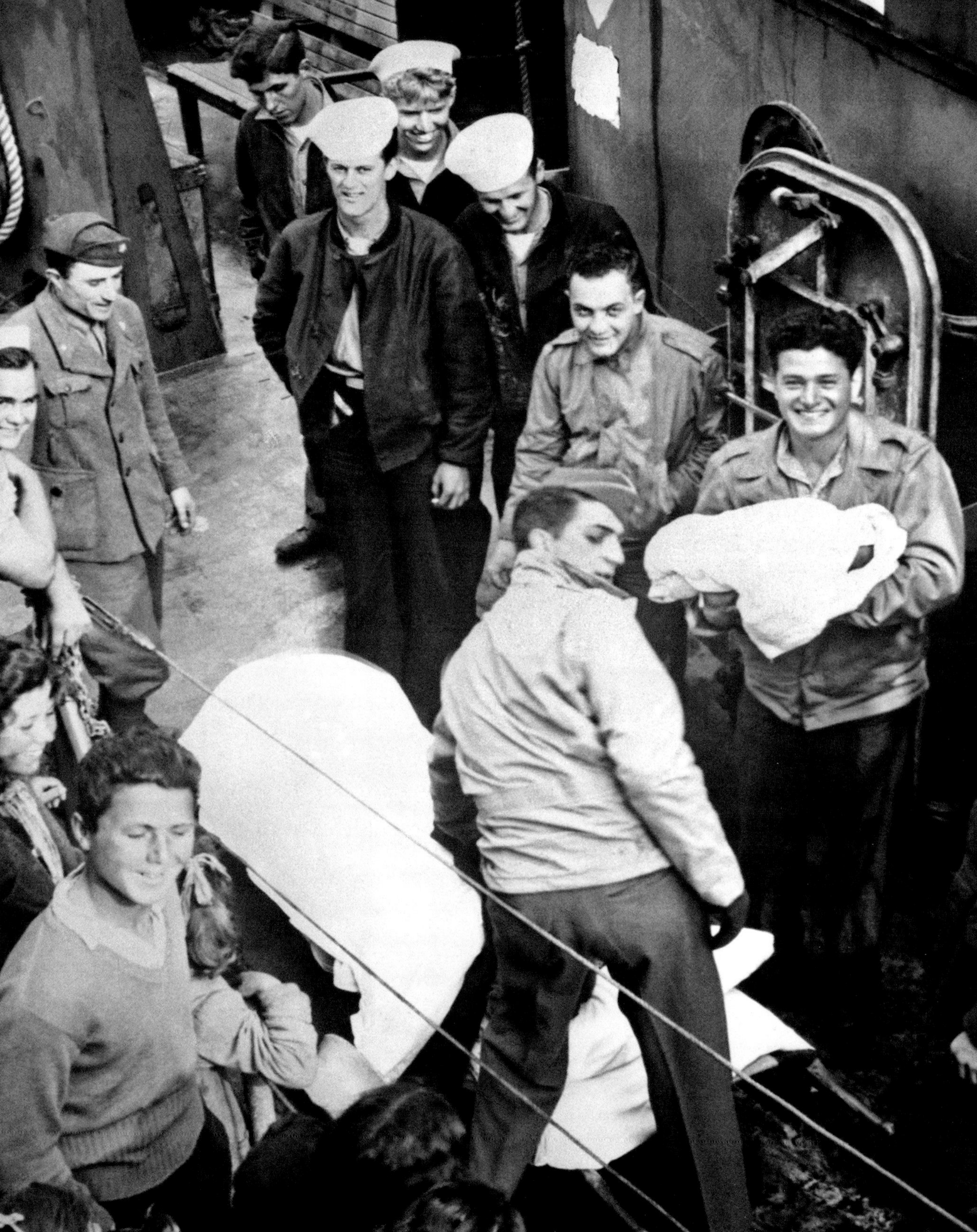

11th April 1944
TOPFOTO CODE: PD3001196
Refugee baby born on landing craft, Anzio. Beachhead baby. En route from the Anzio Beachhead with a load of refugees, pharmacist Mate Anthony Savarese performed his strangest duty as a sailor on a landing craft. On the night of April 10th Mrs. V Camilli, an Anzio refugee, gave birth to a son. Pharmacist Mate Savarese helped the mother, and the child was named Geroge Camilli and baptized on the landing-craft. Photo shows:- Some of the ship's crew with mother and child shortly after the blessed event.

Battle of Anzio and the Beachhead Baby

The Allied forces' liberation of Italy had, at the end of 1943, come to a stalemate. Following the Italian surrender on 8 September, the Germans had retreated and fifteen divisions were dug in deep behind the Gustav Line spanning from coast to coast, preventing any further Allied advance on the strategic objective of Rome.

In December 1943, Churchill was in the north of Africa and while sick with pneumonia he hatched a plan that he hoped would break this deadlock. One month prior, he had secretly met with Stalin and Roosevelt at the Tehran Conference (read more on page 125), where he had committed to Operation Overlord (the D-Day landings).

The Allied top brass met with Churchill at Carthage and considerations on how to land two divisions on the beach of Anzio, some 30 miles south of Rome – without compromising the 'sacrosanct' commitment to Overlord – were discussed (similar to the landings already previously carried out in Sicily). All turned to the option of LSTs.

The landing craft or LSTs (Landing Ship Tank) were vital to the Italian campaign of the Second World War. They were vessels designed for landing men, machines and supplies directly on to beaches, without the need of docks and loading equipment.

At the time, 104 LSTs were present in the Mediterranean and an estimated eighty-eight were needed to carry the two divisions. This would delay the return of fifty-six LSTs to the UK in preparation for Overlord, but Churchill conveyed to US President Roosevelt that he felt that the Mediterranean campaign would be left half-finished (and possibly even ruined) if they did not follow through. Roosevelt agreed and Operation Shingle was given the go-ahead.

Roosevelt sent a telegram to Churchill that he thought no communication about this should be given to 'Uncle J', so as to not disturb the newly sealed agreement in Tehran. Churchill replied that he was in complete agreement. ('Uncle Joe' was the nickname used by Western media for Joseph Stalin.)

The Battle of Anzio began on 22 January 1944, and close to midnight 36,000 men and more than 3,000 vehicles had been put ashore. The attack initially took the Germans by surprise but sadly a cautious US general trusted with the tactical command chose a defensive rather than an offensive strategy. The Germans did not lack initiative, and three days later 40,000 men had surrounded the Allied forces on the beachhead. A protracted and deadly struggle ensued.

In the midst of this was young William H. Fullilove, who was a British Royal Navy seaman aboard the landing craft LST 62. One night in mid-February he was leaving Anzio en route to a harbour near Naples when his craft was hit by LST 416 returning to Naples. At the time they had aboard 419 Italian refugees – one of them a very pregnant woman – who, due to the impact, went into labour. Fullilove recalls that only a 19-year-old ship berth attendant (SBA) was aboard, who was completely unfamiliar with childbirth. Instead, two experienced sailors were assigned the duty of midwives, as the consensus was they might have a better idea of what they were doing. According to Fullilove, this however never happened, as the lady was able to walk ashore where the child was born.

A fiction book called *The Ninety and Nine* by William Brinkley, published in 1966, mentions a similar story where the baby was born on the LST ship, stating that it was delivered by a pharmacist's mate second class (general nursing duties/first aid).

The book might have taken inspiration from the adjacent photo, but it begs the question of whether Fullilove's recollection is wrong, or whether the baby was simply carried back to the ship for a photo op, possibly with the intention of using the story as an Allied propaganda puff piece, at a time where an operation was not going well. There may have been two separate incidents – although this seems highly unlikely. At any rate, a healthy baby boy was born.

The operation was ultimately a success, but the victory came at a heavy cost with more than 40,000 casualties on both the Allied and the German sides. On 5 May 1944, Rome was finally liberated.[3]

The Royal Red Cross has a long history going back to its inception by Queen Victoria in 1883. The first Anglo-Boer War in Africa, some years prior, had caused the demise of many British Army nurses. This alerted the Queen to the absence of an award presented to professional and military women for their efforts in caring for the sick.

Until the beginning of the First World War in 1914, only 246 of these crosses had been presented, making it an exceptionally rare and prestigious award. During the First World War many upper-class women actively participated in caring for the wounded and made room in their private residences for treatment and convalescence. In return, there was almost an expectancy of the bestowal of this recognition upon them, resulting in many unskilled hands receiving the award over the heads of the trained.

In 1915, the Associate Royal Red Cross (ARRC) was instated as a second class for the RRC. A total of 6,741 RRCs and ARRCs were awarded during the First World War, and it clearly shows the shift in how the medal was used to appease these prominent women craving acknowledgement, rather than commending the actual professional women who were acting beyond the call of duty.

This, however, changed at the onset of the Second World War, and from 1939 to 1945 only 1,300 further medals were presented. In 1976, an amendment also made it possible for men to receive the award.

The *British Journal of Nursing*, reporting on January 1944's New Year's Honours, states that Miss A.M. Rodd (in the photo) received the promotion to Second Class ARRC for her services to the Crown.

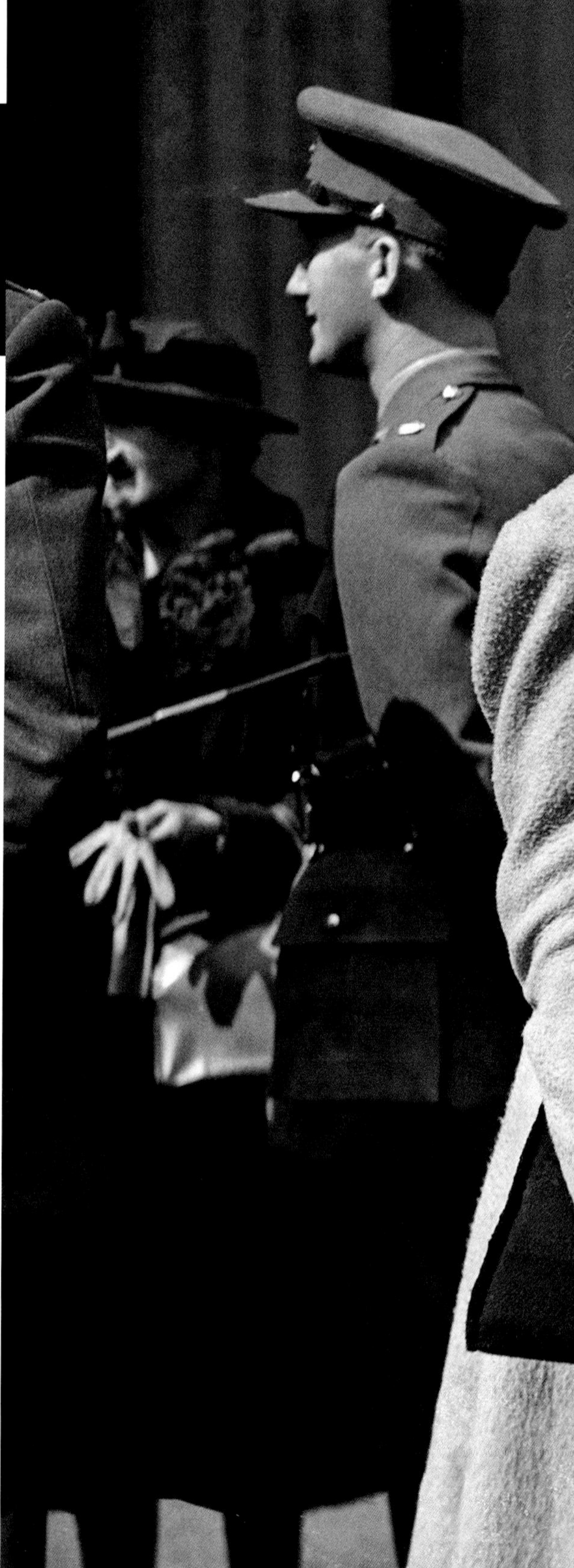

21st April 1944
TOPFOTO CODE: PD3001304
Miss A.M. Rodd (centre), Matron of the R.A.F. Hospital, Innsworth, Gloucester, who was made Associate of the Royal Red Cross, shows her A.R.R.C. decoration to her friends, Miss. P. Taylor and Flight-officer Ramsay, after receiving it from the King at a recent Buckingham Palace investiture.

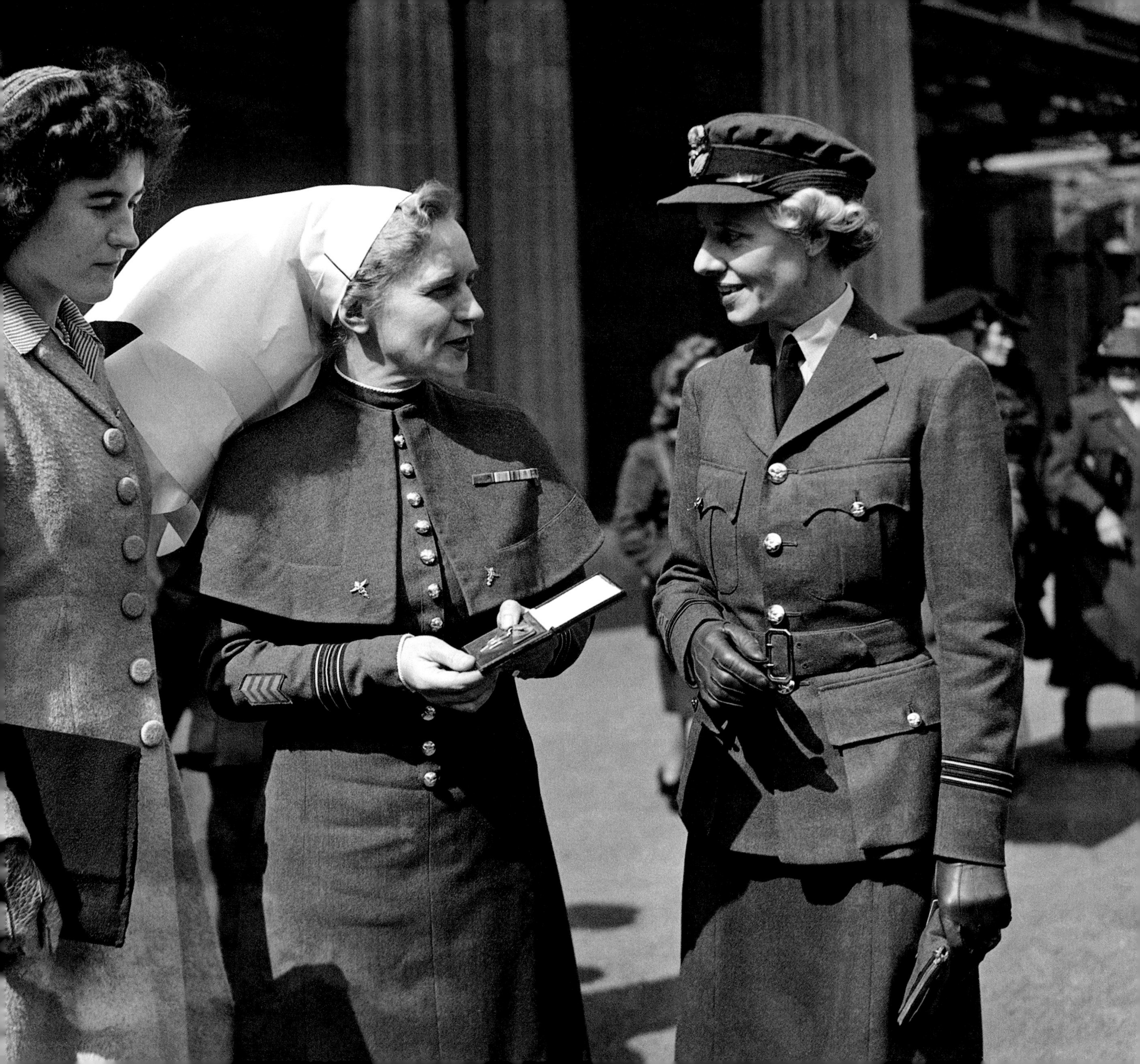

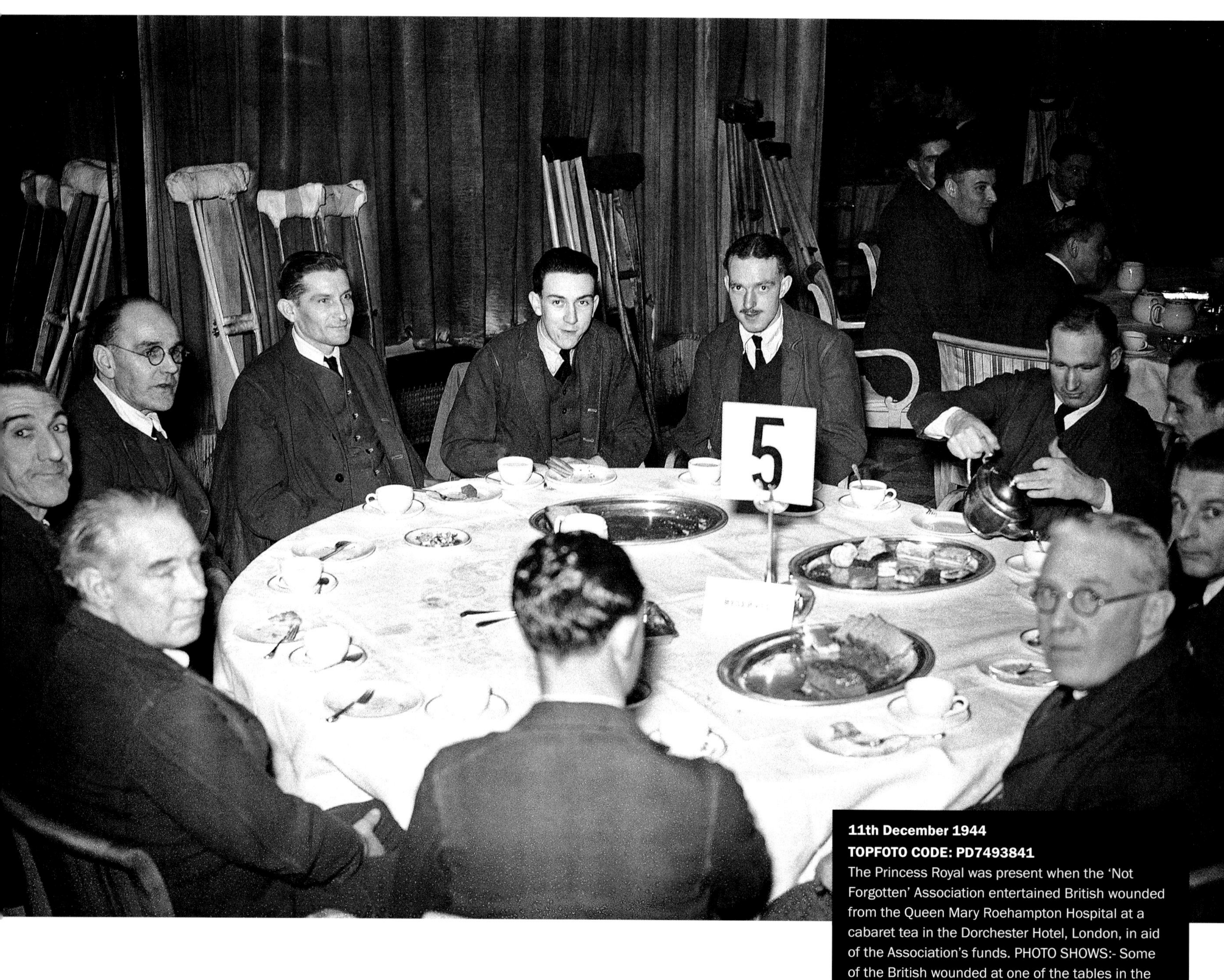

11th December 1944
TOPFOTO CODE: PD7493841
The Princess Royal was present when the 'Not Forgotten' Association entertained British wounded from the Queen Mary Roehampton Hospital at a cabaret tea in the Dorchester Hotel, London, in aid of the Association's funds. PHOTO SHOWS:- Some of the British wounded at one of the tables in the Dorchester Hotel, London.

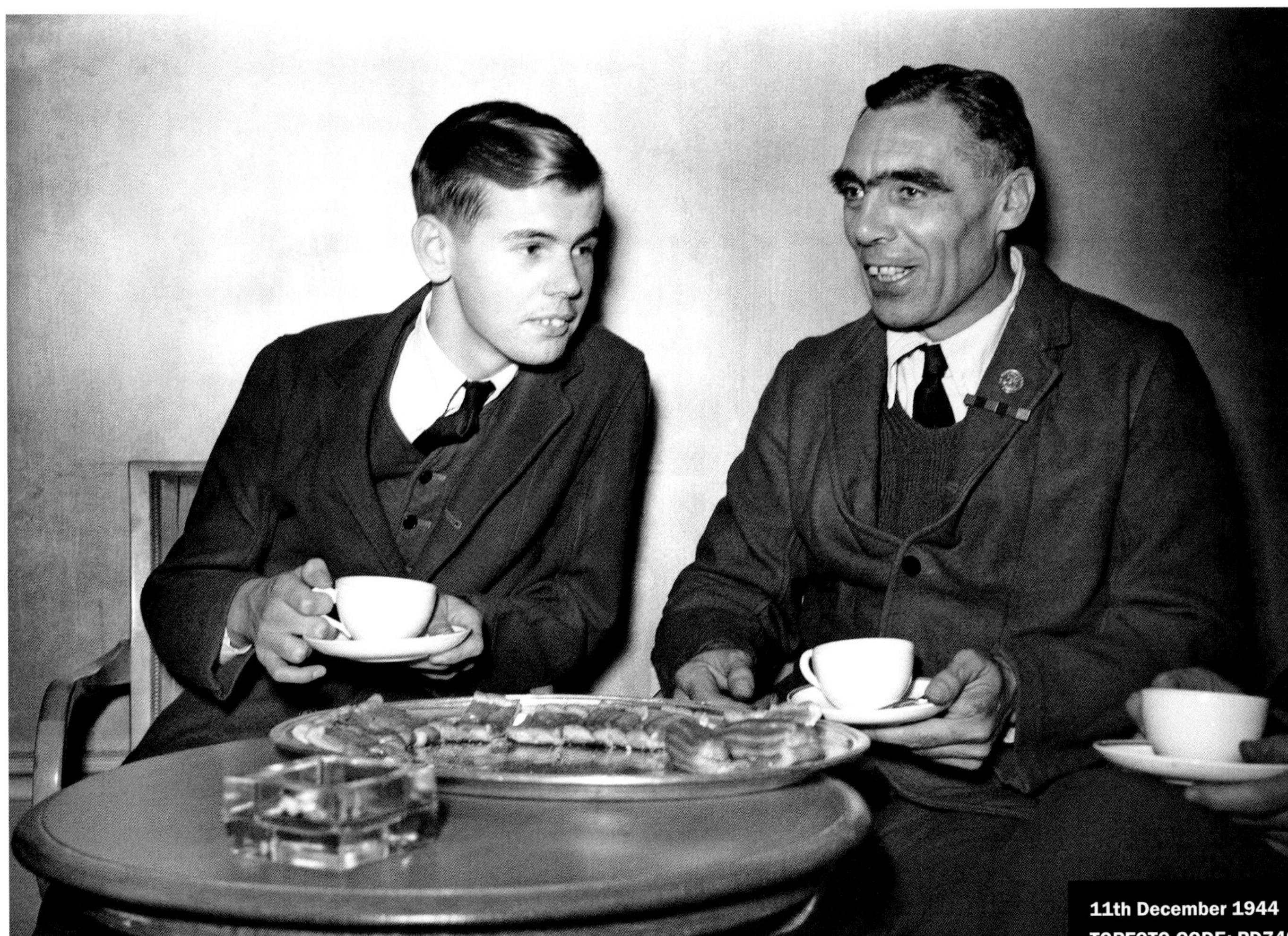

The American-born soprano Marta Cunningham is credited with establishing the Not Forgotten Association. While living in London during the First World War, she took part in charity work, primarily in the East End. After her visit to a hospital in 1919, she discovered that thousands of servicemen, still undergoing medical treatment, were living under-stimulated, lonely and quite destitute lives. With the establishment of the charity, her aim was to provide them with entertainment, encouragement and companionship.

Cunningham's association elicited the support of the Royal Family and supported nearly 10,000 men within its first year of existence. It became her life's work and earned her a CBE in 1929.

The organisation still to this day supports approximately 10,000 people yearly with activities, concerts, social support, and gifts. Thenotforgotten.org happily accepts donations and volunteers who are willing to help and assist the ex-service and currently serving communities.

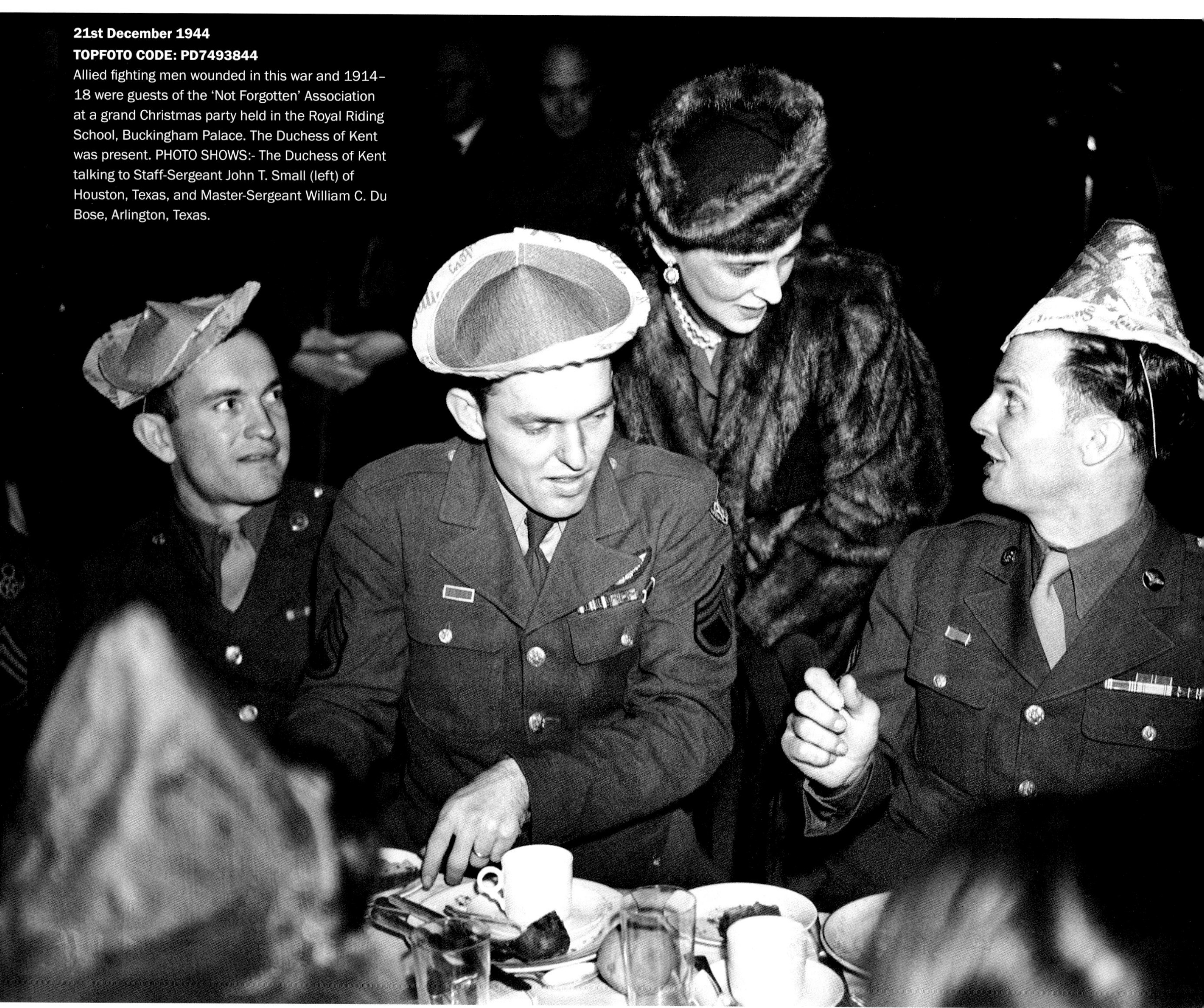

21st December 1944
TOPFOTO CODE: PD7493844
Allied fighting men wounded in this war and 1914–18 were guests of the 'Not Forgotten' Association at a grand Christmas party held in the Royal Riding School, Buckingham Palace. The Duchess of Kent was present. PHOTO SHOWS:- The Duchess of Kent talking to Staff-Sergeant John T. Small (left) of Houston, Texas, and Master-Sergeant William C. Du Bose, Arlington, Texas.

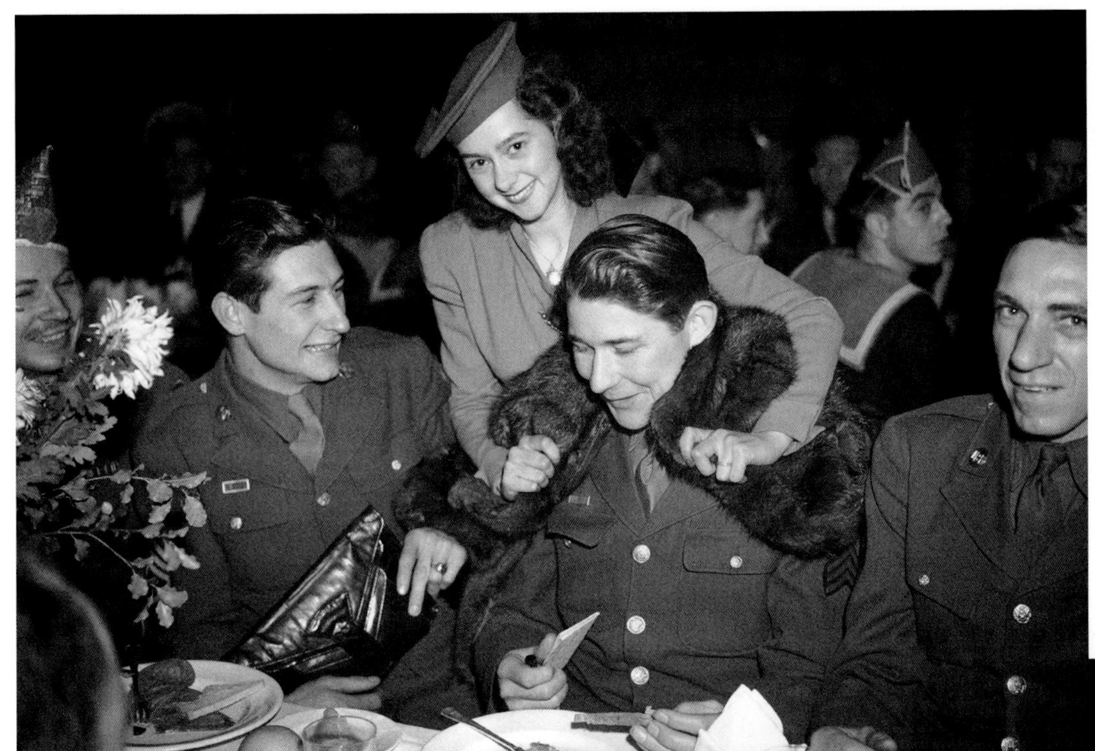

21st December 1944
TOPFOTO CODE: PD7486008
Miss Joan Crawford, the dancer, putting her fur coat round Sergeant J. Tyner, of Tuscaloosa, Alabama, one of the American Guests.

21st December 1944
TOPFOTO CODE: PD7486009
Argo the Clown jokes with Lieutenant Sanford Bailey of Los Angeles, California, and Technical-Sergeant William A. Paschal, of Houston, Texas.

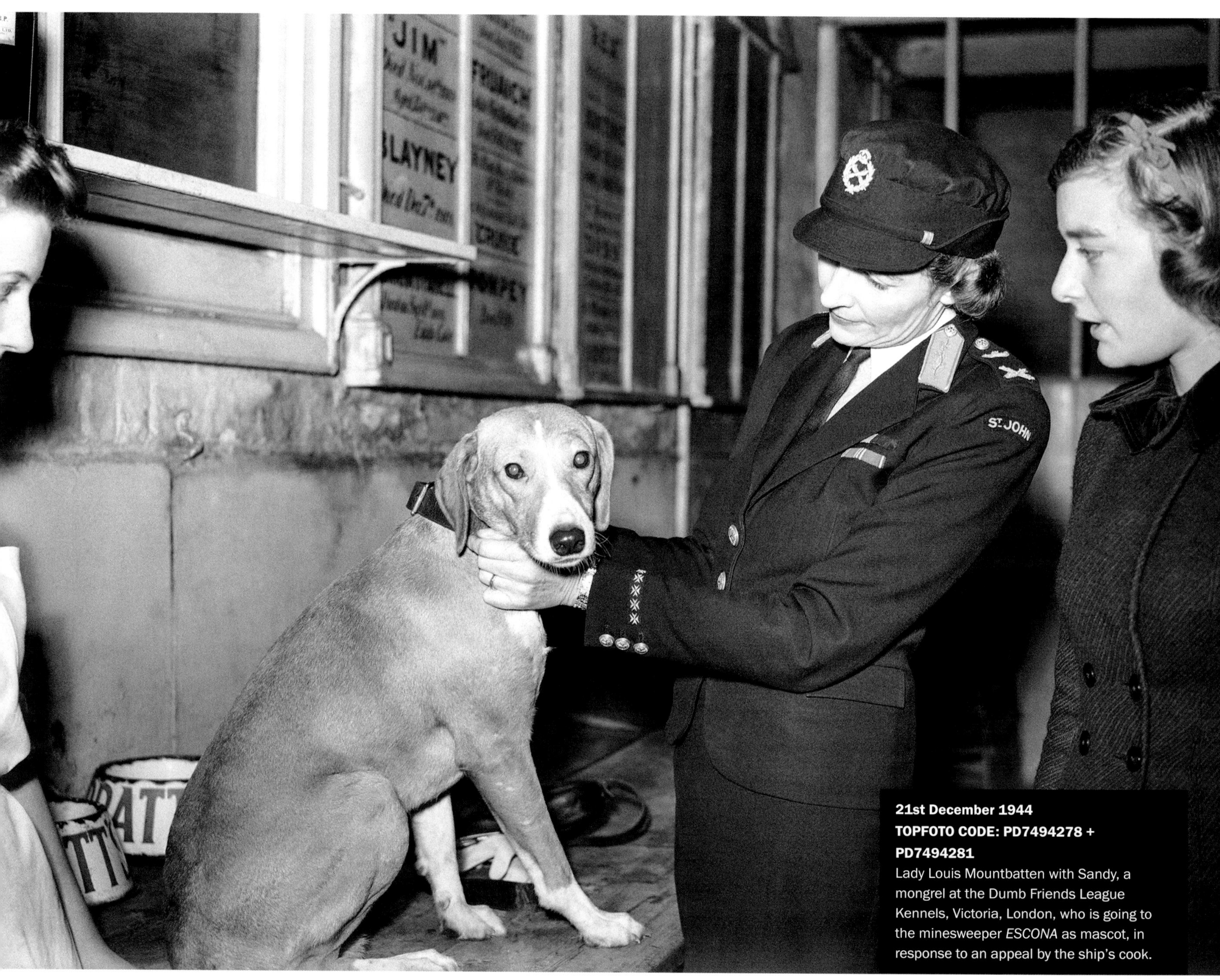

21st December 1944
TOPFOTO CODE: PD7494278 +
PD7494281
Lady Louis Mountbatten with Sandy, a
mongrel at the Dumb Friends League
Kennels, Victoria, London, who is going to
the minesweeper *ESCONA* as mascot, in
response to an appeal by the ship's cook.

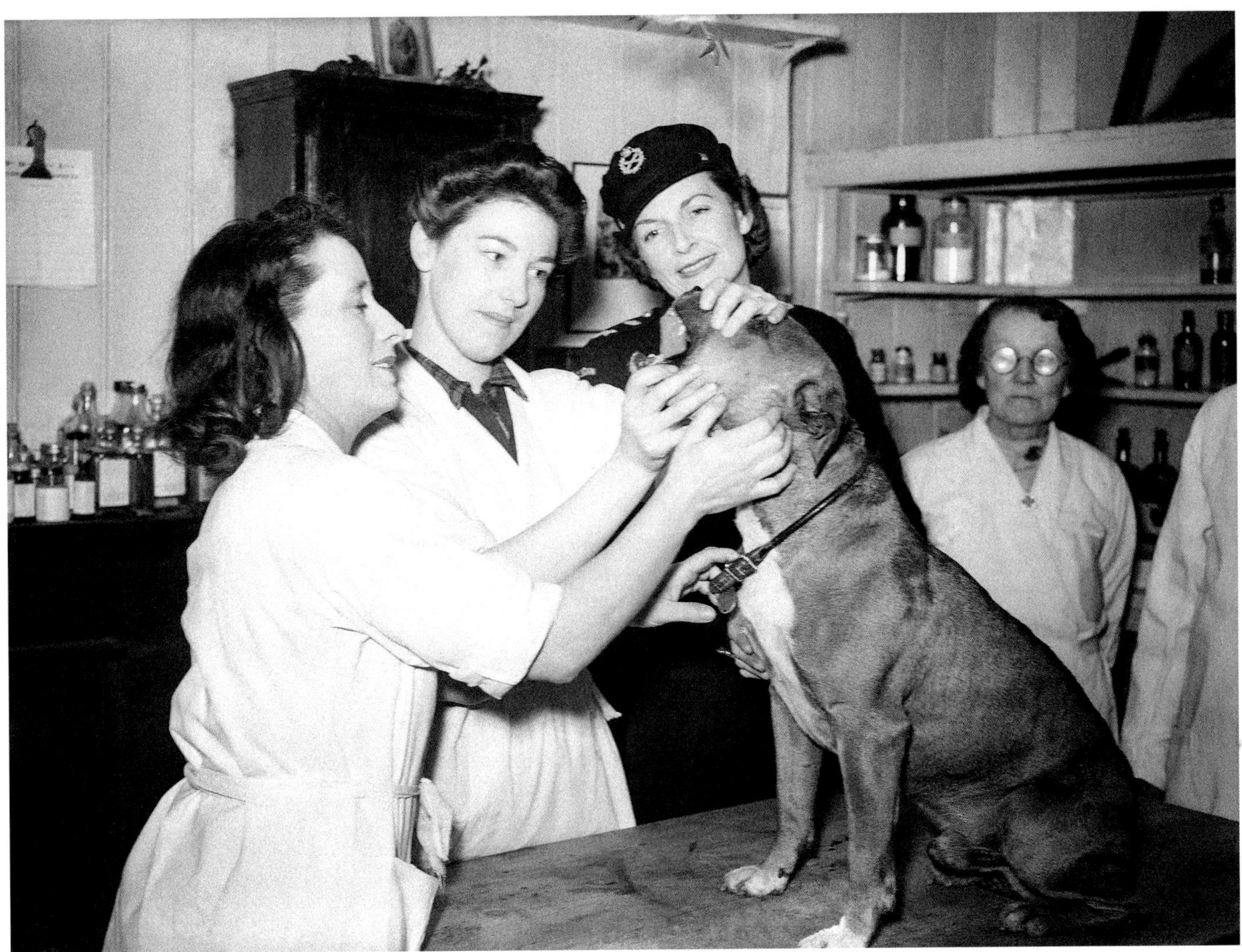

Edwina Mountbatten was a prominent British socialite, who lived a glamorous and privileged life. Being the granddaughter of Sir Ernest Cassel, one of the richest men in Europe, she grew up with extreme wealth. After his death in 1921 she inherited a fortune (equivalent to some £112 million today). One year later she married Louis Mountbatten, 1st Earl Mountbatten of Burma.

When the Second World War broke out, Lady Mountbatten's focus shifted and she became deeply involved in humanitarian work. In 1942 she became the Superintendent-in-Chief for the St John Ambulance Brigade *(see the St John emblem on her shoulder).* Her dedication to social causes grew further and in her capacity as the last Vicereine of India, she worked tirelessly to alleviate the suffering caused by Partition in 1947.

Much has been written about her alleged extra-marital affairs both with Jawaharlal Nehru, the first Prime Minister of India, and other men. Despite the controversies of her and her husband's lives, she is remembered as a very dedicated individual, who had a deep compassion for the underprivileged. Her philanthropic and social commitment earned her not only a CBE and the American Red Cross Medal, but also more importantly the respect of both the British population and the people of India.

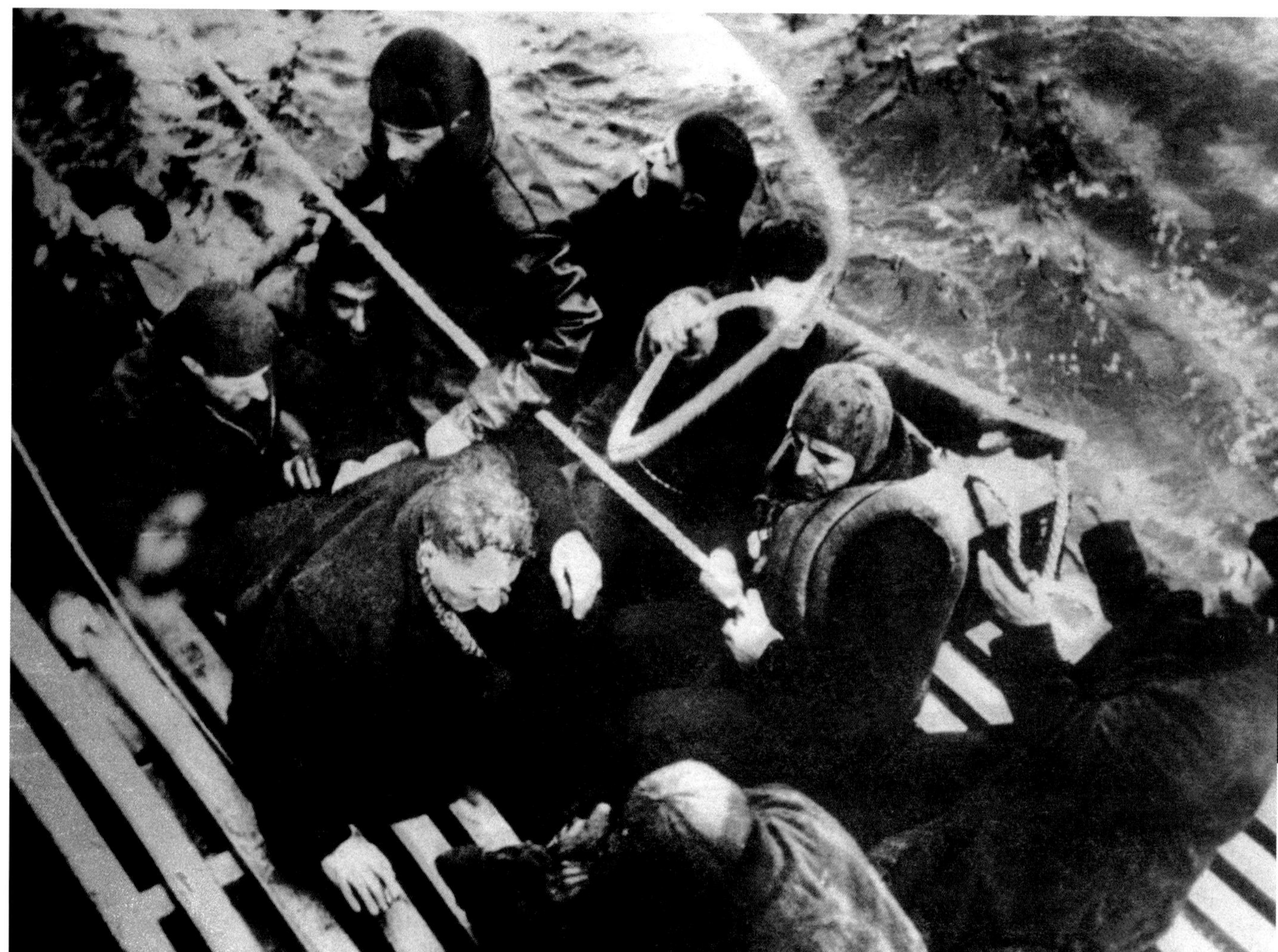

U.S. coast guard in the Atlantic rescue 235 drowning men. U-boats are active in the North Atlantic and this dramatic picture was taken when a U.S. Coastguard cutter captained by Roy L. Raney, of Marblehead, Massachusetts, picked up frozen survivors after a German submarine had sunk their vessel. For rescuing 235 victims from two torpedoed ships, Captain Raney received an official commendation. Photo shows:- Survivors from the torpedoed ship clutch the lifeline as they are taken aboard the rescue cutter.

The story of the sunken transport USS *Henry R. Mallory* has varying facts and perfectly illustrates how different sources can provide very different accounts of an event.

The date of the incident, as well as the number of men rescued, diverge among even reputable sources such as the US Coast Guard, Homeland Security, and the Marine Corps Association.

There seems to be a consensus though that the date the ship was torpedoed and sunk was 7 February 1943 (far from the date of publication on 30 December 1944). The delay could simply be due to the media at the time trying to raise awareness and continued vigilance in connection with German U-boat activity in the North Atlantic.

At 06.59, a torpedo from the German U-boat *U-402* struck the ship and sank it thirty minutes after impact, roughly 680 miles south-south-west of Iceland. *Henry R. Mallory* was sailing in a convoy heading for Reykjavik carrying a total of 494 men, but only three of the ten lifeboats managed to clear the ship with just 175 men, while several others desperately threw themselves in the water.

The US Coast Guard cutter *Bibb*, captained by Roy L. Raney, rescued 205 men, although three later died. A rescue vessel of the convoy was also sunk by *U-402* and the US Coast Guard cutter *Ingham* later rescued twenty-two men, two of whom also passed away.

The MCA-marines.org has a fascinating account of the sinking of *Henry Mallory*.

Operation Stösser and August von der Heydte

Lieutenant Colonel Friedrich August Freiherr von der Heydte was in many ways a very atypical and contradictory personality, far from the conventional interpretation of the archetypical Nazi officer. A man who has been recognised by many historians as, arguably, the most famous German paratrooper ever.

Born a *Freiherr* (baron), into a family of devout Roman Catholics, he was the cousin of Claus von Stauffenberg, the main instigator of the 20 July plot to assassinate Hitler in 1944. It has been suggested that Heydte himself played a part in the plot.

In 1925, he joined the Reichswehr but was released from service in 1927 to pursue an education in law and economics. During his student years, he developed very distinct liberal views. This, however, did not dissuade him from signing up with the NSDAP (Nazi Party) in 1933, as well as the SA (Sturmabteilung, better known as the Brownshirts).

While studying in Vienna, Heydte got into trouble for beating up a Nazi who had insulted the Catholic Church in his presence. Allegedly, that was why he rejoined the army, to evade being arrested by the Gestapo. In 1935, he was promoted to lieutenant within the Wehrmacht, but once again he was released from service to continue his studies.

After a further two years of education, he was recalled and participated in the invasion of Poland as well as the Battle of France, earning an Iron Cross First Class. In May 1940, he was promoted to captain and became a company commander in the 3rd Fallschirmjäger (paratrooper) Regiment. In the Battle of Crete in 1941, the first large-scale paratrooper invasion in history, he led the 1st Battalion and was awarded the Knight's Cross. He continued to serve on the Russian Front and in North Africa, with the Ramcke Parachute Brigade, until its famous escape from the German disaster at El-Alamein. In early 1943, he was transferred to the 2nd Fallschirmjäger Division and shortly after, he crash-landed on Elba during a mission and was badly injured. He recovered and in 1944 he was given command of the 4,500 men of the 6th Fallschirmjäger Regiment.

In June 1944, he led his paratroopers in the Battle of Carentan against the 101st Airborne (now famous from the TV show *Band of Brothers*, with Episode 3 of the same name 'Carentan'). Heydte was given strict orders by Erwin Rommel to defend Carentan at all costs, as the town was a vital intersection between the Allied forces' landing positions at Omaha and Utah Beach. While the fighting was extremely fierce, Heydte ultimately withdrew after two days to avoid being surrounded. He thereby ignored a *Führererlass* (Führer Decree) from Hitler himself to hold out to the last man. Brigade Führer Otto Baum was furious and wanted Heydte arrested, but his connections in high places ended up saving him.

Heydte participated in several other operations and fought against the Allies in the failed Operation Market Garden before he was finally ordered to commence Operation Stösser. While he had been an early adopter of numerous right-wing and paramilitary groups, he later conceded that while he had at first 'enthusiastically agreed to many of the ideas of National Socialism', he ultimately had irreconcilable differences with 'the Nazi worldview and (his) religious and scientific convictions'.[4]

According to his memoirs, he had been a member of Widerstand Gegen den Nationalsozialismus (German Resistance to Nazism) since early 1942. He also claims that he was, indeed, involved in Operation Valkyrie and that he only avoided being targeted after the coup had failed due to 'a mix-up of names'.[5]

Most of the evidence suggests that he never actively took part in the plan to kill Hitler, although the practical circumstances of Operation Stösser suggest that suspicions were still harboured towards Heydte by the German High Command, and very possibly by Hitler himself.

The Battle of the Bulge or the Ardennes counter-offensive was Germany's last desperate attempt on the Western Front before the war ended. They needed to get to Antwerp and halt the Allies' repairs of the deep-water port, to prevent supplies and reinforcements coming in.

Part of the plan involved an elite paratrooper company dropping behind enemy lines. It was a daring plan, involving the first and only night jump by the Germans and what was also to be the final one of the war. They were to parachute in, then take and hold the crossroads at Belle Croix near Malmedy for twenty-four hours until they were relieved by the 12th SS Panzer Division. The code name of the mission was Operation Stösser.

On 8 December, Heydte was given only eight days to prepare for a mission but no further information was provided. He was promised some of the best from each of the regiments of the 2nd Fallschirmjäger Division, but instead he received every single troublemaker and misfit available. Most had little or no experience at all. The jump was to be carried out without prior aerial reconnaissance and at night to further avoid Allied suspicions.

On the night of 17 December, 1,300 men (300 of them straw-filled dummies, to further confuse the Allies) were loaded into 112 Ju 52 transports. They took off in a fierce snow blizzard, heavy winds and almost zero visibility. With little or no experience in night flight, navigation, flight formation, or combat experience, the whole operation was doomed before it began. Most of the planes never even got close to the drop zone. More than 250 men were dropped over Bonn, 80km away, and many men were still in the planes when they landed back at base. Nearly 200 men died that night from being crushed against trees and other obstacles while attempting to land in over 60km/h side winds. Many more were immobilised on the ground with severe injuries. A later German article, infuriated by the poor preparations, referred to the incident as Operation Mass Murder.

Further issues, caused by the men's lack of training, meant heavy weapons and radio equipment had to be dropped in separate containers as they were unqualified to do the jump with them. As a result, most that managed to survive had no firepower – nor any means of communication to reassemble.

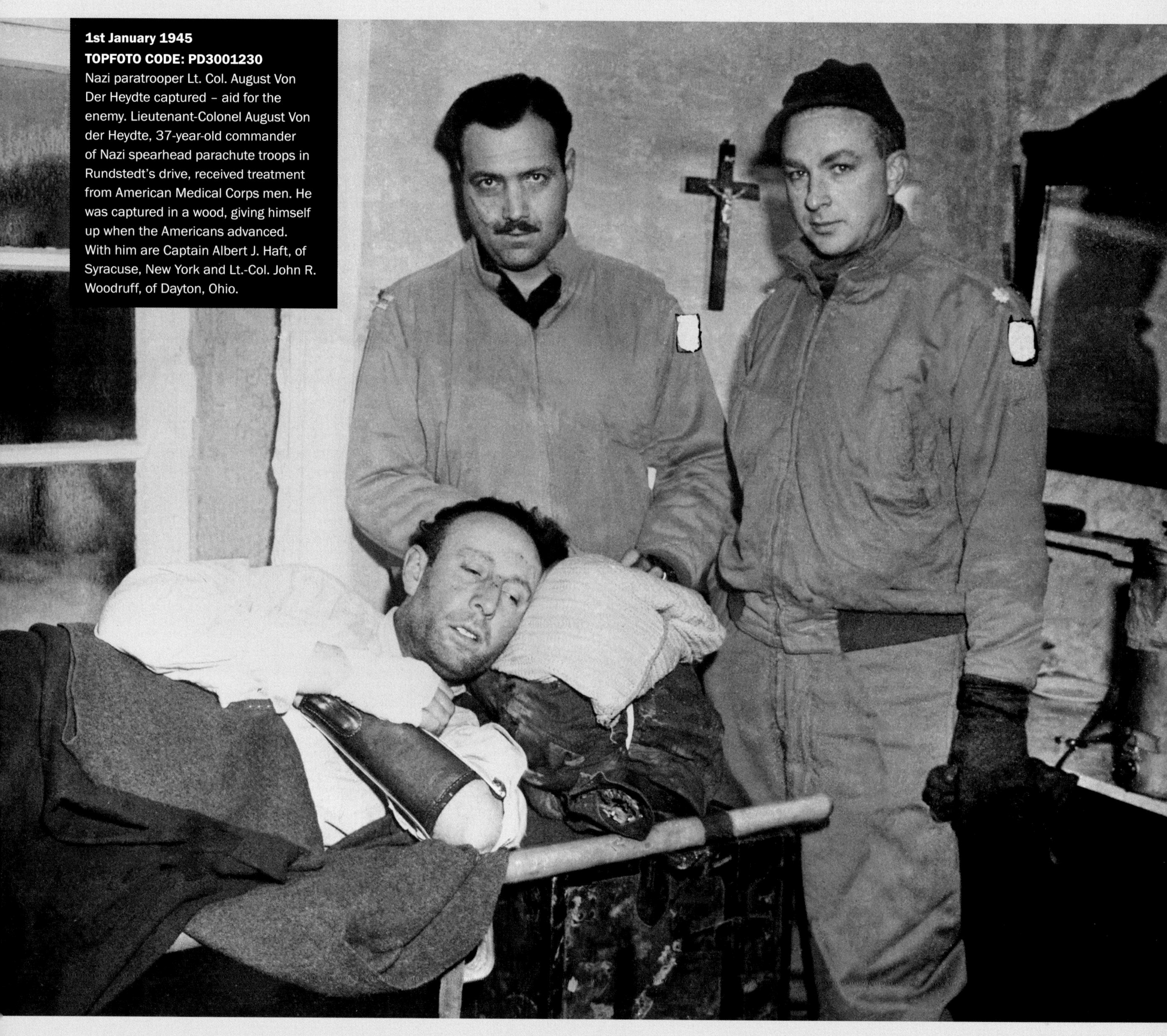

1st January 1945
TOPFOTO CODE: PD3001230
Nazi paratrooper Lt. Col. August Von
Der Heydte captured – aid for the
enemy. Lieutenant-Colonel August Von
der Heydte, 37-year-old commander
of Nazi spearhead parachute troops in
Rundstedt's drive, received treatment
from American Medical Corps men. He
was captured in a wood, giving himself
up when the Americans advanced.
With him are Captain Albert J. Haft, of
Syracuse, New York and Lt.-Col. John R.
Woodruff, of Dayton, Ohio.

Ironically, the inexperience, the lack of precision and bad weather conditions inadvertently helped the Germans momentarily confuse the Allied forces, and made them think that a much larger company had dropped behind the lines. The many small and scattered groups meant reports of the enemy were coming in from all over, and a total of 5,000 Allied soldiers and a combat command of 300 tanks were tied up for days looking for a large force – a force that was never there.

Heydte himself made it to the landing zone, miraculously, with his left arm and shoulder in a splint from a previous injury, although the jump caused him further abrasion. (The brace is clearly visible in the photo of him on the stretcher.)

By the early morning hours, Heydte had only managed to gather 125 soldiers, although later the next day the number was closer to 280. Most had no weapons, many had injuries and all their radios were in containers 80km away in Bonn. By this time the mission had officially failed, and the window for blocking the crossroads had passed. Later, they would learn that their success would have been futile, as the 12th SS Panzer Division had also failed in their task to overcome the Americans at Elsenborn Ridge and would never have come to their rescue.

With the Americans closing around them, Heydte chose to send the worst of the wounded and a few captured men over to the Allied side.

Having previously fought against the 101st Airborne in Carentan, where he had graciously arranged a ceasefire, allowing the Allied recovery of their injured, he sent a letter along with the men, personally addressed to General Max Taylor, asking for the favour to be returned.[6]

A last attempt was made to break through the line, but many died and Heydte, finally seeing the writing on the wall, paired up the remaining survivors in small groups of two to three men with instructions to get back to the German side. By then, none of them had eaten for almost five days. Believing Monschau was still in German hands, Heydte entered the town alone on 21 December. However, it had been occupied by the Allies.

Wounded, frostbitten, starving, and suffering from pneumonia, he knocked on every door. A schoolteacher gave him shelter for one night, but he finally gave himself up on 22 December, having the teacher's son carry a letter of surrender to the town commander. It is estimated that approximately only eighty men of the original 1,000 made it out alive.

Heydte became a POW and from 23 February 1945 he was held in Trent Park POW camp near London. Later interrogations established him as an intelligent Anglophile and although an initial supporter of National Socialism, he had become disaffected with Nazism. He served the rest of his prison time in Belgium, until his release on 12 July 1947.

Following his release, Heydte once again dedicated himself to academic pursuits, and in 1951 he became a Professor of Constitutional Law and International Law at the University of Mainz. He also served as a professor in numerous other institutions, although simultaneously he continued his military career within the West German Army.

It seemed a bizarre turn of events that a man who had very recently been a high-ranking German Nazi officer would now be closely aligned with the West in the ensuing Cold War against the Soviet Union. Many factors could have had an influence on why the Allied forces believed they could trust Heydte, but clearly the consensus was that it was best to have him on their side.

In 1972 Heydte published a very important work with the title *Modern Irregular Warfare: In Defense Policy and as a Military Phenomenon*. As a military insurgency specialist and a professor of law and politics, he had a unique perspective on the boundaries of how to wage war in a modern world. He felt that irregular warfare was gradually replacing large-scale warfare.

As an alternative to the more conventional way that war had previously been conducted, he presented the application of irregular warfare as a strategic model. Heydte argued that irregular war is 'real war', and as such, long preceded the current concept of conventional war that is restricted by, and tied to, international law. Irregular warfare can include multiple types of violence, not all of which are military in nature.

The book was extremely innovative for its time and remains very relevant to this day. A reprint in 1986 added a section where he argued for its continued relevance and spoke of Russian aggression in Ukraine, Chinese belligerence in the South China Sea and radicalised Islamic attacks in the West, arguing that irregular warfare had become the global tool of choice. Sadly this book continues to be exceedingly poignant when you look at the news today. What Heydte referred to as 'irregular warfare' was and is in fact very similar to the more contemporarily used terms 'terrorism' or 'insurgency'. He literally wrote the book on it.

Heydte's later years were somewhat tumultuous as well. In 1962 he was involved in the serious Spiegel Affair, where he accused the editors of the newspaper *Der Spiegel* of treason by allegedly revealing sensitive information to the Russians. Later, in 1985, he was the accused party in the Flick Affair, where speculation over money laundering forced him to appear before a court.

Much can be said about Freiherr von der Heydte. Whether you see him as a Catholic, intellectual aristocrat caught in a violent period in time or a natural-born killer with a penchant for academia, there is no doubt that he was a complex man. No matter what he was involved in, he seemed to have an instinct for survival, and an ability to somehow convince whoever was on the opposite side that he was in fact on theirs.

Heydte is a great example of how any war and its participants cannot merely be observed retrospectively with any clear-cut and simple dualistic distinction of good and evil. Rather, they are a kaleidoscopic grid of convictions, actions and attitudes combined, providing a slightly more nuanced and wholesome understanding of the complexity of mankind.

Heydte was a highly intelligent, well-educated and liberal man of noble descent, yet he was also a brutal and extremely active force within the most despicable, fascist, military regime the world had ever seen. He died in 1994 after a long period of illness at the age of 87.

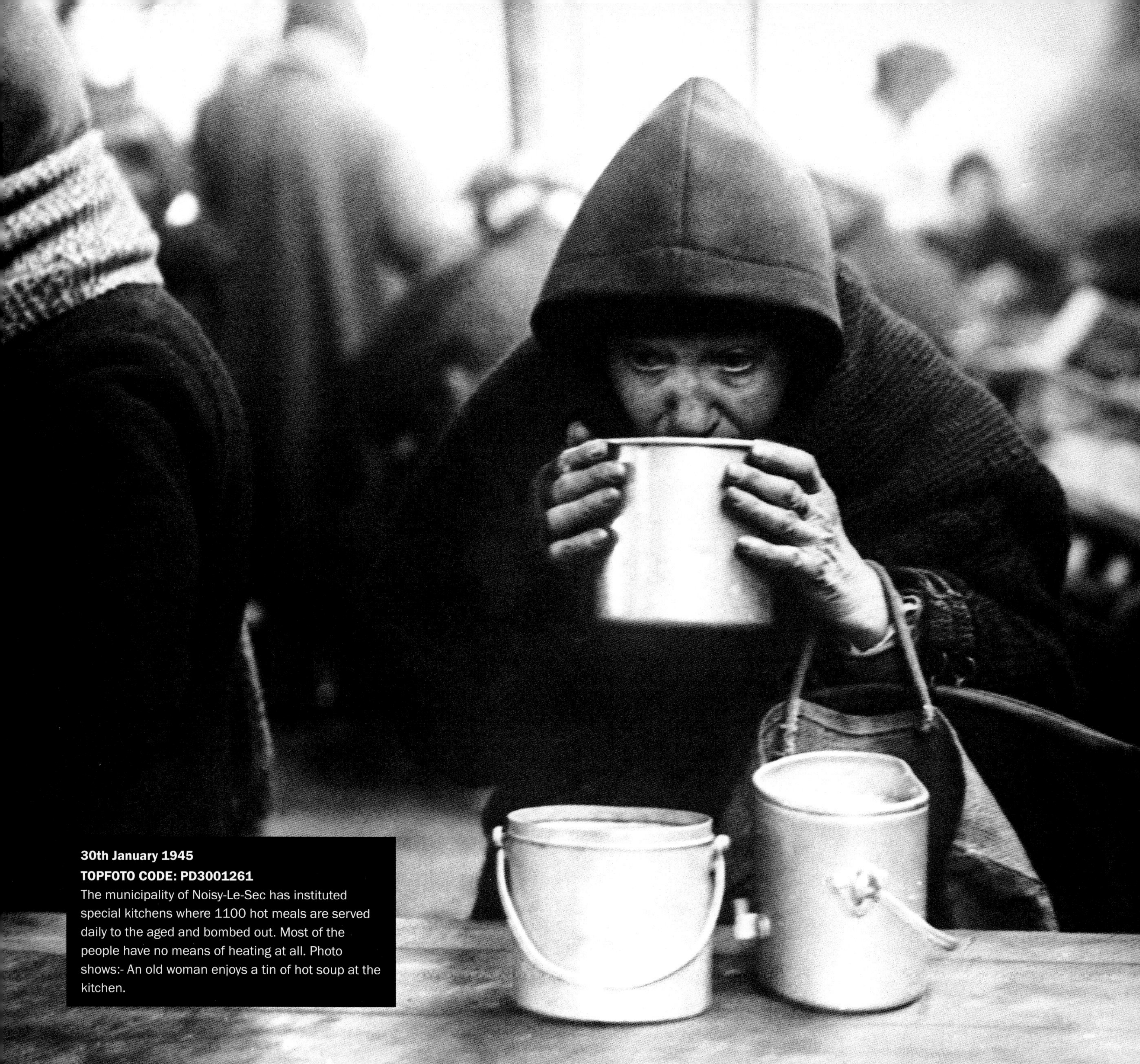

30th January 1945
TOPFOTO CODE: PD3001261
The municipality of Noisy-Le-Sec has instituted special kitchens where 1100 hot meals are served daily to the aged and bombed out. Most of the people have no means of heating at all. Photo shows:- An old woman enjoys a tin of hot soup at the kitchen.

Noisy-le-Sec is a French commune, located 3 miles north-east of Paris. It was the target of a major bombing on 18–19 April 1944. Between 1940 and 1945, Allied forces bombed a total of 1,570 French cities and towns, killing nearly 70,000 civilians in total.

The bombing of Noisy-le-Sec was mainly to destroy its important railway centre and thereby disrupt German logistics in preparation for Operation Overlord, the D-Day landings. Of all the bombings of France performed during those five years, the bombing of Noisy-le-Sec was the eleventh deadliest with 464 people killed, 370 seriously injured and almost 3,000 left homeless.

This raises an important topic, relating to the indiscriminate bombing of cities, both then and now, by all participants engaged in any conflict. Many argue that when the Allied forces bombed the German city of Dresden in February 1945, it was nothing short of a war crime. An estimated 25,000 civilians were killed, and critics state that the staggering 83,900 tons of bombs that were dropped in just three days were completely disproportionate to what was gained from a military point of view.

It is important to remember that no country or alliance stands above the humanitarian laws stated in the Geneva Conventions and that the end does not always justify the means – especially if you are aiming at occupying the moral high ground.

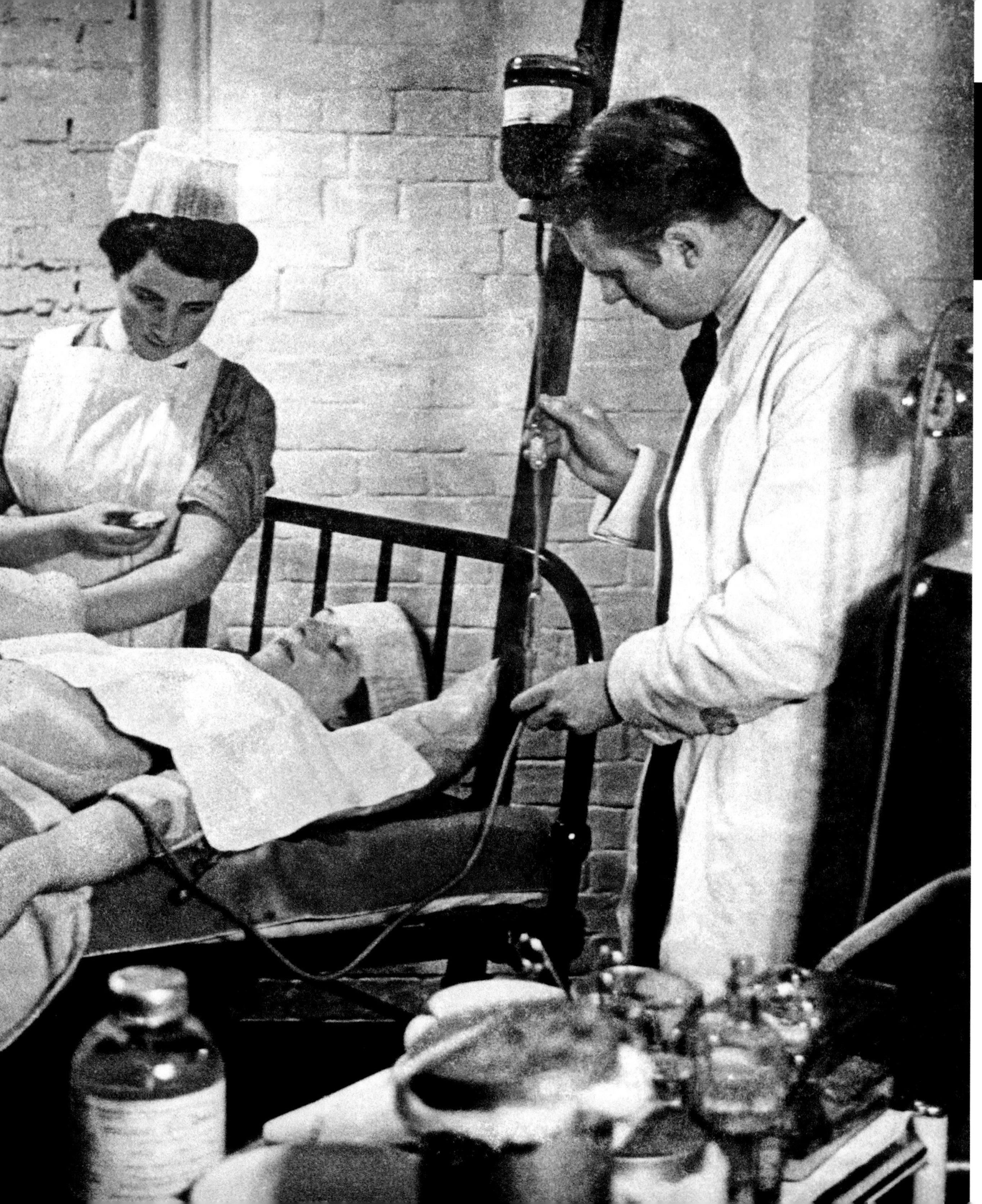

Undated
TOPFOTO CODE:
PD7493835
Air raid victim undergoing
blood transfusion in the
underground ward of
St. Thomas' Hospital,
London.

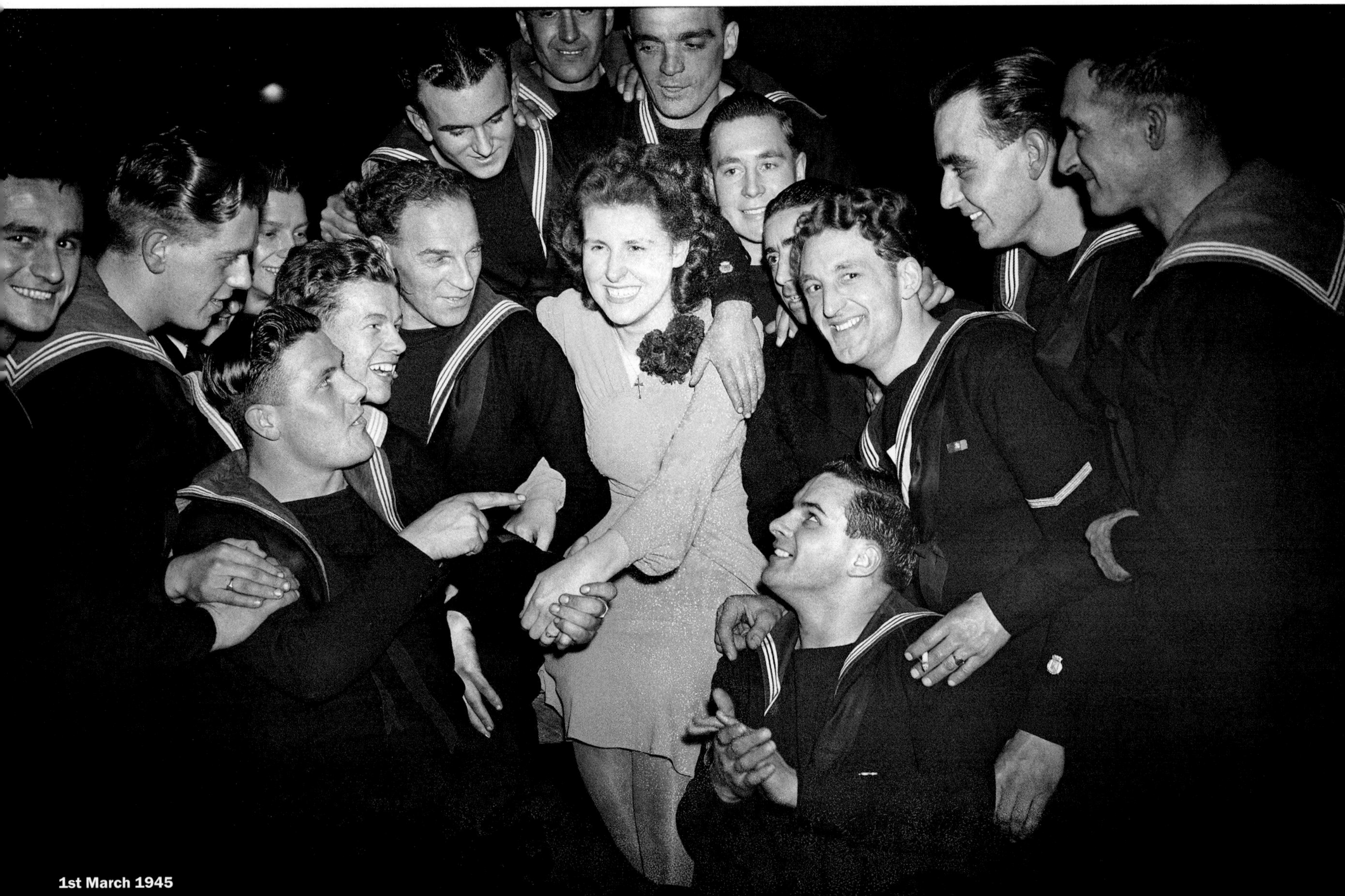

1st March 1945
TOPFOTO CODE: PD3001228
When Walthamstow, north-east London, entertained
150 officers and men of the minesweepers attached
to H.M.S. ST. TUDNO, which the people 'adopted'
three years ago, one of the principal items on the
proceedings was the introduction to the ships'
companies of Miss Joan Butfield, from now on their
own 'pin-up girl'. PHOTO SHOWS:- 'Pin-up girl' Joan
Butfield with some of her nautical admirers.

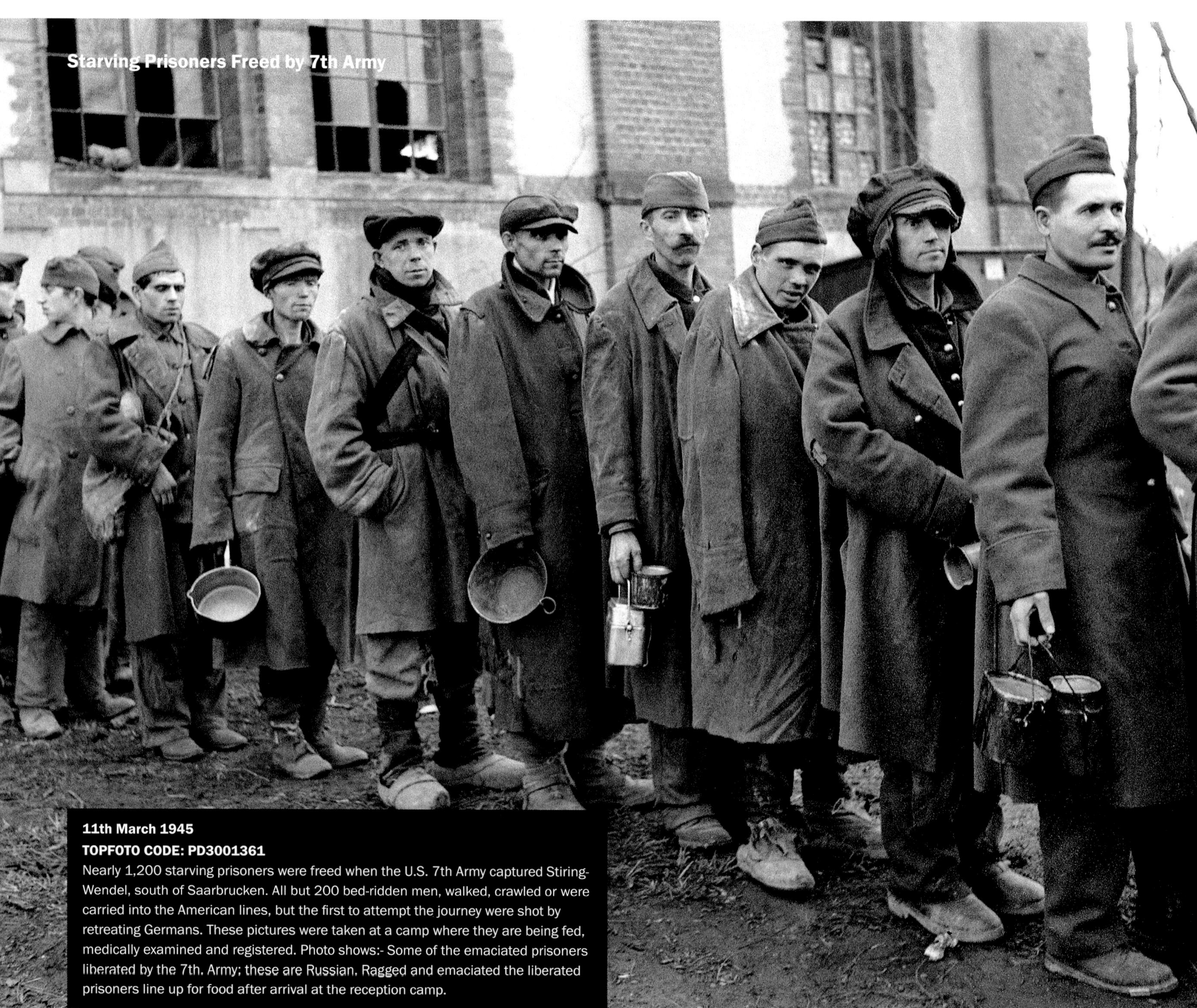

11th March 1945
TOPFOTO CODE: PD3001361
Nearly 1,200 starving prisoners were freed when the U.S. 7th Army captured Stiring-Wendel, south of Saarbrucken. All but 200 bed-ridden men, walked, crawled or were carried into the American lines, but the first to attempt the journey were shot by retreating Germans. These pictures were taken at a camp where they are being fed, medically examined and registered. Photo shows:- Some of the emaciated prisoners liberated by the 7th. Army; these are Russian. Ragged and emaciated the liberated prisoners line up for food after arrival at the reception camp.

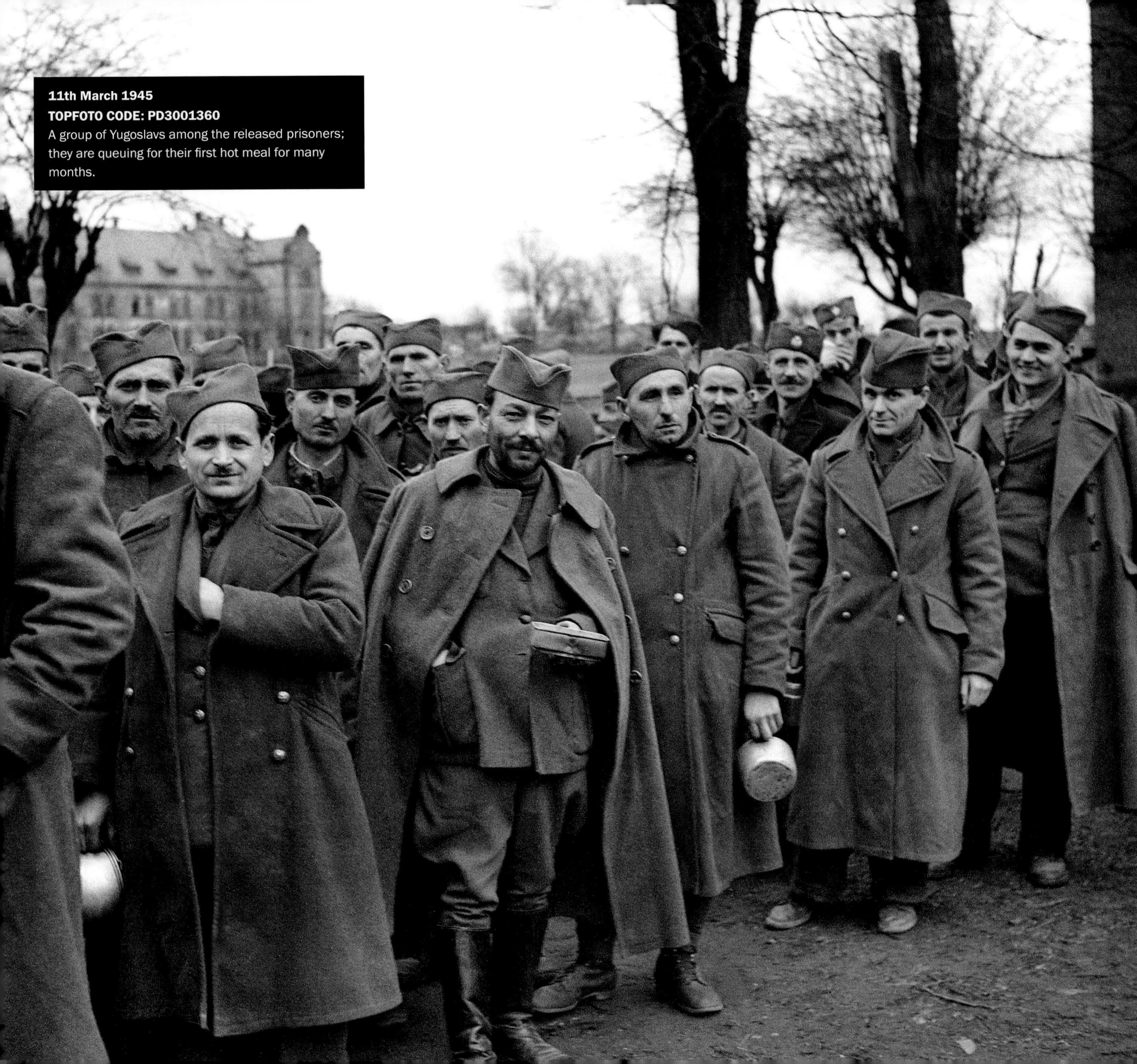

11th March 1945
TOPFOTO CODE: PD3001360
A group of Yugoslavs among the released prisoners;
they are queuing for their first hot meal for many
months.

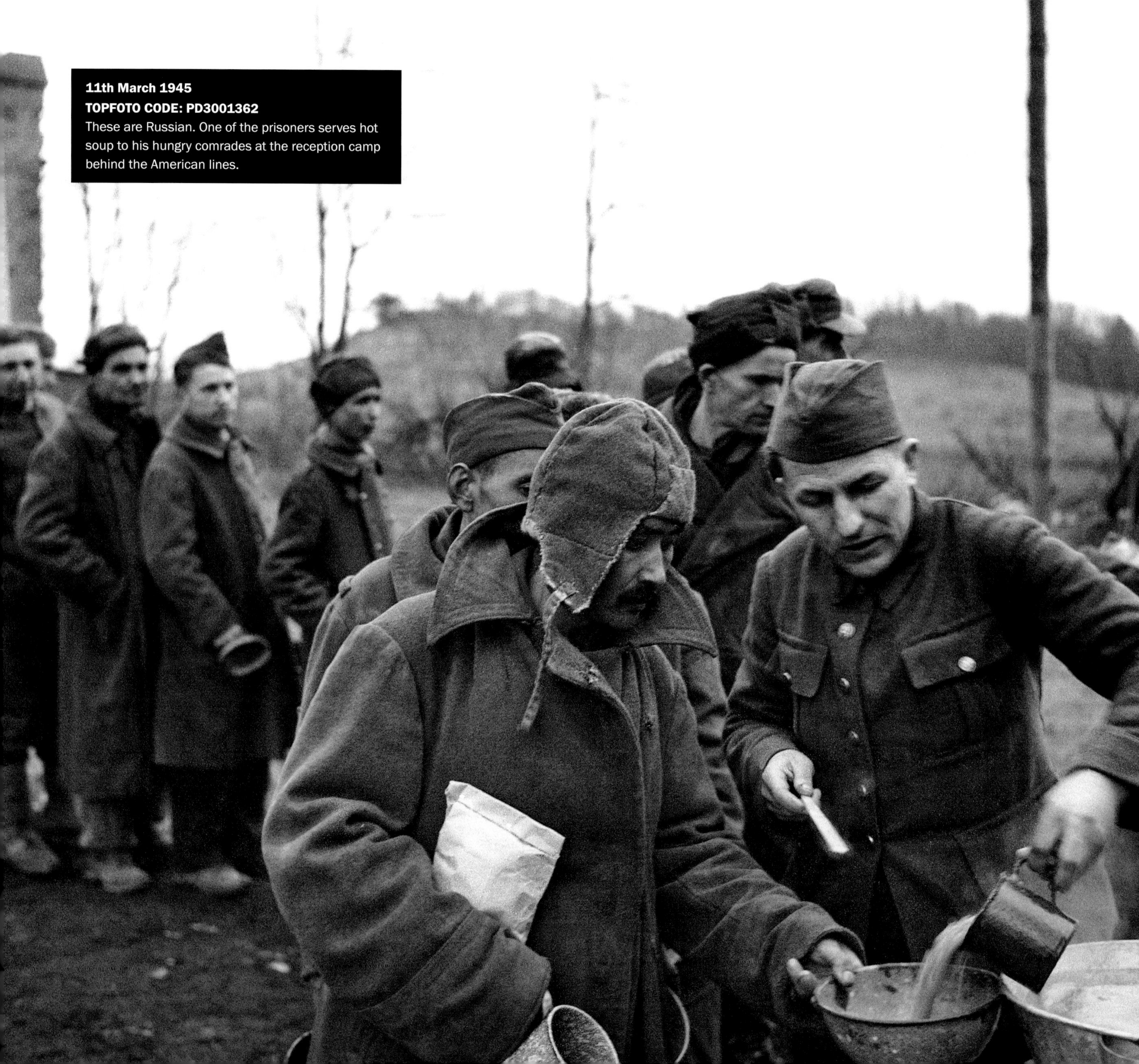

11th March 1945
TOPFOTO CODE: PD3001362
These are Russian. One of the prisoners serves hot soup to his hungry comrades at the reception camp behind the American lines.

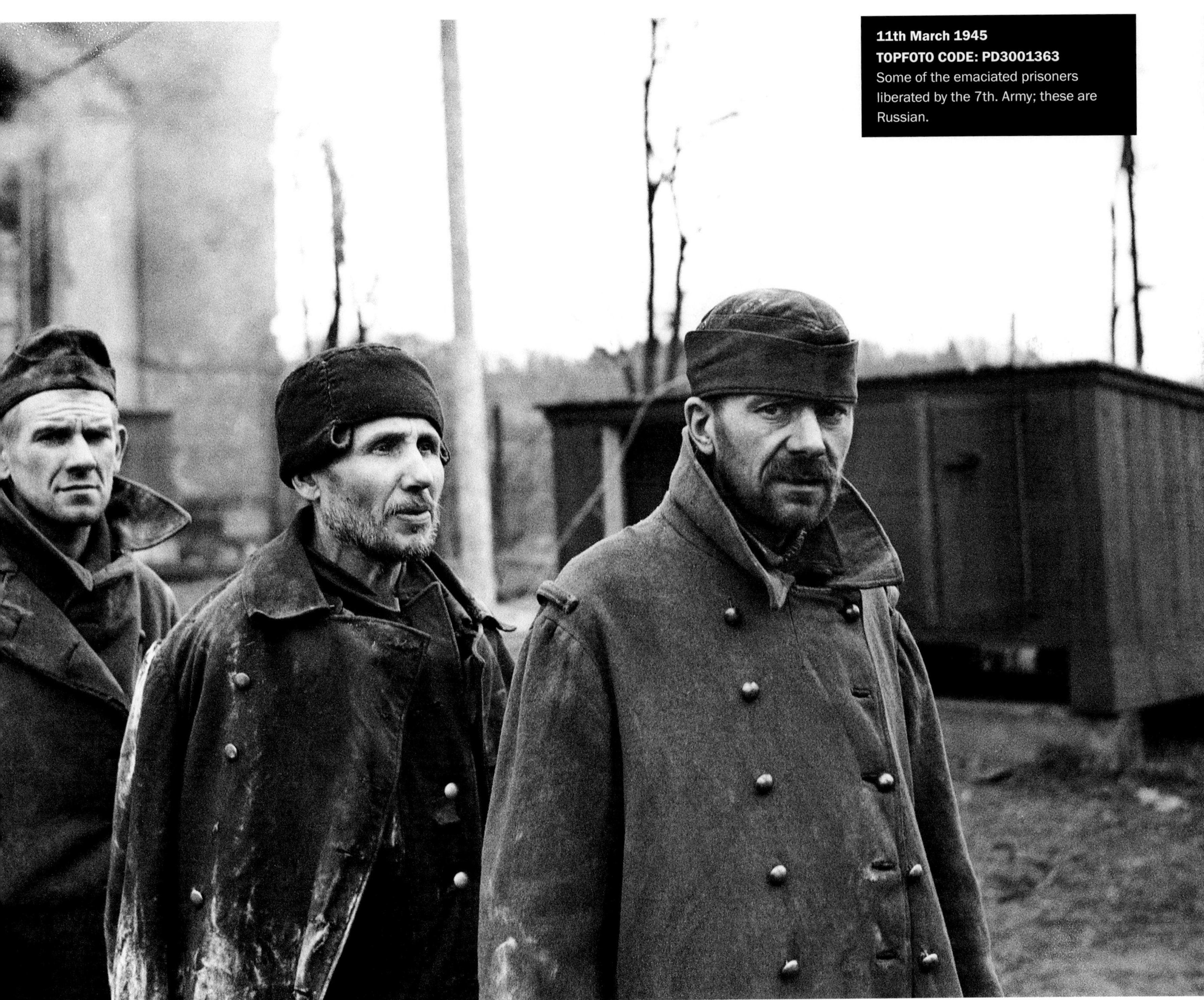

11th March 1945
TOPFOTO CODE: PD3001363
Some of the emaciated prisoners
liberated by the 7th. Army; these are
Russian.

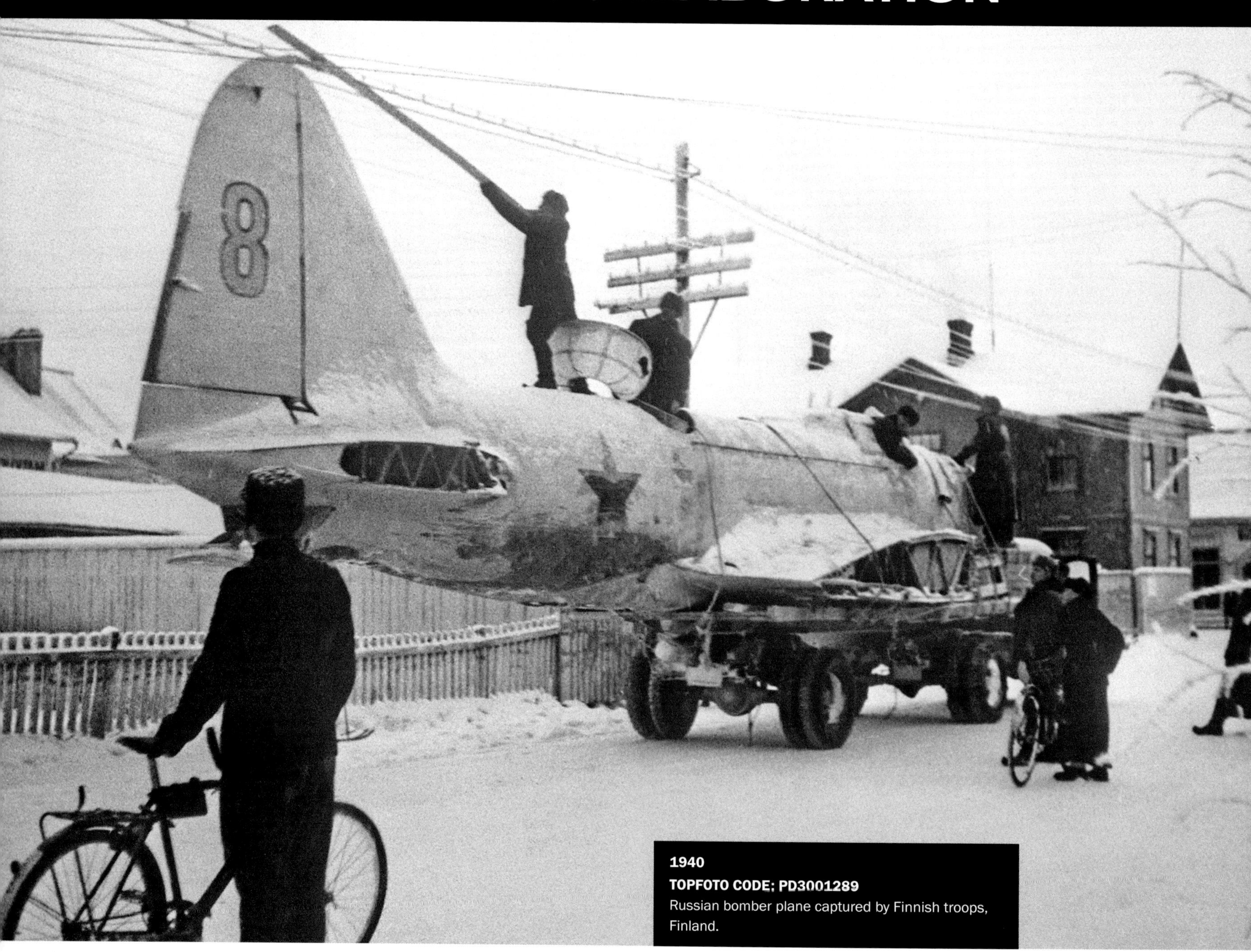

1940
TOPFOTO CODE: PD3001289
Russian bomber plane captured by Finnish troops, Finland.

After a period of political disagreements between Russia and Finland over territory, the Soviet Union chose to invade Finland on 30 November 1939. The invasion and the following nearly four months of fighting became known as the Winter War. It was a battle between David and Goliath, but shrewd guerilla tactics employed by the Finnish along with home advantage made it a hard-won victory for the Russians when the Finns ultimately ceded the disputed borderlands.

The Russian casualties were an estimated 300,000 men against 65,000 Finnish. Fearless flying by the grossly outnumbered Finnish pilots combined with the use of AA guns and the Russian need to fly their bombers low, meant that losses were also higher here. An approximate 500 Soviet aircraft were downed compared to around only seventy Finnish. Some of the Russian Tupolev SB bombers that were shot down were repurposed by the Finns – twenty-four of them in total between 1939 and 1945. The first ten of these were serialled VP-1 to VP-10, with VP-8 the one being transported down the road in the photo.

For Finland, the war years were turbulent – to say the least. It initially saw them fight a defensive battle against Russia, supported vaguely by the Allies. Secondly, an offensive battle ensued, once again against Russia, but this time alongside Nazi Germany (this alliance was a pragmatic and not an ideological one). Finally, they fought against Nazi Germany alongside the Allied forces.

The Finnish fluctuation during the Second World War perfectly illustrates a geographically ill-placed, small nation's need for adaptability, in order to protect themselves against vastly larger belligerents.

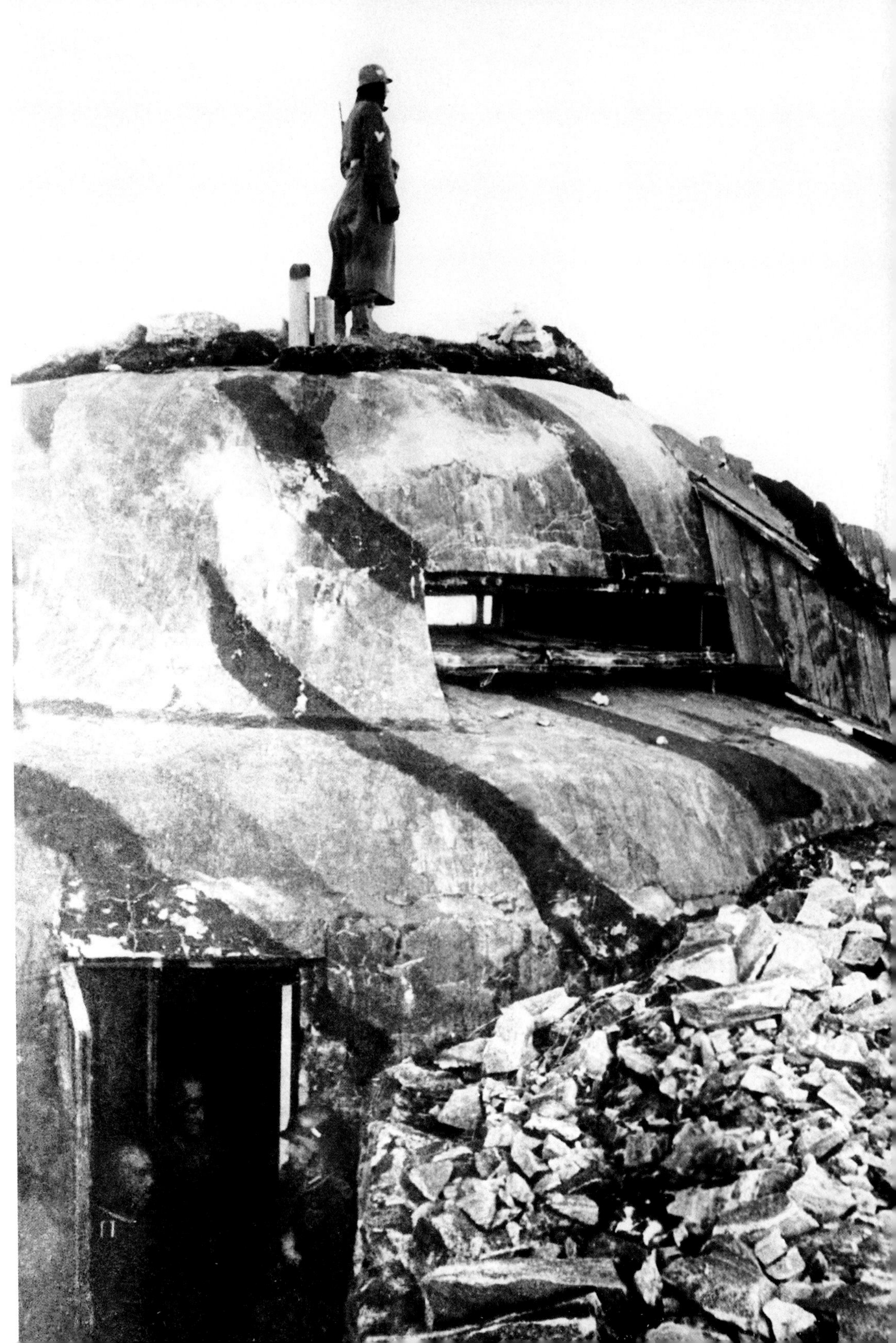

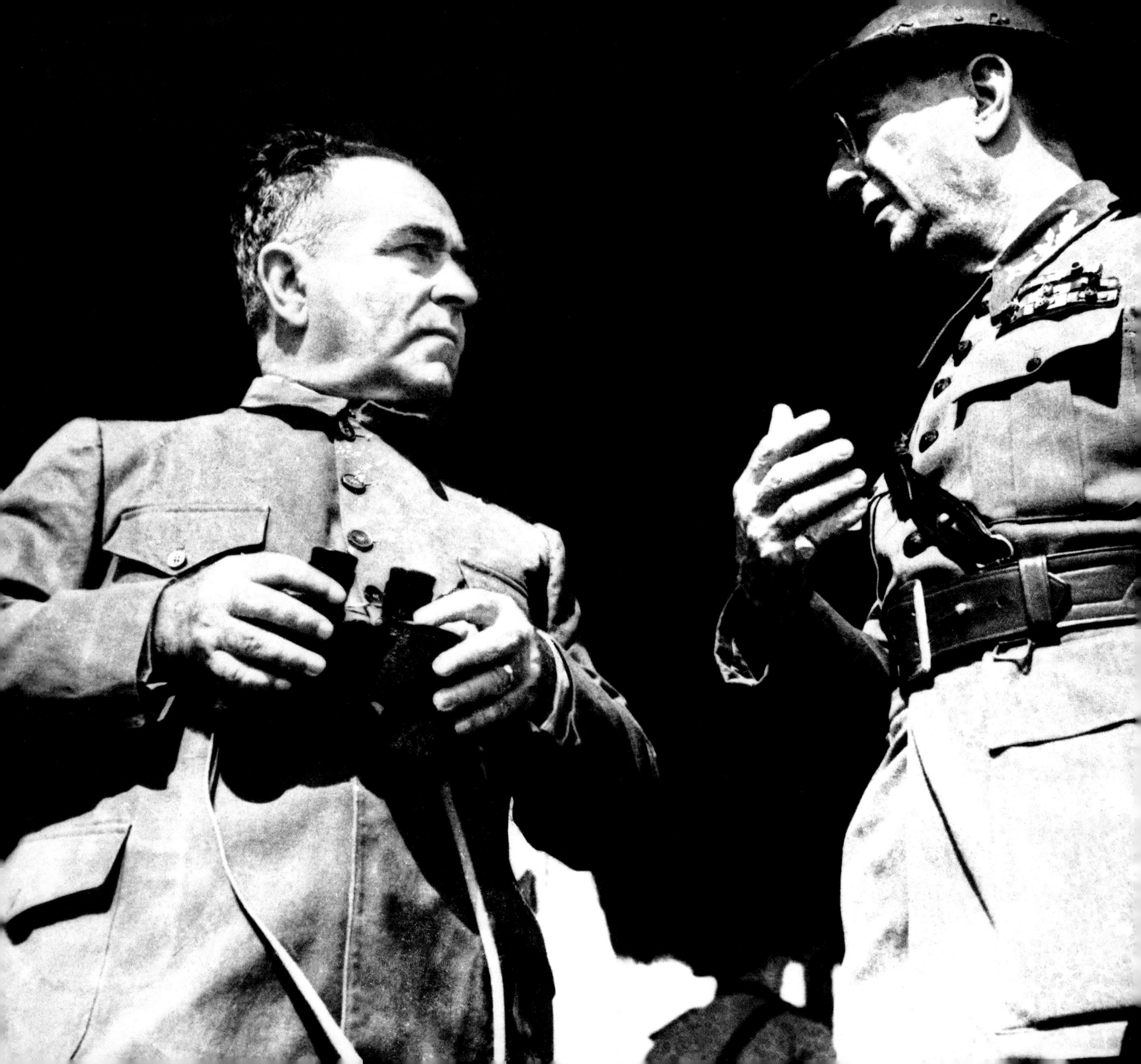

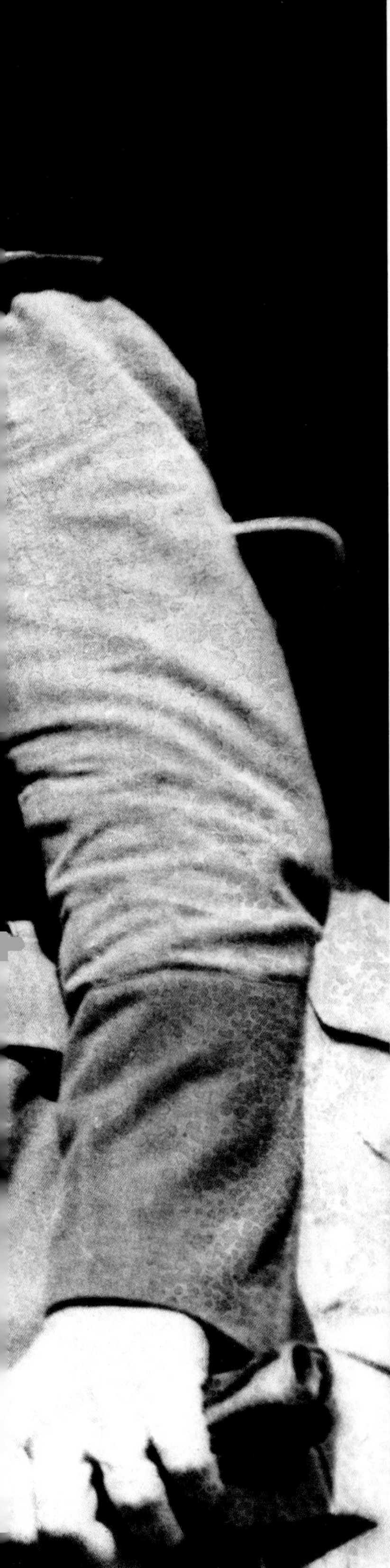

Brazil at War with Germany and Italy: Brazilian Armed Forces

Germany's attacks on Brazilian merchant ships in the first half of 1942 was the final straw that threw Getúlio Vargas into the arms of the Americans and the Allied forces. Even though approximately 80,000 Germans had immigrated to Brazil in the interwar years (and that Brazil counted the largest body of Nazi party members outside Germany), it could not stem the public outrage these attacks had created, and the government saw itself pressured into a strong and firm response.

In the early 1930s, Brazil had been flirting with fascism, and Vargas, himself a controversial and dictatorial leader, had steered the country into an attempted neutrality trying to curry favour with both sides at the beginning of the war.

The attack on Pearl Harbor on 7 December 1941, however, led Brazil, Uruguay, Paraguay, Ecuador and Peru to officially sever ties with the Axis forces in late January 1942. A few months later, the US and Brazil created a quid pro quo deal wherein Brazil was to receive the most generous economic and military aid the US had ever provided to a Latin American country. In exchange, the US was to build air bases in Brazil, in particular one in Parnamirim that later became extremely important to Allied operations in both the Atlantic and North Africa.

The alliance with the United States also came from aspirations of a stronger post-war position on the global scene politically, as well as a hope of a leadership role in Latin America.

In July 1944, Brazil became the first and only South American country to deploy soldiers to Europe during the war, sending the Brazilian Expeditionary Force and its 25,000 men to fight.

After the war, tensions rose politically once more, and the fight against fascism gave way to the Cold War confrontations between Russian communism and American democracy. Anti-communist views, combined with Brazil's ineffective immigration programme, provided an opening for many Nazis to reinvent themselves south of the equator.

The so-called Ratlines leading to especially Argentina, but also a number of other countries, led numerous high-ranking Nazis to safety. Thousands of German war criminals were given a safe haven, and were even supported by rogue elements within the Catholic clergy.

Recently, Brazil has seen a worrying surge in neo-Nazi groups, and their Human Rights Council has voiced concerns to the United Nations with a report showing an alarming 270.6 per cent increase from January 2019 to May 2021 in these cells.

22nd August 1942
TOPFOTO CODE: PD7493831
Brazil declared on August 22 that she was at war with Germany and Italy, and a few hours later Uruguay announced that she would act 'in complete solidarity' with her neighbour. Brazil is the first South American State to declare war on the Axis Powers and the Twenty Ninth nation to do so (See M. of I. Handout No. 23 dated 23.8.42.). PHOTO SHOWS:- The Brazilian President, Getulio Vargas, (left) taken on manoeuvres in Paraiba. He is seen chatting with General Almerio de Moura, C. in C. Manoeuvres. K. 2794. (Picture issued August 1942) ISSUED BY THE MINISTRY OF INFORMATION.

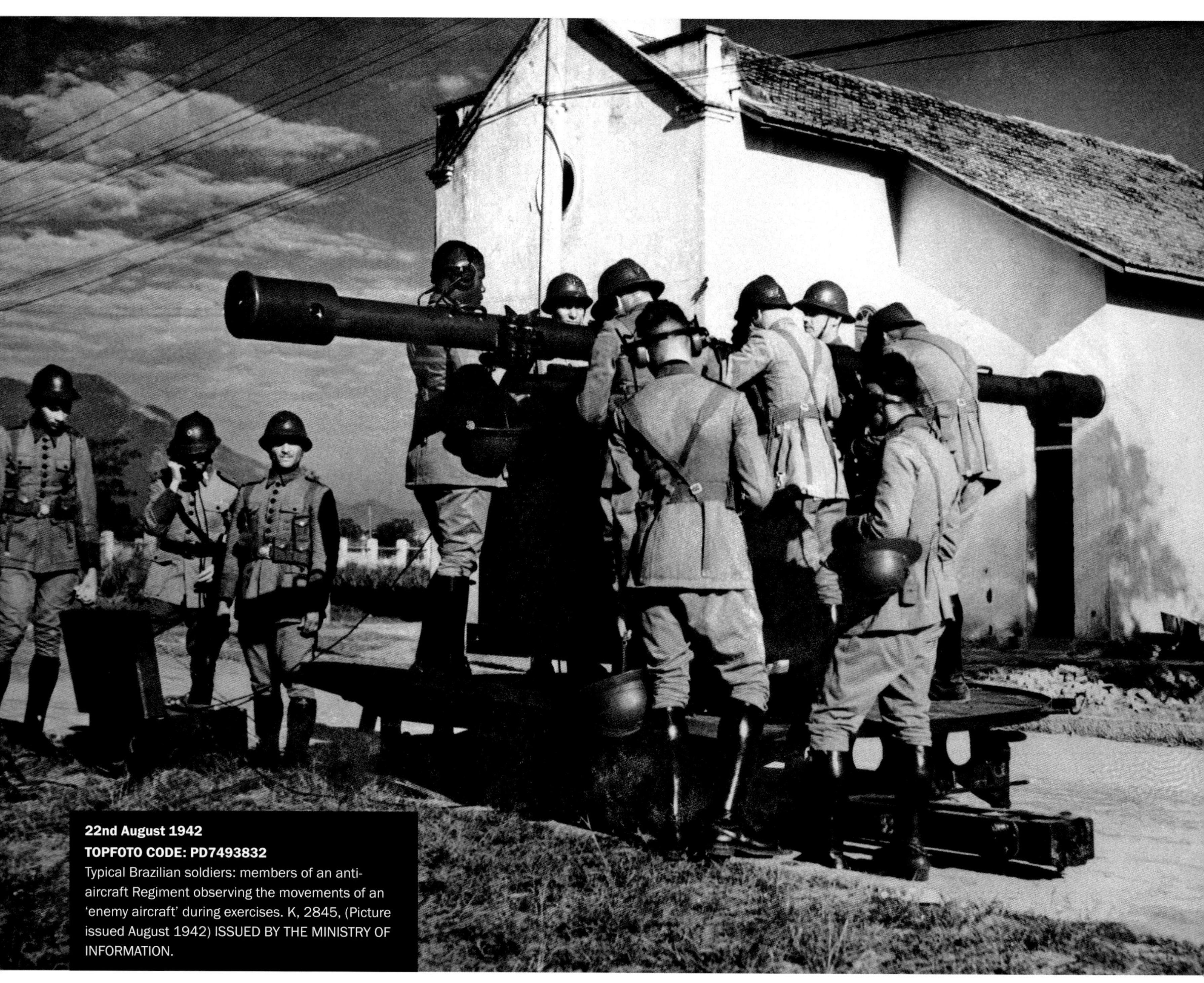22nd August 1942
TOPFOTO CODE: PD7493832
Typical Brazilian soldiers: members of an anti-aircraft Regiment observing the movements of an 'enemy aircraft' during exercises. K, 2845, (Picture issued August 1942) ISSUED BY THE MINISTRY OF INFORMATION.

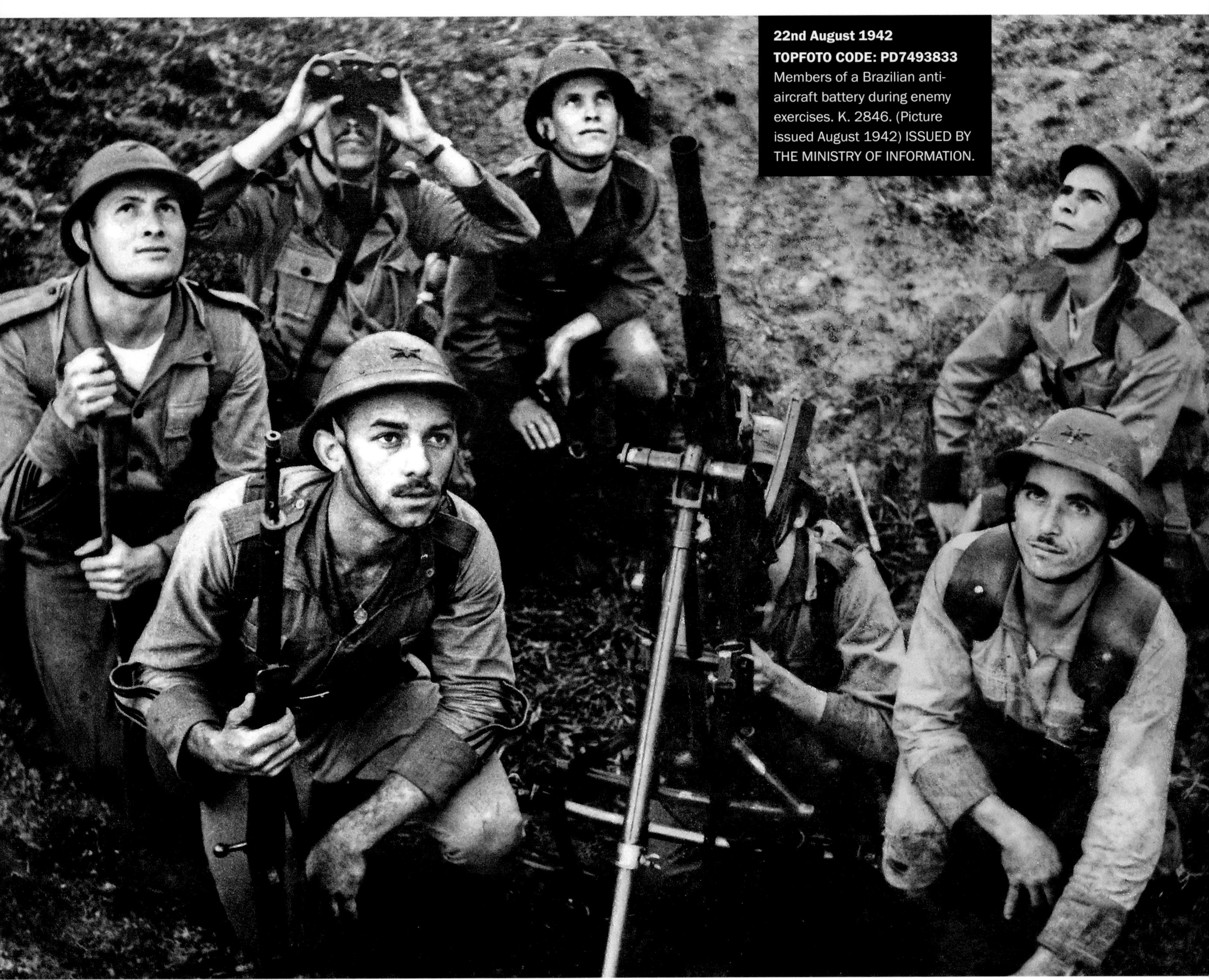

22nd August 1942
TOPFOTO CODE: PD7493833
Members of a Brazilian anti-aircraft battery during enemy exercises. K. 2846. (Picture issued August 1942) ISSUED BY THE MINISTRY OF INFORMATION.

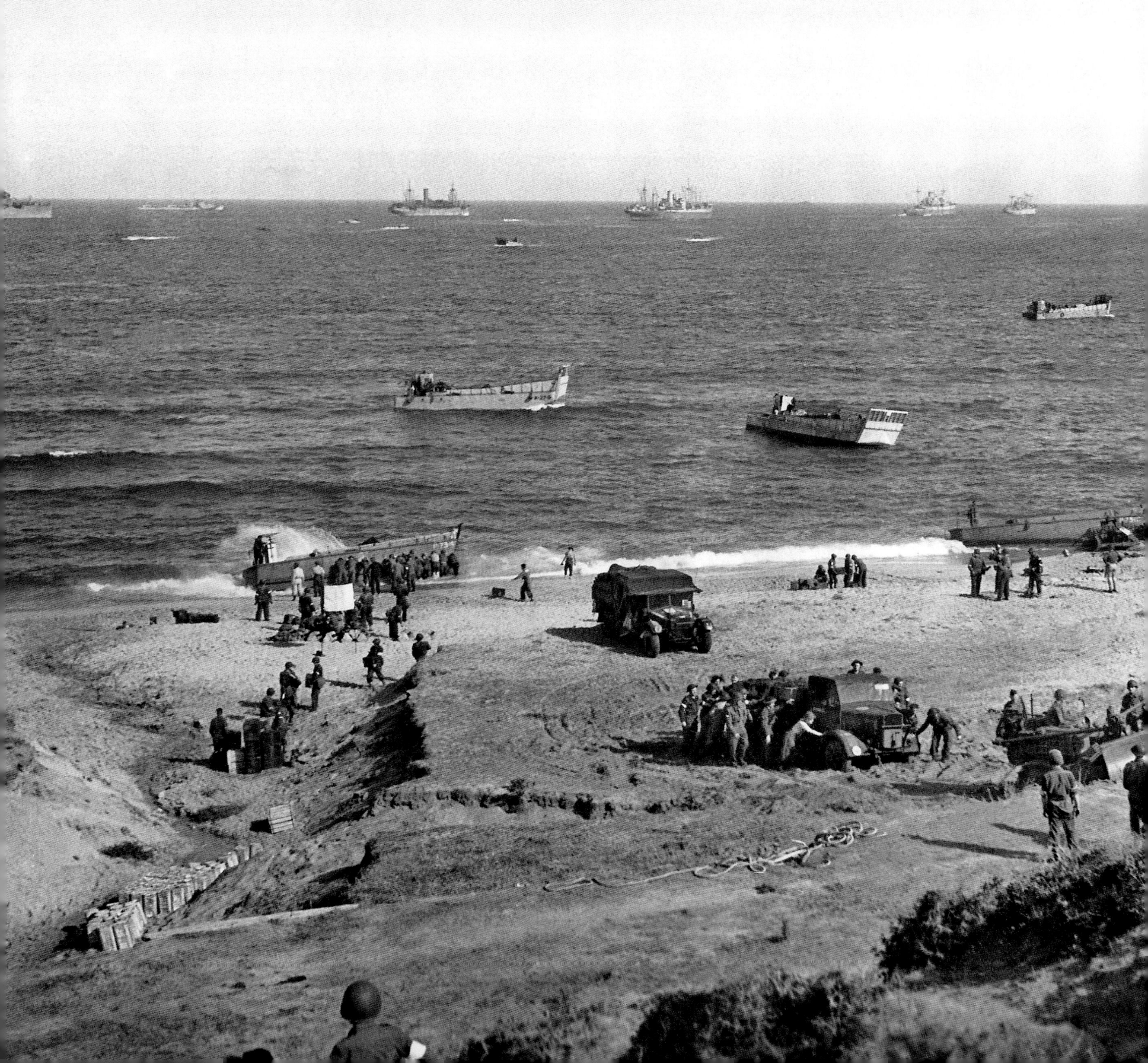

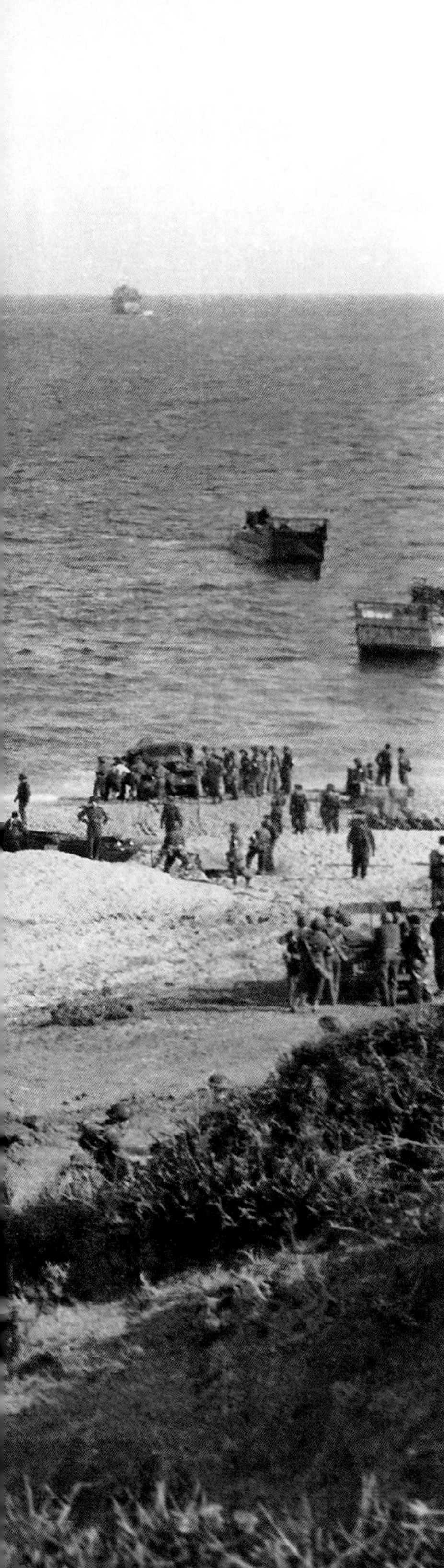

North Africa: Largest Seaborne Expedition in History Opens Allied Move to Sweep Axis from Mediterranean

Operation Torch was launched on 8 November 1942. It was the first major offensive carried out by the Allied forces against the Axis powers in the West. The intention was to open a new front to divert the Germans' attention and relieve the pressure on the Eastern Front.

The operation involved collaborating American, British and French forces and was led by Dwight D. Eisenhower. Its primary objective was to secure key ports and airfields in Casablanca, Oran and Algiers, and establish a foothold on the African continent from where further offensives could be launched. This would put them behind German and Italian forces, and with British forces already fighting them from the east (read more on page 30), a pincer move could be performed. The Vichy French, however, stood in their way.

The operation was complicated by political considerations, as the French Vichy puppet government was collaborating with the Axis. Delicate negotiations had to be performed with key generals to attempt to assure allegiance and minimise resistance from the French forces already present in the region. It was further complicated by the disastrous prior Anglo-French incident in Mers El Kébir in 1940. The British, fearing that the Germans would take the French Navy, had asked the French to place it in British hands. Their unwillingness to do so resulted in the British sinking a battleship and mercilessly killing 1,297 French sailors. This naturally led to suspicion and resistance among the French.

Torch was a massive logistical operation, involving the transport of more than 100,000 US and British troops over 1,500 miles to the beaches of North Africa to fight and pacify the nearly 125,000 Vichy French. Despite resistance, the Allied forces gradually gained the upper hand and by mid-November 1942 the ports of Casablanca, Oran and Algiers were firmly under Allied control, signalling a decisive turning point in the campaign. On 13 May 1943, the last of the Axis forces in North Africa surrendered.

Later speculation on why such an important campaign has been, somewhat, historically overlooked have been attested to the involvement of the French on both sides, obscuring the somewhat common simplistic, dualistic narrative of the Second World War in contemporary history.

November 1942 TOPFOTO CODE: PD7493854
Royal Air Force Fighters gave cover to the Allied shipping at Algiers, where landings were made to effect a bridgehead in preparation for the assault on the airfield at Maison Blanche, a few miles away. When American Forces captured Maison Blanche airfield, fighters were landed and were soon in action, driving off Axis aircraft attacking Allied shipping. R.A.F ground personnel were the first British troops to land in North Africa. Picture shows:- Weapons and equipment being landed on the beach preparatory to the assault on the aerodrome. BRITISH OFFICIAL PHOTOGRAPH. NO. CNA. 9 (XP). AIR MINISTRY PHOTOGRAPH CROWN COPYRIGHT RESERVED.

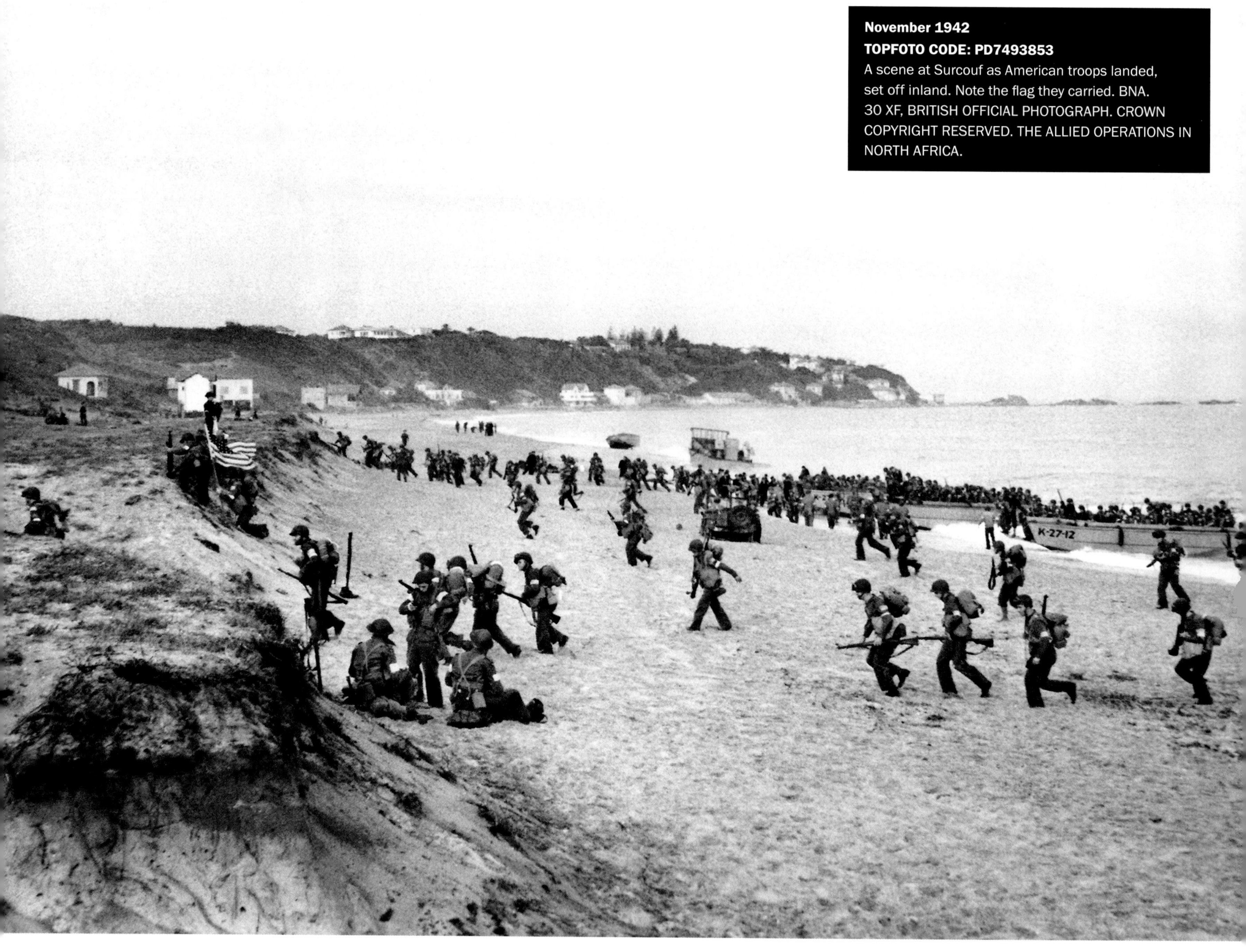

A scene at Surcouf as American troops landed, set off inland. Note the flag they carried. BNA. 30 XF, BRITISH OFFICIAL PHOTOGRAPH. CROWN COPYRIGHT RESERVED. THE ALLIED OPERATIONS IN NORTH AFRICA.

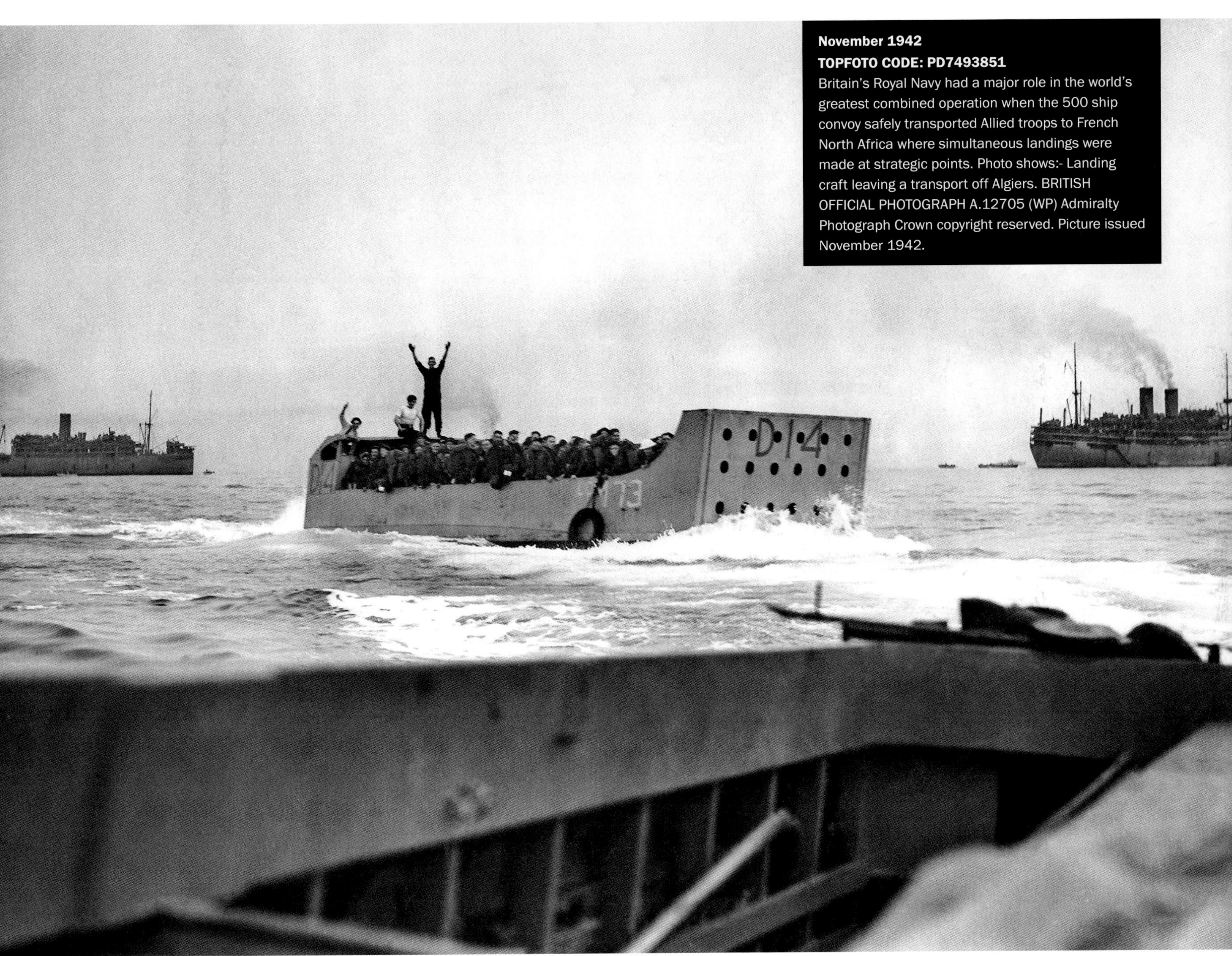

November 1942
TOPFOTO CODE: PD7493851
Britain's Royal Navy had a major role in the world's greatest combined operation when the 500 ship convoy safely transported Allied troops to French North Africa where simultaneous landings were made at strategic points. Photo shows:- Landing craft leaving a transport off Algiers. BRITISH OFFICIAL PHOTOGRAPH A.12705 (WP) Admiralty Photograph Crown copyright reserved. Picture issued November 1942.

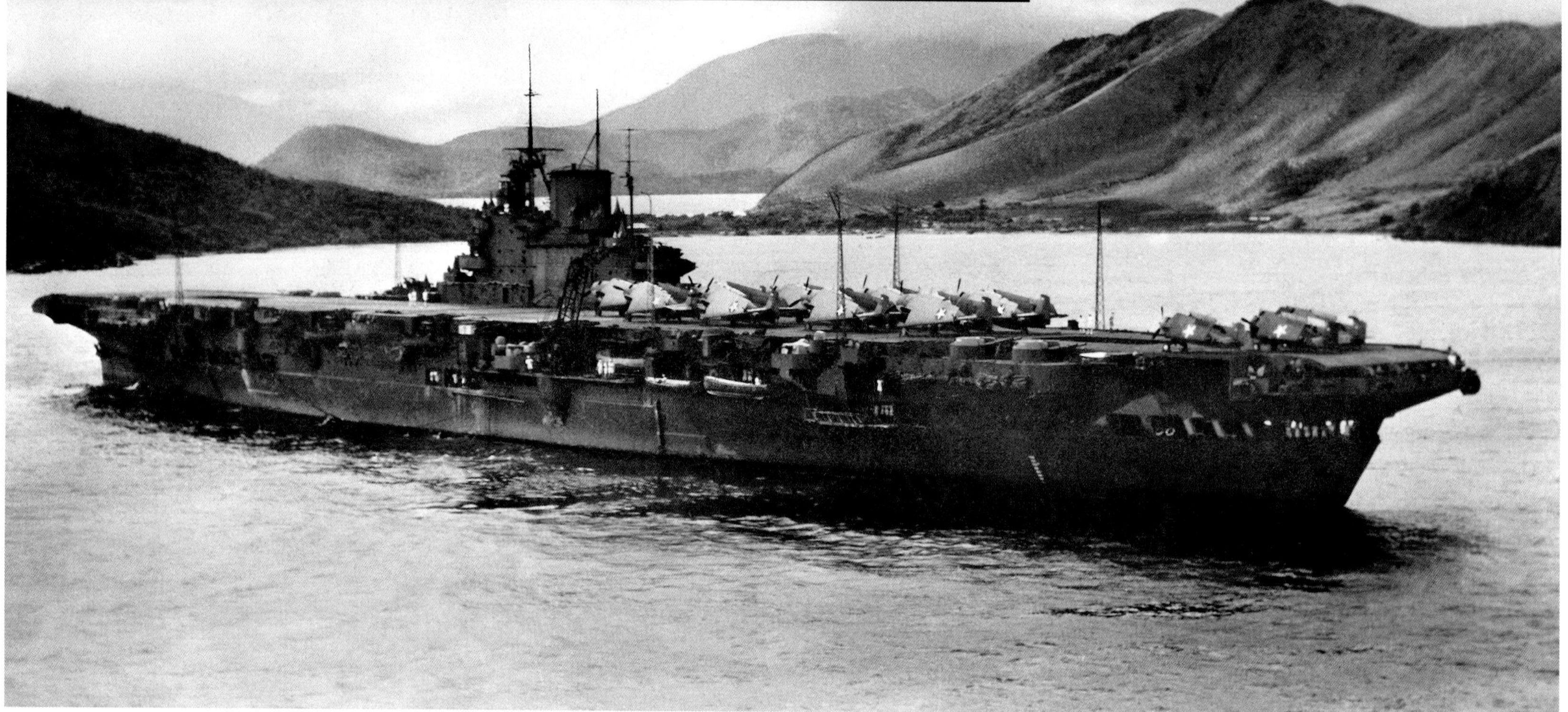

The British aircraft carrier HMS *Victorious* was launched in September 1939 and saw a lot of action during the Second World War. At 673ft long, it could carry more than fifty aircraft at the height of its service.

The US Navy had sustained heavy losses to their carrier fleet during the Battle of Midway in 1942 and the continuing Guadalcanal Campaign, so the only US carrier in the Pacific was USS *Saratoga*. The British, therefore, generously gave HMS *Victorious* on loan to the Americans until their own fleet could be replenished. It was temporarily redesignated USS *Robin*.

The date of the photo is not specified beyond May–September, but naval history annals state that it performed cross-carrier operating procedures with USS *Saratoga* in July 1943 (most likely what we see in the photo). It also states that it was deployed in August 1943 to cover landings in the Solomon Islands as part of Operation Cartwheel. (Read more on page 33.)

Observations by the British sailors aboard USS *Robin* were that not all of the US officers were overly thrilled with the prospects of this transcontinental collaboration; however, capable performances by the crew proved them quite wrong.[7]

As the negative caption notes, the vessel was carrying American pilots at the time and Grumman torpedo bombers and fighters with US markings can be seen in the photo. In September 1943, *Robin* was released from US service and became HMS *Victorious* once again.

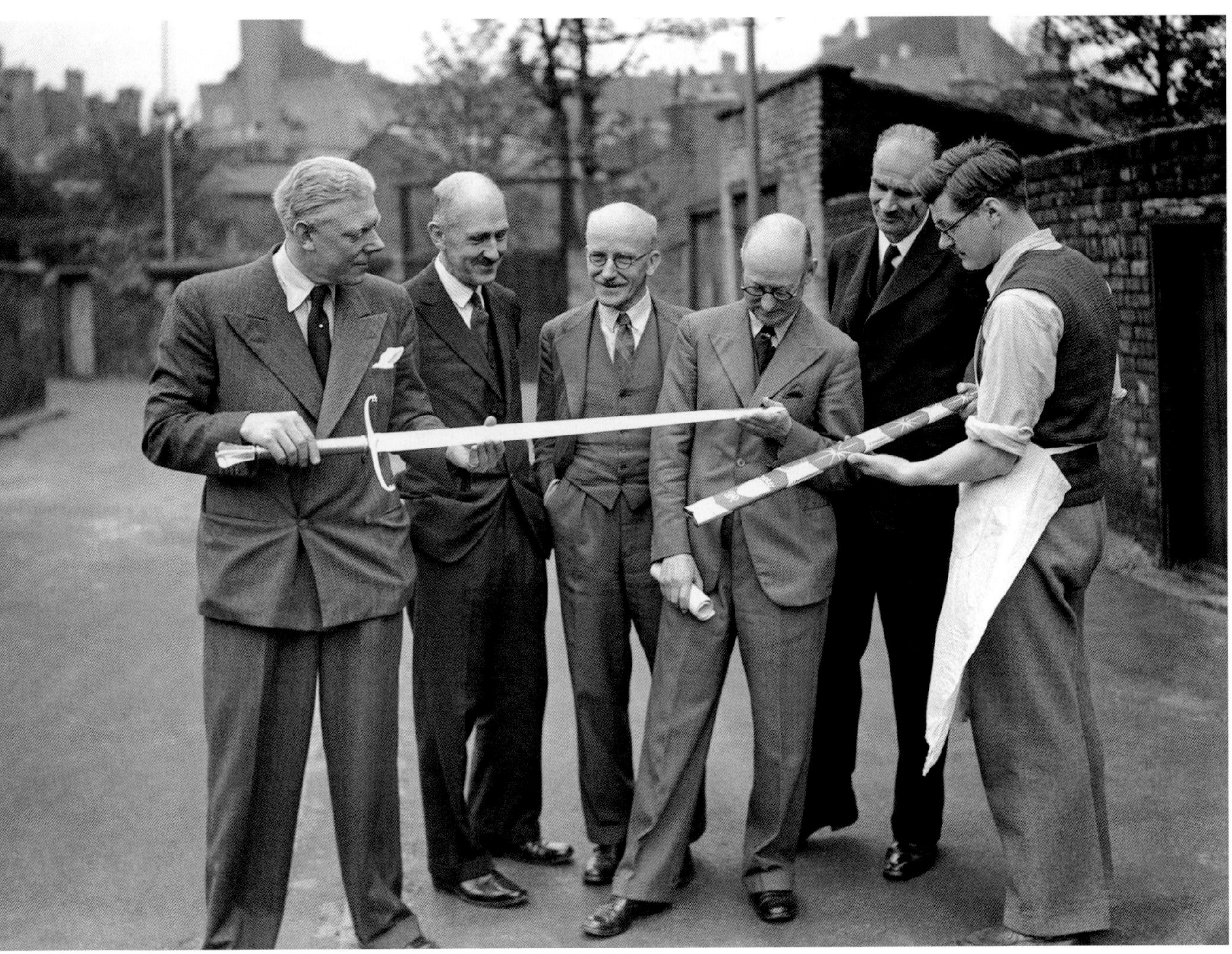

The Stalingrad sword. Putting the finishing touches to the King's gift to the steel-hearted citizens of Stalingrad. The two-handed sword of Honour, to be presented by His Majesty the King to Stalingrad is now completed and on view at the Goldsmith's Hall. These pictures show the experts who have made it, putting the finishing touches. Picture shows:- The experts examine the finished article. They are left to right:- Mr. J.W. Latham (Wilkinson Sword Co.); Mr. G.R. Hughes (Goldsmith's Company); Mr. M.C. Oliver (Lettering expert); Mr. G.T. Friend (engraver of the inscription on the blade); Professor R.Y. Cleadowe (Designer); Mr. L.G. Durbin (responsible for the gold and silver mounts on the scabbard). NOT TO BE PUBLISHED BEFORE 5.10.43. THIS PICTURE IS BEING ISSUED FOR WEEKLY PAPERS ONLY.

The Battle of Stalingrad was arguably one of the most important of the Second World War and marked the first major defeat for Nazi Germany. Fought between July 1942 and February 1943, it is also widely considered to be the bloodiest in human history, with an estimated 2 million combined military and civilian casualties.

Stalingrad was not a city of huge strategic importance but bore the name of the Soviet leader, Joseph Stalin. For Hitler, that made it symbolically irresistible not to attempt to conquer it, and for Stalin it made it equally important not to lose. Both sides, therefore, ordered their troops to not give in and to fight – at all costs. The minus 30-degree temperatures of the Russian winter, combined with the brutal and vicious urban combat, resulted in a horrendously high death toll. The German Sixth Army ultimately surrendered to the Red Army, which was a devastating psychological blow to the Third Reich, and marked the turning point in the fortunes of the war.

Following the battle, King George VI and Winston Churchill came up with the idea of commissioning a sword as a tribute to the Soviet defences on behalf of the British government. The renowned British maker Wilkinson Sword (now probably mostly recognised for their razorblades) was selected to be the creator of the sword – a process that took almost three months. Considered one of the last true masterpieces in modern sword-making, it is a 4ft, two-handed longsword, featuring solid silver, 18-carat gold wire, a giant rock crystal and rubies. Inscribed in both English and Russian, the engraving reads: 'To the steel-hearted citizens of Stalingrad – The gift of King George VI – In token of the homage of the British people.' It was presented to Stalin at the Tehran Conference in November 1943.

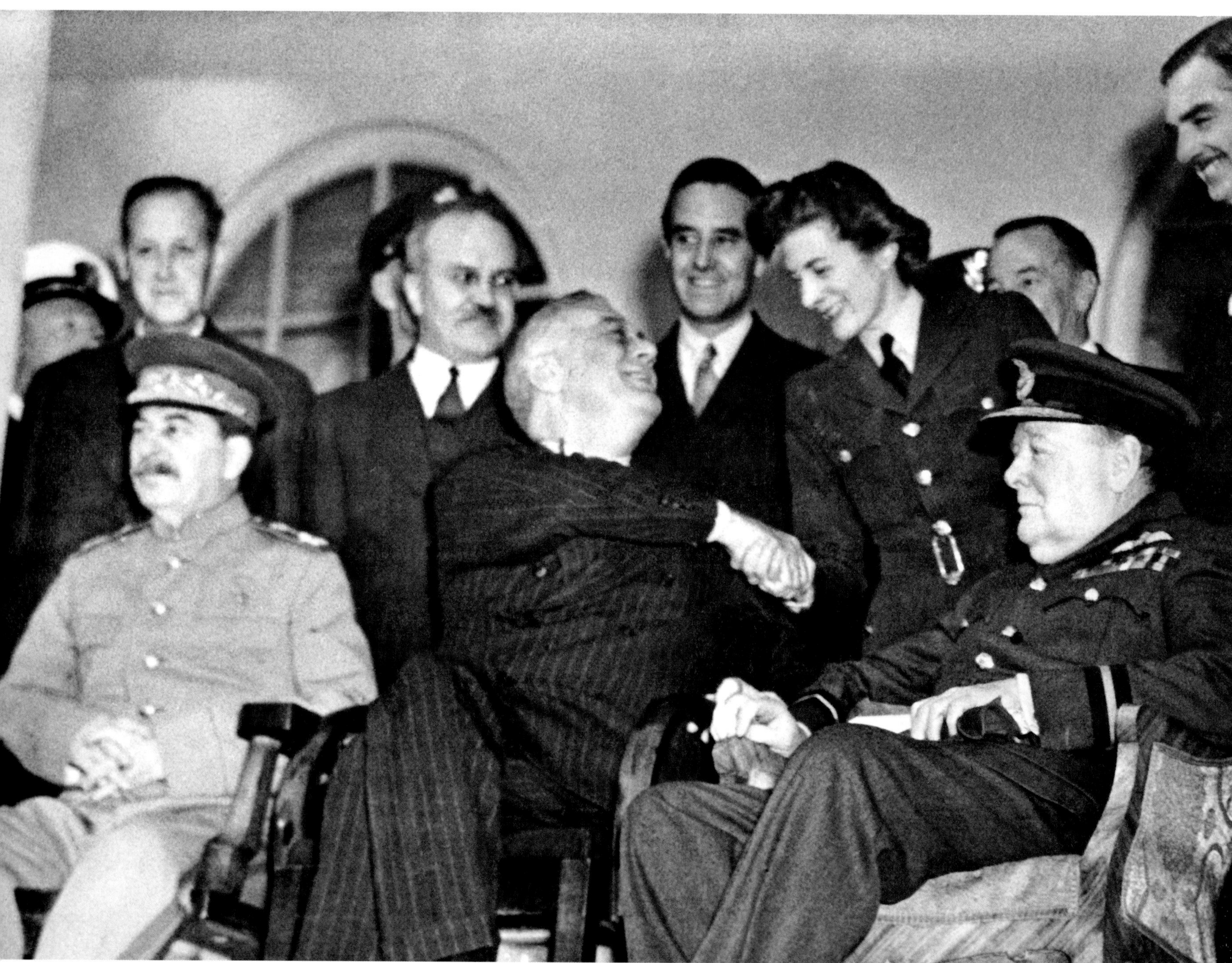

The Tehran Conference in 1943 was the first meeting to take place between the top leaders of the Allied forces of Britain, the US and the Soviet Union – often referred to as 'the Big Three'. It is curious that, while the war began in 1939, it took nearly four years for this assembly to occur.

The main purpose of the meeting was to co-ordinate a united effort against the remaining forces of the Axis powers. At this point in the war the wind had changed, and with major victories in Sicily, Stalingrad, North Africa and the Pacific, the prospects of winning the war were looking brighter than ever. Stalin, Roosevelt and Churchill all had very different agendas but finally came to an agreement on some key issues. Most importantly, it was decided to open a second front in Western Europe and relieve the pressure on the Soviet forces on the Eastern Front. This resulted in the preparation and execution of Operation Overlord – the D-Day landings. In return for this, Stalin committed to enter the war against Japan upon the defeat of Nazi Germany. Discussions on how Germany and Poland should be partitioned post-war were also debated – though not decided. While Allied co-operation was certainly reinforced, clear tensions between Stalin and his Western allies foreshadowed the issues that would eventually lead to the Cold War.

Interestingly, the photo shows Roosevelt shaking hands with Churchill's daughter, Sarah, who acted as her father's aide-de-camp at the Tehran Conference. Sarah was an actor and a dancer, and joined the WAAF (Women's Auxiliary Air Force) during the war. Modern literature seems to have underestimated her importance and she allegedly made a very big impression on Roosevelt, inspiring him to take his own daughter to the next Allied conference in Yalta in February 1945.

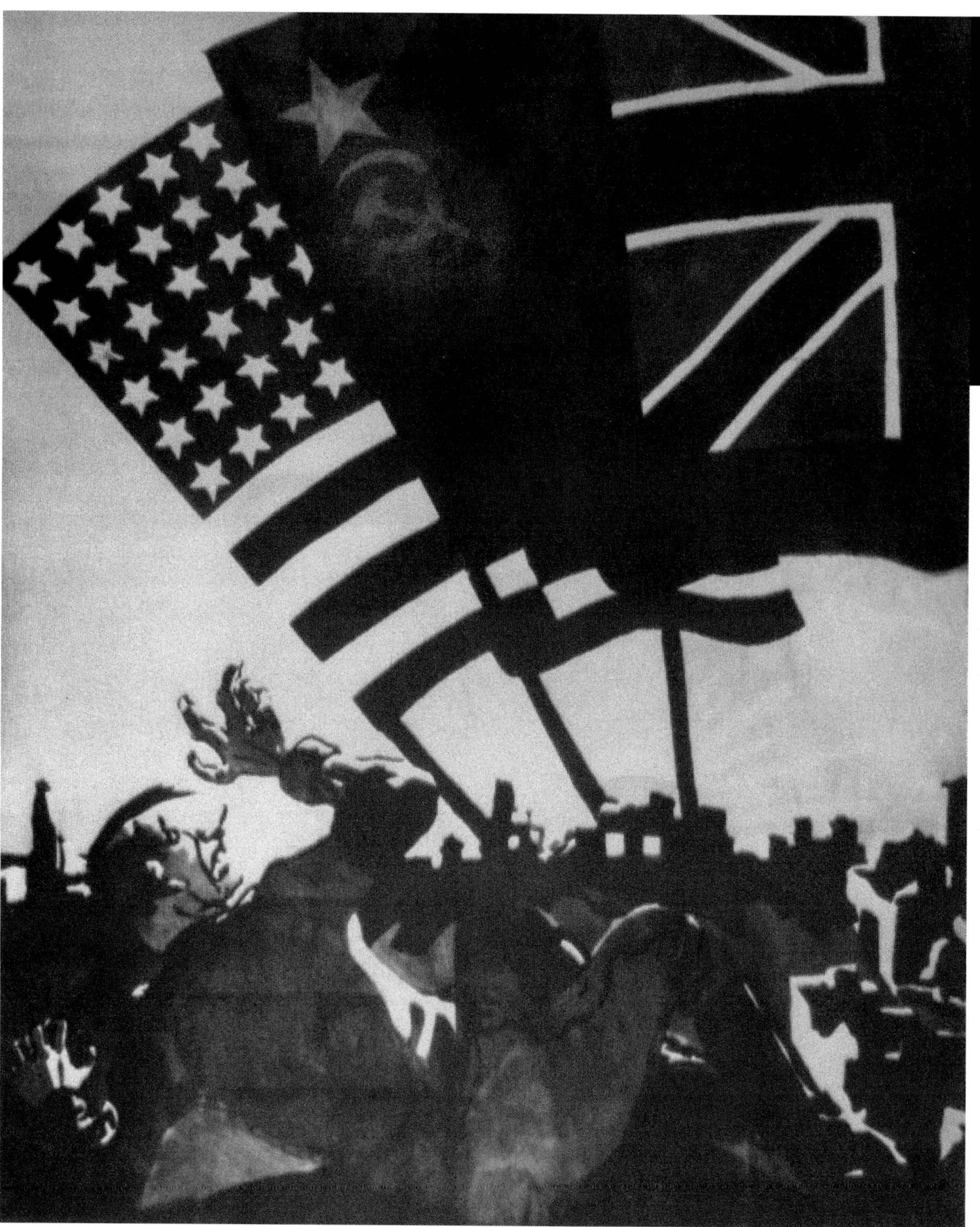

28th November 1943
TOPFOTO CODE: PD3001505
Moscow posters illustrate Tehran declaration.
Following the Declaration of Tehran, after
the conference between Mr. Churchill, Stalin
and President Roosevelt, the official Tass
agency of the U.S.S.R. has displayed large
posters in its windows, each illustrating a
phrase of the Declaration. PICTURE BY RADIO
FROM MOSCOW SHOWS: 'Our attack will be
ruthless and increasing'. The flags of Britain,
the U.S.S.R. and the United States tower over
a caricature of Hitler. One of the huge Tass
posters in Moscow.

1st May 1944
TOPFOTO CODE: PD7486011
Churchill Commonwealth PMs Conference
Cabinet Office Whitehall. Imperial Conference
of 1944. Meeting of the Commonwealth
Prime Ministers held in London, 1–16 May,
during the Second World War. Left to right:
General Jan Smuts of South Africa, William
Lyon Mackenzie King of Canada, British Prime
Minister Winston Churchill, John Curtin of
Australia, and Peter Fraser of New Zealand.
Consensus was reached to support the
Moscow Declaration, and agreement was
made regarding the respective roles in the
overall Allied war effort.

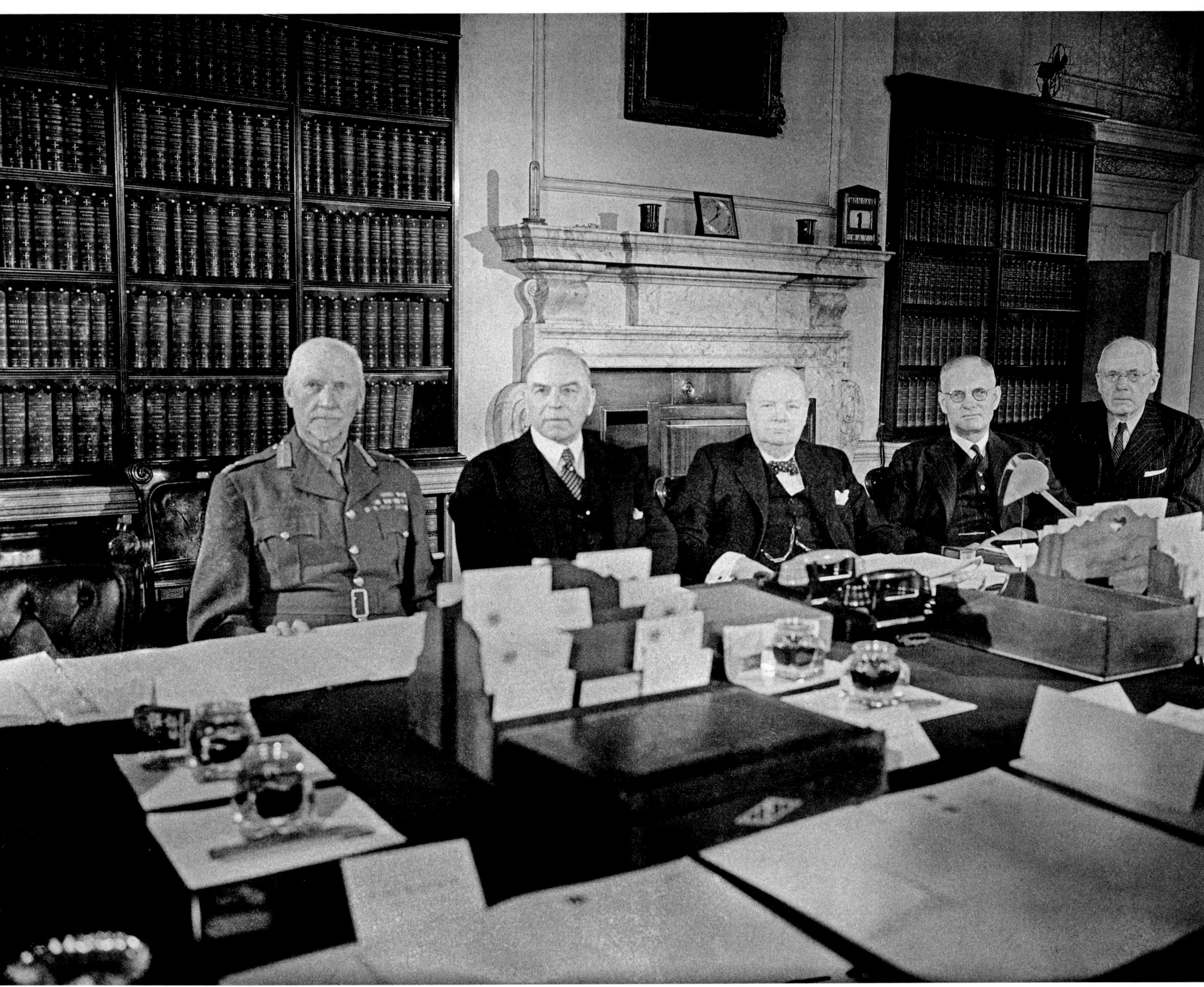

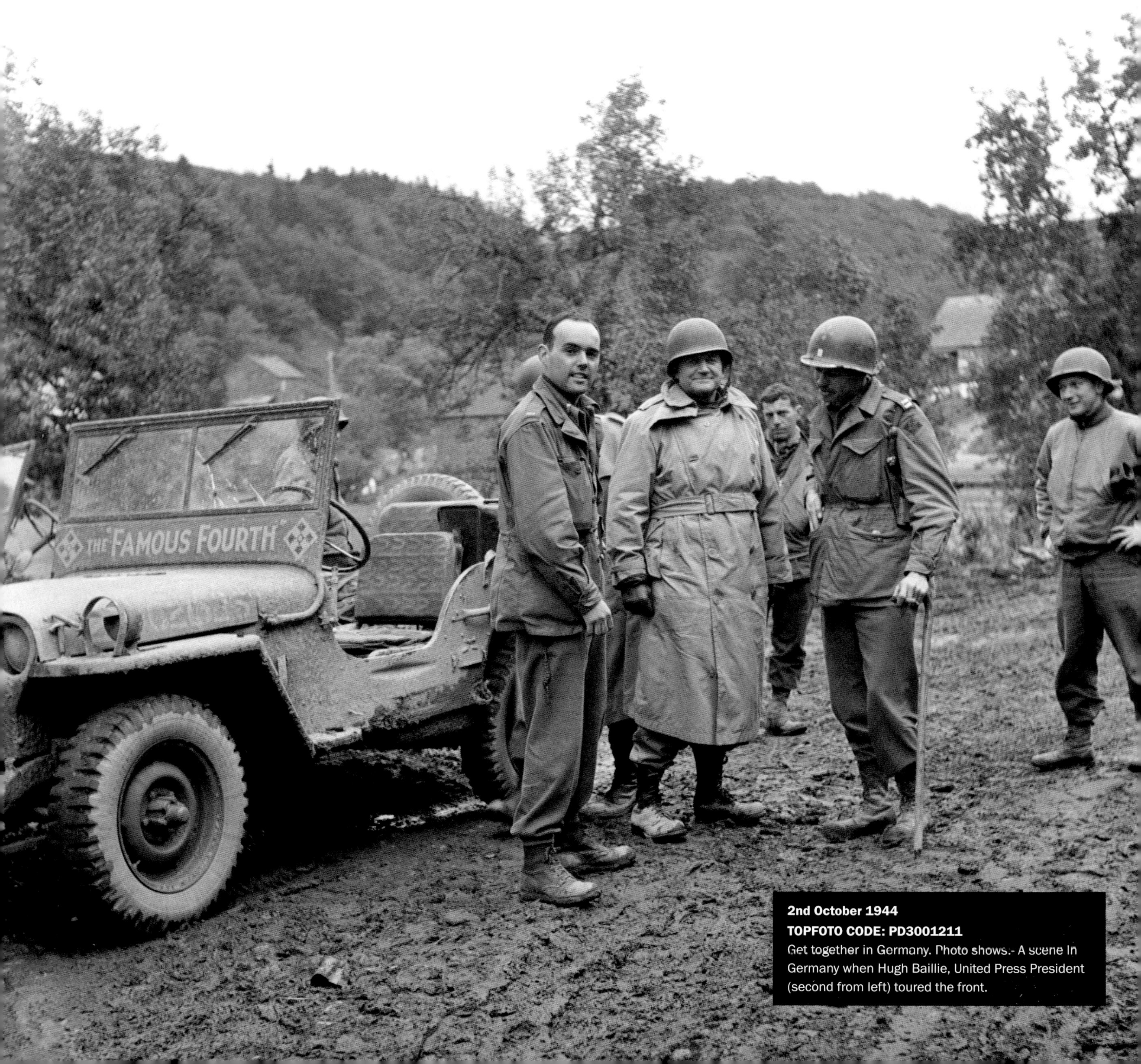

2nd October 1944
TOPFOTO CODE: PD3001211
Get together in Germany. Photo shows.- A scene In Germany when Hugh Baillie, United Press President (second from left) toured the front.

Hugh Baillie began as a journalist for United Press in 1915 at the age of 25. He eventually rose to become its president, a position he held from 1933 to 1955. His father had been a noted journalist himself, who had also been the literary secretary for Andrew Carnegie (industrialist, philanthropist and one of the richest men in US history).

While growing up, Hugh accompanied his father on numerous interviews and was introduced to many famous people such as Theodore Roosevelt, Mark Twain and Thomas Edison.

He developed his own style of in-depth reporting and in 1937 he interviewed both Hitler and Mussolini. He was a firm believer in the freedom of the press and the Fourth Estate as something separate from the interference of government. During part of the Second World War he was reporting from the front line and in 1944 he was wounded in Belgium. In 1953 he was honoured with a Distinguished Service in Journalism from the Missouri School of Journalism. After stepping down as president of United Press in 1955, he went on to publish an autobiography in 1959 called *High Tension*.

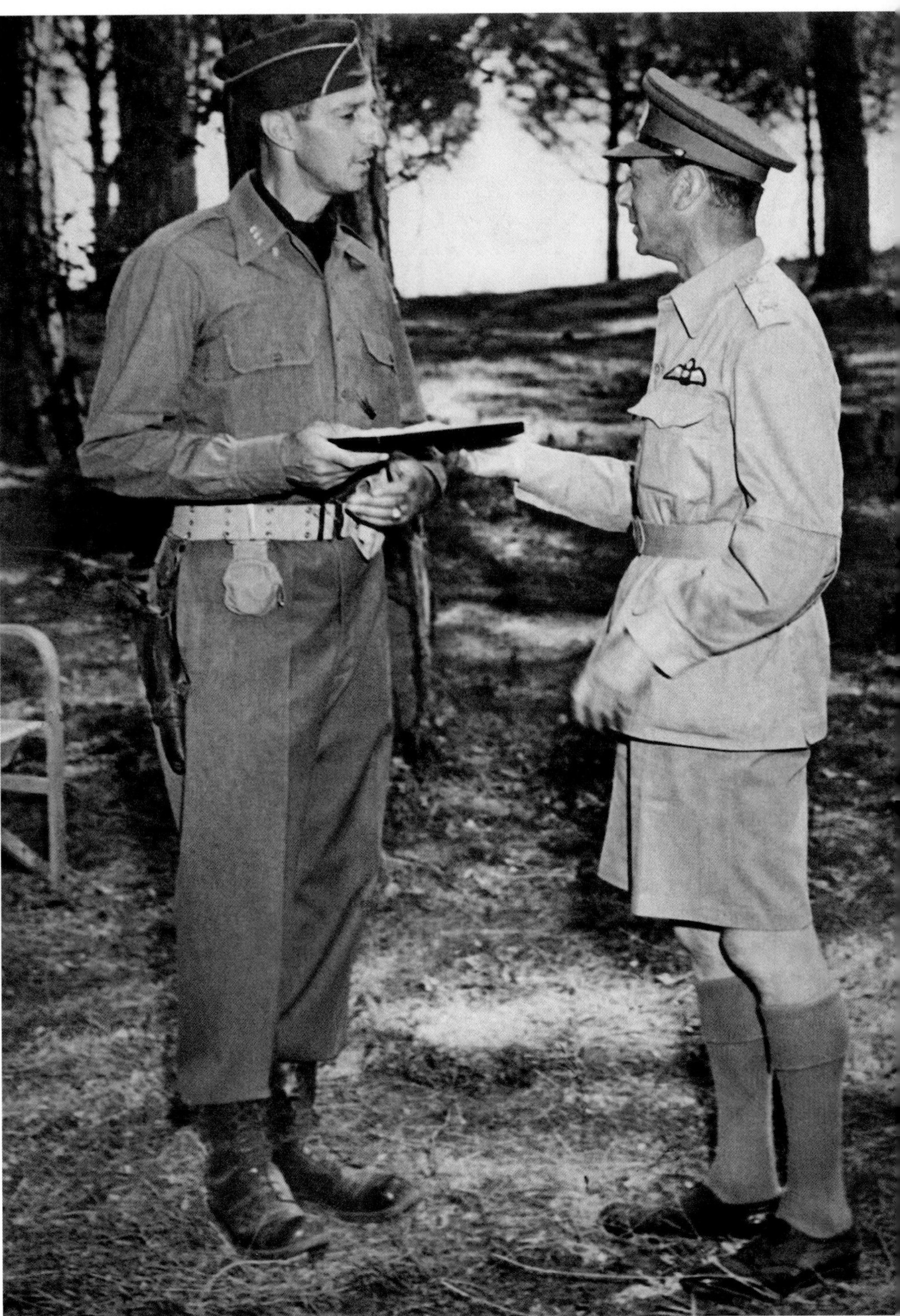

7th October 1944

TOPFOTO CODE: PD7485099

U.S. general honoured by British King. U.S. Lieutenant General Mark. W. Clark (left), Commander of the Allied Fifth Army in Italy, receives the Medal of the Honorary Knight of the British Empire from King George VI of England. King George arrived in Naples on July 23rd, 1944, from England for his fourth trip to a war zone and his first trip to Italy since 1930. He inspected the Italian fronts, reviewed units of all the Allied Armies and visited the Allied Mediterranean Fleet. By appropriate U.S. authority. RELEASED TO AFTERNOON PAPERS 1/9/44. (U.S Office of War Information picture/Library of Congress, Prints & Photographs Division, Farm Security Administration/Office of War Information Black-and-White Negatives)

Mark W. Clark was a participant in both the First World War, the Second World War and the Korean War, serving thirty-six years in the US Army. He was the Deputy Commander for Operation Torch (read more on page 119), and led the Fifth Army in the capture of Rome in 1944 – the first of the Axis capitals to fall. In 1945, he became the youngest ever US officer with the rank of four-star general, and therefore was probably also the last surviving Second World War four-star general when he died in 1984.

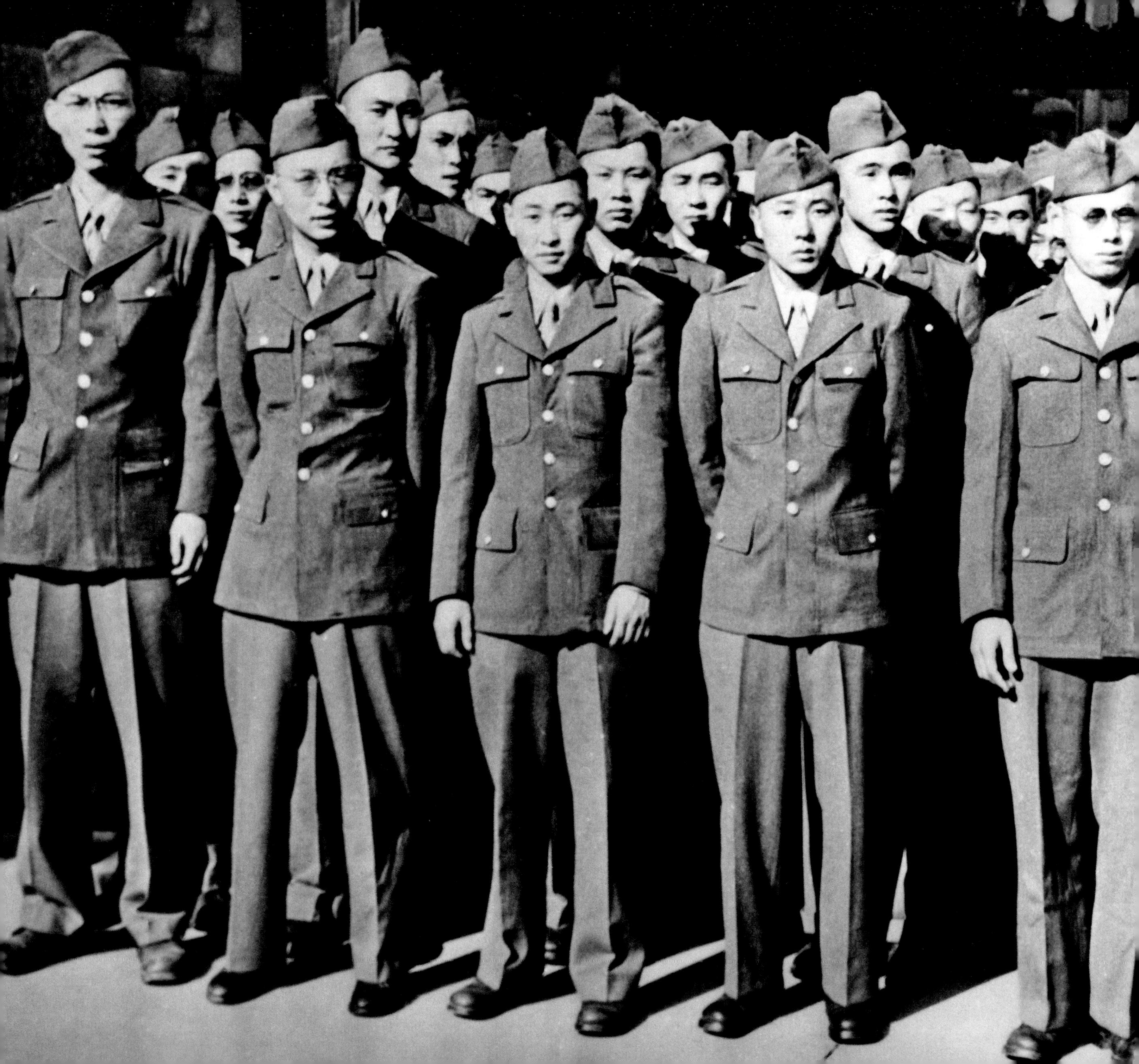

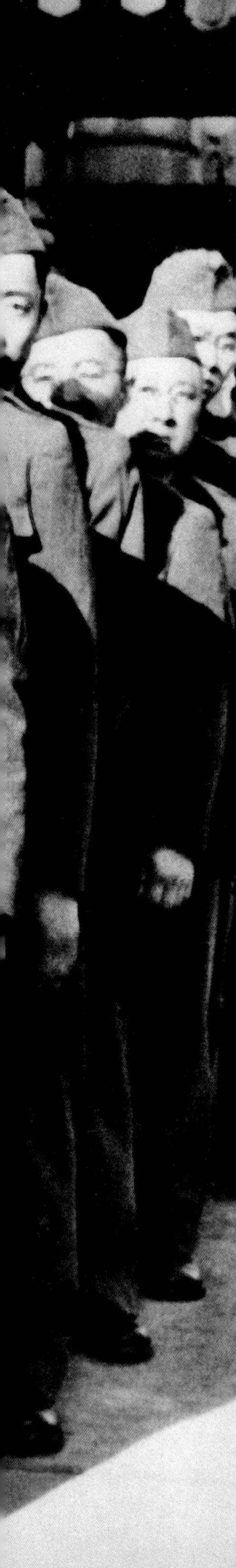

Following Imperial Japan's attack on Pearl Harbor on 7 December 1941, there was not much love lost for the US Japanese citizens. The next day, the United States declared war on Imperial Japan and formally entered the Second World War. It sparked an immediate widespread suspicion of, and discrimination towards, those of Japanese descent living in America.

Executive Order 9066 was signed by President Roosevelt on 19 February 1942, authorising the forced removal and internment of over 100,000 Japanese Americans, primarily from the West Coast. Unwarranted prejudice and racial bias meant that completely innocent, hard-working immigrants were moved to remote camps, where they would live under harsh conditions and with severe restrictions. As a result, many of them lost their homes, businesses and lives.

The 100th Infantry Battalion was activated on 12 June 1942 and consisted of 1,400 Japanese Americans, all second-generation US citizens, known as 'Nisei'. ('Nisei' means 'second generation'; 'Issei' means 'first generation', so born in Japan).

The unit was deployed in the Italian campaign in September 1943, under their own banner that read 'Remember Pearl Harbor'. It was a strong statement, clearly intended to leave no doubt as to where their allegiances lay. They fought with tenacity and bravery from Cassino to Rome and suffered such heavy casualties that they earned the nickname 'Purple Heart Battalion'. (The Purple Heart is the US military medal bestowed upon a serviceman wounded or killed in combat.) In mid-1944 they were merged with the 442nd Infantry Regiment and continued to fight in the south of France.

The 100th Infantry Battalion became recognised as the most highly decorated American unit (relative to its size and duration of service), and provided an opportunity for Japanese Americans to demonstrate their patriotism and loyalty to the US. It probably also played an important role in changing long and persistent negative perceptions within the US population, as well as creating a strong sense of identity and pride within the Japanese American community – even in post-war America.

In 1988, the Civil Liberties Act was signed by President Ronald Reagan, acknowledging and apologising for the injustices committed against Japanese Americans during the Second World War. Restitutions were made financially in the form of a $20,000 compensation, awarded to anyone who had survived the internment camps. Though it was an important admission on behalf of the US government, it still did not fully rectify the clear violations of American civil rights inflicted upon its citizens of Japanese origin.

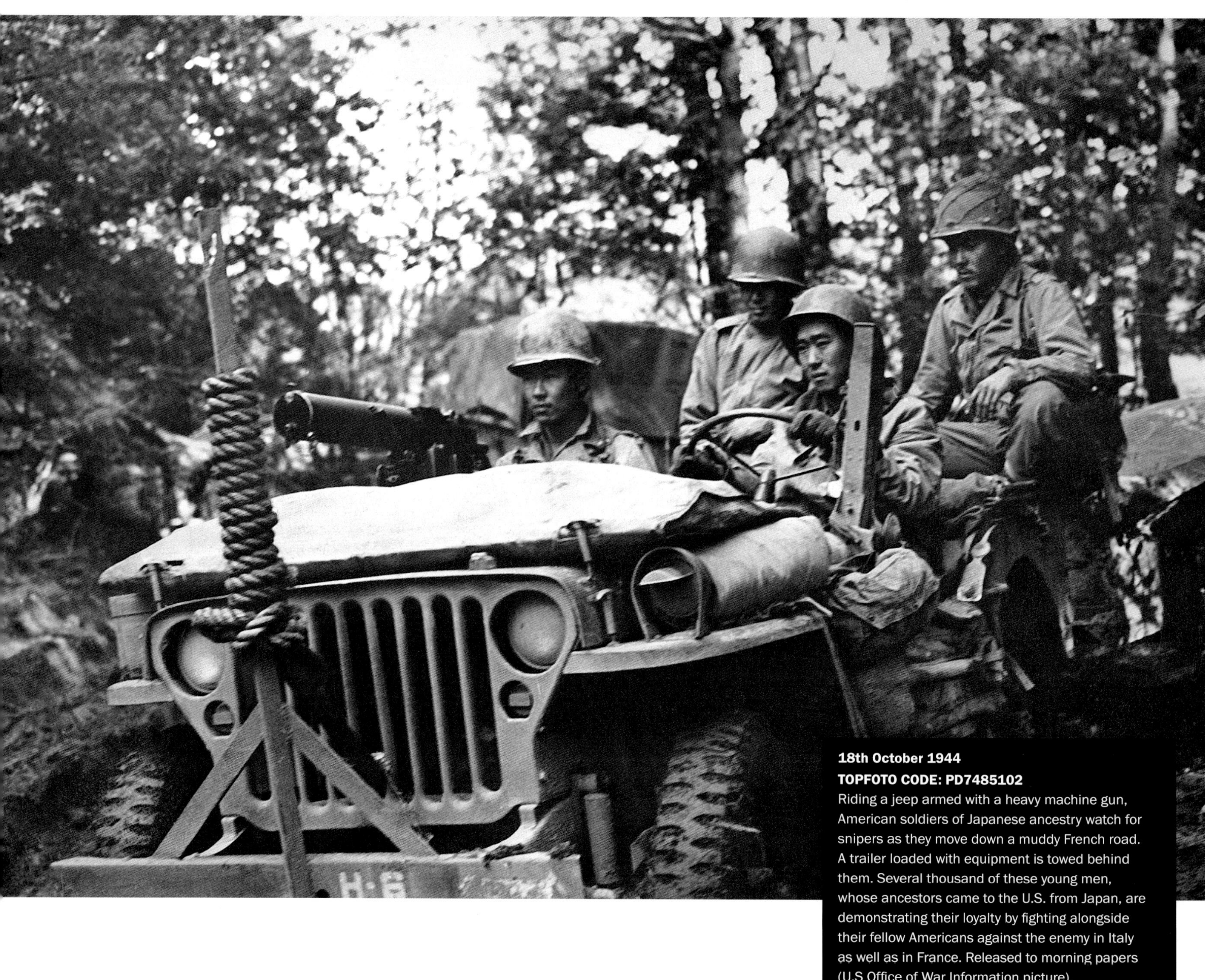

18th October 1944

TOPFOTO CODE: PD7485102

Riding a jeep armed with a heavy machine gun, American soldiers of Japanese ancestry watch for snipers as they move down a muddy French road. A trailer loaded with equipment is towed behind them. Several thousand of these young men, whose ancestors came to the U.S. from Japan, are demonstrating their loyalty by fighting alongside their fellow Americans against the enemy in Italy as well as in France. Released to morning papers (U.S Office of War Information picture).

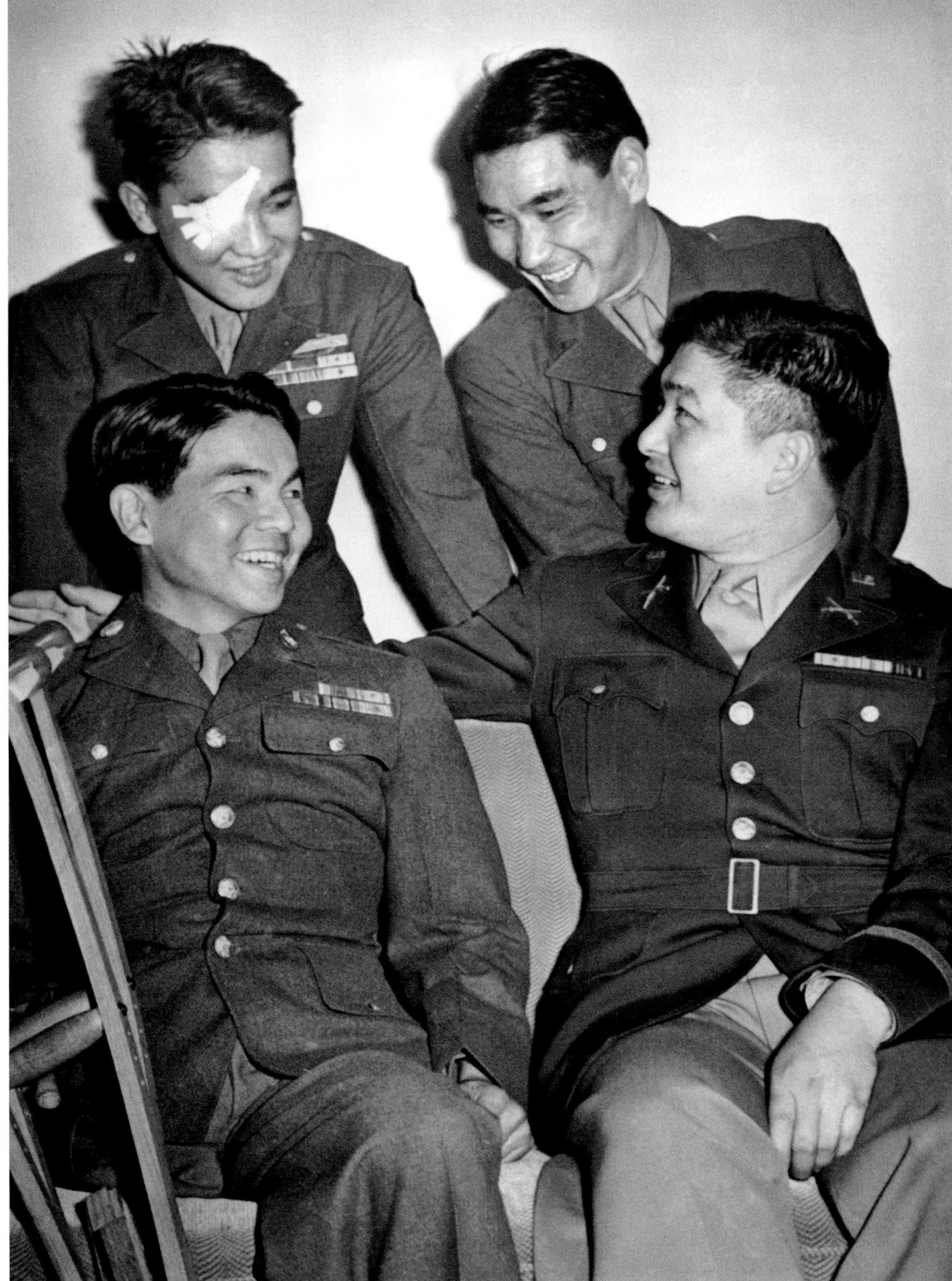

Peter II Karađorđević was the last of the Karađorđević dynasty to rule Yugoslavia. When he was just 11 years old his father was assassinated, leaving the throne empty. Due to his young age, Peter's cousin, Paul Karađorđević, became the temporary ruler in 1934, until Peter was to reach adulthood. Prince Regent Paul tried to navigate the contemporary complex European political situation, not diminished by Yugoslavia's geo-political position and the raw materials it possessed. Courted by both Germany and Britain, he attempted to reach the best possible solution for his country but ultimately succumbed to Hitler. On 25 March 1941, Yugoslavia signed the Tripartite Pact – the 'unholy' alliance between the three primary Axis powers of Nazi Germany, Italy and Japan.

Just two days later, a pro-Western coup d'état saw Prince Paul deposed and the 17-year-old Peter Karađorđević assumed his throne as Peter II of Yugoslavia. His reign lasted just eleven days as Germany, Italy and Hungary, unwilling to accept this turn of events, resolutely invaded Yugoslavia. Their Operation Retribution saw Belgrade viciously and ruthlessly bombed, leaving an estimated 3,000–4,000 civilians dead and both military and non-military targets ground into the dirt. Among these targets was the Yugoslavian National Library, with hundreds of thousands of books turned into dust.

King Peter escaped to London, by way of Greece, Palestine and Egypt, and established a government in exile in June 1941. In 1942, King Peter met Princess Alexandra of Greece and Denmark in a London club. The press used the image of the two royal lovers' war-torn romance, and their subsequent quick engagement, for front-page propaganda. This caused a major stir on the Yugoslavian home front. As a leader of a nation in a state of emergency, the people believed his engagement was breaking with traditions and that he was abandoning his country while living it up in London. Peter and Alexandra pursued the relationship undeterred, and eventually married in March 1944.

His choice of 'love over country' had a devastating effect on his credibility among his subjects, and in November 1945 King Peter was officially deposed and Yugoslavia declared a republic. A pro-communist leadership took over, with Josip Broz, better known as Tito, in charge.

Peter went off to live in the United States, initially a curiosity for the Americans, although the novelty quickly wore off. Perceived by many as a helpless, hopeless man, who lacked charisma and vigour, he became a sad textbook symbol of the bygone era of monarchies and monarchs. He was a man desperately clinging on to the absurd hope of winning back his long-lost country – a country that no longer wanted him. With a problematic relationship with his wife and son, his fortunes squandered and, suffering from depression and issues with alcohol, he eventually died from a liver disease at the young age of 47.

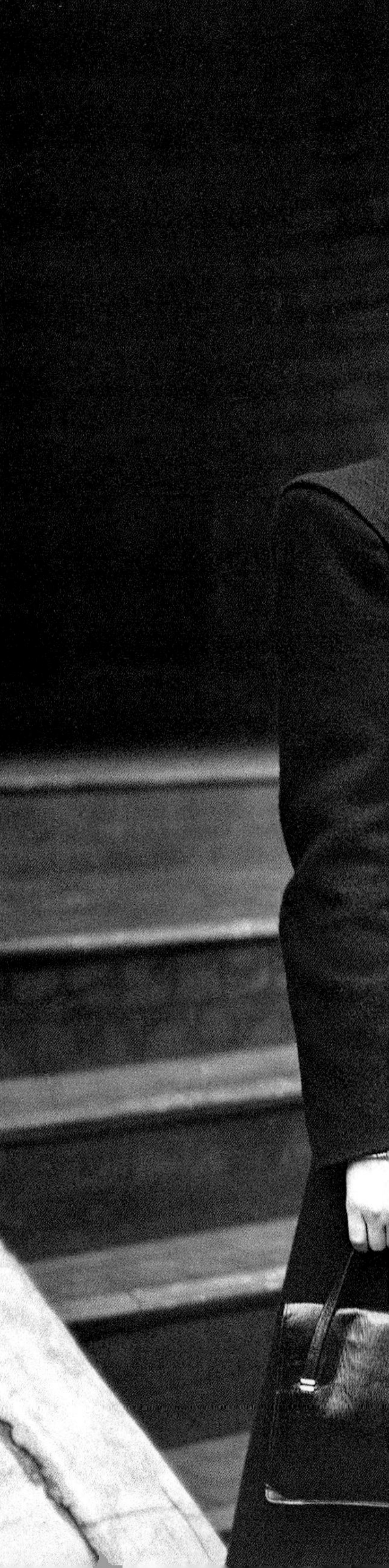

1st December 1944
TOPFOTO CODE: PD7486010
King Peter and Queen Alexandra of Yugoslavia leaving the Serbian Orthodox Church, Lennox Gardens, West London, after attending the Yugoslav National Day service.

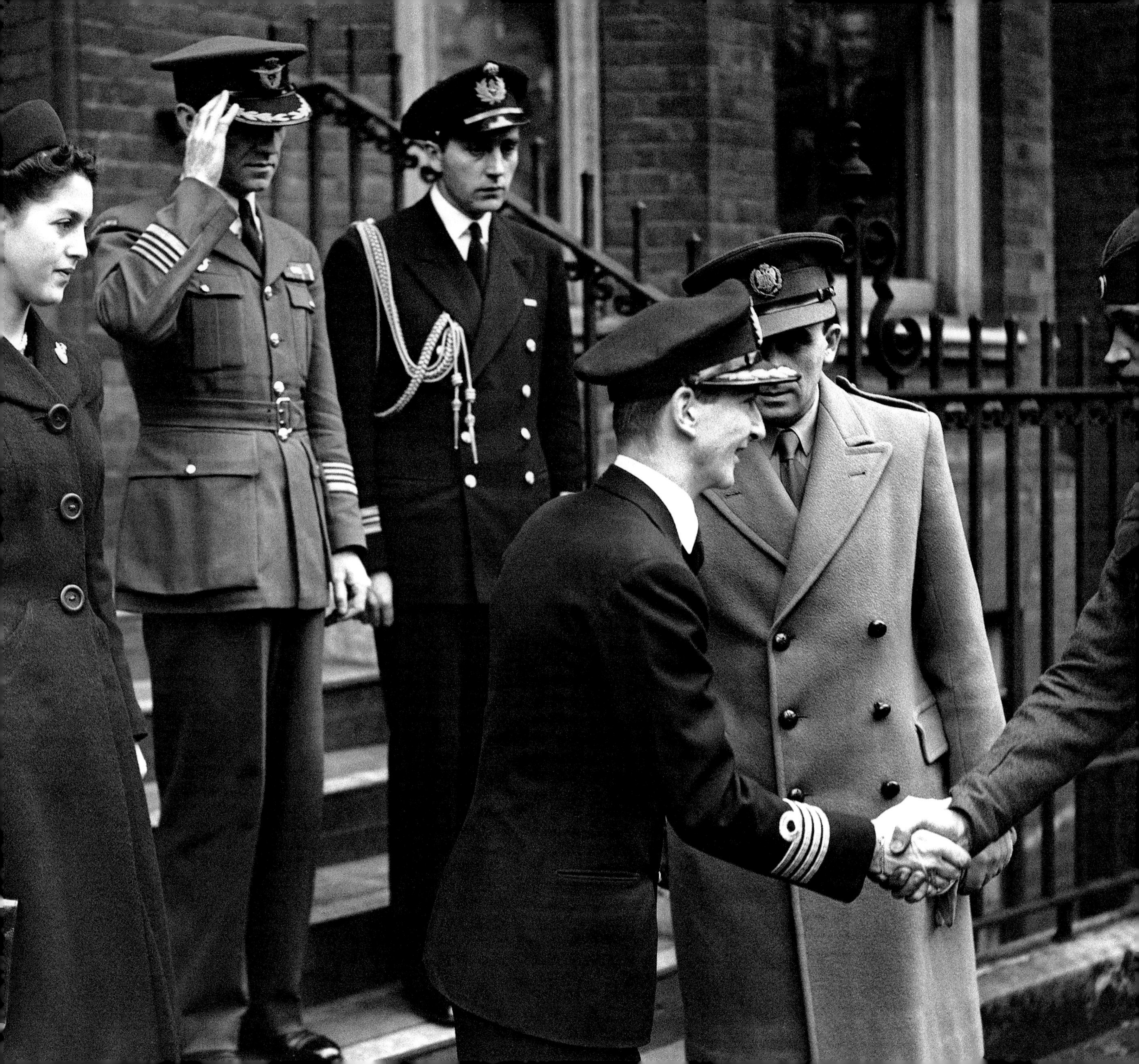

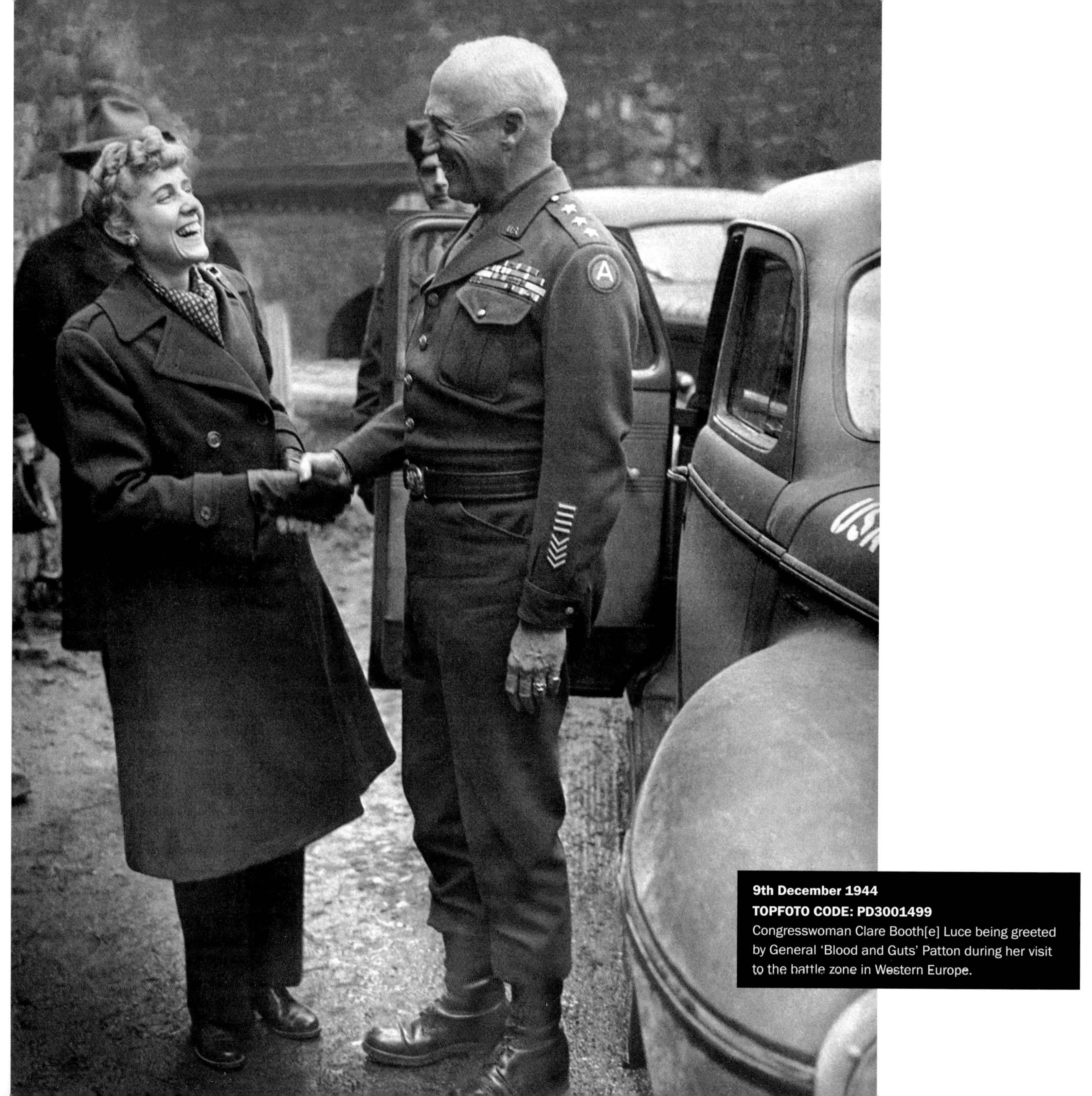

9th December 1944
TOPFOTO CODE: PD3001499
Congresswoman Clare Booth[e] Luce being greeted
by General 'Blood and Guts' Patton during her visit
to the battle zone in Western Europe.

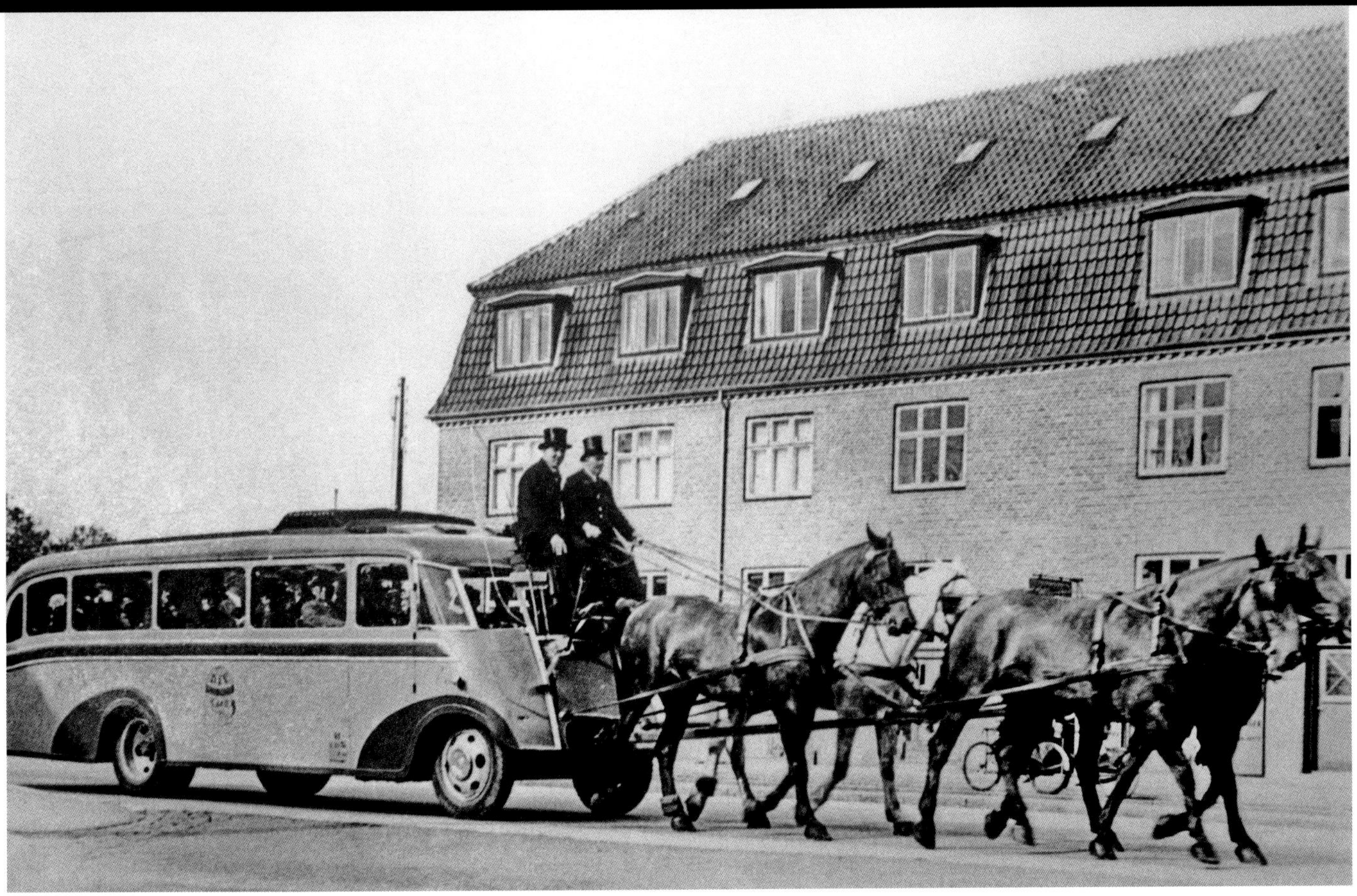

Following the quick surrender by the Danish armed forces on 9 April 1940, a fairly unique agreement came into place. With a policy of co-operation with the Germans, the Danish government and its monarchy were allowed relative sovereignty, and life carried on somewhat as before – at least for the first few years. Danish underground resistance, however, steadily grew over time, in spite of the government's discouragement.

By 1943 things really began to change. Sabotage intensified and the Danish general population became increasingly resistant to Nazi control. In August 1943, a revolt resulted in the resignation of the government and the Germans declared martial law. A much harsher use of force was instilled across the board.

Just two months later, orders came to initiate the implementation of Himmler's Final Solution and start the deportation of the Danish Jews. However, a remarkable incident took place. A tip came, allegedly from the German civilian administrator of Denmark, SS-Obergruppenführer Werner Best, to none other than his Jewish tailor. The Danish resistance and the Danish civil population rallied the Danish Jews and in one night managed to assist in the escape of over 7,000 to nearby neutral Sweden. This was nearly the entire Danish Jewish population.

Danish resistance and sabotage continued to increase until Denmark was finally liberated by British forces on 5 May 1945.

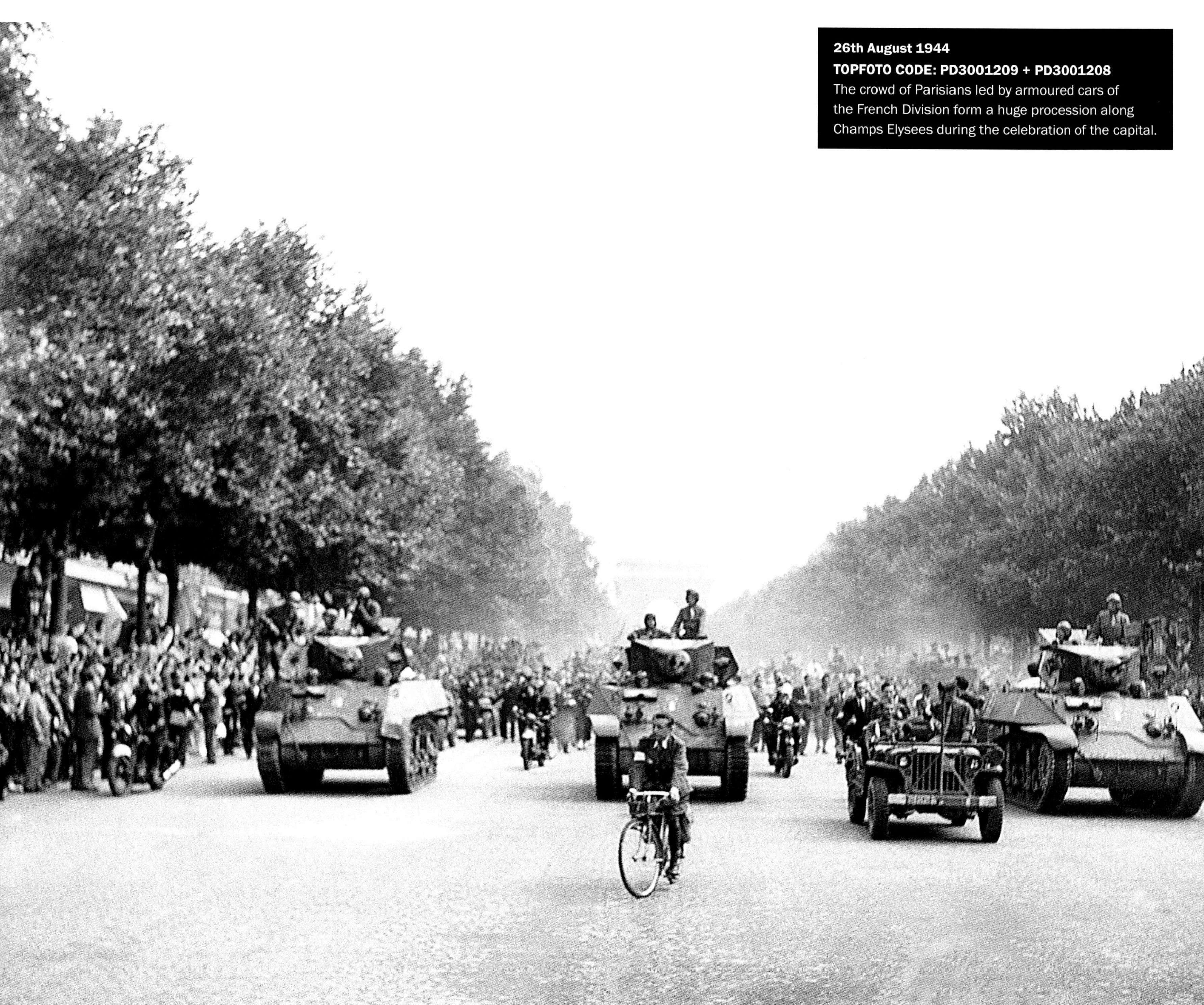
26th August 1944
TOPFOTO CODE: PD3001209 + PD3001208
The crowd of Parisians led by armoured cars of
the French Division form a huge procession along
Champs Elysees during the celebration of the capital.

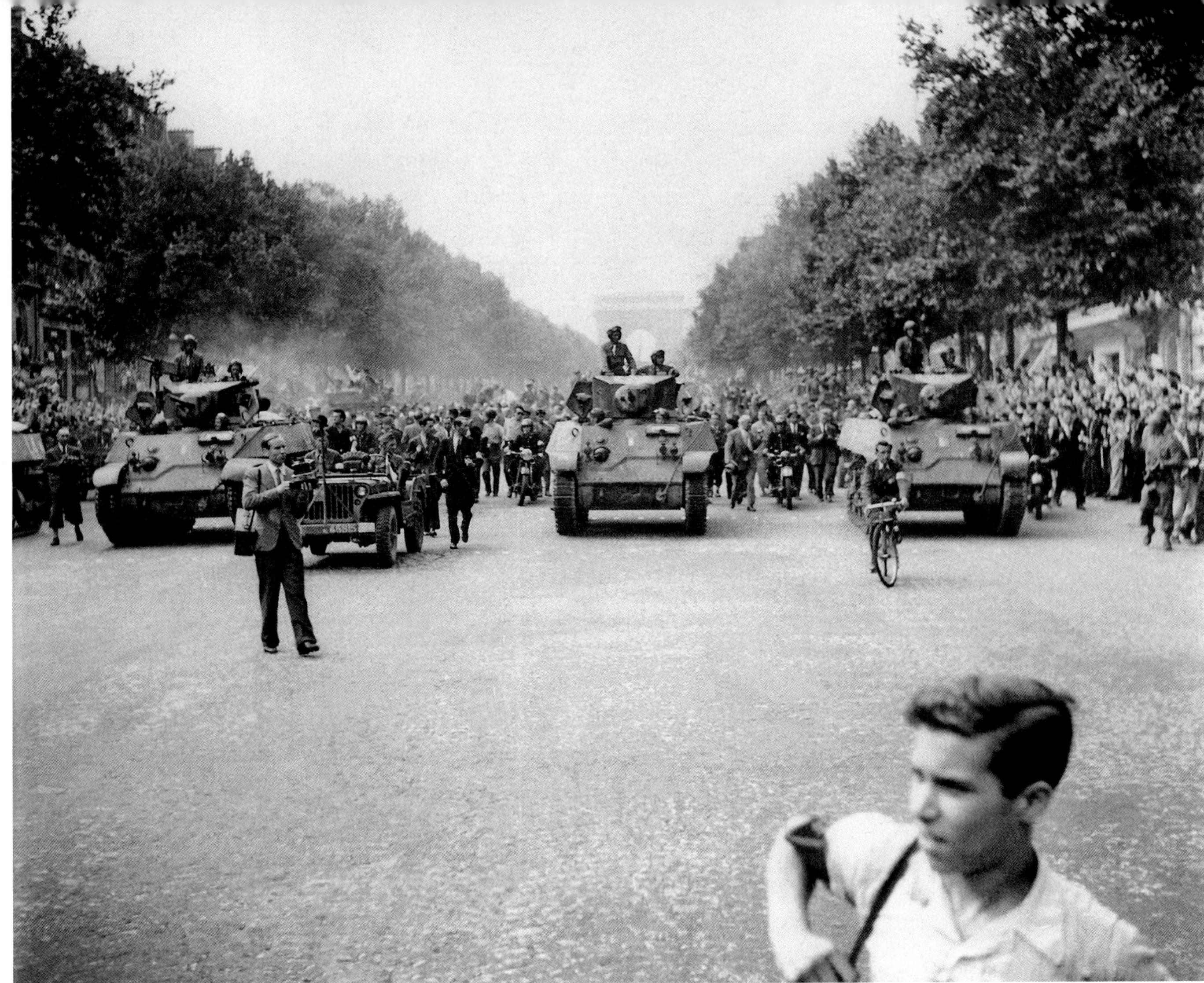

Liberation of Paris, 26 August 1944

In 1940, Nazi Germany invaded France and quickly defeated the French army. The country was divided into occupied and unoccupied zones, with the northern part of France, including Paris, falling under German control. For four long years the 'city of light' was in the hands of Nazi Germany until 26 August 1944, when it was finally surrendered. The liberation was a collaboration between the Allied forces and the French Forces of the Interior (FFI, the French Resistance).

The German commander of Paris, Dietrich Hugo Hermann von Choltitz, had reportedly been under strict orders by Adolf Hitler to defend Paris at all costs, or leave it in ruins. According to sources, Choltitz had various motivations to disobey the Führer. He was aware that he had little chance in successfully repelling the attack, he had a deep respect for the history of Paris and its architecture, and, maybe more importantly, he was all too aware that Hitler was no longer making rational decisions. He chose instead to hand over Paris undamaged. In 1950 he published a book titled *Is Paris Burning?*, in which he stated that he defied his orders mainly because he believed Hitler was mentally ill. He died in 1966 and was hailed as 'the Saviour of Paris', and the main reason why Paris is still standing today.

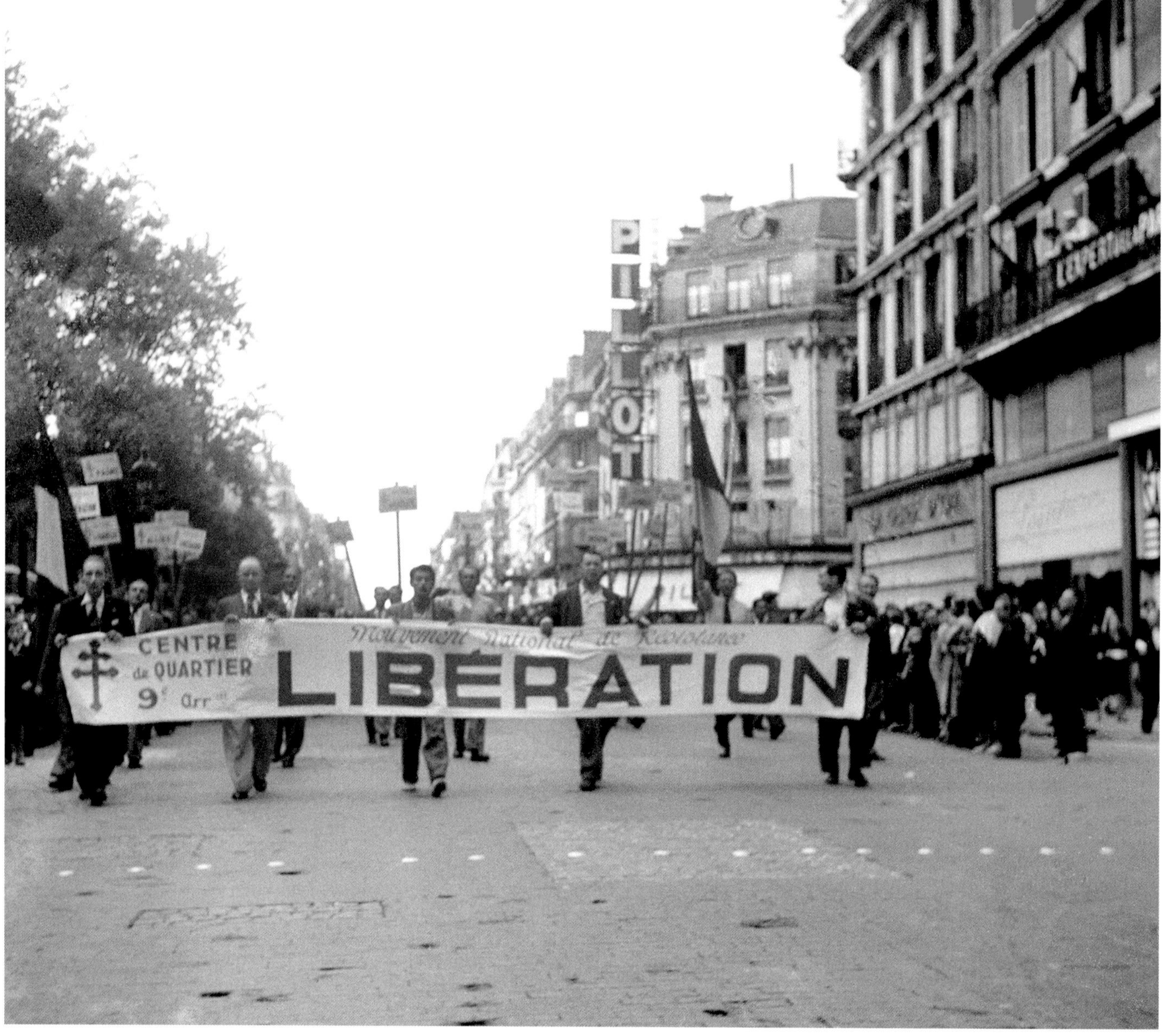

26th August 1944
TOPFOTO CODE:
PD3001353
Men of the Maquis march down a Paris street carrying before them a huge banner proclaiming the city's liberation.

When Germany occupied France in 1940, an 'independent' French government known as Vichy France was established. The Men of the Maquis were the angry French youths' opposition to this puppet government that openly collaborated with the Germans. Specifically it was the rebellion against a 'compulsory work service' (Service du Travail Obligatoire, STO), formally created by the Vichy government, but abused by the Germans to bolster their own depleting workforce. It was the systematic deportation of men aged 21 to 35, destined to essentially become slaves. The Nazis promised that for every three French workers they were given, they would free one French POW. On 1 March 1943 a French paper published the headline, 'French Youth replies: Go To Hell!'

Many of these young men chose to become Maquisards instead, and worked for the French Resistance, later given the name FFI (French Forces of the Interior). They hid in the mountains or the hills, hence the word Maquis ('*Prende le Maquis*', 'to go into the bush'). By June 1944, they had an estimated 100,000 members. Poorly armed but relatively highly skilled, they were instrumental in the liberation of Paris.

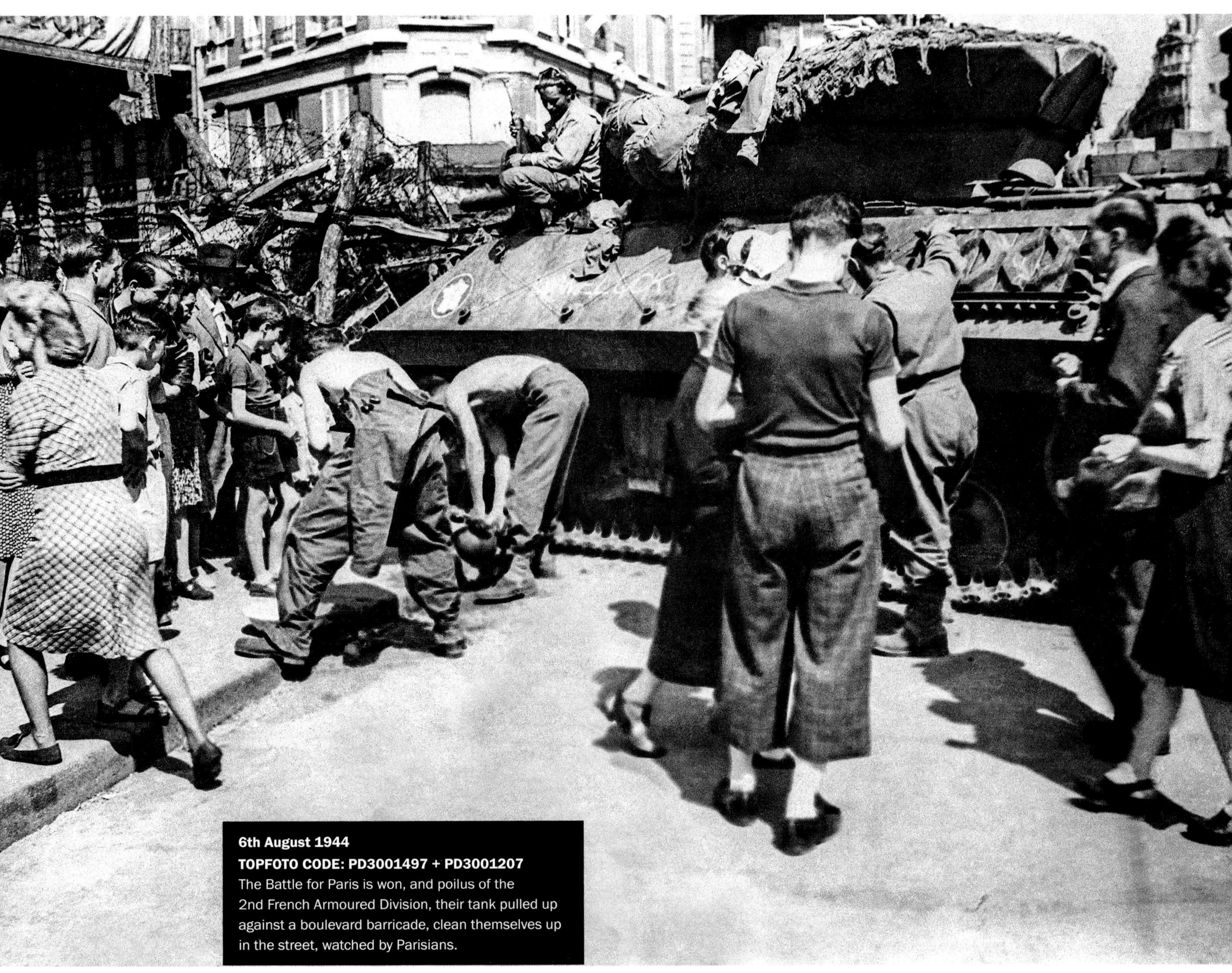

6th August 1944

TOPFOTO CODE: PD3001497 + PD3001207

The Battle for Paris is won, and poilus of the
2nd French Armoured Division, their tank pulled up
against a boulevard barricade, clean themselves up
in the street, watched by Parisians.

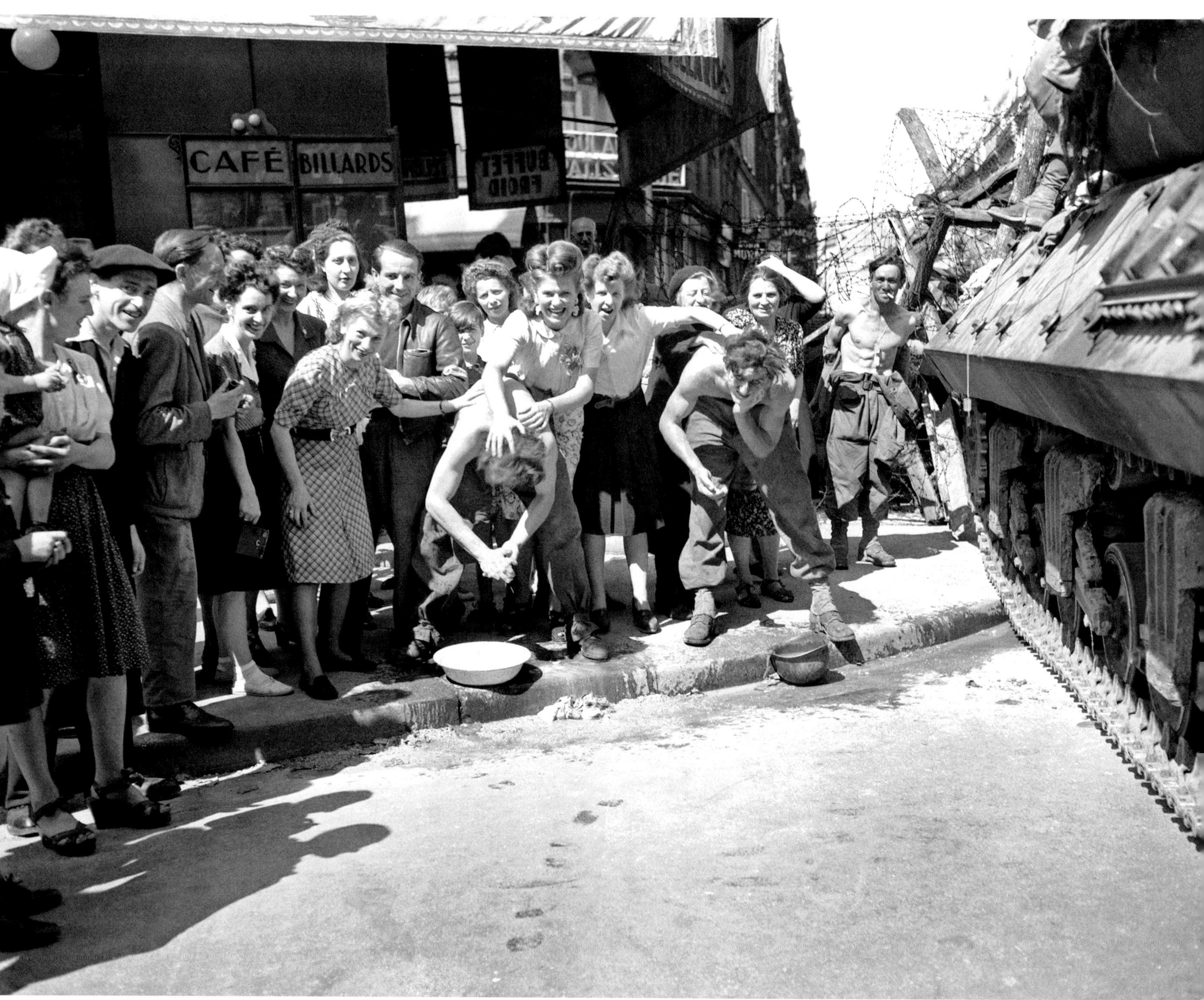

CAFÉ BILLARDS
BUFFET FROID

The Hidden Art Treasures of Holland

Deep under Mount Saint Peter in the Netherlands lies Saint Peter's caves, also known as the Maastricht Underground; they date back over a thousand years. During the Second World War, an estimated 45,000 individuals were hidden in this underground. Along with them were thirty tanks (to be deployed at the time of liberation), various armaments, and about 800 of the country's most priceless pieces of art and artefacts. These represented almost the entire national art treasures of the Netherlands by artists such as Rembrandt, van Gogh and Monet. The caves were in themselves a work of art that had already served as a hideaway since the sixteenth century, boasting 330 artworks carved and painted in the tunnels. Today's figures show that an estimated 650,000 paintings were stolen by the Germans across Europe from 1933 to 1945, which is why it was imperative to hide these invaluable pieces from the Nazi invaders.

Originally, the caves were dug by the Romans to mine marl (a type of limestone) for buildings and construction. Located some 30m underground, they now house more than 60km of intricate tunnel systems and approximately 8,000 passages. Between the sixteenth and eighteenth century, Maastricht was continuously invaded by first the French and then the Spanish, due to its important strategic location. Large fortifications were built on the hill to defend the town, but in times of crisis the caves continuously provided shelter for the local civilian population.

In the eighteenth century, the caves were further extended to house up to 25,000 refugees. A wealth of graffiti from this time still survives. In the 1880s, a local order of Jesuits started occupying a section of the caves, now referred to as Jezuietenberg (Jesuit Caves). As a distraction, and as a recreation from their hard work, the order let the monks have Wednesdays off to pursue artistic practices.

They slowly converted the passageways into workshops and galleries with hundreds of artworks. They chiselled, carved and painted the walls in these dreamlike catacombs, and left some of the most wondrous and breathtaking art behind. Although most of the works were of Christian origin, curiously and uncommonly for a religious Catholic order, they recreated many works taken from other religions too. In an almost idolatrous admiration, statues of Egyptian pharaohs, Buddhas and Hindu deities were created, along with obscure and phantasmagorical sculptures.

The beginning of the Second World War, sadly, led to the expulsion of the monks by the invading forces. In May 1940, the Germans took Holland by surprise, during the Battle of Maastricht. Yet again, the city's strategic position made it one of the first targets for occupation by invaders. Maastricht would remain occupied until the Allied forces finally liberated it on 14 September 1944. During this time of occupation, the population of Maastricht once more found shelter and safety in the depths. They hid their most prized and important art within this treasure vault that, over time, had become a national treasure itself.

The Nazis hungered for art, though not all art was equal, nor considered art to them. In his youth, Hitler had wanted to be an artist but failed twice to be accepted into the Academy of Fine Arts in Vienna due to his 'unsatisfactory' drawing skills. He continued to paint, but it came to an end in 1914 when he was picked up by the police, having avoided registration for the military draft. He also failed his Austrian military fitness exam, but nevertheless enlisted voluntarily in the German (not the Austrian) army at the outbreak of the First World War. Subsequently, during his rise to power, Hitler railed against 'degenerate' and 'deviant' art. He believed non-representational and experimental artworks to be products of mere 'Jews and Bolsheviks', in stark opposition to the stereotypically 'Aryan' and more conventionally 'beautiful' art.

Art was a powerful tool in Nazi rhetoric. A firm position was taken that any true German would immediately be able to tell the difference between what was 'right and wrong'. Visual symbolism and storytelling were at the core of the conveyance of Nazism, and it became vitally important to not just destroy the opposition, but to also completely erase the traces of its existence. By opening the Entartete Kunst Exhibition (Degenerate Art Exhibition) at almost the same time as the Große Deutsche Kunstausstellung (Great German Art Exhibition), Hitler made it quite clear what was classed as 'acceptable' art and what was 'dangerous and impure iconography' that 'threatened the very fabric of the Aryan nation' and fuelled its cultural disintegration.

The Degenerate Art Exhibition was cleverly staged and marketed as a 'freak show'. It gave the German population a 'last chance' to publicly mock, scorn and reduce previously highly regarded artworks to simplified, decadent and perverted objects of ridicule before their imminent destruction. There would be no room for reinterpretation.

Slogans were painted on the walls in between the art to enhance the shock and outrage the viewer should be left feeling. Among these slogans were sentences such as 'Nature as seen by Sick Minds', 'Deliberate Sabotage of National Defence' and 'Revelation of the Jewish Racial Soul'. More than 2 million people attended. Later, historians argued that the majority of the visitors were most likely forced to attend.

Paradoxically, many within the highest echelons of the Nazi Party strongly disagreed with Hitler's ideas of 'degenerate art'. Among them were powerful men such as Reichsmarshall Hermann Göring (the second-highest-ranking Nazi) and Propaganda Minister Dr Joseph Goebbels. They eventually, officially, adhered to the party line.

Goebbels was so eager to redeem himself that he became the one to conceive the idea of the Entartete Kunst Exhibition, although many of the paintings that were mocked had strangely first been selected by him for the original Great German Art Exhibition.

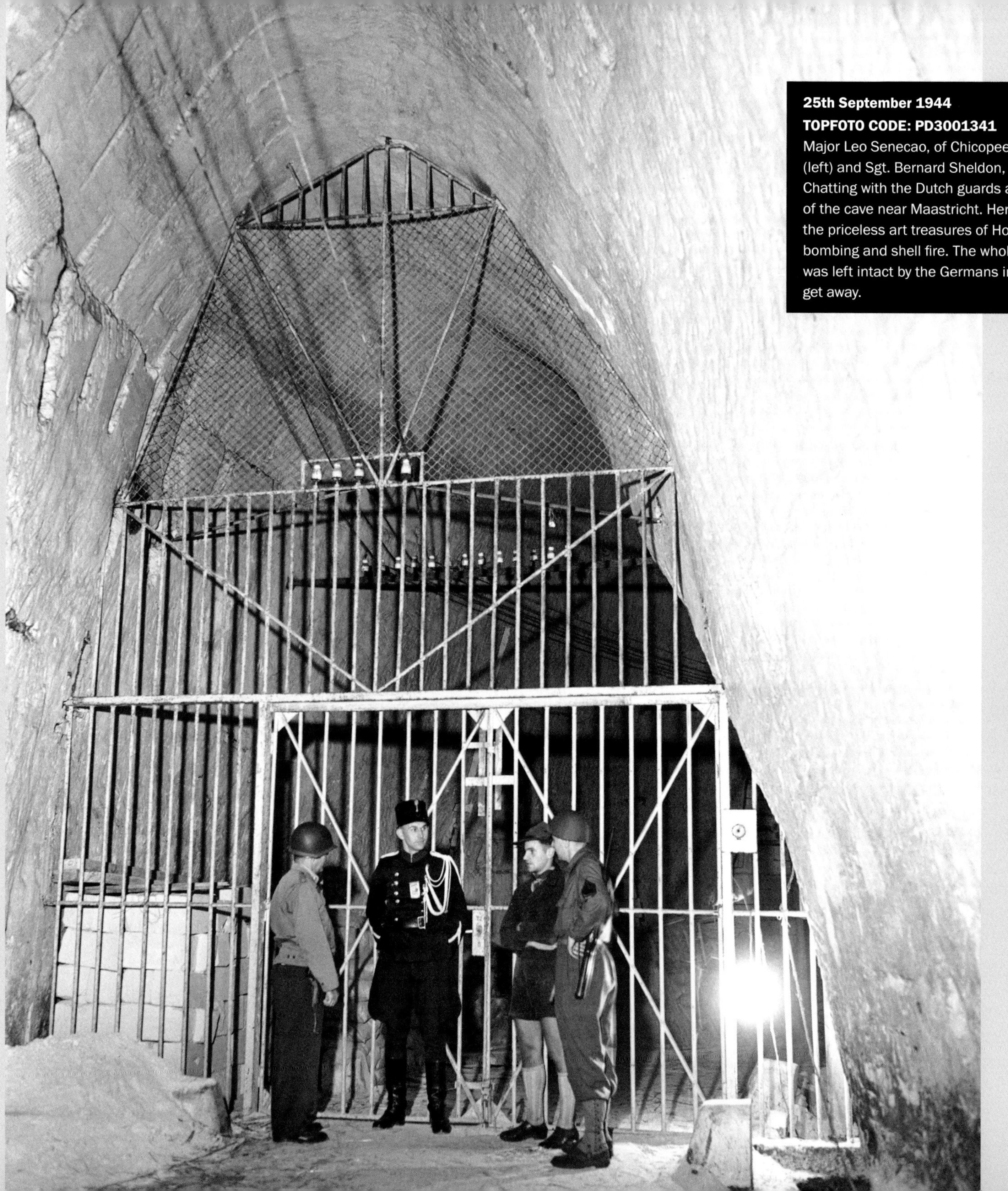

25th September 1944
TOPFOTO CODE: PD3001341
Major Leo Senecao, of Chicopee, Massachusetts:
(left) and Sgt. Bernard Sheldon, of New York, N.Y.:
Chatting with the Dutch guards at the steel gates
of the cave near Maastricht. Here were stored all
the priceless art treasures of Holland, safe from
bombing and shell fire. The whole treasure house
was left intact by the Germans in their hurry to
get away.

In only two weeks, more than 5,000 works were seized, and in total over 16,000 pieces were put on display, derided and, ultimately, burned in the same way the Nazis had done with much of the opposing literature in Germany. According to Hitler's beliefs, all the art, literature, music and philosophies of the decadent Weimar period were to be permanently erased and replaced by traditional ideals.

Hitler also had a clear vision for what was to happen with all the esteemed 'Aryan' art. He had long had a plan of what was eventually to be the Führer Museum. All the art treasures that were bought, appropriated or simply stolen were to become the foundation of this great bastion of culture in his home town of Linz. Fortunately, this never happened and the museum, intended to be finished in 1950, was never built.

For the people of Maastricht, it had, therefore, been imperative to hide their art, to stop the Germans from stealing or destroying their heritage. In recent years, some paintings have resurfaced that were purportedly destroyed during the war, but were actually 'acquired' by certain contemporary, unscrupulous art dealers.

Some will have seen the 2014 film *The Monuments Men*, a movie loosely based on the book *The Monuments Men: Allied Heroes, Nazi Thieves and the Greatest Treasure Hunt in History* by Robert M. Edsel. His book was based on a true initiative, started by the Allied leaders in 1943. By then, it was widely known that the Germans were systematically looting art.

Allied leaders created the MFAA, an acronym for Monuments, Fine Arts and Archives Program. Its task was to protect and safeguard cultural property and historic buildings along with finding, identifying and later returning works of art the Nazis had stolen during the war. Among the works in the caves were Rembrandt's 'The Night Watch' and 'Titus at his Desk', as well as his rendition of 'Saul and David'. There was van Gogh's 'Poplars Near Nuenen', several Claude Monet paintings, 'The Lamentation of Christ' by Rogier van der Weyden, and 'The Wayfarer' by Hieronymus Bosch.

'The Night Watch' was placed on a roll that had to be turned to prevent damage, due to the extreme humidity in the caves. At 12 × 14ft, it is the largest and most famous of Rembrandt's works. Interestingly, the Jesuits, some sixty years prior to 1944, had copied several of Rembrandt's works on to the walls. As fate would have it, decades later the master's original works would occupy the very same space.

Hidden in the vault was also one of Han van Meegeren's most successful forgeries ever: 'Supper at Emmaus' by Caravaggio. Meegeren was considered to be arguably the greatest art forger of the twentieth century. He was famously arrested and put on trial in 1945 for collaborating with the enemy, having traded a supposed original Vermeer painting with none other than Luftwaffe commander Hermann Göring for a total of 200 original Dutch paintings. When faced with prison, van Meegeren came clean and purportedly exclaimed the painting in Göring's hands was not a Vermeer, but a van Meegeren. Although he was undisputedly a criminal, Meegeren was eventually hailed as a national hero rather than a Nazi collaborator for having ingeniously saved the precious paintings that Göring himself had stolen earlier in the war.

Additionally, while serving as a refuge for civilians and treasures, the caves were also a hiding place for downed Allied pilots. The many passageways, previously extended to the Belgian side of the border, now served as part of an elaborate escape route out of Holland. Once on the other side, in Belgium, the airmen would be provided with new papers and clothing and sent on from there.

The Caves of Maastricht were never on the official list of art repositories by the MFAA, as this was not a cache of stolen goods made by the Germans but rather a treasure vault, hidden from the Nazis. So while the individuals responsible for the hiding, safeguarding and preservation of these pieces were never really technically 'Monuments Men', their work was nevertheless invaluable. These men preserved the very foundation of modern humankind by protecting these paintings. For what is art, but the most fragile, pure and elevated expression of human emotion and capability? The cradle for the advanced ability to freely – and without inhibition or repercussion – observe, imagine and create. The very essence of what was in danger of disappearing, had the outcome of the war been different.

As a sad footnote, the caves were excavated again after the Second World War and were extended to more than 230km and over 20,000 corridors. Large parts of the caves were regrettably demolished during this time. Excavations ceased in 2006 and luckily since then Dutch Heritage has taken over the site and now provides guided tours to tourists to show off this remarkable place.

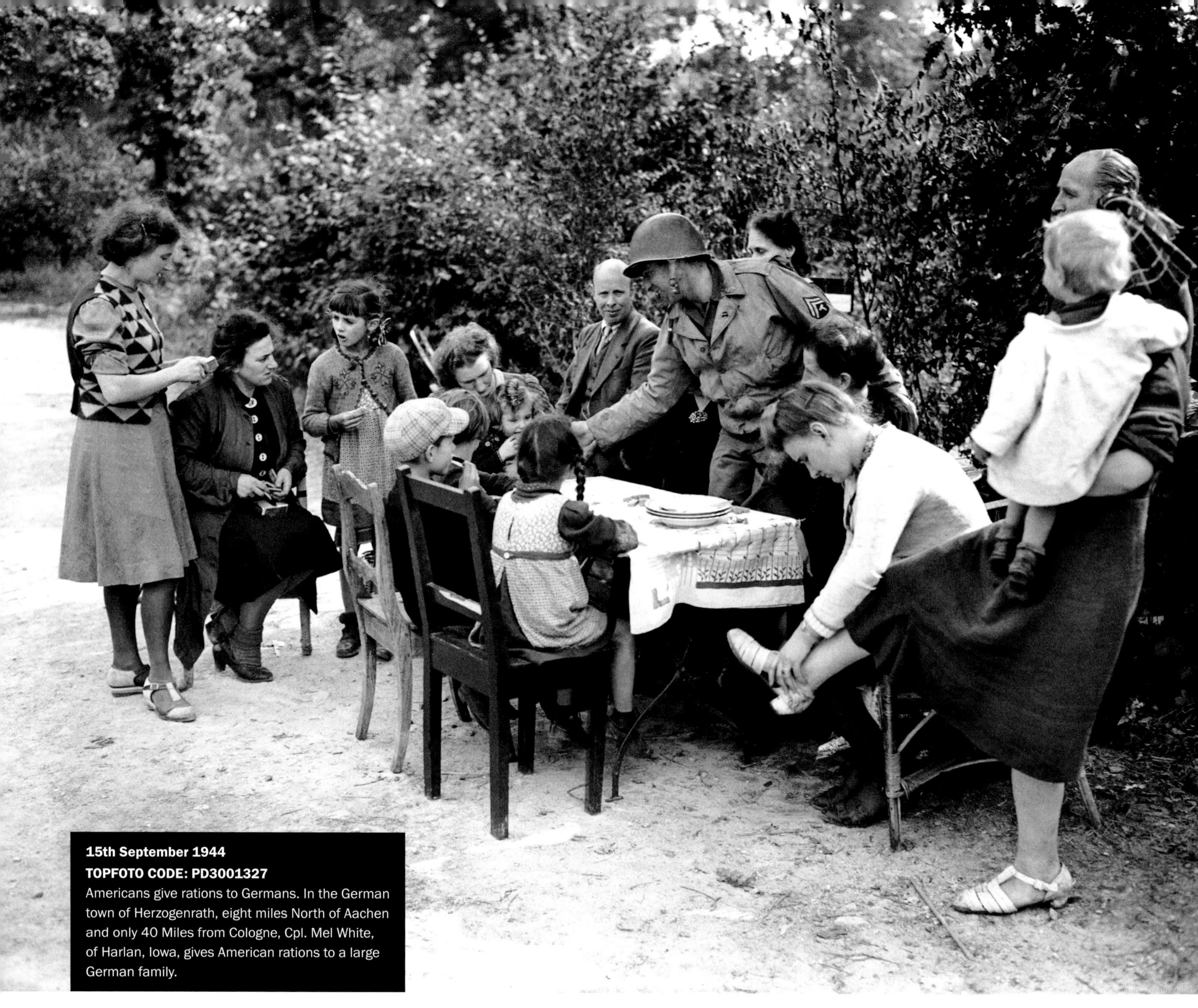

15th September 1944
TOPFOTO CODE: PD3001327
Americans give rations to Germans. In the German town of Herzogenrath, eight miles North of Aachen and only 40 Miles from Cologne, Cpl. Mel White, of Harlan, Iowa, gives American rations to a large German family.

By the beginning of autumn 1944, the Allied forces had fought their way to Germany's western border. The city of Aachen stood on the Siegfried Line (The Westwall, Germany's line of defence) and while possessing little strategic importance, it had immense symbolic value for the German Reich.

Nazi lore and propaganda had elevated Hitler to be the person who would reunite the lost empire of the eighth-century King Charlemagne, whom the Nazis hailed and proclaimed to be the founder of the first German empire. As Aachen had been the capital of Charlemagne's old empire, it was imperative for the Germans to defend this city at all costs. Hitler had even gone so far as to having plates produced, which were given to collaborating French Vichy soldiers in an SS division, inscribed in Latin: 'The Empire of Charlemagne, which was divided by his grandsons in 843, was defended in 1943 by Adolf Hitler, together with all the people of Europe.' One of the few surviving plates is currently located in the German Historical Museum in Berlin.

The Battle of Aachen began on 12 September and was to be a 'foot in the door' for the Allied forces. Following the failure of Operation Market Garden, it was a way into Hitler's boot-stomping Germany – but it came at a heavy cost.

It was a fierce urban battle, arguably one of the hardest fought during the Second World War, with heavy casualties on both sides. On 21 October, American forces finally took control of the centre of Aachen and the German garrison laid down their arms. After almost six weeks of intense and gruelling warfare, the Americans had lost an estimated 5,000 men, as had the Germans, with another 5,600 captured – but American boots were on German soil and Aachen became the first city to be taken by the Allies. This was also the first time during the war that German soldiers had fought to defend their 'own' land, and possibly why their resistance had been so particularly fierce.

As recent as February 2024, a 500lb Second World War bomb was discovered and had to be safely defused on a construction site near Königshügel Stadium in Aachen. This is not an unusual occurrence, as on average more than 1,800 tons of unexploded Second World War ordnance is discovered in Germany every year. Estimates calculate that almost half of all the bombs dropped by the Allies during the war fell in Germany.

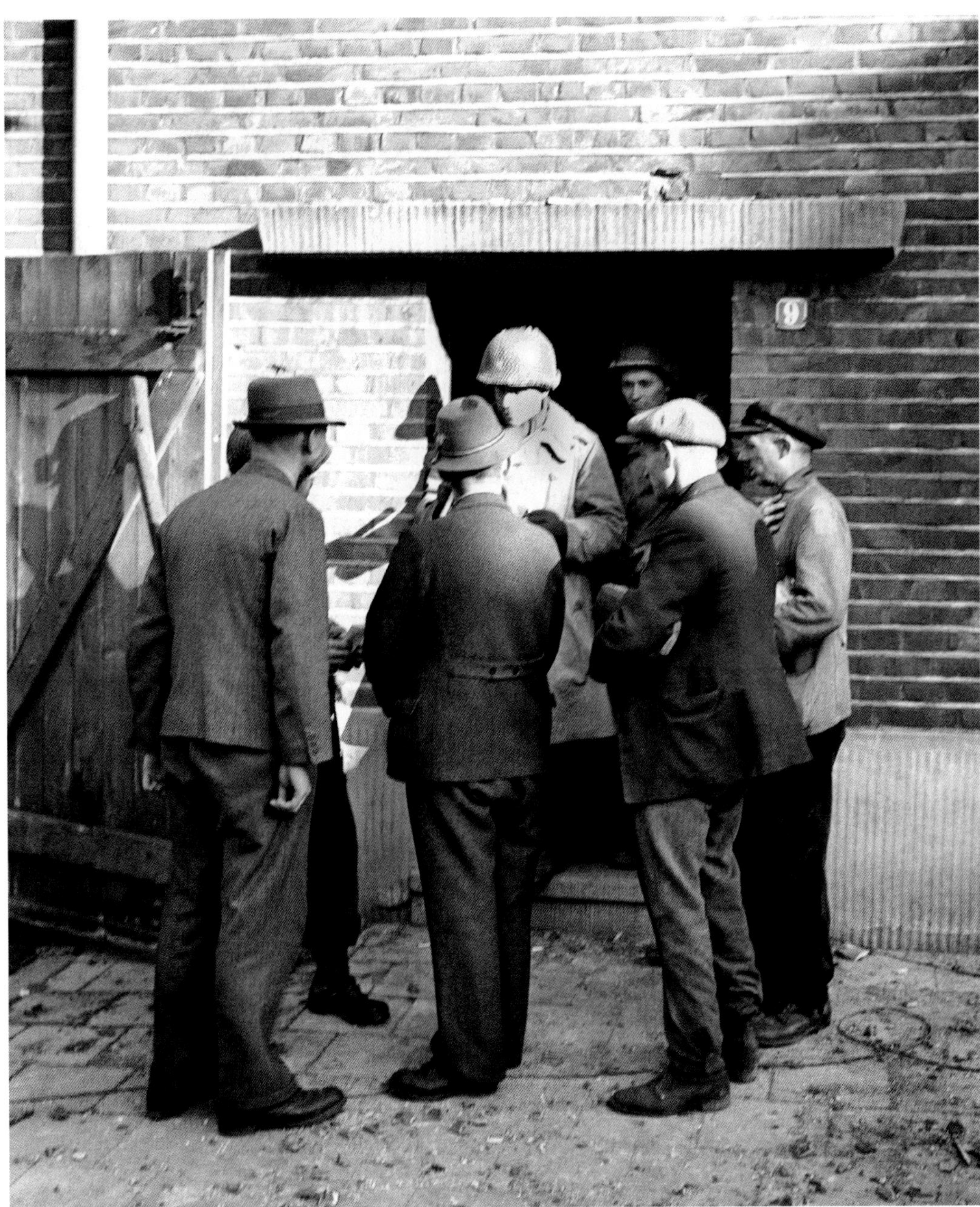

8th October 1944
TOPFOTO CODE: PD3001329
German civilians in the town of Uebach, North of Aachen, being questioned by an American officer, after the capture of the town by the advancing First Army.

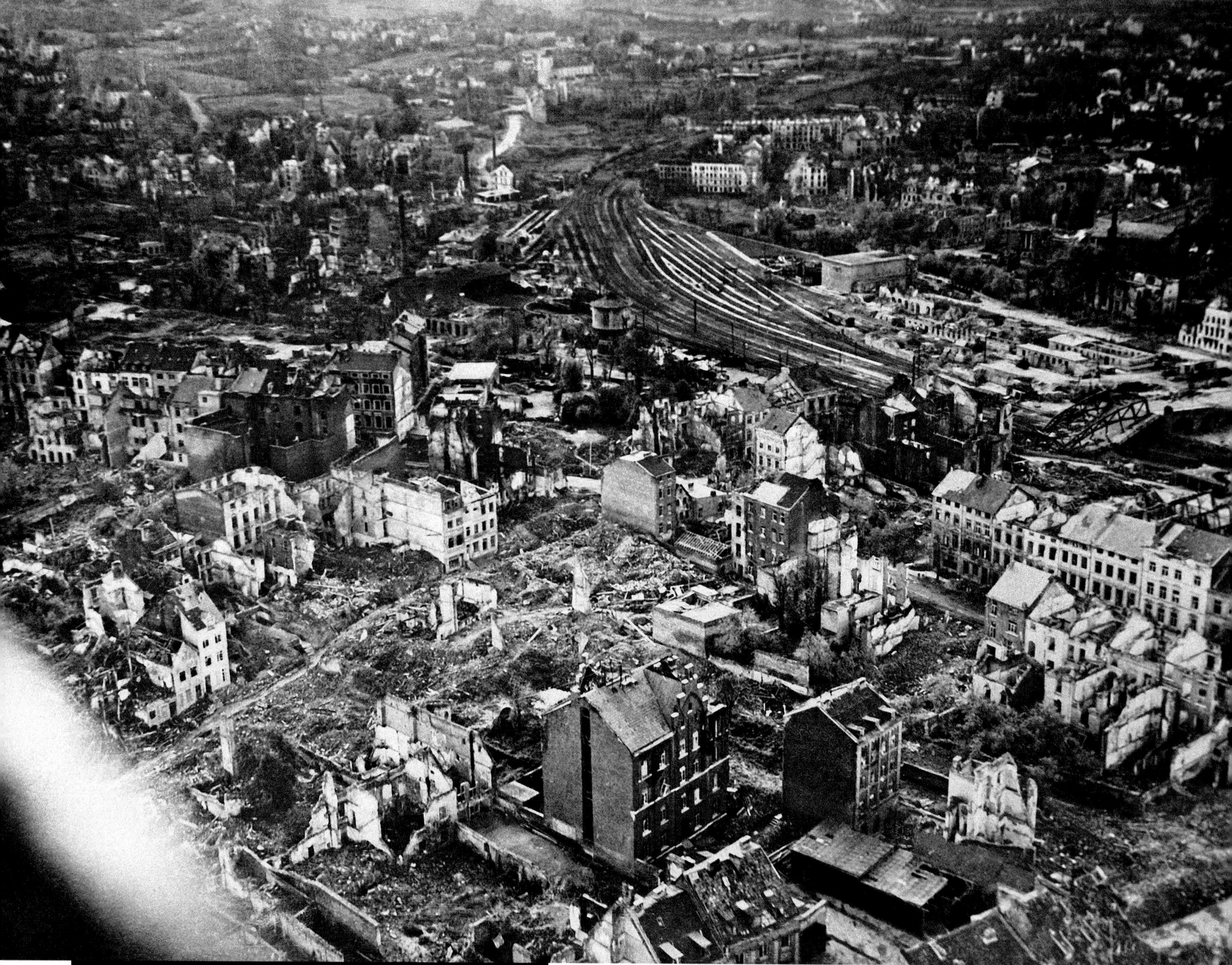

Devastation among buildings skirting the railway in Aachen. An aerial photograph, taken after the surrender of the German garrison.

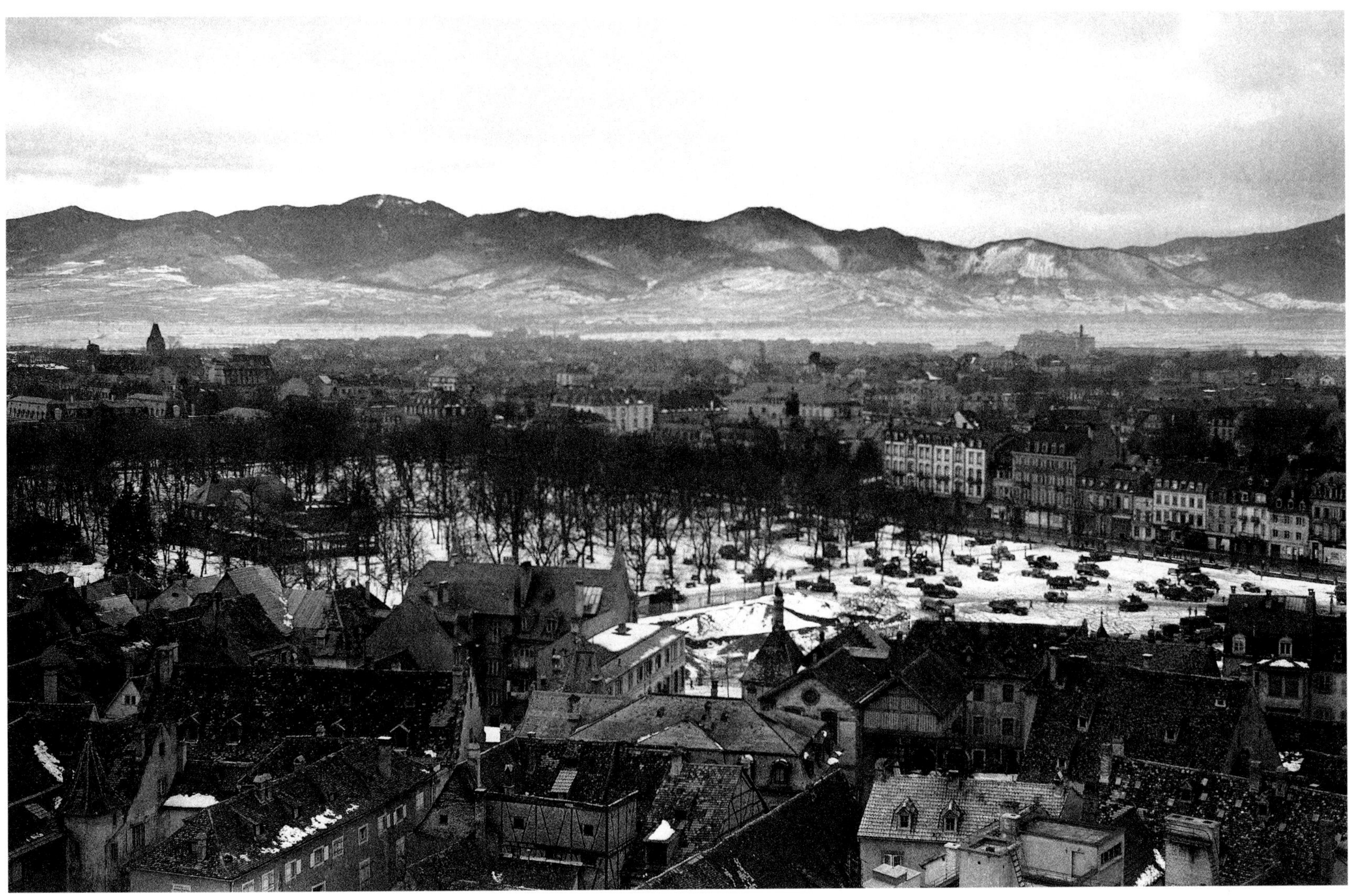

In November 1944, the Allied forces pushed back the Germans from Lorraine and northern Alsace; however, the German 19th Army stubbornly held on to the town of Colmar and the surrounding areas. This little patch, roughly 30 × 40 miles, became known as the Colmar Pocket.

The fighting continued through the winter, making the terrain and conditions even more difficult, right up until February 1945, when the French First Army, assisted by US troops, eventually drove the Germans out into the Rhineland. More than 40,000 French, American and German soldiers lost their lives in the battle for Colmar.

February 1945
TOPFOTO CODE: PD3001325
Germans flee Colmar.

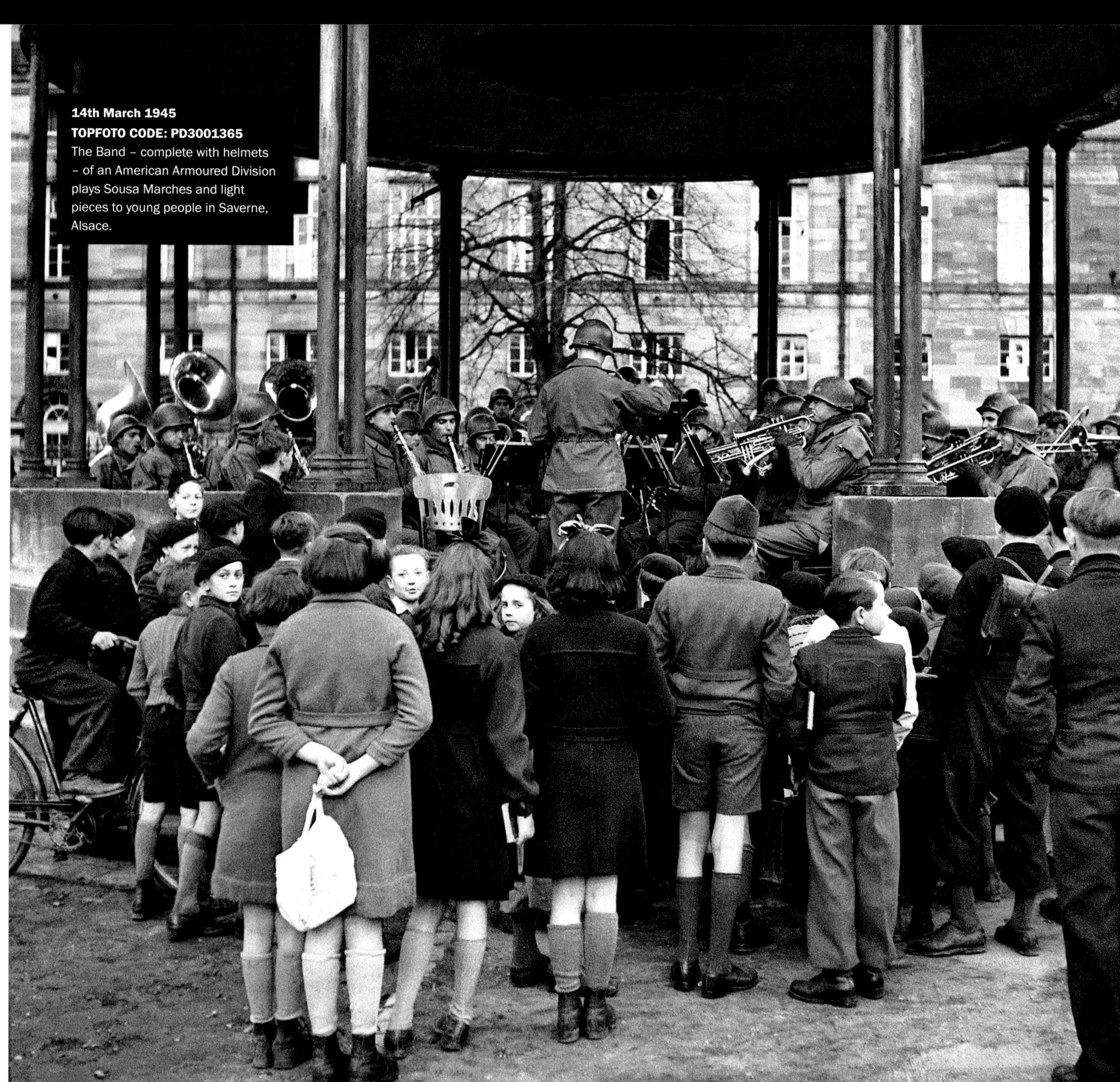

14th March 1945
TOPFOTO CODE: PD3001365
The Band – complete with helmets – of an American Armoured Division plays Sousa Marches and light pieces to young people in Saverne, Alsace.

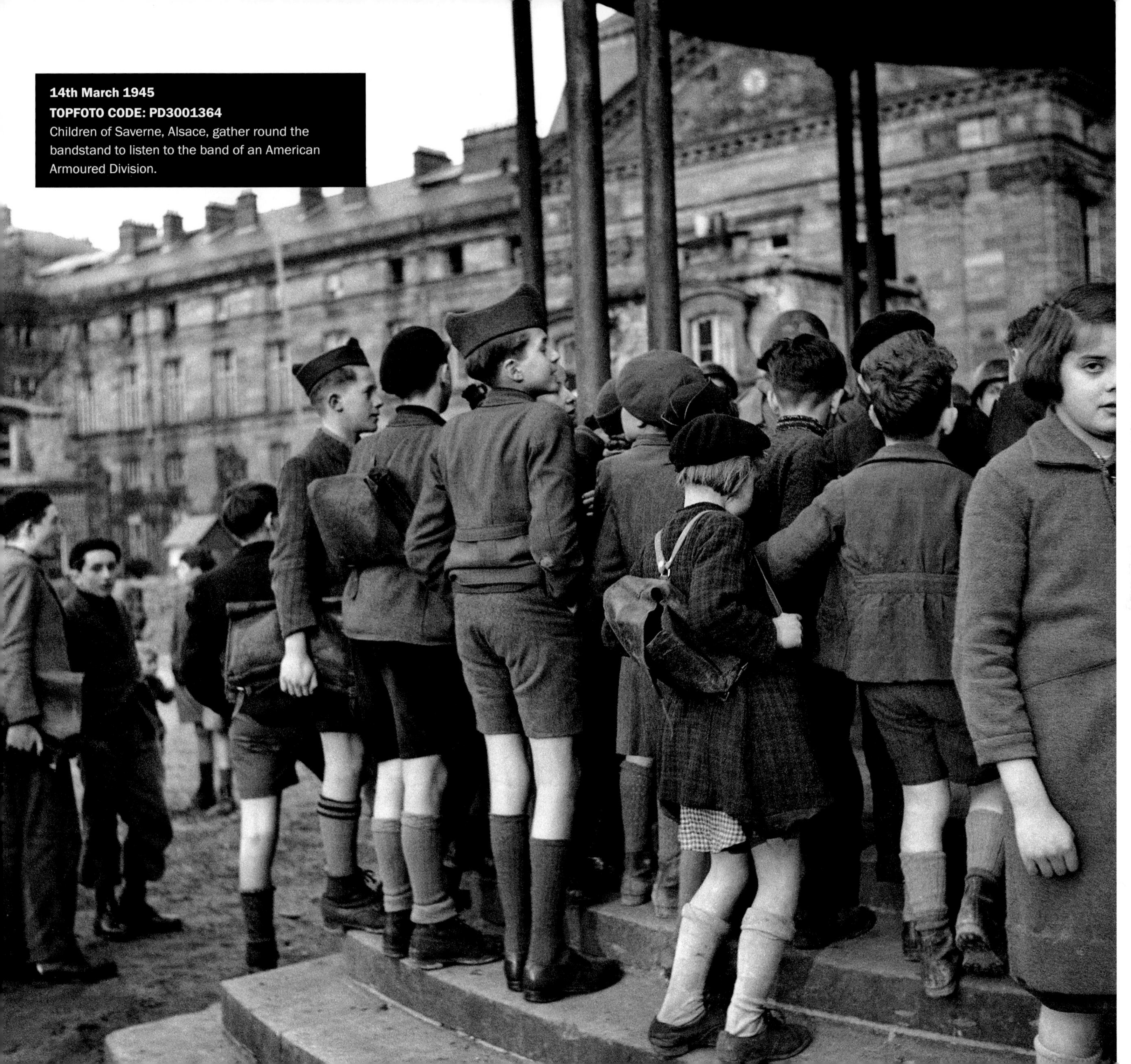

14th March 1945
TOPFOTO CODE: PD3001364
Children of Saverne, Alsace, gather round the
bandstand to listen to the band of an American
Armoured Division.

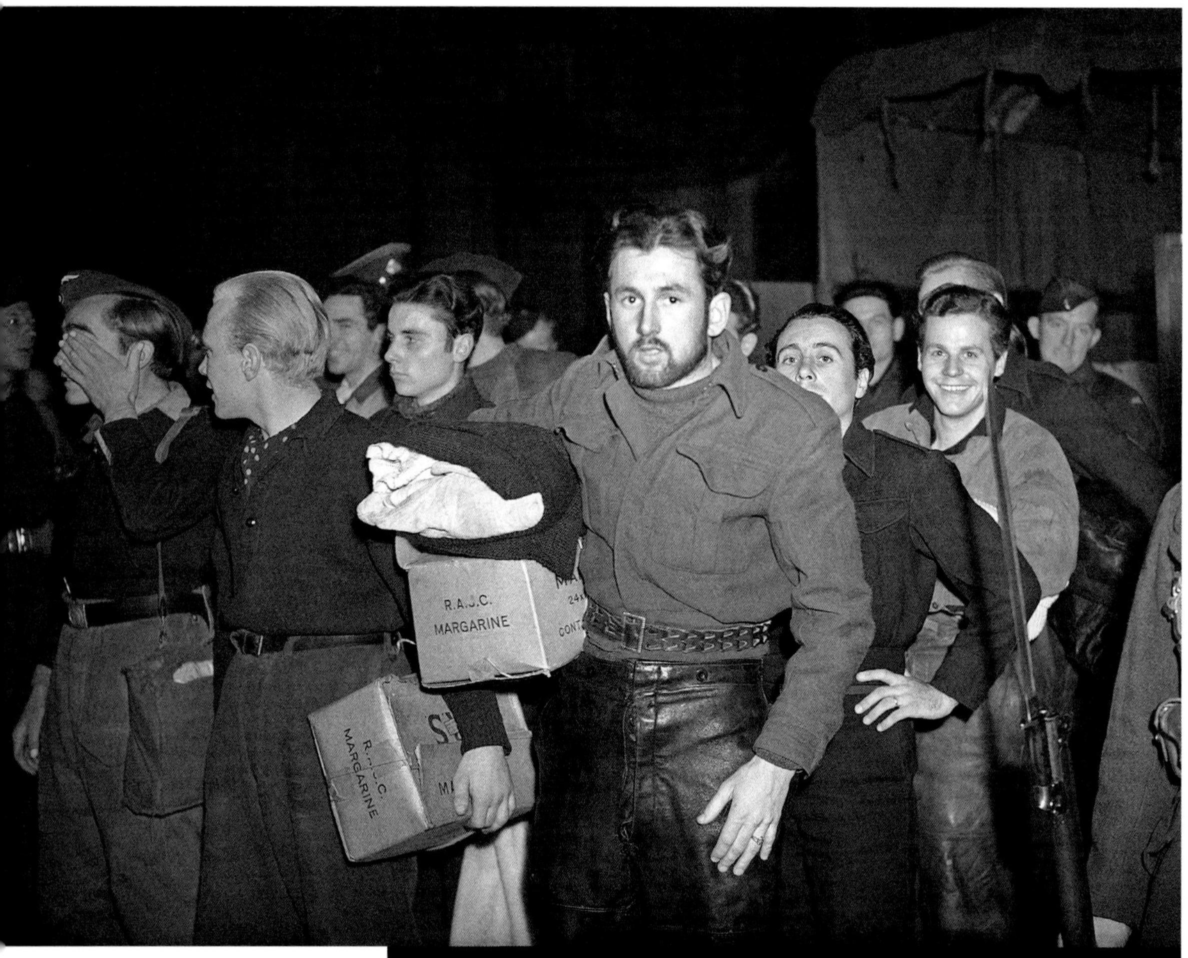

23rd October 1943
TOPFOTO CODE: PD3001219
Nazis in London. Photo shows:- Once it was 'Guns before butter', now these young Nazis, disinterested, apprehensive, cheerful and – in one case – camera-shy, are glad to use R.A.S.C. margarine boxes to hold their few possessions as they are escorted along a platform of a London station, to board a train that will carry them to a prison camp.

At the beginning of the war, most POWs were transported to the outskirts of the British Empire and not many were held on British soil. This changed around mid-1941 and by the fall of the Italian fascist regime in 1943 Britain hosted more than 100,000 Italian prisoners.

These prisoners were used to relieve the domestic labour shortage and assisted primarily with farming. Following the Normandy landings, a huge number of German POWs were subsequently also held in Britain and by 1946, one year after the war had ended, there were still more than 400,000 POWs in the UK, held in more than 1,500 camps.

For various political reasons, the repatriation of the prisoners was deliberately slow. The labour they provided, their democratic 're-education', and the continued occupation of their home country, meant that many stayed until 1948 – some even chose to permanently settle.

Henry Faulk was the British officer in charge of this re-education of the German prisoners, and his book about the subject provides valuable insight. The fact that the Second World War was mainly an ideological war meant that the intention with the reformative education was to replace the authoritarian indoctrination they had been subjected to with democratic values and a better understanding of freedom and human rights – thus hopefully avoiding a repetition of the war by future generations. Though the degree of success varied, arguments were made that former POWs later participated in the erection of democratic institutions in post-war Germany upon their return.

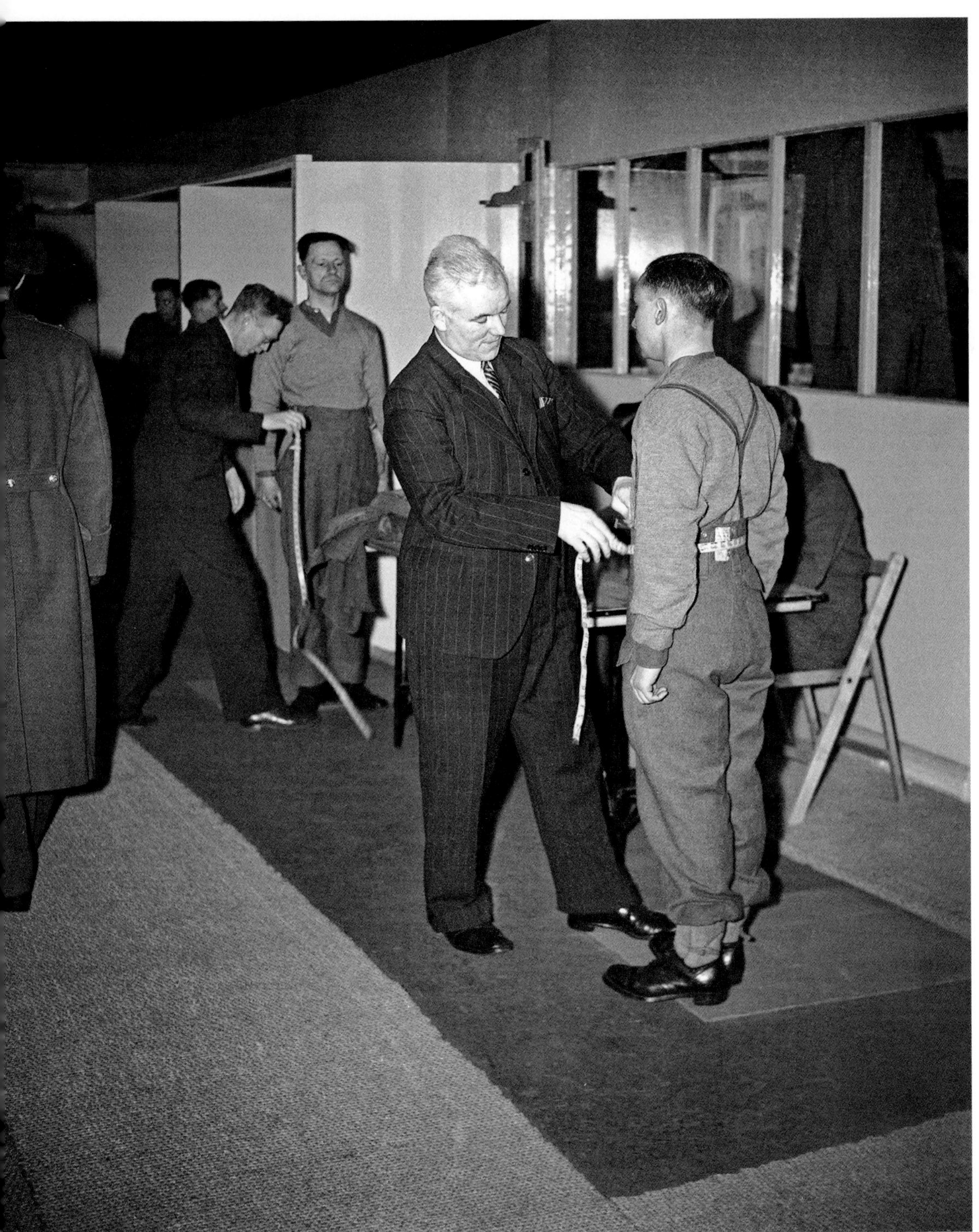

Demobilisation Clothing for the Forces Demonstrated in London

After years of wearing mostly uniforms, many British soldiers no longer possessed a decent and presentable suit – an essential garment to re-enter civilian life and gain post-war employment. As clothes and fabrics were rationed, it would have been very difficult and taken a long time to acquire one, even if you had the means. That is why, upon demobilisation (standing down from combat readiness), the British forces were provided with so-called 'demob suits' – in some cases tailor-made. Additional to the suit, some were provided with a variety of other garments such as a shirt, shoes, tie, raincoat, hat, gloves and even underwear.

The demand to suddenly clothe millions of men in all sizes presented a huge problem and invariably led to quite comical situations, as men simply ended up taking what was available – resulting in sometimes very poorly fitting attire. The men were allowed to keep their uniforms after demobilisation and a burgeoning black market was ready and eager to relieve the men of their demob suits, often directly outside the distribution centres, at an alleged price of £10 (£540 in today's money).

Today, demob suits have become a real collector's item and will set you back quite a lot more than a black-market price of £10.

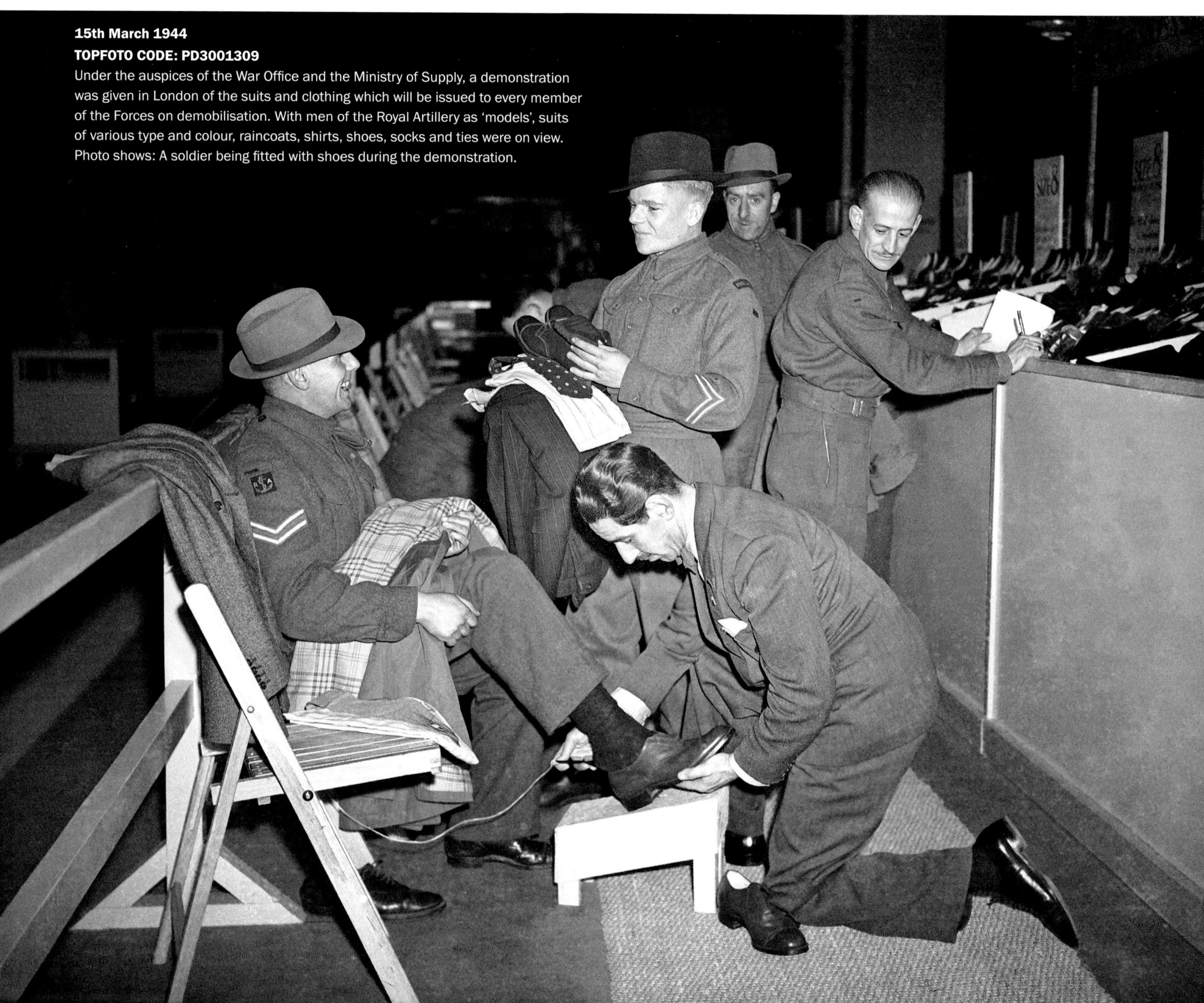

15th March 1944
TOPFOTO CODE: PD3001309
Under the auspices of the War Office and the Ministry of Supply, a demonstration was given in London of the suits and clothing which will be issued to every member of the Forces on demobilisation. With men of the Royal Artillery as 'models', suits of various type and colour, raincoats, shirts, shoes, socks and ties were on view. Photo shows: A soldier being fitted with shoes during the demonstration.

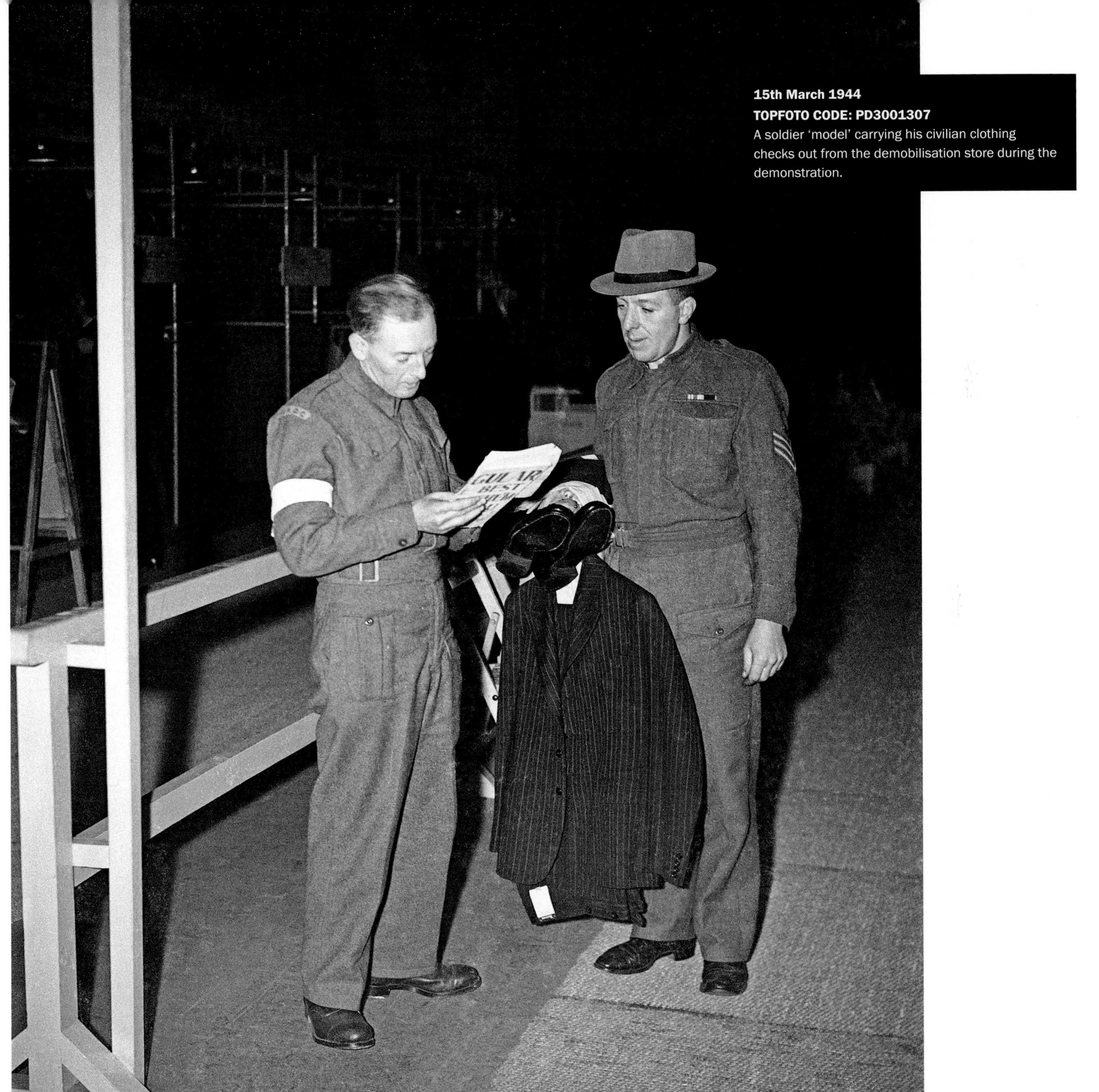

15th March 1944
TOPFOTO CODE: PD3001307
A soldier 'model' carrying his civilian clothing checks out from the demobilisation store during the demonstration.

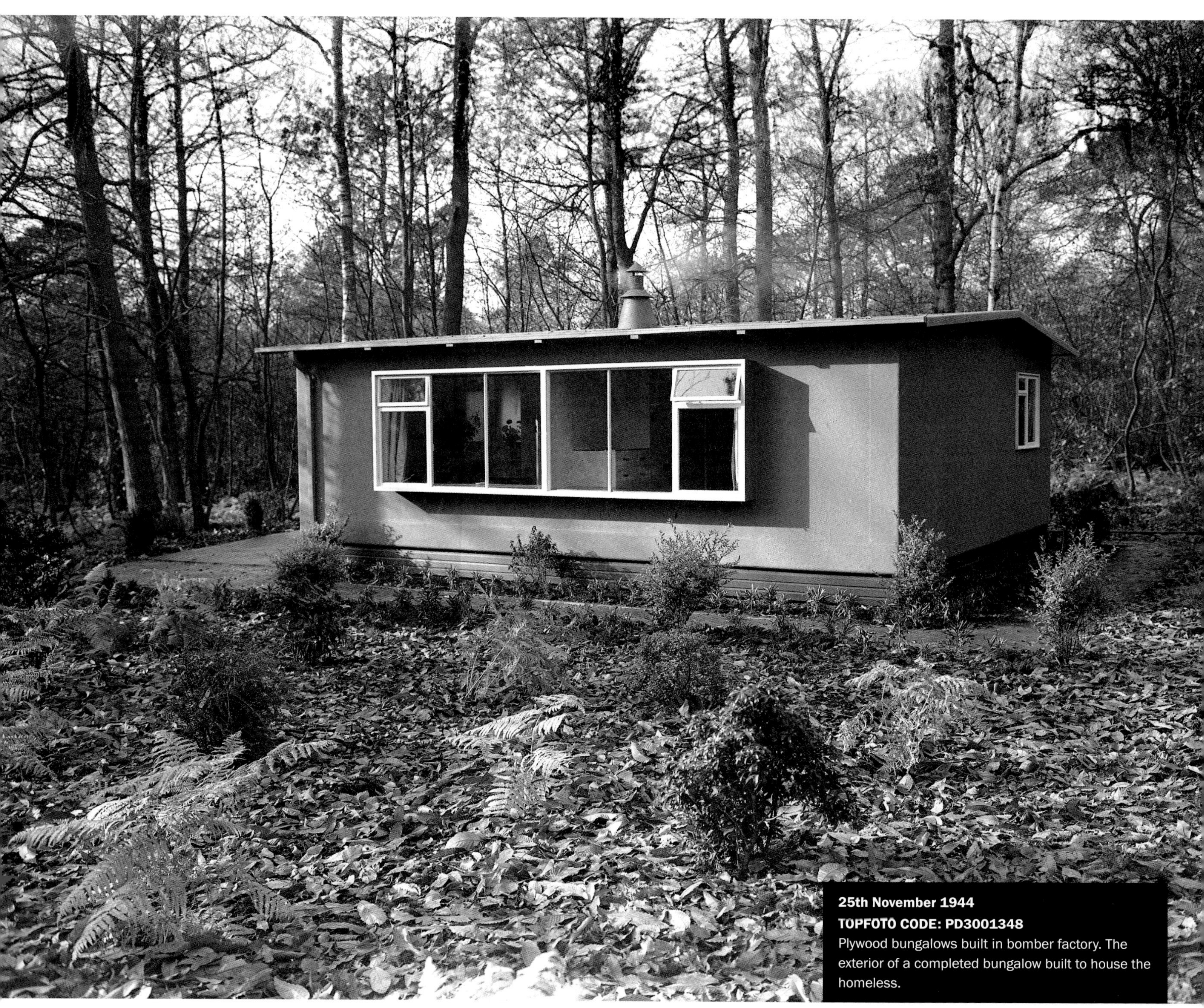

25th November 1944
TOPFOTO CODE: PD3001348
Plywood bungalows built in bomber factory. The exterior of a completed bungalow built to house the homeless.

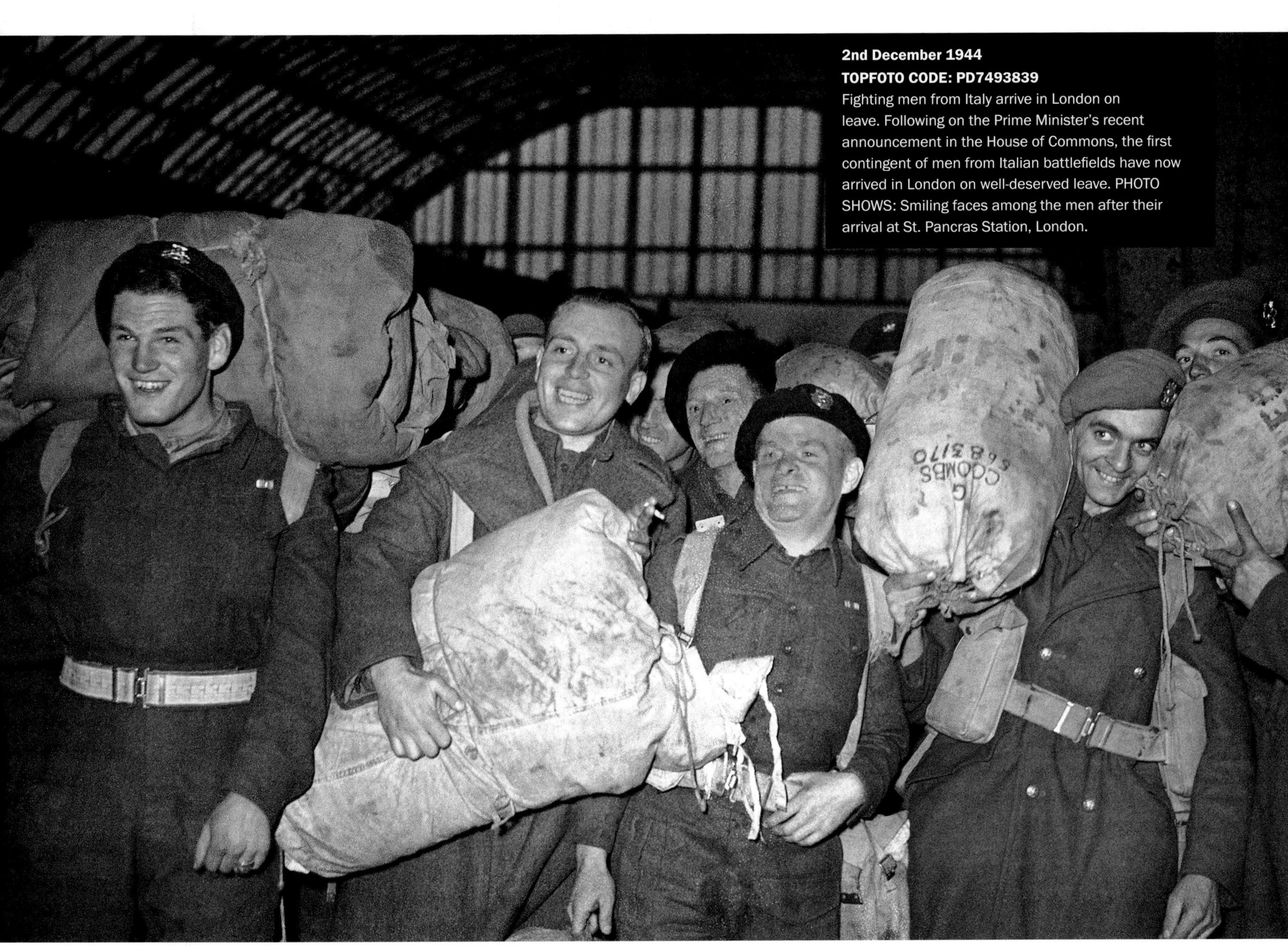

2nd December 1944
TOPFOTO CODE: PD7493839
Fighting men from Italy arrive in London on leave. Following on the Prime Minister's recent announcement in the House of Commons, the first contingent of men from Italian battlefields have now arrived in London on well-deserved leave. PHOTO SHOWS: Smiling faces among the men after their arrival at St. Pancras Station, London.

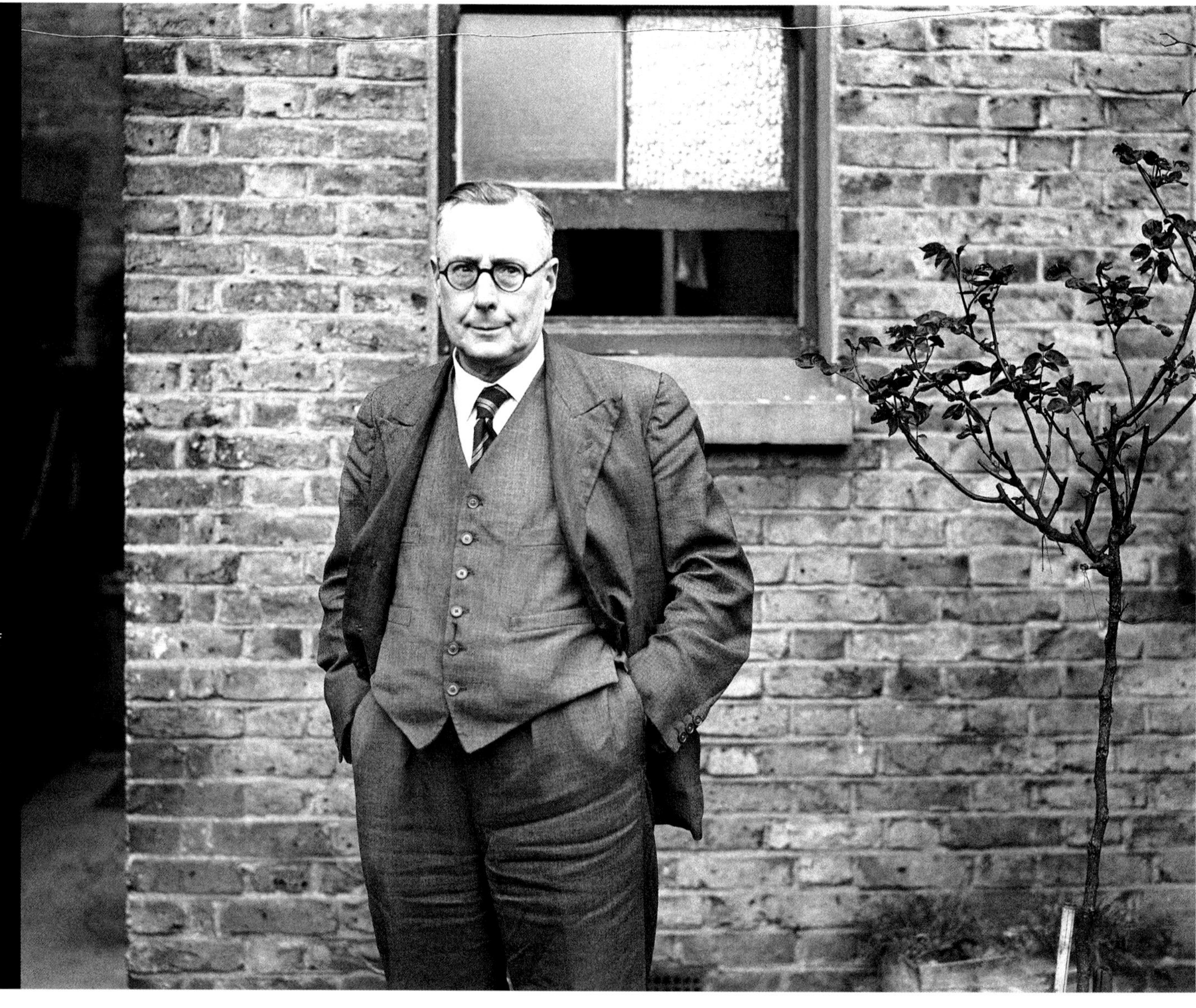

Historically, bells have been used not only for calling the people to prayer but also for the signalling of danger approaching. Introduced into churches around AD 400, they became more widespread in Britain around the mid-eighth century.

Though it is said that all bells in Britain fell silent during the Second World War, only to be used as a warning of an invasion by the Germans, that is not entirely true. The bells stopped ringing on 13 June 1940, but rang out on 15 November 1942, on the order of Winston Churchill, to celebrate the Allied victory in Egypt; on a few occasions, some were simply rung by mistake. In April 1943, the restrictions were relaxed somewhat, allowing for bells to be rung on Sundays, Good Friday and Christmas, but eventually all bans were lifted on 27 May 1943.

In 2020, due to the COVID-19 pandemic, for the first time since the Second World War bells fell silent once again as campanologists could not get to churches or cathedrals.

As a footnote, campanology is the study of bellringing (originating from the Latin word *campana*, meaning bell) and a campanologist is a person who studies the art of bellringing.

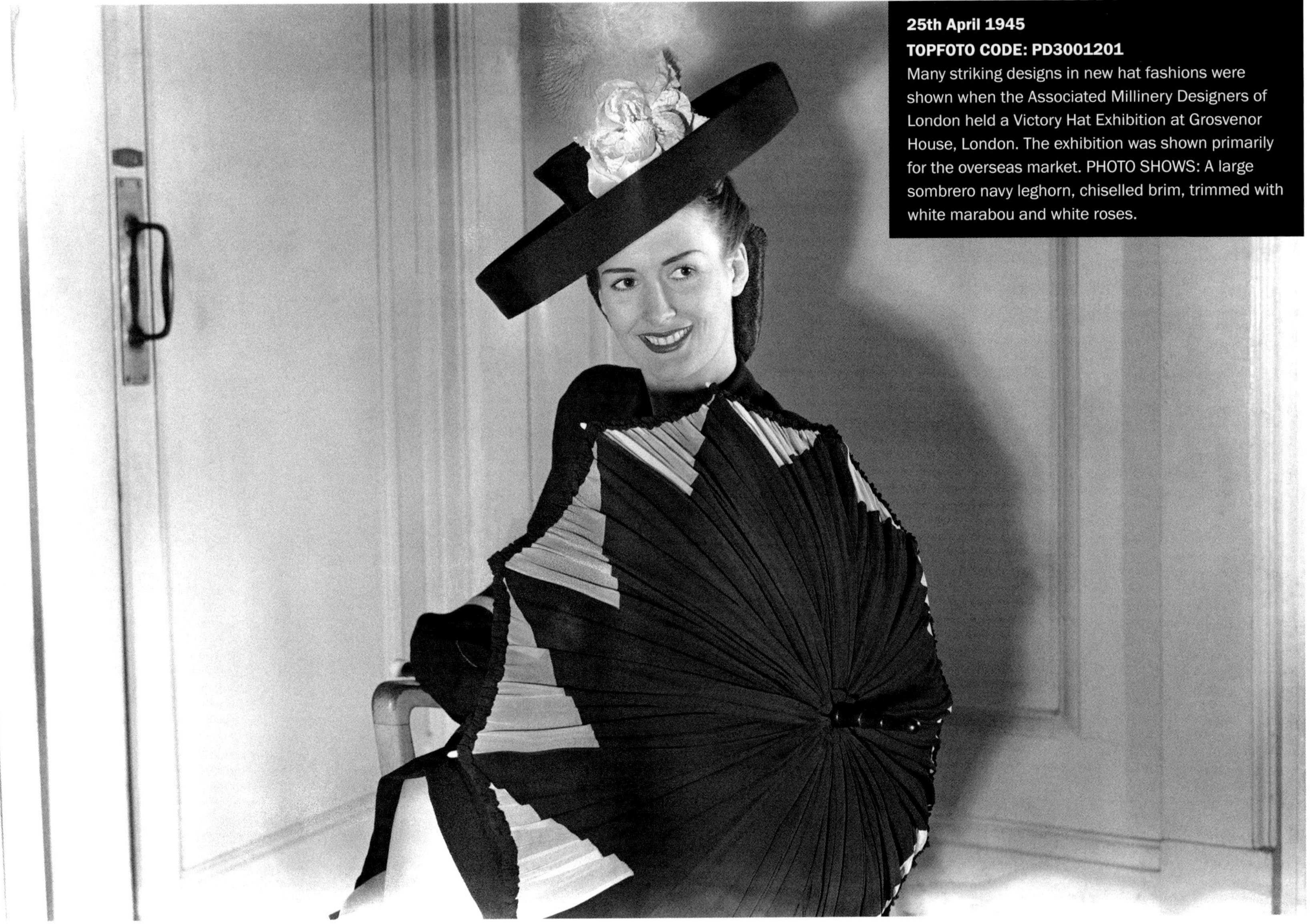

Just a few weeks before VE Day (Victory in Europe Day) and the formal surrender of Nazi Germany, the world already knew which way the wind was blowing. On the same day as this picture was taken, Harry S. Truman had been US President for just thirteen days, following the sudden death of Roosevelt. On this day, he addressed the United Nations Conference on International Organisation (UNCIO) and told them the following:

You members of this Conference are to be the architects of the better world. In your hands rests our future. By your labours at this Conference, we shall know if suffering humanity is to achieve a just and lasting peace. Let us labour to achieve a peace which is really worthy of their great sacrifice. We must make certain, by your work here, that another war will be impossible.[8]

The world was fed up with war. A monumental task awaited, but people were ready for peace and prosperity. The people were ready to wear big and ostentatious hats again.

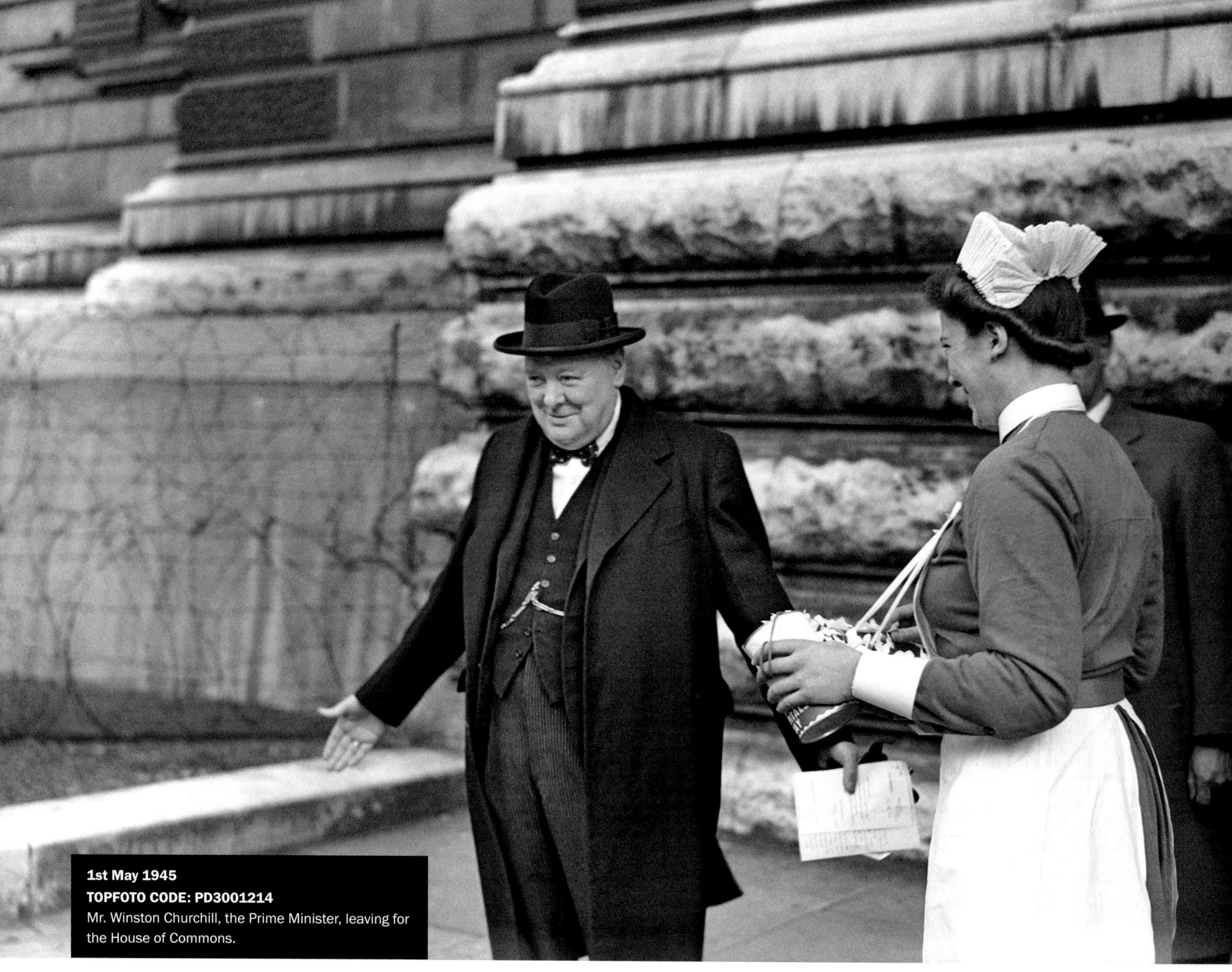

In the evening hours of 1 May 1945, Hamburg Radio announced the death of Hitler. It was later to be made known that it had in fact been suicide. Things moved rapidly after this. Many high-ranking Nazis committed suicide the following day and a domino effect of surrender struck the rapidly sinking German ship.

On 2 May, almost a million men surrendered in Italy and Austria, followed by the surrender of all German forces in Denmark, the Netherlands and north Germany. It all culminated on 8 May 1945, when Germany officially capitulated and seized all operations. Hence, 8 May became known as VE Day.

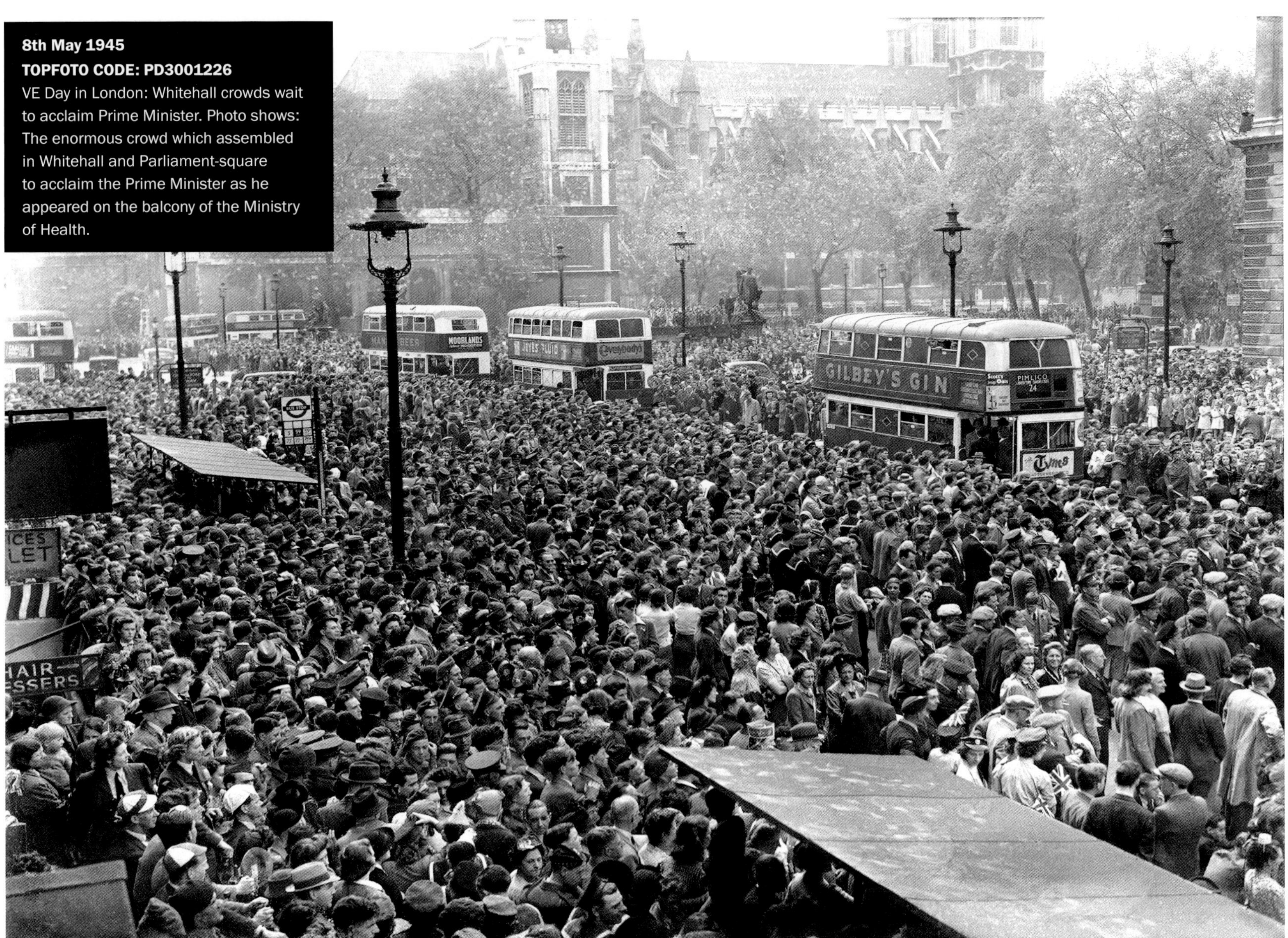

In London, and all over Britain, people came out into the streets to celebrate that years of fear, death and uncertainty were over at last. Though the war in the Pacific would continue to rage for another three months, the war in the European Theatre had finally come to an end. Churchill declared the day a public holiday and large crowds began impromptu rejoicing, dancing and singing. They gathered in Trafalgar Square, at the Houses of Parliament and in front of Whitehall.

Churchill famously came out on to the balcony wearing his boiler suit and gave the V for Victory sign before addressing the jubilant masses in a powerful speech, expressing gratitude to the British people for the many sacrifices made and hopes for a better future. He also warned that one should never bow down to violence or tyranny and that many challenges remained. At the end, he gave the V sign once more and exited to the tunes of the people singing 'For He's a Jolly Good Fellow'.

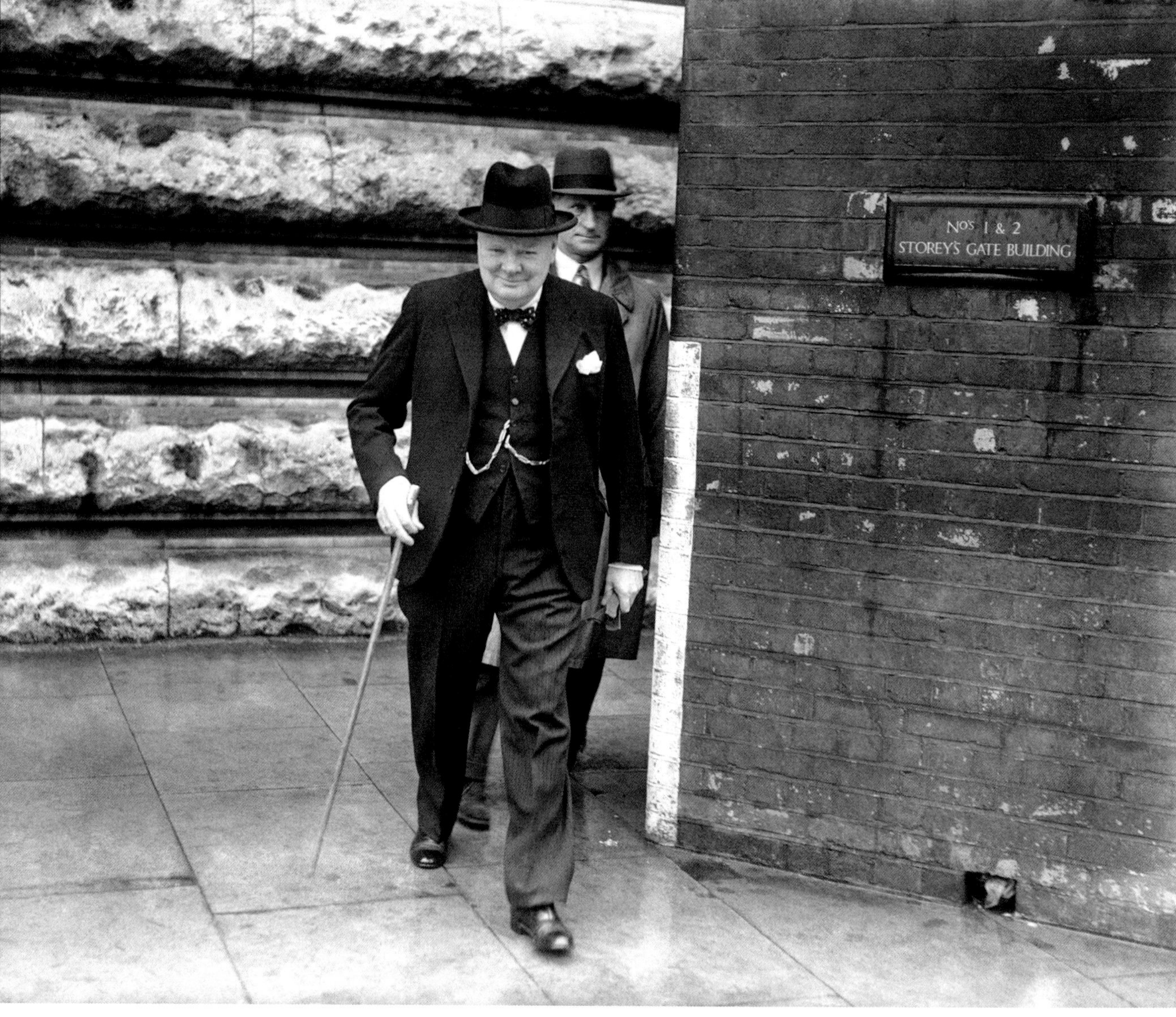

Churchill resigns: forming caretaker cabinet.
Mr. Winston Churchill has handed his resignation to the King. The Prime Minister visited Buckingham Palace to advise the dissolution of parliament, and a notice that the King has agreed will be made soon. Mr. Churchill's resignation means that the whole government goes, and every office becomes vacant. It is understood that the King immediately commissioned Mr. Churchill to form a new Government. A proclamation of the Dissolution, to be announced in three weeks time, will be the first formal beginning of the General Election campaign, which Mr. Herbert Morrison, Home Secretary and Minister of Home Security, described at the Blackpool conference of the Socialist Party as the most important of all time. Photo shows:- Mr. Churchill leaves Downing Street to visit the King at Buckingham Palace and tender his resignation.

Just two weeks after VE Day, Churchill resigned as Prime Minister. The Conservative Party had been leading a coalition government with multiple political parties and following the end of the Second World War that coalition rapidly began to crumble. Churchill had been an immensely popular leader during the war years, but the British public had a desire for social reform. An important body of work known as the Beveridge Report, published in 1942 by the economist William Beveridge, laid the groundwork for the post-war welfare state that Britain was to become. A vital part of this was the creation and implementation of the National Health Service (NHS).

Churchill had been perceived as a strong and resolute leader who could govern the country in a time of war, but in a time of peace the domestic policies of the Labour Party, emphasising the needs of the people and a more equitable society, resonated strongly with the voters. The leader of the Labour Party, Clement Attlee, had already held the position of Deputy Prime Minister since 1942, and while being seen by some as quiet and shy (even mocked by fellow Labour MP Hugh Dalton as 'a little mouse'), he had proven himself tenacious. The war was over and things were about to change: it was time for an election.

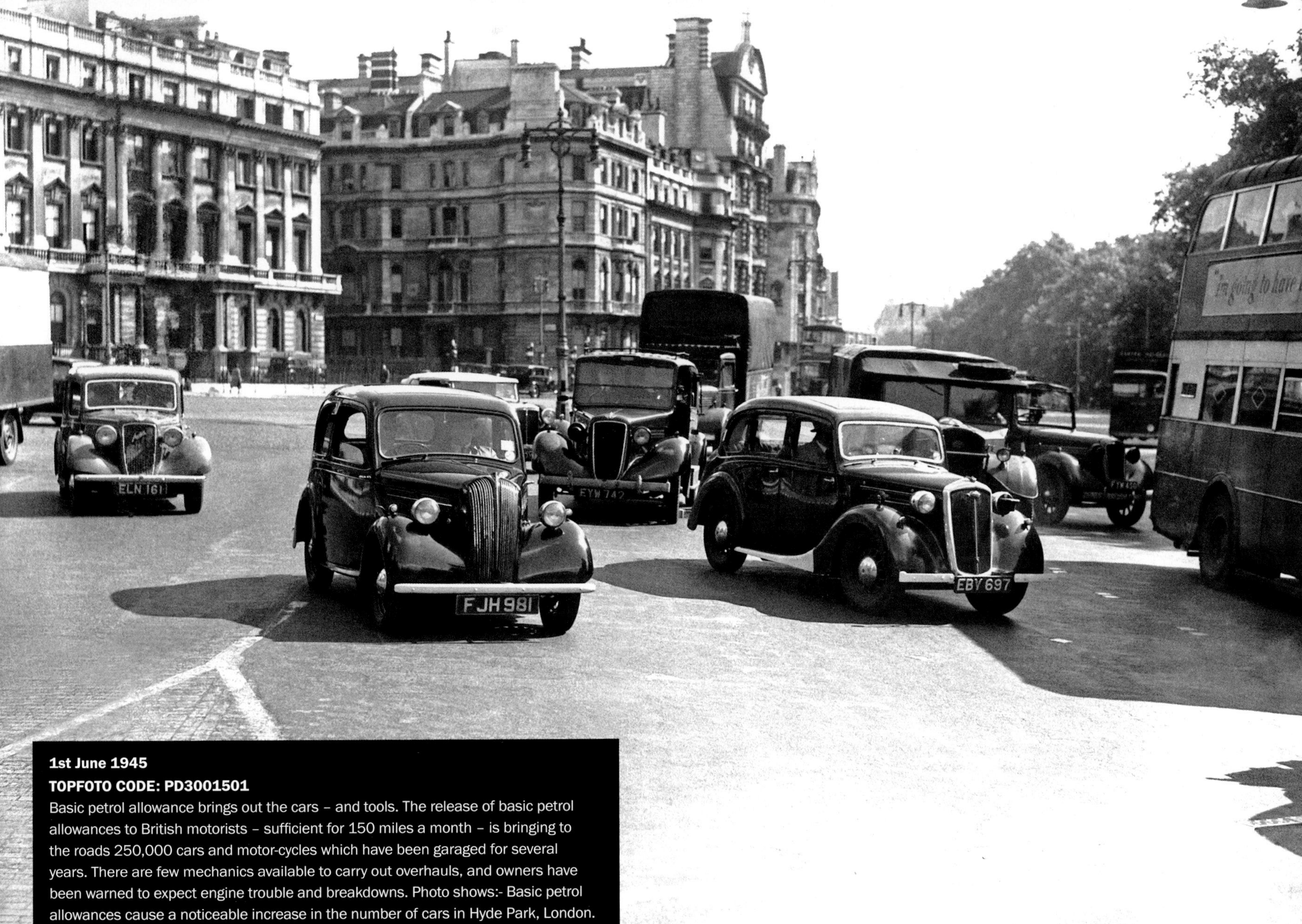

1st June 1945
TOPFOTO CODE: PD3001501
Basic petrol allowance brings out the cars – and tools. The release of basic petrol allowances to British motorists – sufficient for 150 miles a month – is bringing to the roads 250,000 cars and motor-cycles which have been garaged for several years. There are few mechanics available to carry out overhauls, and owners have been warned to expect engine trouble and breakdowns. Photo shows:- Basic petrol allowances cause a noticeable increase in the number of cars in Hyde Park, London.

In September 1939, British car and motorcycle owners were hit with wartime petrol rationing. It was the first commodity that was impacted, and it meant that you would only be able drive around 200 miles per month. In July 1942, this ration was also removed, and all non-essential motoring was suspended until 1 June 1945, when a cautious 150-mile a month limit was instilled.

Many other stable commodities were also rationed during the war to help with the war effort and due to limited supply. Some continued to be rationed even after the war. A standard ration for one person per week when rationing was at its highest was: 1 egg, 4oz of bacon, 8oz of sugar, 1oz of tea, 2oz of cheese, 8oz of preserves (per month), 2oz of butter, 4oz of margarine, 2oz of lard, 8oz of sweets (per month) and around £3 worth of meat, in today's money. Exceptions were made for vegetarians, who would receive an increase in certain food groups to compensate for the animal products.

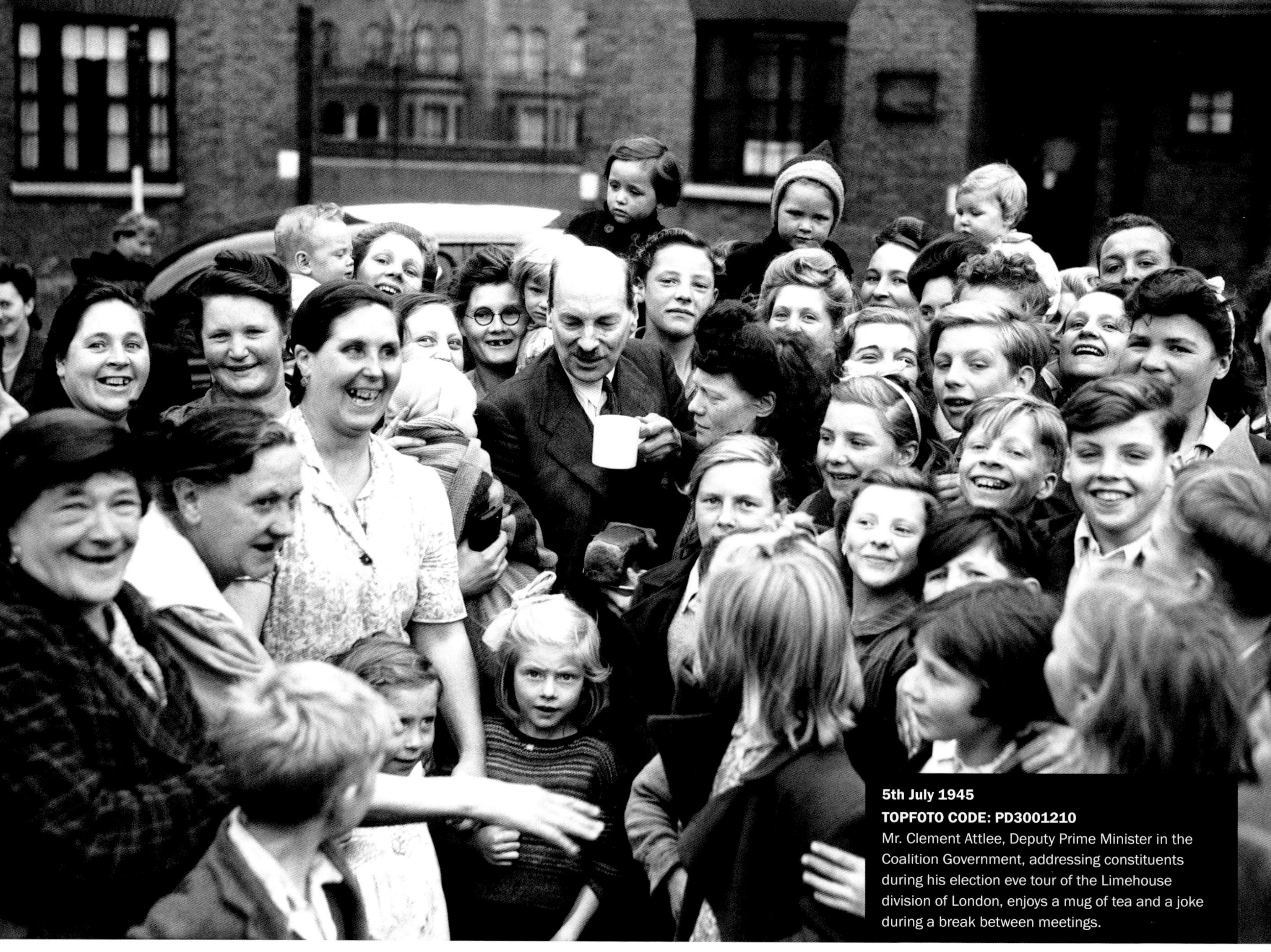

Mr. Clement Attlee, Deputy Prime Minister in the Coalition Government, addressing constituents during his election eve tour of the Limehouse division of London, enjoys a mug of tea and a joke during a break between meetings.

The date of the 1945 UK general election was 5 July and it ultimately resulted in a landslide victory for Labour. Clement Attlee became Prime Minister and immediately started making good on the promises of his party's new political manifesto 'Let us face the future'. It was an ambitious and comprehensive plan of social change, addressing issues of housing and healthcare, education and employment. It also began the nationalisation, and hereby public ownership, of industries such as coal, steel and railways, and laid the foundations for improving social security, unemployment benefits and pensions.

Attlee became the little mouse that roared, and put to bed any doubts people might previously have had about his capabilities. Viewed by many as one of the most influential Labour politicians of the twentieth century, he is generally credited with transforming Britain into the welfare state it is today.

"These men preserved the very foundation of modern humankind by protecting these paintings. For what is art, but the most fragile, pure and elevated expression of human emotion and capability?

The cradle for the advanced ability to freely – and without inhibition or repercussion – observe, imagine and create. The very essence of what was in danger of disappearing, had the outcome of the war been different."

On the Hidden Art Treasures of Holland (page 145)

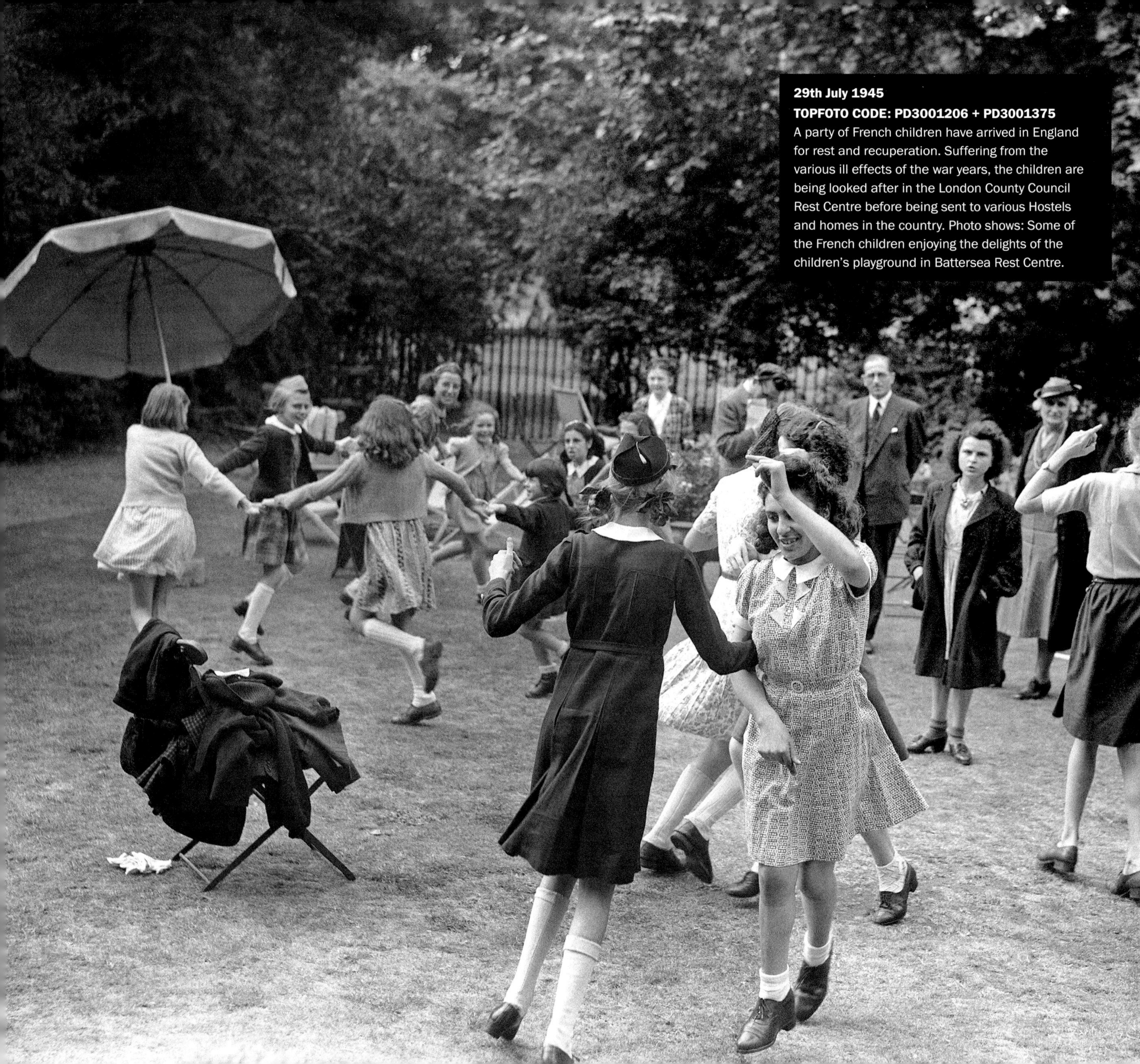

29th July 1945
TOPFOTO CODE: PD3001206 + PD3001375
A party of French children have arrived in England for rest and recuperation. Suffering from the various ill effects of the war years, the children are being looked after in the London County Council Rest Centre before being sent to various Hostels and homes in the country. Photo shows: Some of the French children enjoying the delights of the children's playground in Battersea Rest Centre.

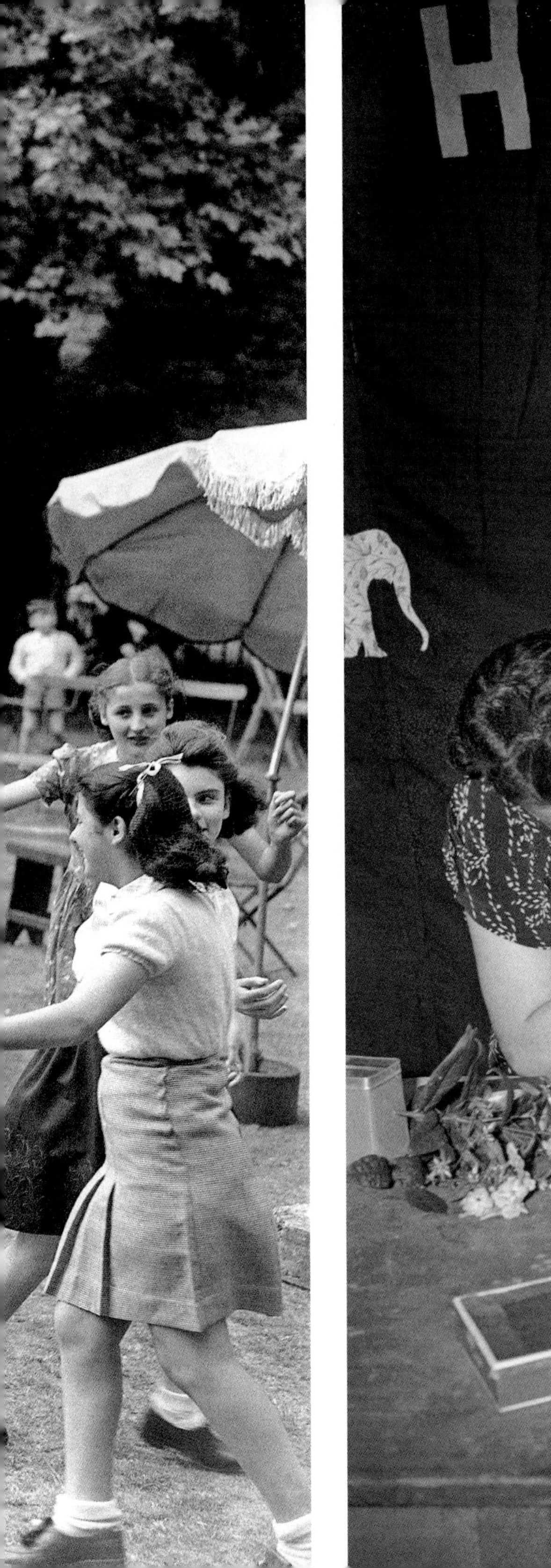

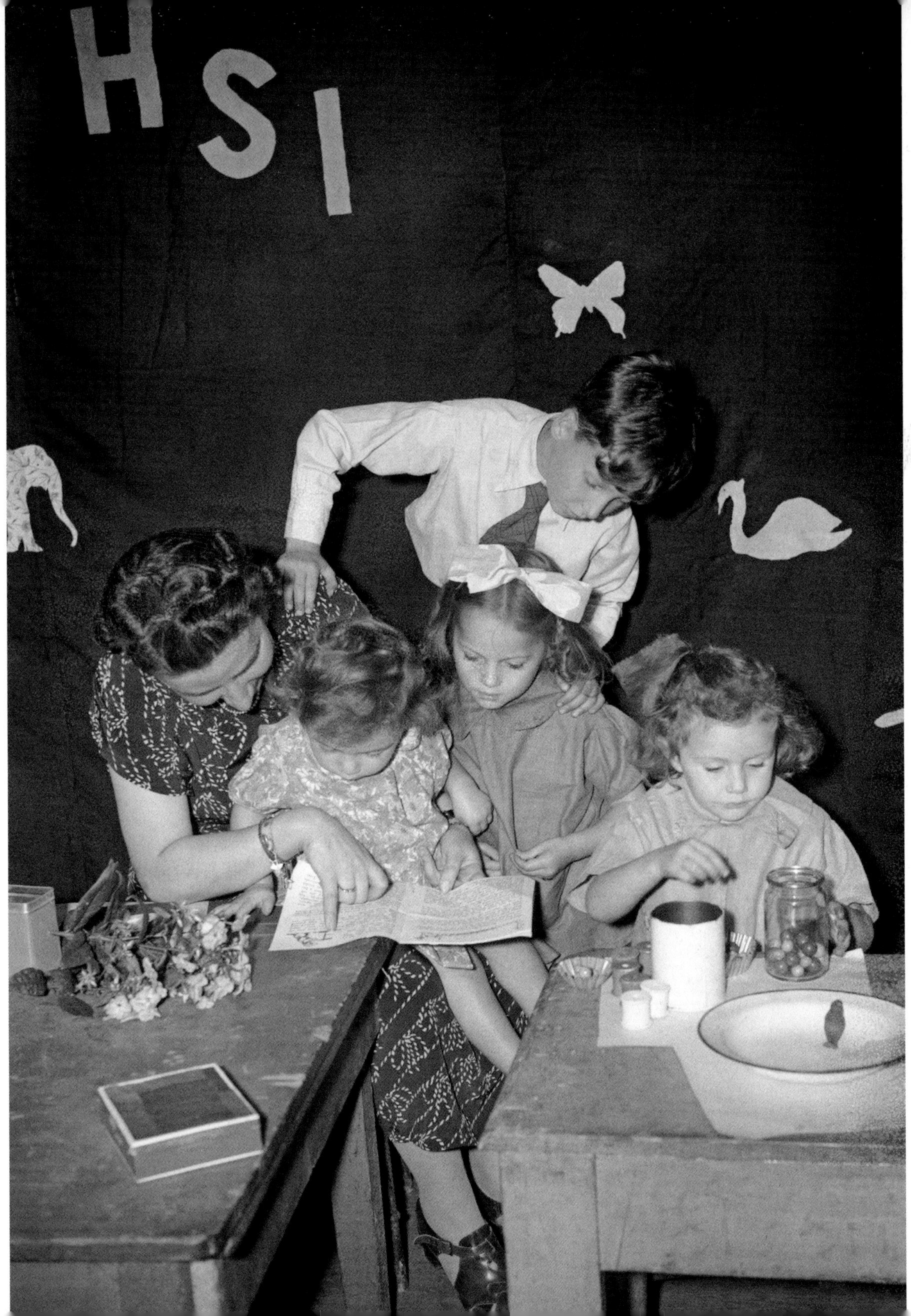

From Normandy Trenches to School Benches

On VE Day, 8 May 1945, Germany unconditionally surrendered to the Allied armed forces, officially ending the Second World War in the European Theatre. More than 2½ million US soldiers, whose sole purpose for years had been to win the war, had now contributed to achieving that. Standing at the finish line, many were wondering what to do next.

PFC Robert N. Haire (in the photo opposite) would have found himself waking up from a four-year 'rite of passage' in a foreign land. It was a new world very unlike the one he had entered four years earlier, and probably in many ways he was a very different man than he had been before the war.

Twelve weeks later, three American-style universities were opened in Europe. The army was bringing education to the GIs – directly from the Normandy trenches to the school benches. These post-war US Army universities in Europe were created to build a bridge between military experience and academic life, and to assist veterans in rebuilding their mental adaptability. The first GI university was created in Florence, Italy, the second in Biarritz, France, and the third in Shrivenham, England.

On 22 June 1944, the Servicemen's Readjustment Act, known as the GI Bill, was passed. While the American Legion was pushing to help veterans from various wars, President Roosevelt was trying to focus on a programme that would help all the poor and less fortunate, regardless of their military service. The outcome, despite his efforts, still became a bill that largely favoured the men in service. It allowed benefits for any veteran who had served on active duty for a minimum of ninety days during the war.

The benefits (provided that the soldier had been honourably discharged) included areas such as education, vocational training and guaranteed low-cost mortgages. It covered living expenses and tuition associated with enrolment in high school, low-interest loans for business start-ups and unemployment payment for up to a year.

Robert Haire worked as a meat packer before the war started and had been with the 29th Infantry Division, 155th Regiment through D-Day, the Battle for Brest and Operation Cobra, until the very end of the campaign. Through the GI Bill, he now had the opportunity to get an education, improve himself and better his chances for the future. From having dodged bullets and dug trenches only weeks prior, he would exchange guns with school books, and foxholes with comfy cushions, along with three square meals per day.

This was an intermission for soldiers, either on their way back to the States or, if you did not have enough points in the Adjusted Service Rating Score System, a welcome respite before redeployment to the Pacific Theatre and the battle against Japan. Students, therefore, attended for one term only. The only requirement was a High School Diploma and enlisted men were given preference (only 10 per cent enrolled were officers).

In Shrivenham, the previous army camp was converted into a university. It was functional for two terms only, until December 1945. During this period an estimated 8,000 students attended – roughly 4,000 each term. While it was a school, it was still created on military grounds, and military discipline continued in many ways. Reveille was sounded every morning and while the GIs had nice warm beds, clean sheets, good food, a beer tavern and American football, you could still be court-martialled for skipping classes.

Three hundred different courses were available in eight main fields, and 130 civilian professors along with 100 Army officers were hired or given leave to teach. Most of the grunt work associated with the daily running, cooking and maintenance work on the premises was done by German POWs. The heroes studied while the defeated did the hard labour. (Read more about this on page 152.)

Oxford University also contributed by allowing use of the Bodleian Library (by professors only though), and a local postman generously donated 1,000 volumes for the institution. The open and informal teaching style created a lot of excitement and interest within the British more formal and intellectual environment, and brought many visiting academics and dignitaries on site to observe.

One of the initiatives was a journalism course, the only one on British soil at the time, and the first student radio show ever in Britain. It was, in fact, a full fifteen years before Hertfordshire's Crush Radio, which is traditionally regarded as the first student broadcaster in Britain. A state-of-the-art language laboratory with phonographs and lots of records was also made available on campus for nearly fifteen hours every day. As a student, you were allowed to take three courses. Midterms and final exams were given and a 'no pass' got you booted back to your unit.

As Shrivenham is located in the middle of the pastoral countryside of Oxford, the students had immense opportunities to visit a multitude of historical and cultural sites and cities. Special trains and buses were there to ensure that they made good use of the opportunities. Many more offerings were made available at the university, some more popular than others. A young girl by the name of Diana Fluck modelled for the art classes in the nude, perhaps making it a particularly interesting study for the men. She was later to be known as none other than Diana Dors, the British actress and blonde bombshell who took Hollywood by storm in the 1950s.

Despite the initial less than optimistic forecast of this relatively short and unique educational experiment, most students, against popular belief, passed their courses with top marks. The British political magazine the *New Statesman* implored Shrivenham American University to continue. They lobbied for the development of an equivalent British institution at the time. Sadly, nothing ever came of this.

Twelve years later, nearly 8 million vets had benefited from the GI Bill, which was praised for its significant contribution to raising the US stock of human capital. The GI Bill was, however, also criticised widely for its racial discrimination in its invariable accommodation of Jim Crow laws (American statutes that made racial segregation legal). While the GI Bill was a fantastic opportunity at its inception, at least for some, the historian Ira Katznelson described it as merely 'an affirmative action for whites',[9] a bill that actually ended up increasing the already existing racial wealth and social imbalance. As an example, the sad statistics show that while 67,000 mortgages were insured by the GI Bill in the New York area alone, fewer than 100 of these were provided to non-whites.

The inequalities that have existed between races for centuries are still ingrained within the very roots of modern society. It was there long before, it was there then, and it is still here today. This is particularly and tragically ironic when we look at some of the fundamental reasons for what caused the outbreak of the Second World War in the first place.

In spite of the clear criticism, the programme was a roaring success and provided a multitude of young, battle-torn soldiers with a very welcome respite: a chance to acclimatise and re-enter society again through the introduction of higher education and cultural offers. Since then, Congress has approved a number of expansions to the benefits within the GI Bill, ensuring that all American military veterans can receive proper help and assistance.

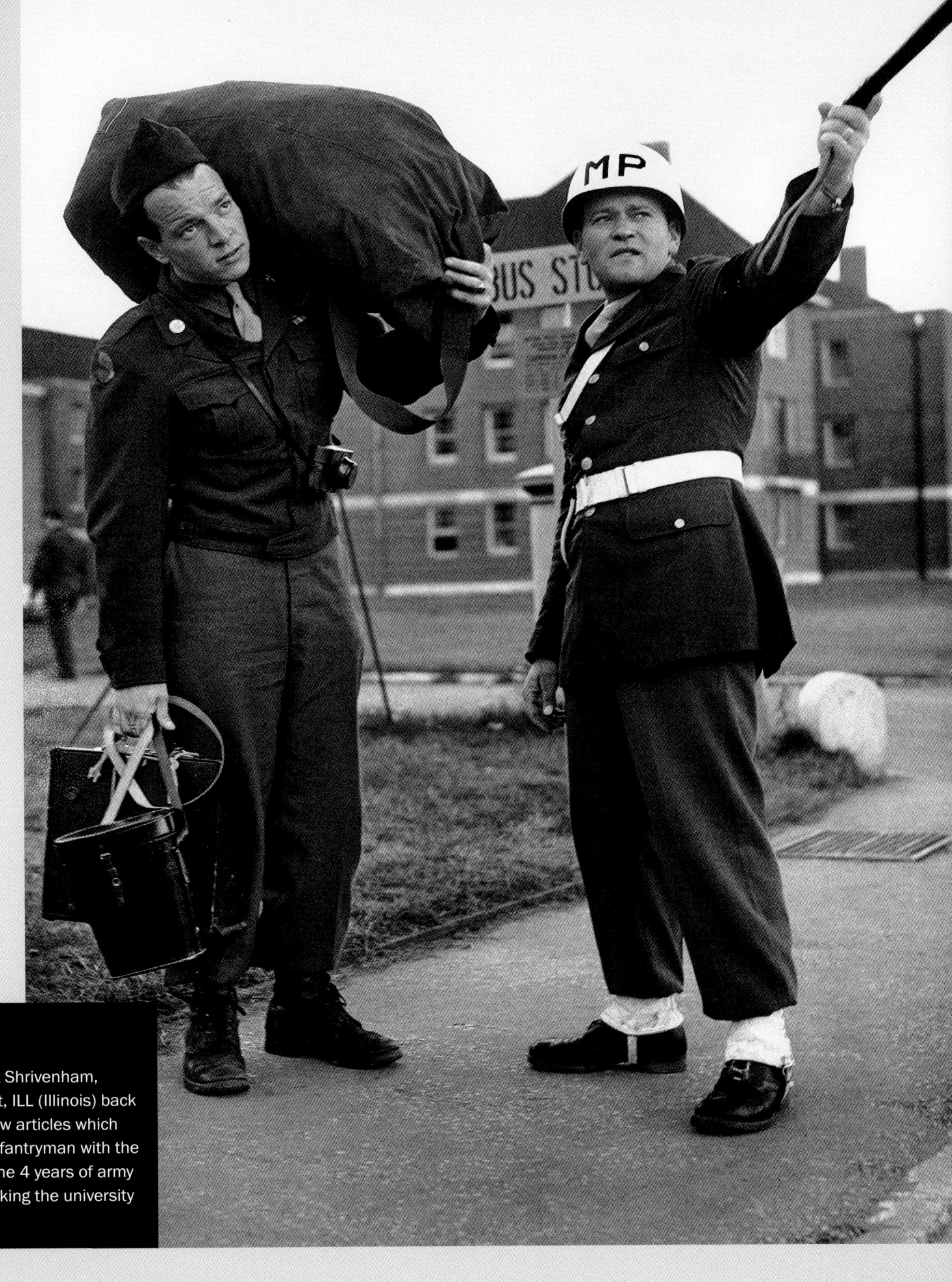

1945
TOPFOTO CODE: PD3001223
29th Infantry 115th regiment U.S Army University centre at Shrivenham, England. Photo shows:- PFC. Robert N. Haire of Lake Forest, ILL (Illinois) back from the war on the European Front with all his kit and a few articles which he 'liberated', arrives at the university centre. He was an infantryman with the 29th Infantry Division and the 115th Regiment. He has done 4 years of army service. In peace time he was a meat packer and is now taking the university course to study business methods.

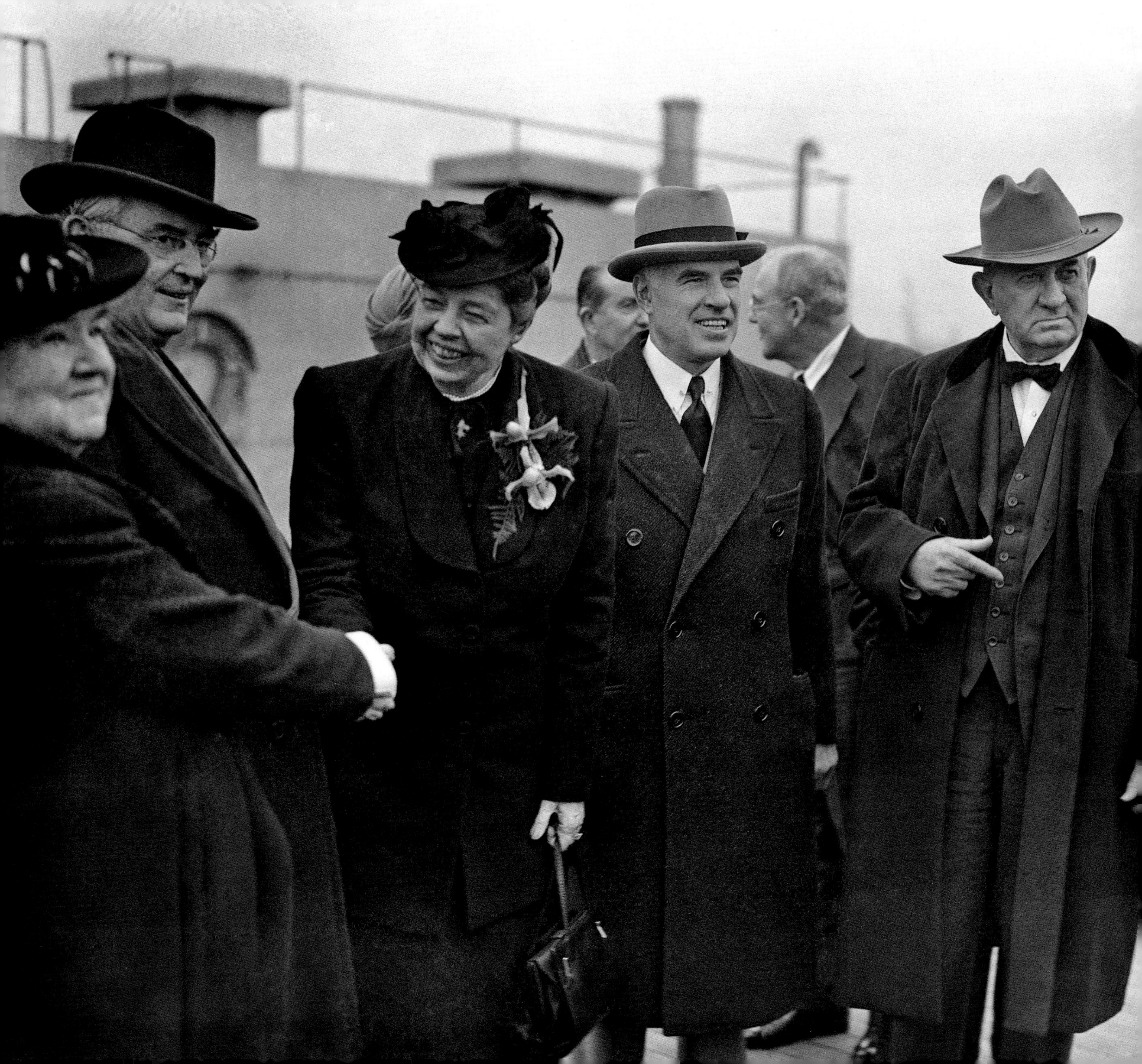

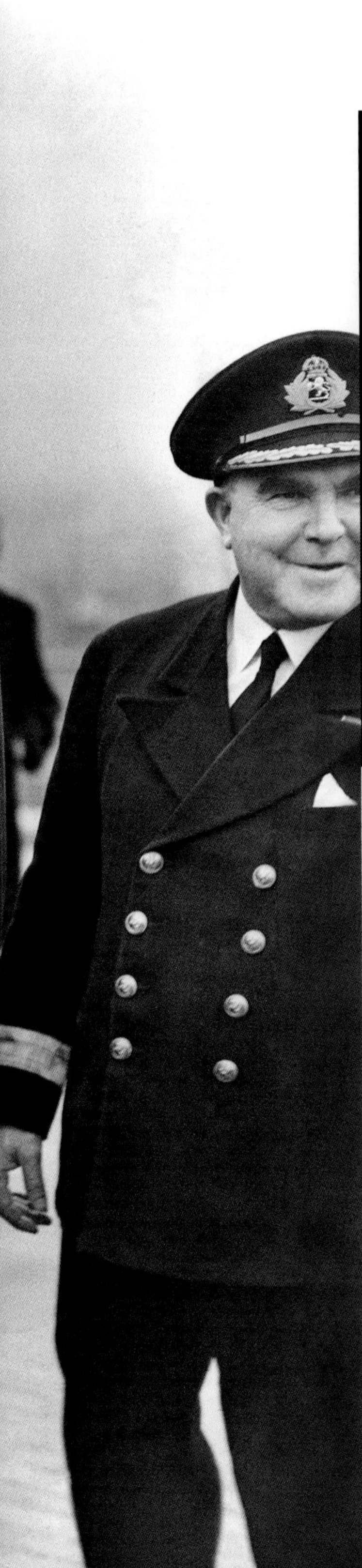

Eleanor Roosevelt was the First Lady of the USA from 1933 to 1945, and in many ways redefined this role in American society. She was deeply involved in politics and was very outspoken on the subjects of civil, workers' and women's rights. Additionally, she was also an early supporter of the civil rights movement and advocated strongly for racial equality and integration.

Following the death of her husband on 12 April 1945, Eleanor was appointed a delegate to the newly established United Nations by the new US President Harry S. Truman. She played a vital role in drafting the Universal Declaration of Human Rights in 1948, as she served as the chair of the Human Rights Commission. The declaration is a fundamental text in the basic rights and fundamental freedoms applying to every human being. The day before arriving in the UK, Eleanor wrote in her published, diary-like column 'My Day':

5th of January, 1945

I have been thinking of the serious responsibility which lies not only on the delegates to the United Nations Organization but on the nation as a whole as we gather for our first meeting of the UNO Assembly ... The greed, suspicion and fear which have created wars in the past will create them again unless, through education and understanding, human beings can be brought to see that their own best interests lie along new lines of development. If we hope to prosper, others must prosper too, and if we hope to be trusted, we must trust others ... The building of this organization is the greatest challenge that civilized man has ever faced ... No people are secure unless they have the things needed not only to preserve existence, but to make life worth living. These needs may differ widely now. They may change for all, from time to time. But all people throughout the world must know that there is an organization where their interests can be considered and where justice and security will be sought for all.[11]

Eleanor served as a delegate for the UN for more than ten years. Later president John F. Kennedy nominated her for the Nobel Peace Prize, and while she did not receive it, Eleanor arguably remains one of the most admired American women in history.

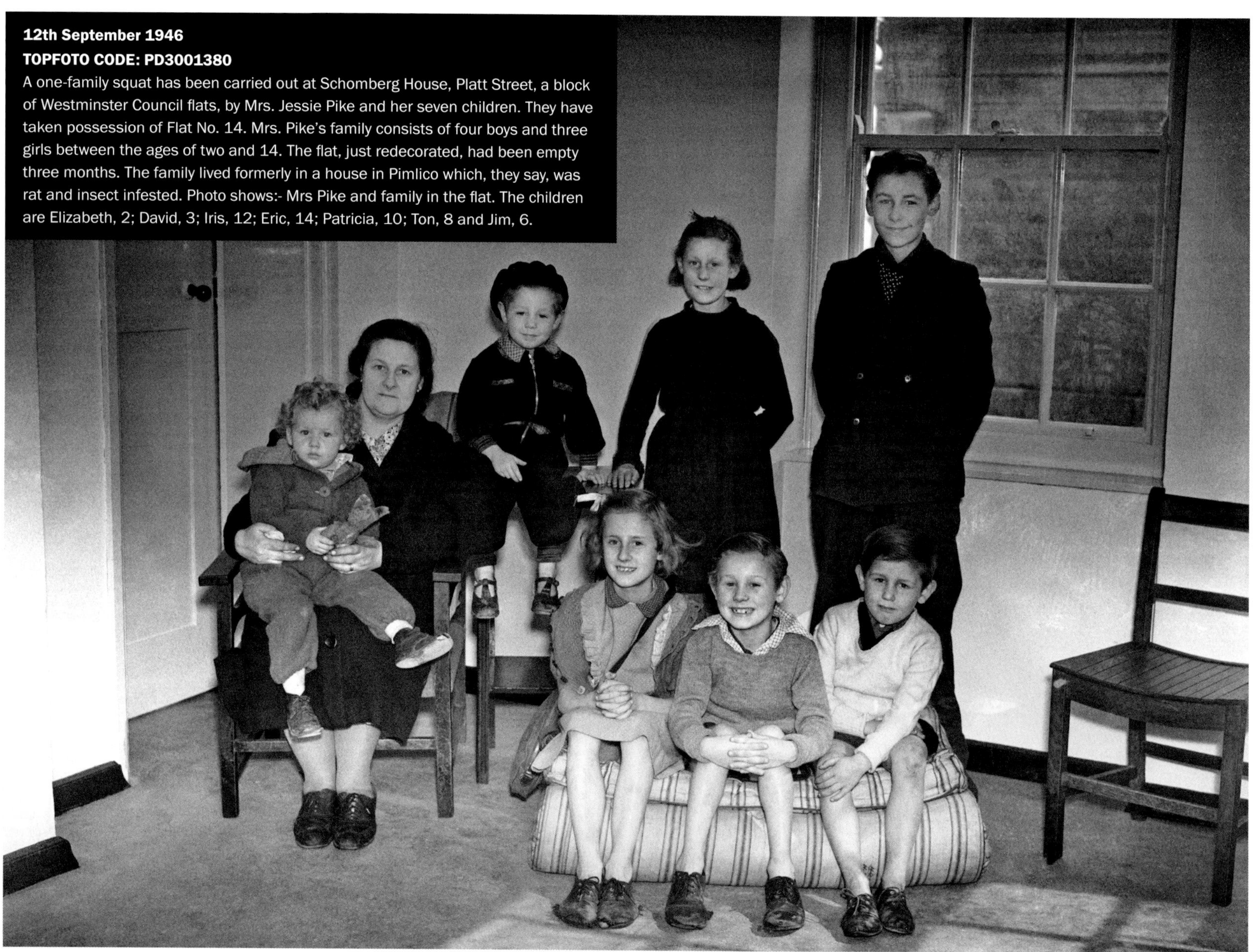

Already prior to the Second World War, the UK had insufficient housing for its population. Post-war it became an even bigger issue due to many factors. With their win in the general elections in 1945, Clement Attlee and the Labour Party inherited a country with strained finances and a people that were crying out for homes.

From 1945 to 1951, they managed to build over 1.2 million new homes, but with the destruction caused by Luftwaffe bombings, servicemen returning home, limited resources, the post-war baby boom, and a lack of skilled labour it simply didn't suffice. Even with prefabricated houses and temporary solutions, 1946 in particular saw an explosion in mass squatting across Britain. (Notice the condition of the children's shoes in the photo).

(See the example of a pre-fab house on page 156.)

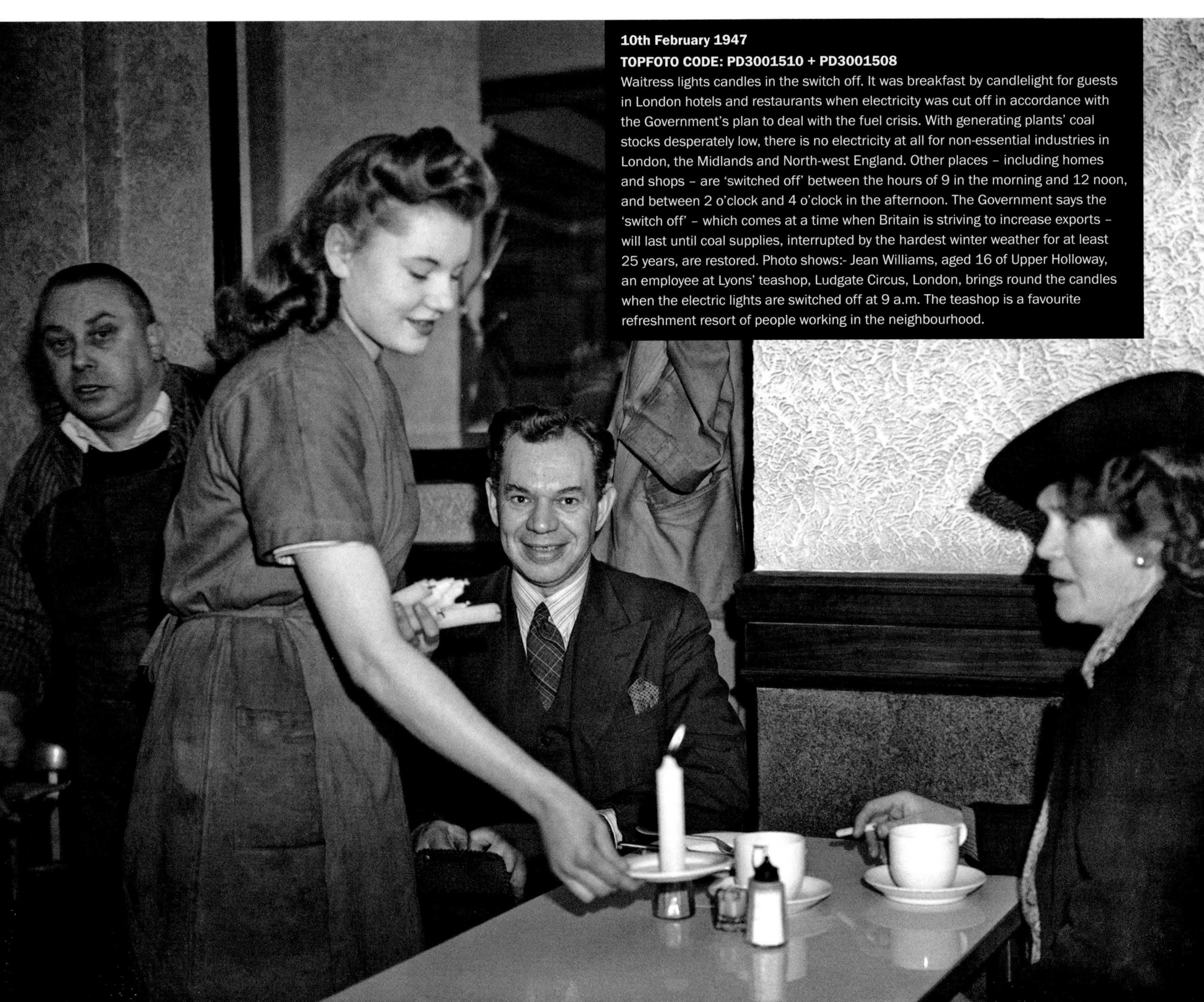

10th February 1947
TOPFOTO CODE: PD3001510 + PD3001508
Waitress lights candles in the switch off. It was breakfast by candlelight for guests in London hotels and restaurants when electricity was cut off in accordance with the Government's plan to deal with the fuel crisis. With generating plants' coal stocks desperately low, there is no electricity at all for non-essential industries in London, the Midlands and North-west England. Other places – including homes and shops – are 'switched off' between the hours of 9 in the morning and 12 noon, and between 2 o'clock and 4 o'clock in the afternoon. The Government says the 'switch off' – which comes at a time when Britain is striving to increase exports – will last until coal supplies, interrupted by the hardest winter weather for at least 25 years, are restored. Photo shows:- Jean Williams, aged 16 of Upper Holloway, an employee at Lyons' teashop, Ludgate Circus, London, brings round the candles when the electric lights are switched off at 9 a.m. The teashop is a favourite refreshment resort of people working in the neighbourhood.

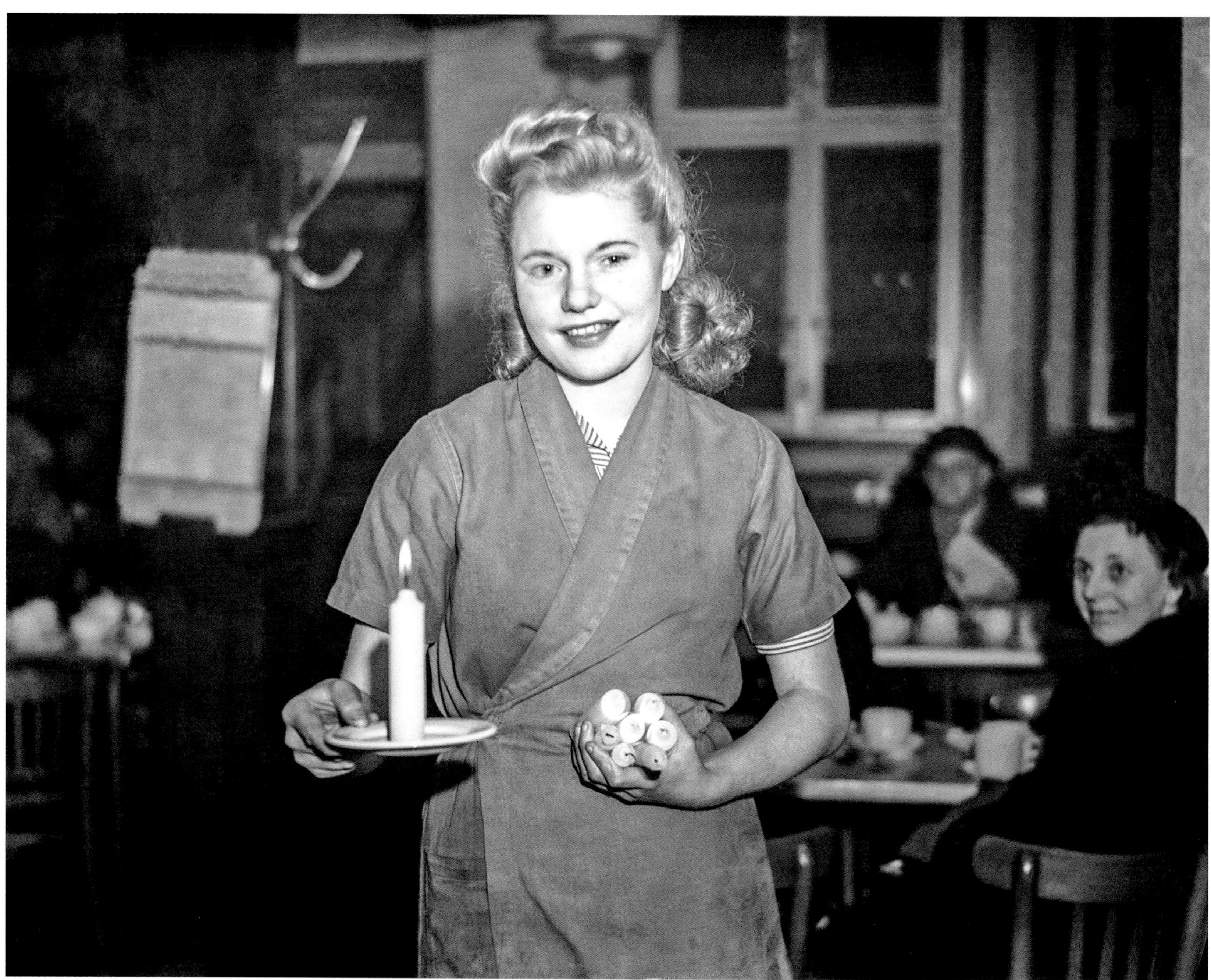

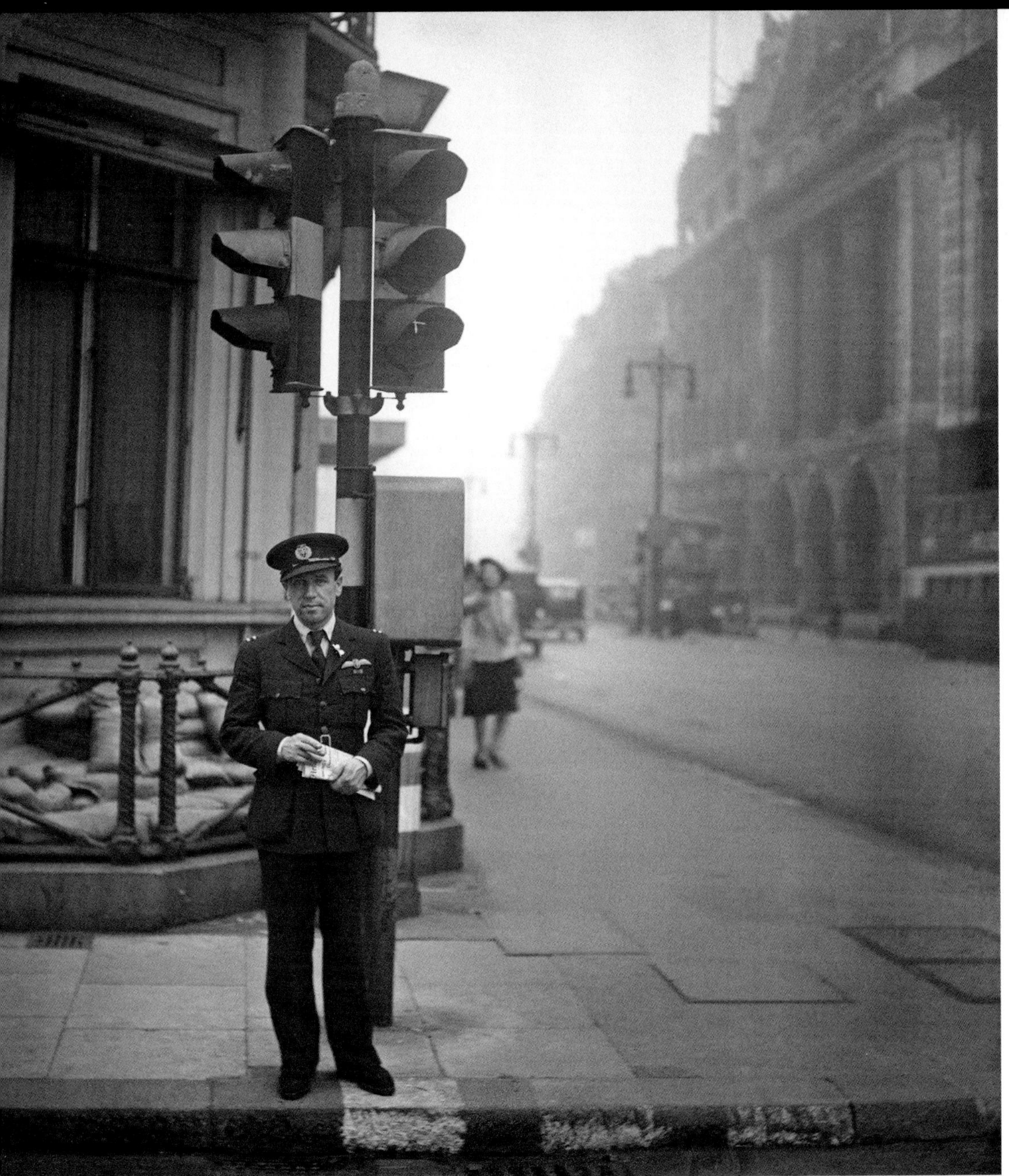

Jim Mollison, who was known for his record-breaking solo flights in the 1930s, is here captured during a rare moment of respite in war-torn London. At only 18 years of age, he obtained his RAF Short Service Commission and was at the time the youngest officer in the service.

Known as a bit of a playboy, he encountered the also famous pilot Amy Johnson on a passenger plane and asked her to marry him within eight hours of them meeting. They married in 1932 and became favourites of the press, who gave them the name 'the Flying Sweethearts'. They divorced in 1938, mainly due to their competitiveness (they were continuous rivals, always attempting to break the same aviation records), but also because of Mollison's increasing consumption of alcohol.

Johnson died in a crash in 1941 during a routine flight. Her plane was never found. In February 2024, eighty-three years later, the only known fragment of her plane was uncovered and sold at auction.

Mollison was eventually appointed a Member of the Order of the British Empire (MBE) in recognition of his dedicated service with the Air Transport Auxiliary (ATA), but later spiralled downwards. In 1953 he had his pilot licence taken away due to his drinking, which only subsequently increased. In 1956 he passed away in a mental health hospital, his ill health caused by alcohol-related issues.

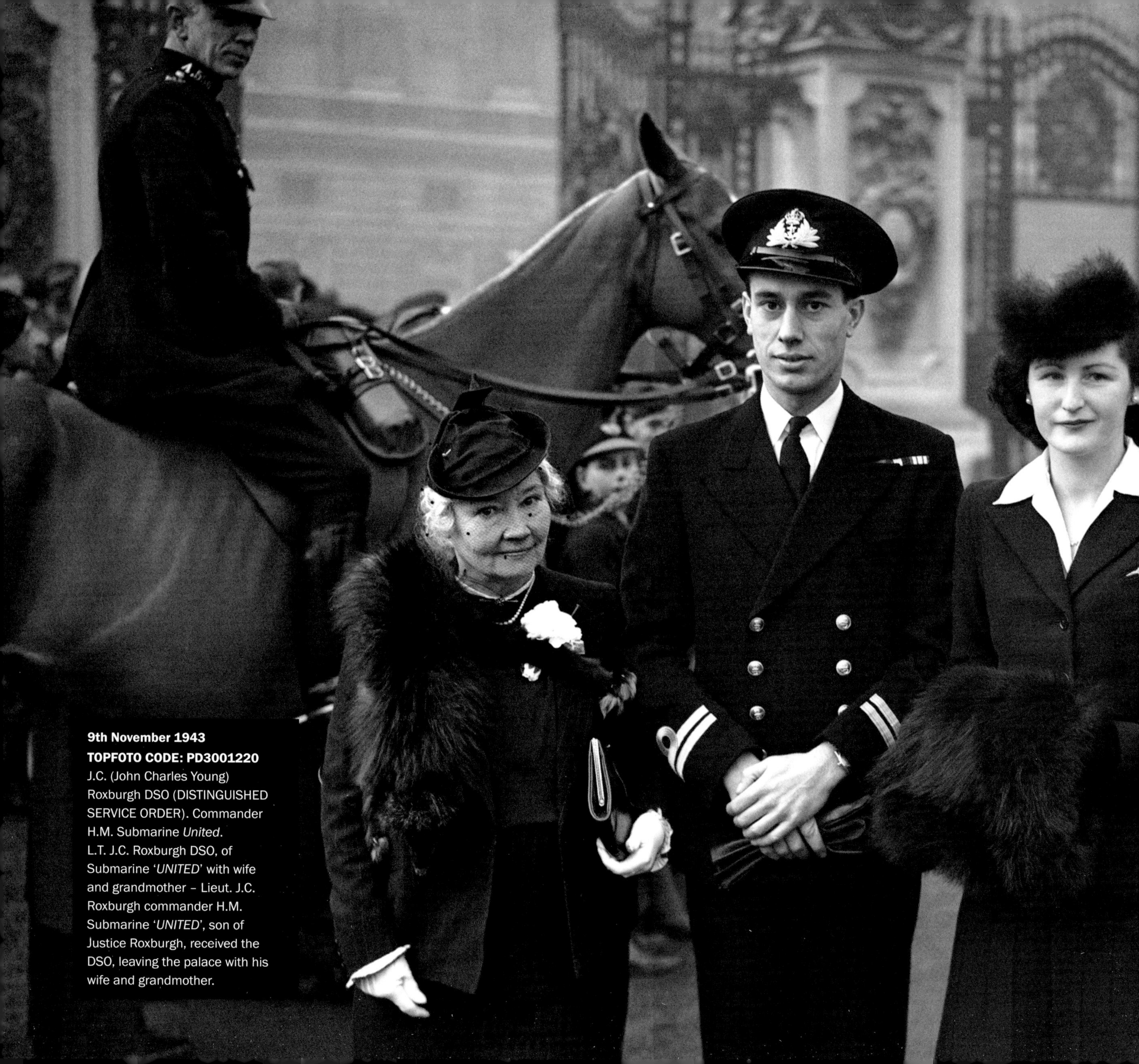

9th November 1943
TOPFOTO CODE: PD3001220
J.C. (John Charles Young) Roxburgh DSO (DISTINGUISHED SERVICE ORDER). Commander H.M. Submarine *United*.
L.T. J.C. Roxburgh DSO, of Submarine '*UNITED*' with wife and grandmother – Lieut. J.C. Roxburgh commander H.M. Submarine '*UNITED*', son of Justice Roxburgh, received the DSO, leaving the palace with his wife and grandmother.

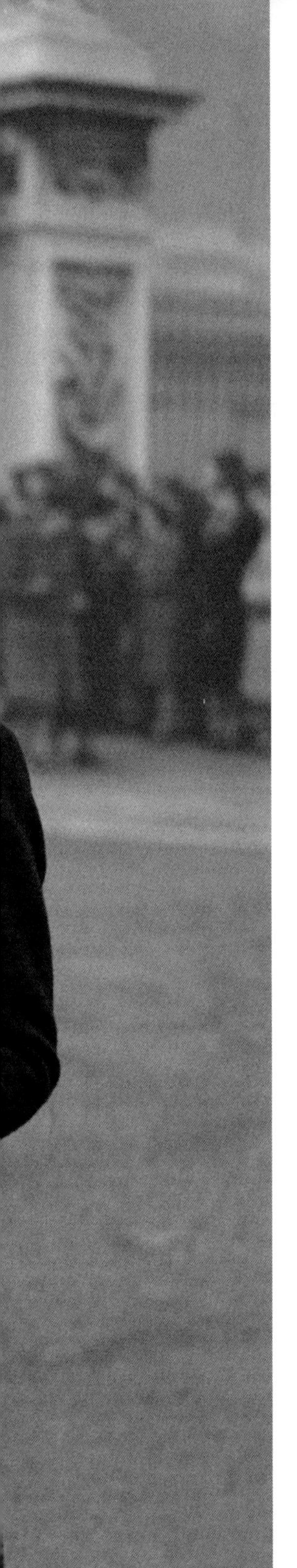

John Roxburgh was the son of the Honourable Sir Thomas James Young Roxburgh, Justice Judge in the Calcutta High Court and Knight Indian Civil Servant.

He was sent to the Royal Naval College Dartmouth at the tender age of 14 and in 1940 he joined the Submarines at just 21. Shortly after, he was awarded a DSC (Distinguished Service Cross) for service in the Bay of Biscay and Norway.

In 1942, at only 23, he took command of HM Submarine *P44*, later known as HMS *United*. Leading Seaman Cyril Balls remembered, 'When we first saw him, I think all our hearts sank; he looked so young and was, in fact, only 23, just a few months older than myself! Our first patrol with him proved very eventful and we soon realised that there was a new name over the door and that we had a cool customer in charge!'[12]

During Roxburgh's first patrol of Italy's coast, he encountered a massive flotilla of eleven enemy merchant vessels accompanied by air patrols, destroyers and anti-submarine craft. Based in Malta, and having only vintage First World War torpedoes at his disposal, he had to make a run for it with a series of difficult manoeuvres. He was later praised for his skill and calm during this incident.

On his second patrol, however, he successfully downed an Italian destroyer in a large convoy and was subsequently, brutally, depth-charged for more than half a day. His submarine resurfaced for only a few minutes during the night, the entire crew suffering with severe headaches, sickness and loss of concentration from the deprivation of fresh air. Seaman Cyril Balls wrote in his diary, 'It was some time before there was sufficient oxygen for the first all-important cigarette.'[13]

It is hard to imagine the mental strength required to have to fight an entire war in the confined quarters of a submarine, deep below the sea, in virtual silence and with limited oxygen. Commander William King recalls, 'At the end of the war I was thirty-five but I looked fifty-five … I was a wreck physically, morally, socially, financially, and in every other way. I wanted to get out of the navy, but of course, they wouldn't let us go. It took me two years to struggle out by writing letters.'[14]

In 1943, Roxburgh led HMS *United* during Operation Husky, the Allied Sicily landings, one of the most important campaigns of the war. It was the Allies' first assault on Europe, and where Roxburgh downed the Italian submarine *Remo*, one of the two largest submarines the country had ever built. Roxburgh watched through his periscope as the Italian boat's stern reared high, its propellers spinning before it sank. He recalled that he felt 'no elation after such a rapid end to one's own kind, but a momentary awe'.[15] His crew managed to save and imprison *Remo*'s captain.

On the way back to base, HMS *United* received a single signal saying 'Grommet', which meant that Roxburgh's wife had given birth to a daughter (it would apparently have been 'Toggle' had it been a boy). The captain of *Remo* also had a pregnant wife, and during his nine-day stay in *United* he joined the celebrations.

Returning to Malta, as per custom, *United* flew the Jolly Roger flag, but additionally also a flag of a stork carrying a baby! All British submarines returning from successful missions flew the Jolly Roger (it is, in fact, the emblem of the Royal Navy Submarine Service), and additional flags had further embroidered annotations, signifying the specific activity the submarine would have succeeded in. A dagger would indicate a 'cloak and dagger' operation, a white bar equalled a sunk merchant ship, a torch meant the sub would have acted as a guide, a red flower would have meant minefield reconnaissance – the list goes on and on. (For more information, pay a visit to the National Maritime Museum Cornwall.)

Roxburgh was one of only a very few submarine commanders to have sunk not just one but two enemy submarines, the second being a German U-boat in April 1945. This sinking was the last successful British submarine mission of the Second World War and earned him a bar to his DSC. The U-boat was none other than the infamous *U-486*, which had on Christmas Day 1944 sunk the American SS *Leopoldville*, resulting in the death of 816 Allied soldiers. (That same day, *U-486* had also crippled HMS *Affleck* and sunk the frigate HMS *Capel*.)

Upon his final mission, Roxburgh had survived torpedoes, bombs and depth charges. Out of the sixteen people on his submariners qualifying course in 1939, only three escaped with their lives. After eleven months he had sent 21,000 tons of enemy ships to the bottom of the sea and sunk a further 12,000 tons of shipping. He was awarded the DSO (which he had just received in the photo).

After the war Roxburgh was appointed Deputy Director of Plans at the Ministry of Defence in 1964, Flag Officer, Plymouth in 1967, and went on to be Flag Officer Submarines in 1969 (the Commanding Officer of the Royal Navy Submarine Service, one of the five fighting armies of the Royal Navy), before retiring in 1972. He was later awarded CBE and ultimately, KCB (Knight Commander).

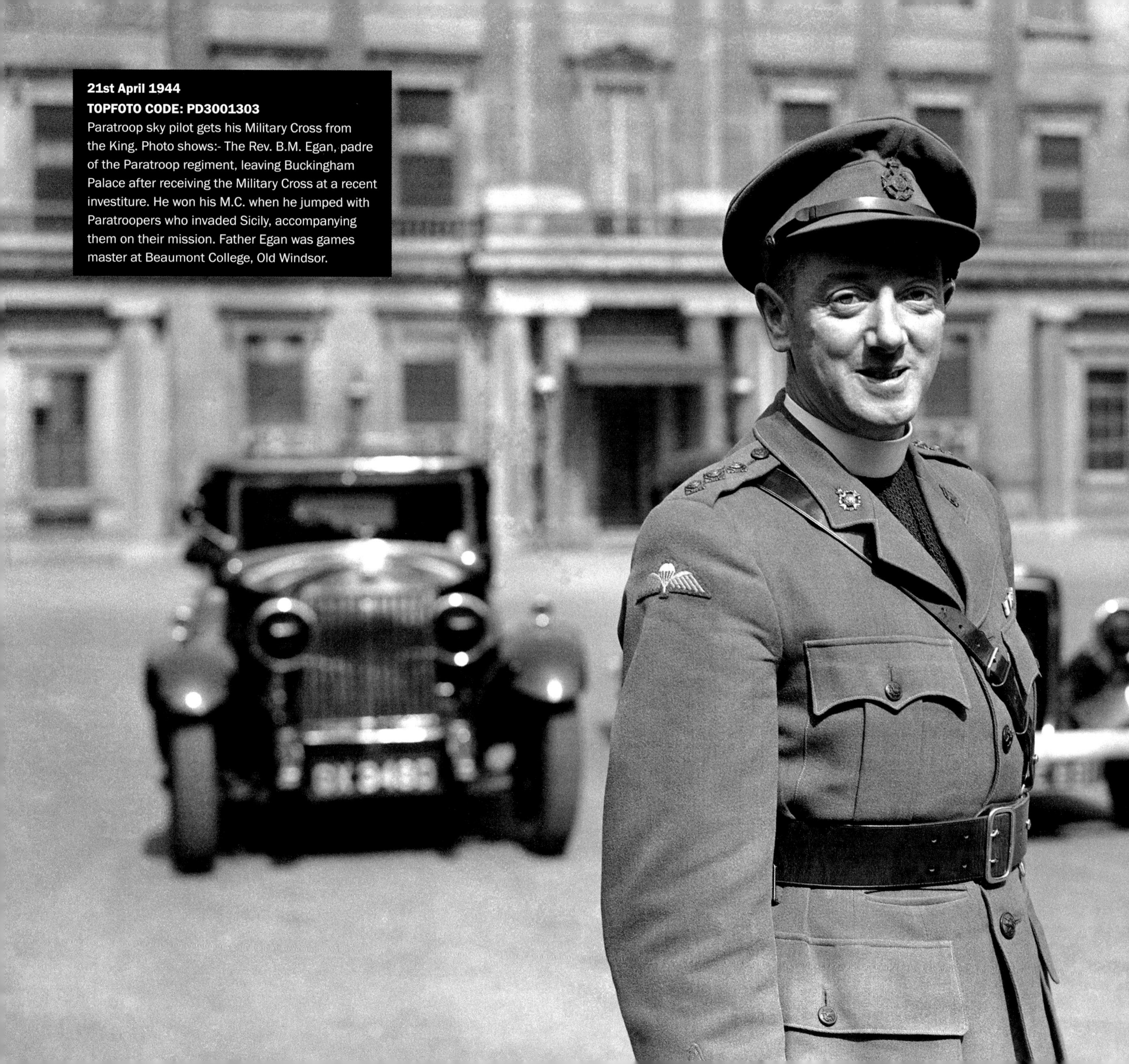

21st April 1944
TOPFOTO CODE: PD3001303
Paratroop sky pilot gets his Military Cross from the King. Photo shows:- The Rev. B.M. Egan, padre of the Paratroop regiment, leaving Buckingham Palace after receiving the Military Cross at a recent investiture. He won his M.C. when he jumped with Paratroopers who invaded Sicily, accompanying them on their mission. Father Egan was games master at Beaumont College, Old Windsor.

After the outbreak of the Second World War in September 1939, the Roman Catholic priest Bernard Egan signed up to become a chaplain for the armed forces. Two years later he volunteered when more men were needed in the Special Air Service. B.M. Egan thus became the very first chaplain (and the very first Roman Catholic chaplain) to complete the course and get his para-wings.

He served with his battalion in North Africa, Sicily, Italy and Arnhem, and was awarded the Military Cross for his service in Sicily in 1943. The photo was taken on 21 April 1944, just five months before his participation in the Battle of Arnhem, part of the failed Operation Market Garden. While Egan made it to the road bridge in Arnhem, he was wounded on 19 September and subsequently captured by the Germans. He spent the remainder of the war in a POW camp. During his time as a prisoner and still wounded, he was laid up with his CO, Lt Col Johnny Frost. The colonel later conveyed a story relating to the character of Egan:

> After our second operation and with the absence of modern drugs, these [the wounds] had to be swabbed out twice daily. A painful business and I so well remember our argument as to whether it was best for the orderly giving the treatment to come to us at the beginning or the end of his round. I wanted to get it over as quickly as possible but he [The Rev Egan] felt that, hearing others suffering first, strengthened him to bear the pain too.[16]

When Egan was liberated in 1945 and returned to the UK, he left the service and spent twenty years as headmaster at Wimbledon Prep School in London. His old wounds from the war became an increasing problem and in his later years he completely lost the use of his legs. He died in 1988 at the age of 83.

In the UK National Archives, a copy of the original army form exists, pertaining to Chaplain 4th Class, Reverend Bernard Mary Egan of the 1st Parachute, 1st Airborne Division, 2nd Battalion. The document states the actions for which he received his Military Cross (only 10,386 of these were awarded during the Second World War):

> For conspicuous gallantry and devotion to duty. Since joining this Battalion in February 1943, Captain Egan has fulfilled his duties as a Battalion Chaplain with courage and determination. During the heavy fighting in the Northern Sector in Tunisia in March 1943, he was often in the forefront of the battle, comforting the wounded and encouraging all ranks under heavy fire. On the night July 13–14th 1943, this officer took part in a parachute operation, South of Catania in Sicily, and was dropped among enemy positions many miles from the remainder of the Battalion.
>
> He collected a small party of parachute troops. After laying up in the near vicinity of the German positions he managed to extricate his party. By cool leadership and initiative, he conducted it over difficult country and through enemy lines, eventually reaching the British positions with his complete party.[17]

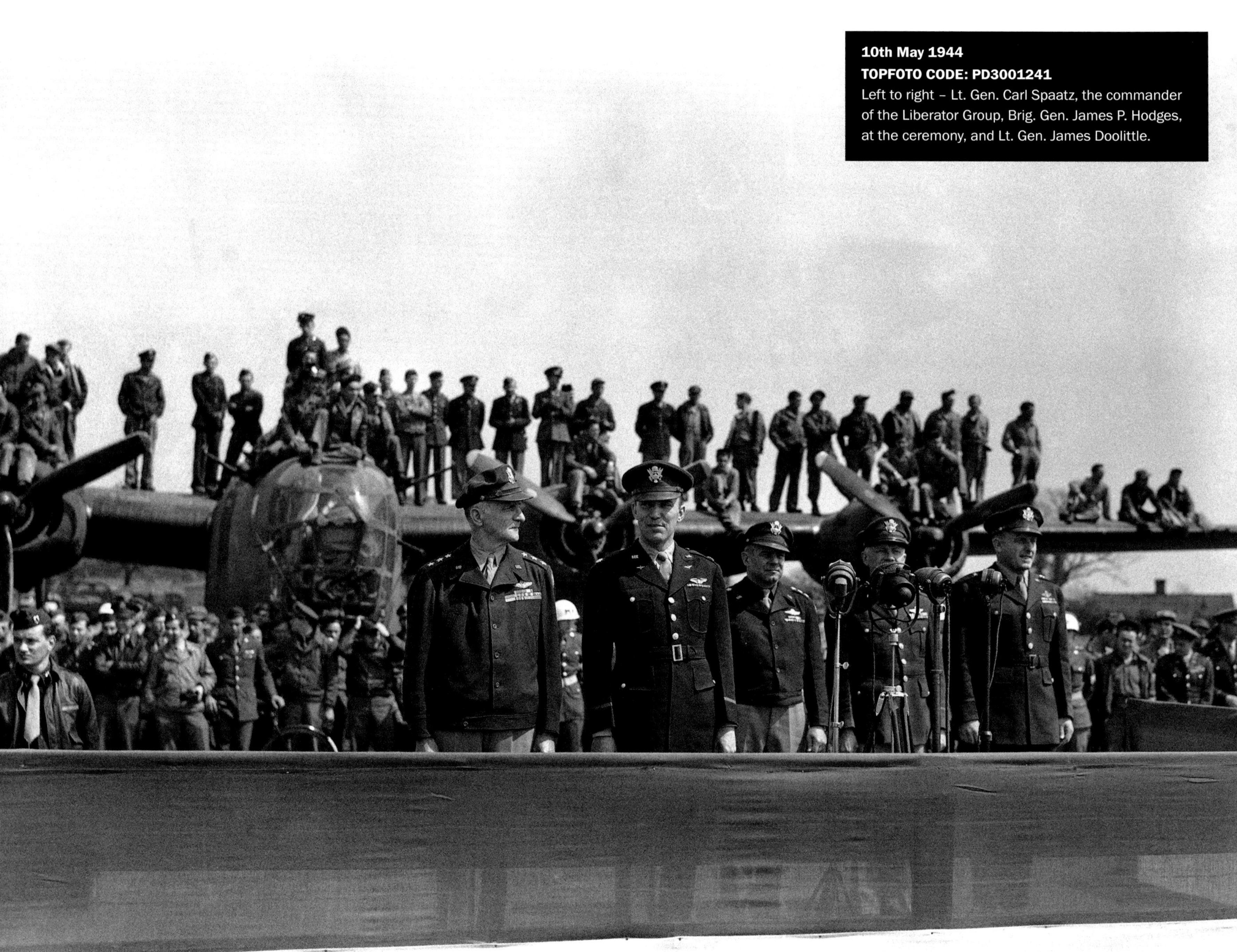

10th May 1944
TOPFOTO CODE: PD3001241
Left to right – Lt. Gen. Carl Spaatz, the commander
of the Liberator Group, Brig. Gen. James P. Hodges,
at the ceremony, and Lt. Gen. James Doolittle.

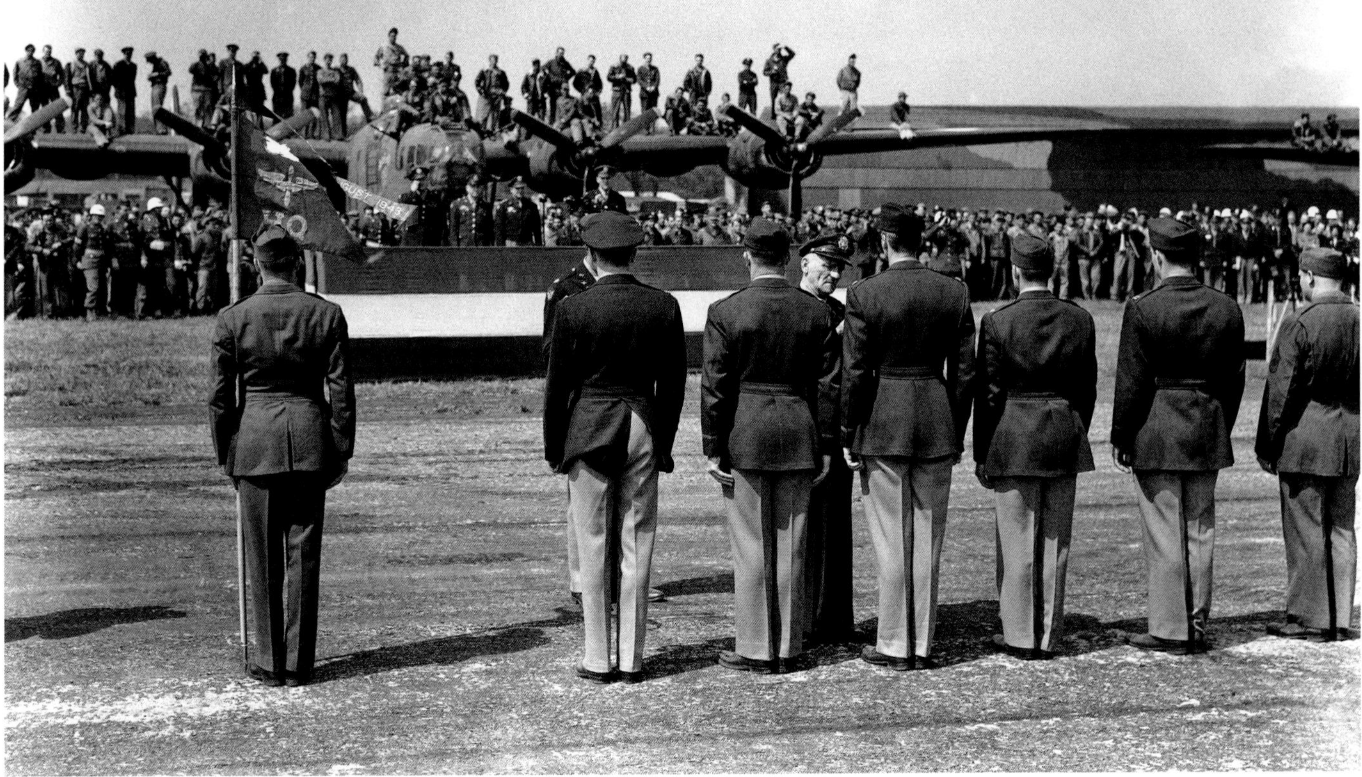

Lt. Gen. Carl Spaatz decorating one of the group representatives with a War Department Citation medal, at the ceremony.

Carl 'Tooey' Spaatz is considered a pioneer within American military aviation. He graduated from West Point in 1914 and served as a combat pilot in the First World War, during which he downed three enemy planes. During the Second World War, Spaatz played an important role in overseeing the bombing campaigns in both Europe and the Pacific Theatre.

As the commander of the US Strategic Air Forces in Europe, he directed the Allied bombing raids on Germany. His personally determined targeting of Germany's oil infrastructure is believed to have played a huge part in significantly weakening the Nazi war machine.

In 1947, with the establishment of the independent United States Air Force, Spaatz was appointed its first Chief of Staff. Under his leadership, he helped shape the policies and strategies that became a guide for the Air Force in the early stages of the Cold War period. He retired in 1948 with the rank of general.

James Harold Doolittle was likewise an aviation legend. He served as a flight instructor during the First World War and in the interwar years performed many daring and record-breaking flights. Doolittle was one of the first to identify that due to the rapid technological development within flight, pilots could no longer entirely rely on their human senses and thus became a spearhead in the early stages of instrument flying. In 1929, he was the first pilot to perform a take-off, flight and landing without any outside view. This type of flying became vital in overcoming limitations to visibility such as clouds, fog, rain and darkness.

Following the detrimental attack on Pearl Harbor on 7 December 1941, he won a Medal of Honor for his planning and execution of the Doolittle Raid, where he commanded a group of bombers in a retaliation attack against the Japanese. From January 1944 to September 1945, he commanded the Eighth Air Force (effectively giving him control of more than 42,000 aircraft), and made a radical decision to alter the strategy for fighters escorting bombers. Previously their protocol had been to remain with the bomber formations at all times. Doolittle changed this by allowing the fighters to fly ahead of the bombers and actively engage German fighters before they could attack. This new and bold tactic effectively neutralised the Luftwaffe's heavy fighter groups, and very likely saved a lot of lives and machinery. Between 1957 and 1958, Doolittle was the Chairman of NACA (the predecessor to NASA). In 1958 one of his two sons, James Jr, also a pilot, tragically committed suicide. Doolittle was later offered the opportunity to be the first administrator for NASA but declined. He retired in 1959.

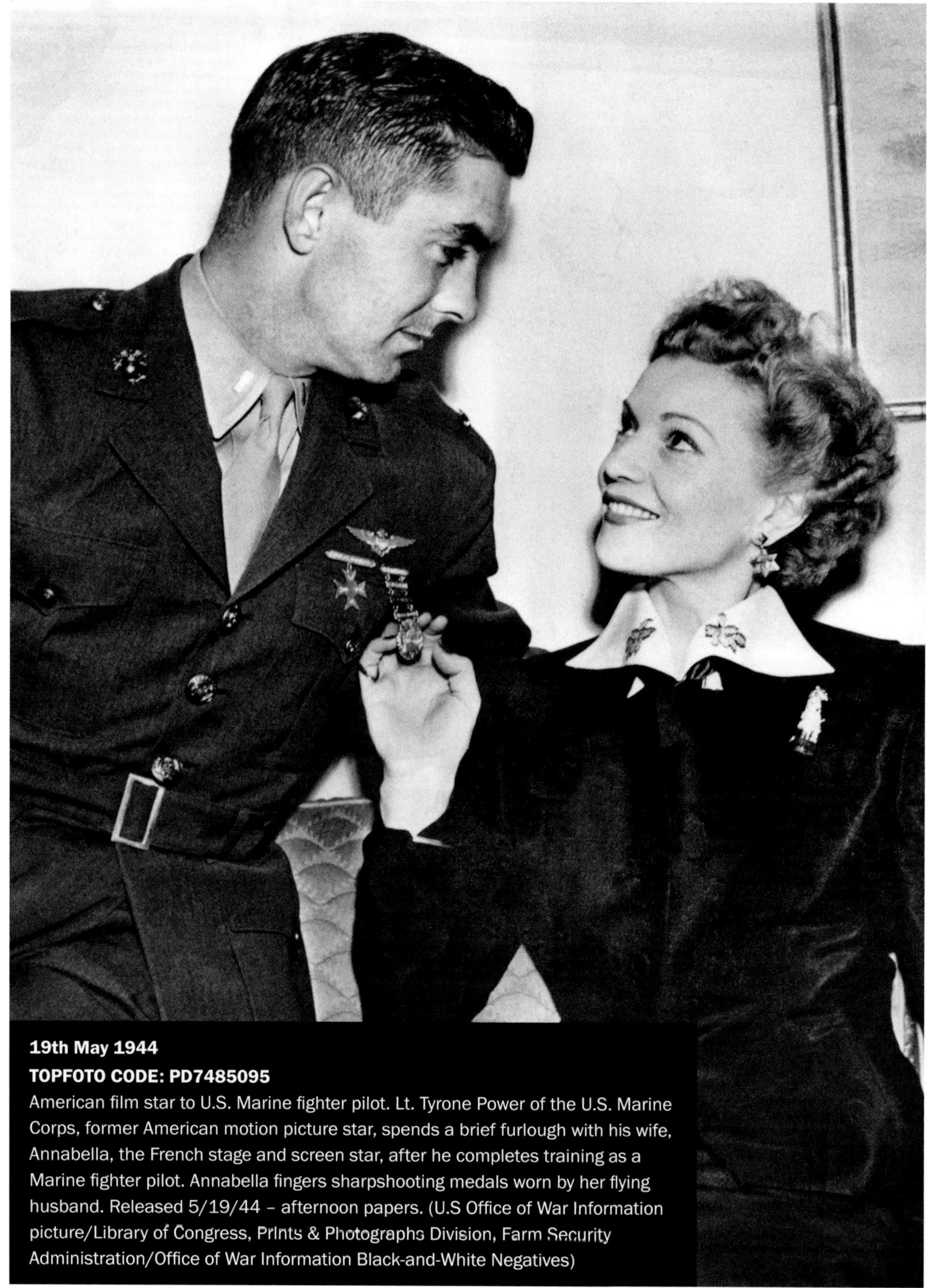

19th May 1944

TOPFOTO CODE: PD7485095

American film star to U.S. Marine fighter pilot. Lt. Tyrone Power of the U.S. Marine Corps, former American motion picture star, spends a brief furlough with his wife, Annabella, the French stage and screen star, after he completes training as a Marine fighter pilot. Annabella fingers sharpshooting medals worn by her flying husband. Released 5/19/44 – afternoon papers. (U.S Office of War Information picture/Library of Congress, Prints & Photographs Division, Farm Security Administration/Office of War Information Black-and-White Negatives)

Tyrone Power was the archetypical handsome, swashbuckling movie star of the Golden Age of Hollywood. Films, musicals and theatre productions, with him as the lead protagonist, were a big draw for the matinee crowds.

Both Power's parents had been actors and, encouraged by his father, he aspired early on to follow them. Tyrone and his father even got to perform together for a short while – until his father suddenly fell ill and died in young Power's arms during preparations on a movie set.

After some tough years, things started looking up for Tyrone though, and 20th Century Fox signed him in 1936. It became a strong collaboration and by the time he met the French actress Annabella (real name, Suzanne Georgette Charpentier), he could have married virtually anyone in Hollywood.

Annabella and Tyrone married on 23 April 1939. Their marriage infuriated their boss, Darryl F. Zanuck, as he foresaw Tyrone's lost appeal to the female fanbase, and therefore penalised Annabella by refusing her work.

In 1942, as an already accomplished pilot, Tyrone enlisted in the US Marine Corps and became a first lieutenant in 1943. At the age of 29, he did not qualify for active combat but instead flew supply runs and carried wounded soldiers in the Pacific Theatre.

After the war, he attempted to reconcile an already troubled marriage but the couple divorced in 1946. He later had a romance with the pin-up model and actress Lana Turner but ended up marrying the Mexican actress Linda Christian in 1946 (she is credited with being the earliest James Bond girl, in an early TV version of *Casino Royale* from 1954).

Affairs on both sides eventually led to yet another divorce and he began seeing the Swedish actress Mai Zetterling, although his affairs continued. In 1958 he got married for a third time – to Debbie Minardos, who fell pregnant shortly after.

Fate would have it that he would exit this world much like his father. In late 1958, while filming in Madrid, Power had a heart attack and died in the midst of a fencing scene. His wife gave birth to a son just a few months later. Although he might be largely unknown today, Power is ranked number twenty-one on the list of the most popular male leads in history.

"I was fighting for freedom ... World War II, that was for freedom.

We fought Nazism, fascism, and imperialism, and all three nations

(Germany, Italy & Japan) became democracies after the war was over."

S/Sgt Walter D. Ehlers, Medal of Honor recipient (page 195)

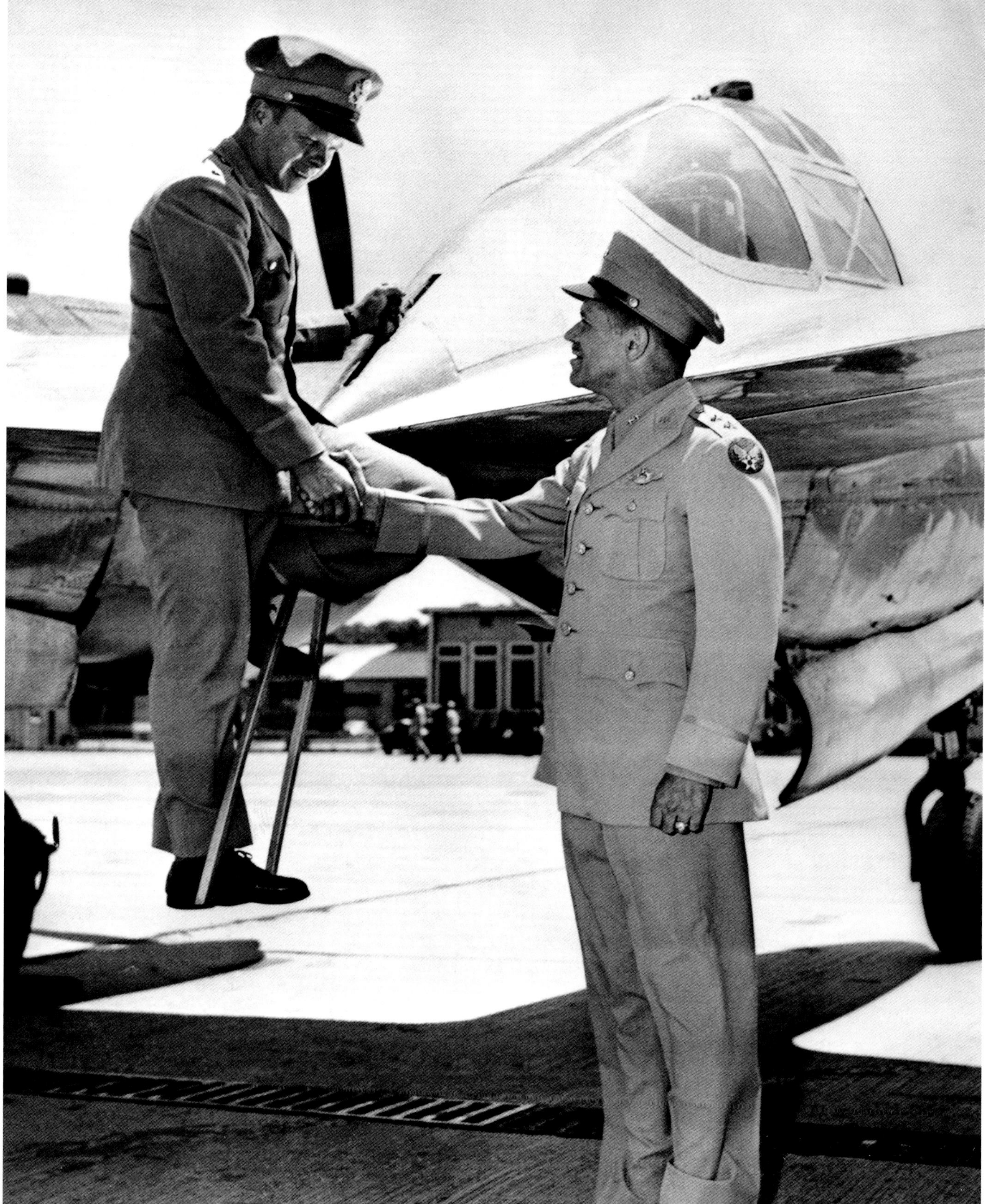

Anyone who has seen the film *Top Gun* will know the term 'ace'. This term originates from the First World War when aerial combat engagements, known as dogfights, first began. An aviator who engaged in combat and came out victorious, shooting down at least five enemy planes, was generally considered an 'ace'. Major Richard I. Bong was appropriately known as the Ace of Aces.

The American pilot Edward Vernon Rickenbacker scored twenty-six aerial combat victories during the First World War, making him the most successful US pilot ever up until that point. Bong surpassed that by lengths. During the Second World War, Bong had forty confirmed kills and logged more than 500 combat hours in his P-38 fighter. (Sources suggest that the number of kills was much higher than forty, but that Bong would regularly 'give away' kills to other members of his squadron.)

A farm boy from Wisconsin, he was known as a daredevil and a thrill seeker. Allegedly, he was once reprimanded and grounded in 1942 for looping his plane around the Golden Gate Bridge in San Francisco and later flying through its Market Street, blasting people's laundry off their clothes lines. In late 1942, he was specially chosen by General George C. Kenney and sent to Australia to fly P-38s in the Pacific. He earned his first ace title within just a few weeks of his first encounter with the enemy. In early 1943, he and six other pilots were protecting a group of bombers when they encountered heavy Japanese resistance. Together the seven of them shot down an estimated twenty planes. By mid-1943, he did the same again and engaged another twenty aircraft with just ten P-38s. Suddenly an additional fifteen Japanese planes entered the fight and Bong and his wingmen took down eleven of the thirty-five planes – without losing a single man themselves. Bong personally shot down four of these eleven planes.

Bong had near-fatal encounters but always seemed to get away quite unscathed and just kept rising in rank and fame, earning every medal in the process. By 1944, he had been promoted to major and was utilised by the top brass for promoting the sales of war bonds, while paraded around as a national hero to raise the spirit of the civilian population. He was made an instructor, and was himself instructed to not partake in any more dogfighting – except in the event of self-defence. However, self-defence was a matter of interpretation for Bong. Six weeks later he had shot down yet another ten Japanese planes, in just a few but particularly breakneck sorties.

On 12 December 1944, he was awarded the highest military decoration bestowed by the US Armed Forces: the Medal of Honor. (Read more about this on page 195.) This he could add to his Purple Heart, two Silver Stars, DSC (Distinguished Service Cross), seven DFCs (Distinguished Flying Cross) and a staggering fifteen Air Medals, making him one of the most highly decorated pilots in US history. Six months later, at the age of just 24, he would be dead.

On 6 August 1945, while test flying a new P-80A jet fighter plane, something went terribly wrong and Richard Bong went down in a blaze of flames, the cause of the crash still questioned by many today.

The P-38 that Bong flew for years, which he named 'Marge' after his wife, was later flown by a different pilot, Tom Malone, who crashed it in Papua New Guinea in 1944. In May 2024, a team discovered the very same plane in the jungle, identified by the nose art drawing of Bong's wife.

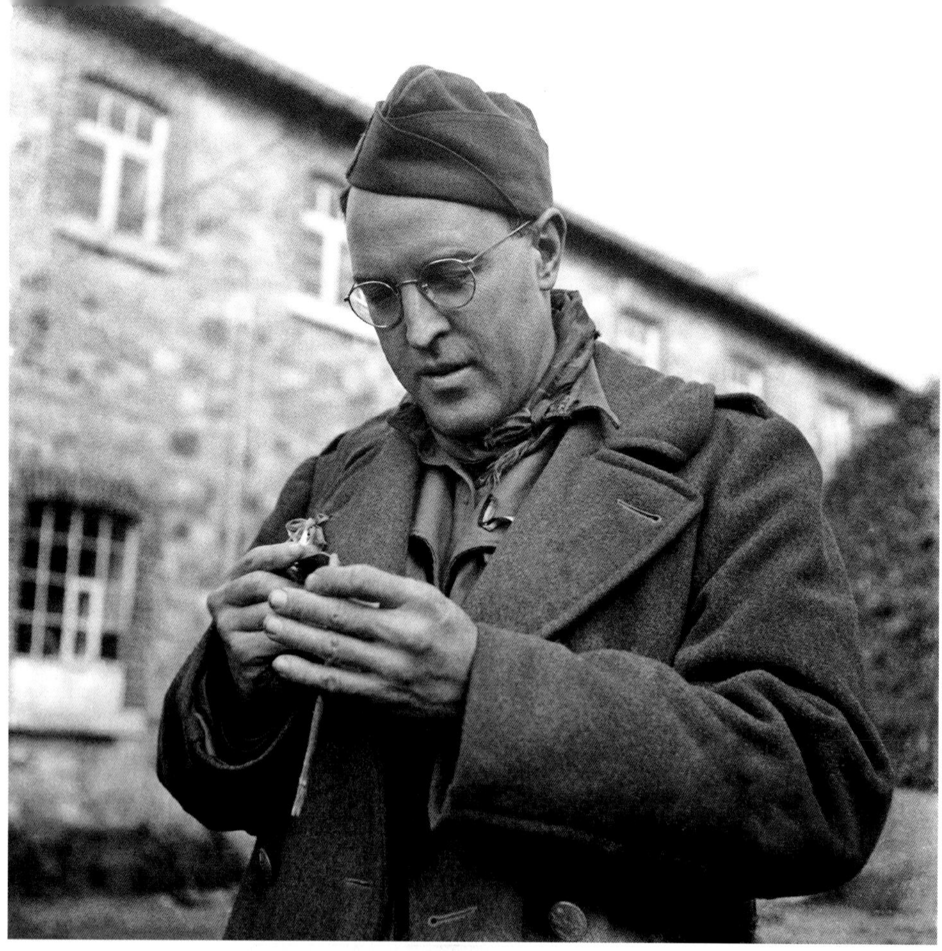

George Hicks was an American reporter and journalist who became famous for his live broadcast during D-Day, commenting from aboard USS *Ancon*, which was stationed at Omaha Beach in support of the landing forces. The recording was broadcast unedited around midnight, on 6 June 1944, on CBS, NBC, Mutual and Blue Network (for whom George was working at the time). Naturally, many fellow reporters also gave their own interpretation of the battle, but what made his so special was that he did it live as opposed to a later report of what he had observed. His clear description of the events – how the fire was raging, how smoke was rising, how objects were falling from the sky – combined with his own encouragement to the soldiers, gave the audience a feeling of being present themselves to witness the devastation unfold at first-hand.

The reportage won him numerous awards and *The New York World-Telegram* referred to it as 'the greatest recording yet to come out of the war'. (*Broadcasting*, Volume 26. Broadcasting Publications, 1944, p.9.) Blue Network later sent his wife a cheque for $1,000 (nearly $18,000 in today's money), in addition to his salary, as a token of appreciation for his work.

Hicks had a month in England but returned to the front to cover the advances of the Allied forces. The photos (left) showing Hicks sharpening his pencil and writing on his pad were taken on 18 October, just two months before he was wounded at the Battle of the Bulge.

Hicks passed away in 1965, aged 59. In 2019, his original thirteen-minute recording from D-Day was discovered in the cellar of a summer house on Long Island. It was later donated to the D-Day Foundation in Virginia, USA.

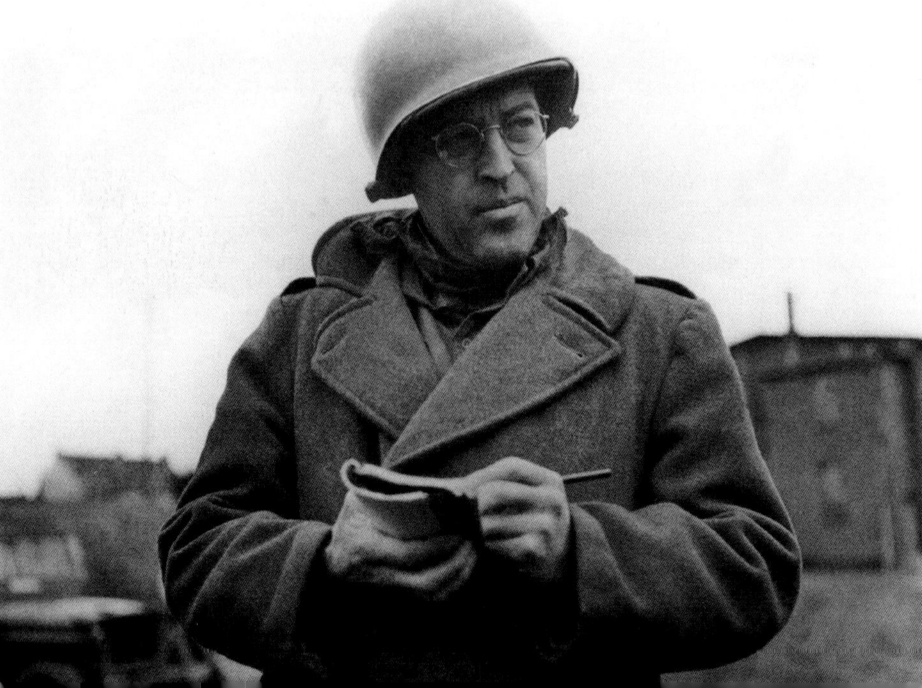

18th October 1944
TOPFOTO CODE: PD3001334 + PD3001332
George Hicks, of Blue Network, photographed in Germany as he gathered copy for a story.

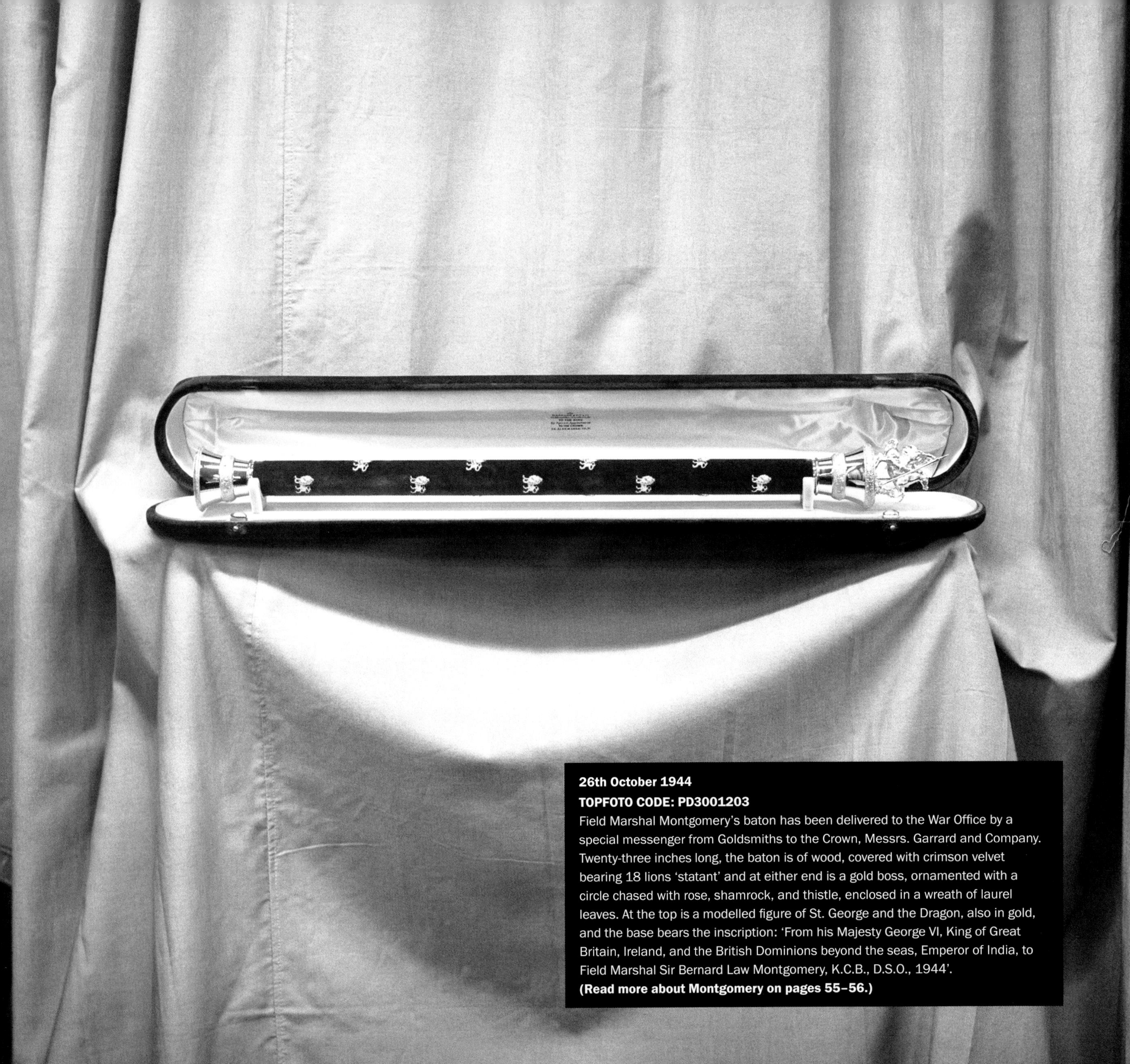

26th October 1944
TOPFOTO CODE: PD3001203
Field Marshal Montgomery's baton has been delivered to the War Office by a special messenger from Goldsmiths to the Crown, Messrs. Garrard and Company. Twenty-three inches long, the baton is of wood, covered with crimson velvet bearing 18 lions 'statant' and at either end is a gold boss, ornamented with a circle chased with rose, shamrock, and thistle, enclosed in a wreath of laurel leaves. At the top is a modelled figure of St. George and the Dragon, also in gold, and the base bears the inscription: 'From his Majesty George VI, King of Great Britain, Ireland, and the British Dominions beyond the seas, Emperor of India, to Field Marshal Sir Bernard Law Montgomery, K.C.B., D.S.O., 1944'.
(Read more about Montgomery on pages 55–56.)

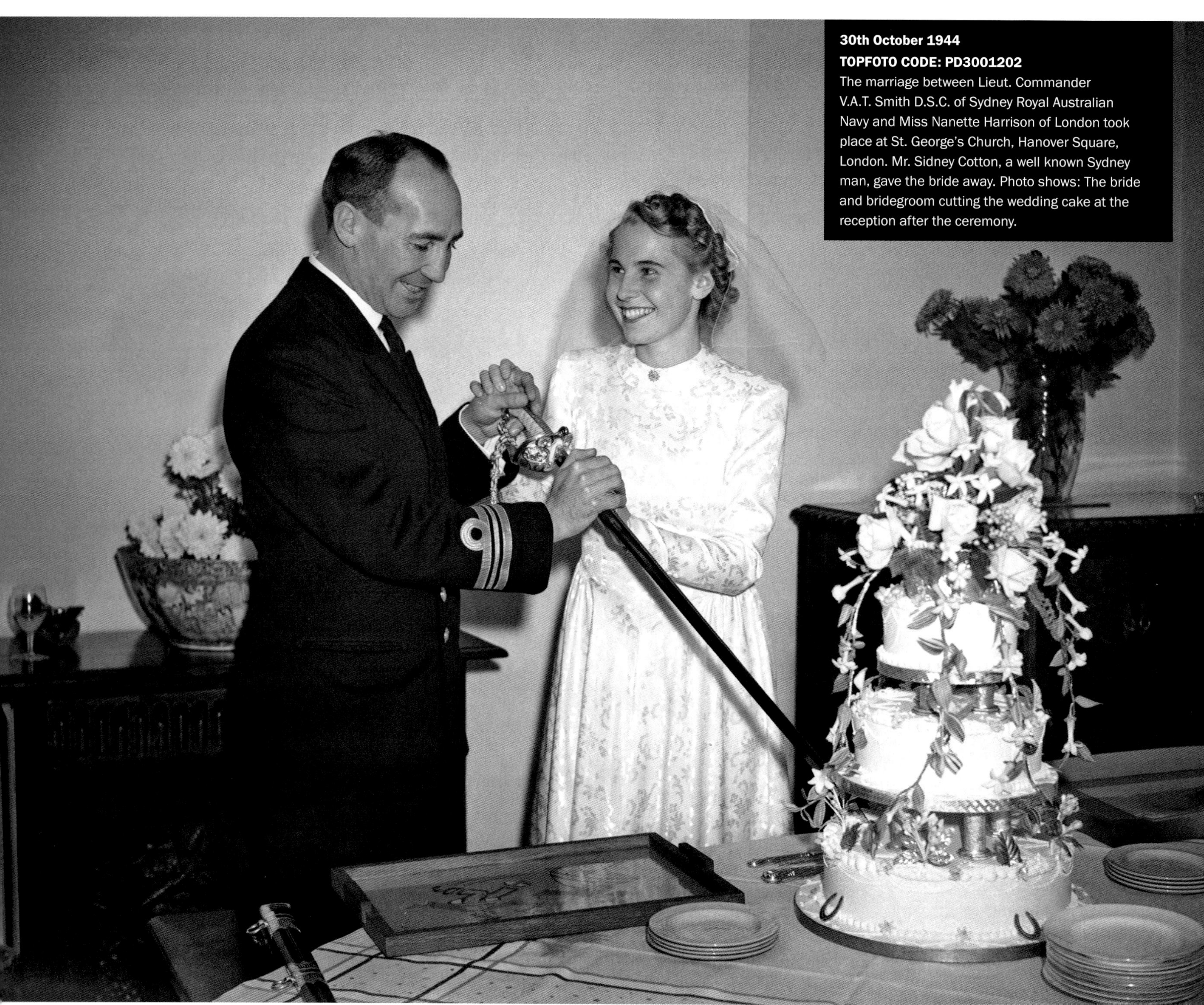

30th October 1944
TOPFOTO CODE: PD3001202
The marriage between Lieut. Commander
V.A.T. Smith D.S.C. of Sydney Royal Australian
Navy and Miss Nanette Harrison of London took
place at St. George's Church, Hanover Square,
London. Mr. Sidney Cotton, a well known Sydney
man, gave the bride away. Photo shows: The bride
and bridegroom cutting the wedding cake at the
reception after the ceremony.

Admiral Sir Victor Alfred Trumper Smith was rightfully regarded as a true legend in his own time. Extremely well respected, he is considered to be the father of the Australian Navy's Fleet Air Arm (FAA), as well as being instrumental in the planning of D-Day.

During the war, he served in several different fighter squadrons, and on a number of different destroyers. In 1940 he commanded six Swordfish biplanes and conducted the first ever air-to-sea torpedo attack against the German battleship *Scharnhorst* in Norway. He served on HMS *Ark Royal*, aka HMS *Pegasus*, which was the first-ever purpose-built seaplane carrier (for more about this, read the story on page 18). In 1970, he became the first Australian ever to receive the full rank of admiral.

Smith was shot down twice yet managed to be picked up at sea by friendly destroyers both times. In the New Year's Honours of 1942, he was awarded the Distinguished Service Cross (DSC) for 'outstanding zeal, patience and cheerfulness and for setting an example of whole-hearted devotion to duty'. Commanding several cruisers to boot, he served in both the European Theatre and the Pacific Theatre, as well as in the Korean War.

He was promoted to acting lieutenant commander in 1943 and later Air Staff Officer aboard HMS *Tracker*. Here he assisted in the sinking of the submarines *U-355* and *U-288* and in the downing of six German long-range planes. This led to yet another promotion to lieutenant commander in 1944 and a posting as the Air Planning Officer on the staff of the Flag Officer BAA (British Assault Area) for the Normandy invasion.

During his time in England, on the planning staff for the Normandy landings, Smith met Miss Nanette Susan Harrison. Smith and Nanette were engaged in September 1944: she was 21, he was 31. Less than one month later he was ordered to return to Australia. With only ten days to spare, he grabbed the phone, called Nanette and proposed a shotgun wedding the following Saturday. Within those ten days, they got married and had their honeymoon; Smith was then shipped off to Australia. More than a year was to pass before they would see each other again.

Smith received the DSC, KBE (Knight), CB and the Companion of the Order of Australia, before finally retiring in 1975 after forty-nine years of naval service. After retirement, Smith became President of the ACT/Queanbeyan Division of Birthright, an Australian organisation that assists single parents with dependent children. He died in 1998 aged 85.

Nanette survived her husband by nineteen years and died at the age of 94. She is remembered as a most stylish and proper lady of her time, and recalled by countless people as someone who always looked after sailors, officers and their families. She was also famous for her legendary dinner parties and her strong and undying dedication to the FAA.

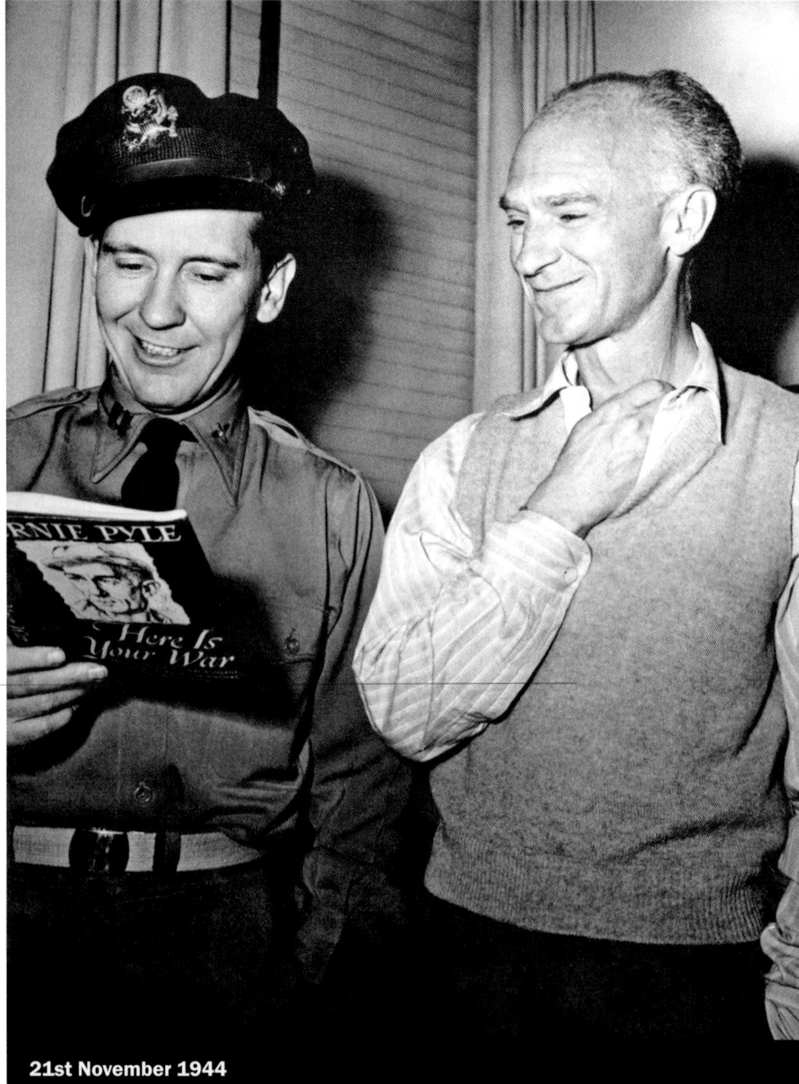

21st November 1944
TOPFOTO CODE: PD7485105
Motion picture to be made from U.S. newsman's book. Captain Burgess Meredith of the U.S. Army Air Forces (left), formerly an American stage and screen actor, skims through pages of 'Here Is Your War' as the author of the book, Ernie Pyle, looks on. Captain Meredith, who has been placed on inactive duty by the U.S. War Department, will play the role of Mr. Pyle in a motion picture based on this book and the writings of other American war correspondents. Mr. Pyle has become famous in the United States through his human interest writings about the ordinary soldier and his part in the war. Released to afternoon papers – 11/29/44. (U.S Office of War Information picture/Library of Congress, Prints & Photographs Division, Farm Security Administration/Office of War Information Black-and-White Negatives)

Ernie Pyle is perhaps one of the most overlooked writers of the Second World War. In the company of giants like Steinbeck, Hemingway, Heller and Gellhorn, he is almost unanimously acclaimed as the one who truly got under the skin of the average GIs and told the war from their perspective. A quiet, soft-spoken but restless young man, people warmed to him quickly and shared their thoughts with him quite easily.

The human interest articles became his signature and the underdogs of the world his heroes. He was the editor of *Washington Daily News* for a few years but hated being tied to a desk and eventually convinced his boss to let him become a roaming reporter. From 1935 to 1941 he travelled the world (by his own estimate more than 200,000 miles) and told the stories of the people in it.

In 1942, he became a war correspondent for Scripps-Howard and covered nearly every major European Theatre event from North Africa to the Normandy landings. His popularity steadily increased as his observations and publications continuously hit the mark with the public. The book *Here Is Your War* (pictured in the photo, left) was based on his interviews with the men who fought in the North Africa campaign and it became such a big hit that the publishers had to ask the government for a dispensation for more paper (as it was rationed like most things) in order to keep up with the demand. More than 400 daily newspapers posted his articles during the war, and in 1944 he received a Pulitzer Prize – very much to his own surprise.

The fame, however, was taking its toll and Ernie was suffering from fatigue, depression, PTSD and had issues with alcohol. After a brief convalescence in the States, he returned to the front line, this time in the Pacific Theatre. This was where Ernie's war would end. On 17 April 1945, he arrived in Le Shima near Okinawa. Riding in a jeep with a number of officers, they came under sudden Japanese fire and Pyle was killed by a shot to the temple.

In 2008, an unseen photo emerged that showed Pyle's body lying on the ground. This renewed the public interest in a 'regular guy' who died at the age of just 44, having spent his life portraying ordinary folks with extraordinary tales. Countless tributes have been made to him, from ships, planes, programmes and awards bearing his name to a stamp honouring him and his achievements.

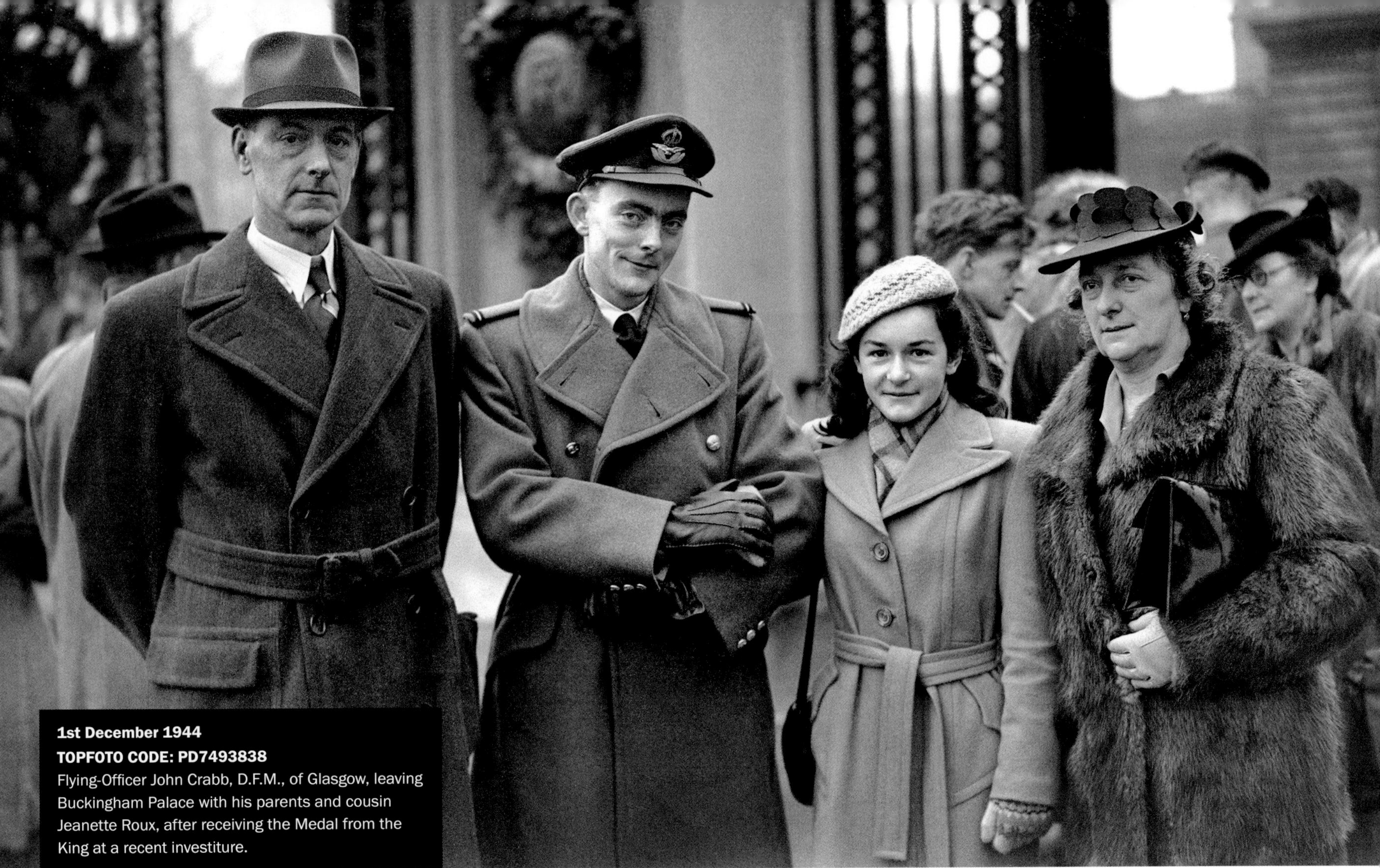

Flying-Officer John Crabb, D.F.M., of Glasgow, leaving Buckingham Palace with his parents and cousin Jeanette Roux, after receiving the Medal from the King at a recent investiture.

John Louis Crabb served with 49 Squadron as an observer, and later on De Havilland Mosquitos with 162 Squadron. On 12–13 July 1943, Crabb was to participate in his thirteenth bombing mission: a raid on Turin. However, both he and his bomb aimer, Leslie Philips, caught severe colds and were unable to fly. This was a stroke of luck for them, as the plane went down and the crew tragically died and was never found. Crabb joined another crew and completed his full tour of thirty missions on 30 October 1943.

He continued as a flight instructor for a year but was recalled for operations and had the choice between an additional twenty bomber missions in Lancasters or fifty missions in a Mosquito. Crabb, well knowing the dangers of Lancaster missions, chose to fly in Mosquitos instead. He managed to complete an additional forty-three missions before the war was over. He was awarded the Distinguished Flying Medal (DFM) in December 1944, and later the Distinguished Flying Cross (DFC). A total of 6,637 DFMs were awarded during the Second World War.

The International Bomber Command Centre Digital Archive holds a great interview with Crabb, conducted in 2017, where he explains in detail his experiences during the war.[18] Crabb died on 19 October 2022 at the age of 102.

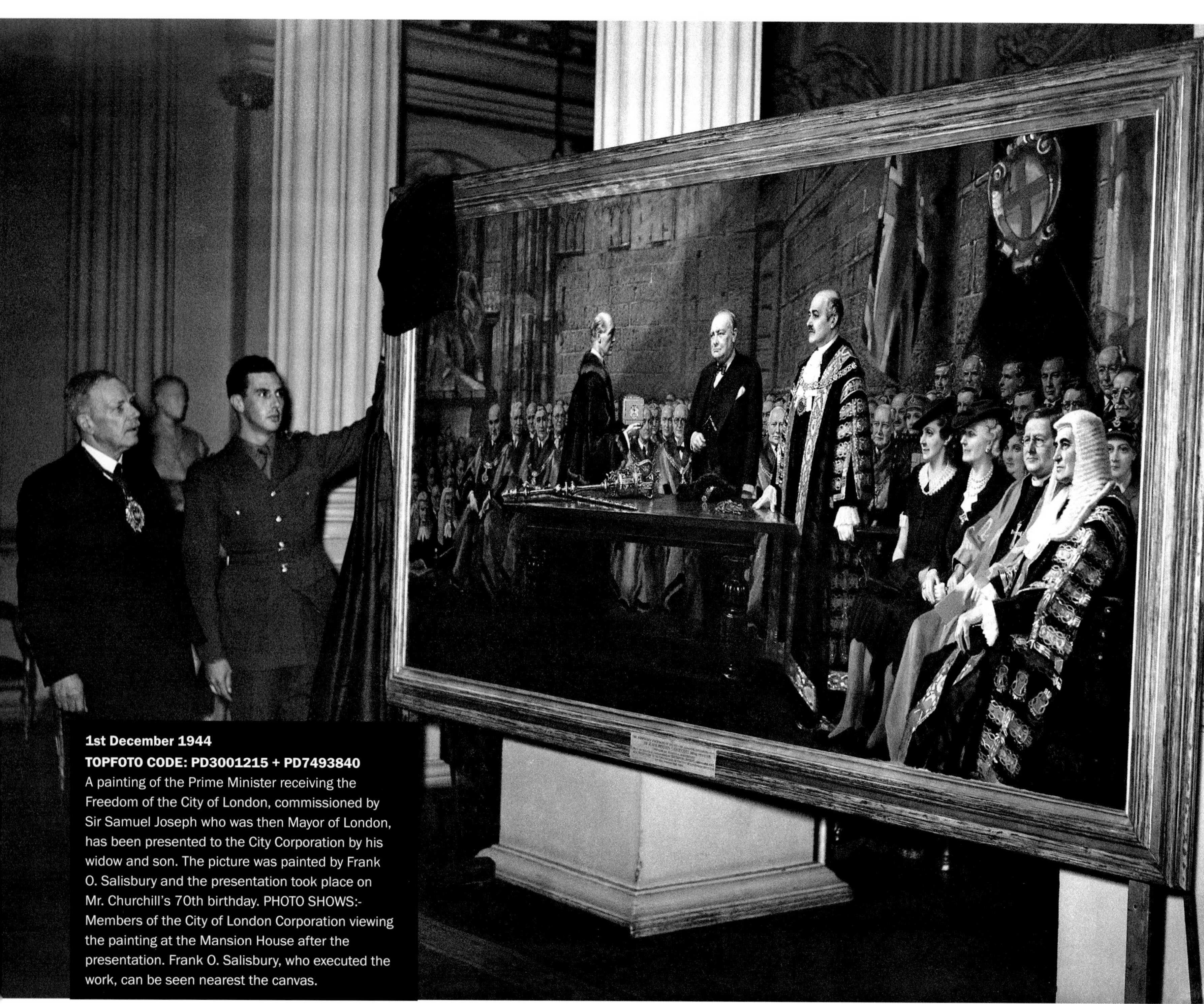

1st December 1944

TOPFOTO CODE: PD3001215 + PD7493840

A painting of the Prime Minister receiving the
Freedom of the City of London, commissioned by
Sir Samuel Joseph who was then Mayor of London,
has been presented to the City Corporation by his
widow and son. The picture was painted by Frank
O. Salisbury and the presentation took place on
Mr. Churchill's 70th birthday. PHOTO SHOWS:-
Members of the City of London Corporation viewing
the painting at the Mansion House after the
presentation. Frank O. Salisbury, who executed the
work, can be seen nearest the canvas.

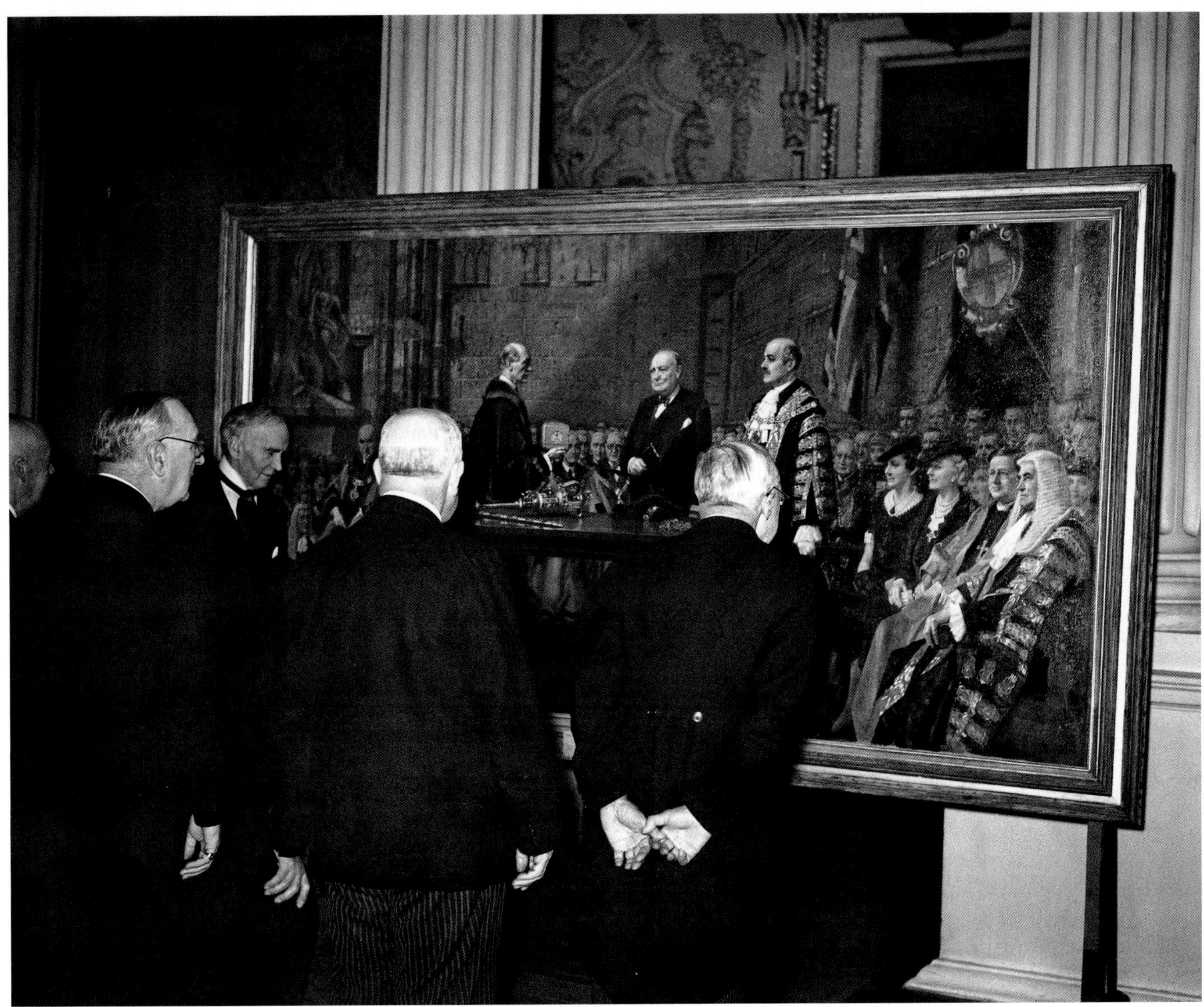

Frank O. Salisbury was a renowned portrait artist who painted eleven portraits of Churchill during his lifetime. Many other artists attempted to paint him, but none really came as close to capturing the intensity and depth of his character and personality as Salisbury did with his 'Blood, Sweat & Tears' painting from 1943 or the iconic piece featuring Churchill in his 'Siren Suit' from 1942.

Salisbury painted a total of twenty-five members of the Royal House of Windsor, six US presidents, as well as a long list of actors, politicians, industrialists and other significant people.

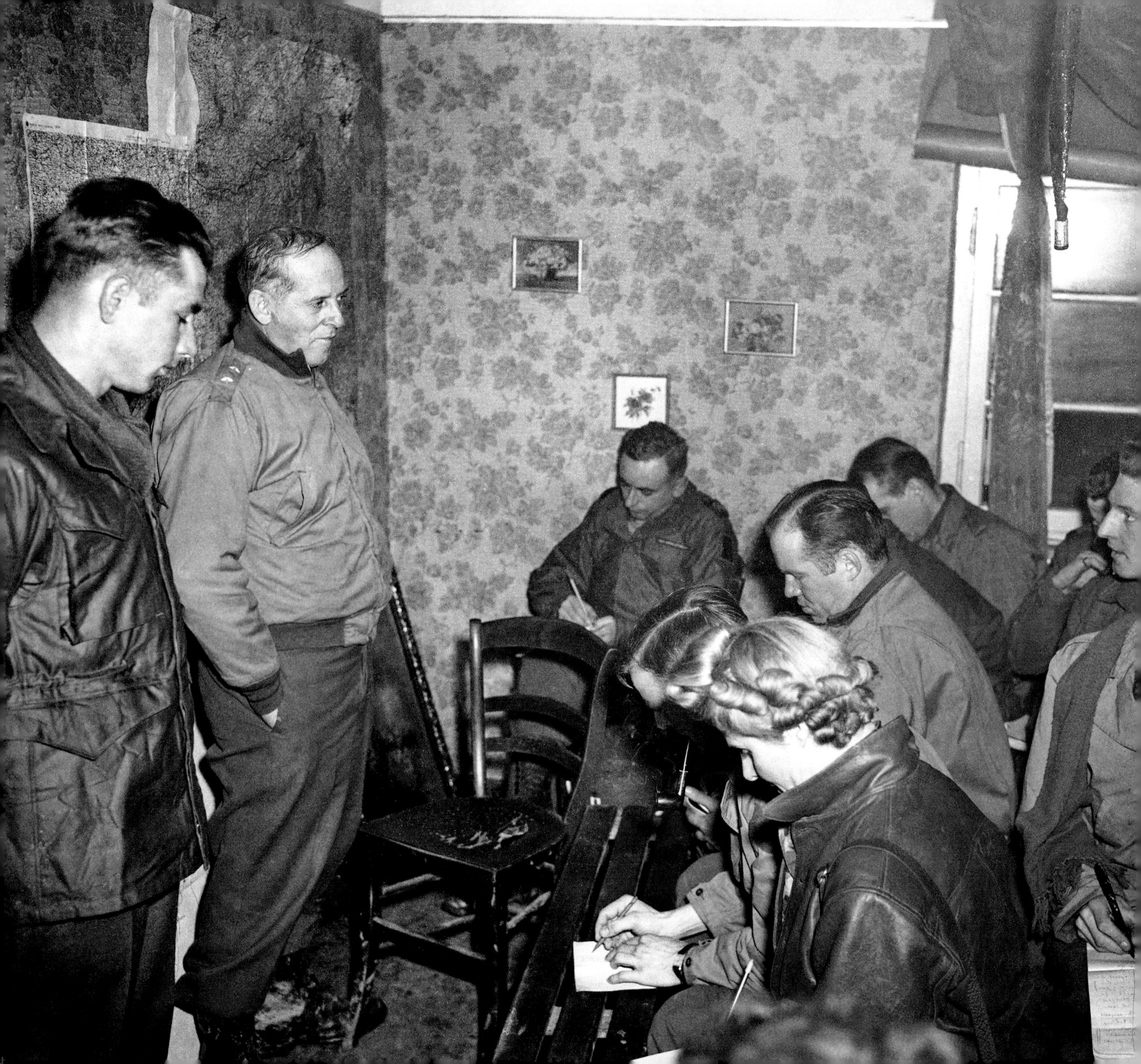

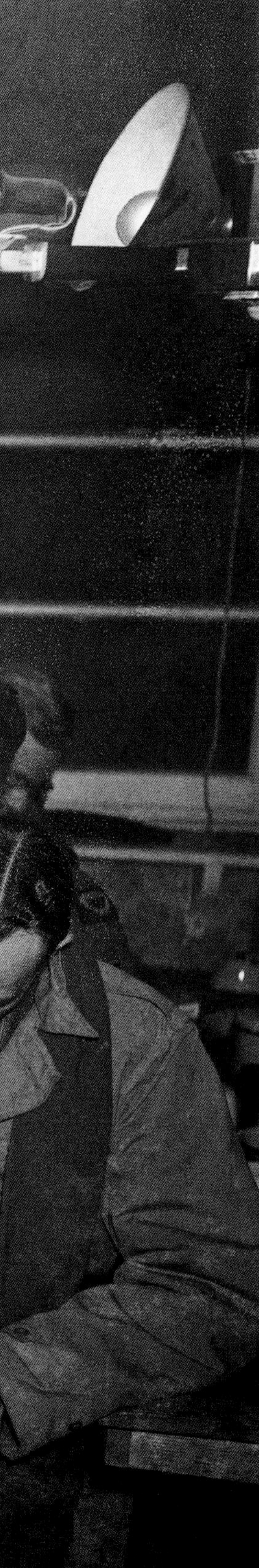

The Medal of Honor (MOH) is the highest and most prestigious military decoration that can be bestowed upon a person belonging to the US Armed Forces and is given for services beyond the call of duty. It was first presented more than 150 years ago and since then only 3,538 medals have been awarded, nearly half of these during just four years of the American Civil War. In comparison, a mere 472 were given for the actions of soldiers serving during the Second World War.

In October 1940, both Walter Ehlers and his brother Roland enlisted in the US Army. Due to Walter's young age, consent from his parents was required and his mother signed, only on the condition that he would vow to act as a 'Christian soldier'. He later expressed the immense difficulty of performing his tasks as a soldier while keeping this promise:

> I was fighting for freedom ... World War II, that was for freedom. We fought Nazism, fascism, and imperialism, and all three nations (Germany, Italy & Japan) became democracies after the war was over.[19]

Both the brothers saw action in North Africa and Sicily and were serving in the 1st Infantry Division (Big Red One). Upon preparations for D-Day, they went into different companies and while they both participated in the landings in Normandy, it would take a month before Walter learned how his brother Roland had died on Omaha Beach – en route to the beach in one of the now notorious Higgins landing vessels. Walter, as a squad leader of a twelve-man team, was part of the second wave to land and was assigned the task of reconnaissance within the nearby town of Trévières. Three days later, outside the French town of Goville, he was to earn his medal for gallantry:

> On the 9th of June, we were sending out a platoon in this field ... I went up on the bank, and I heard some rattling, and I came face-to-face with four Germans on patrol. All of them had their guns pointed at me. They were pretty close together ... and I didn't have any choice. I had to make a real fast decision. Either I shot them or they're going to shoot me. So I just went like this, pulled my trigger four times, and got all four of them.[20]

Ehlers proceeded to advance under heavy fire and knocked out a gun crew, subsequently leading his men to eliminate two mortar positions covered by heavy machine guns, personally killing a further three men. After this, he single-handedly took out yet another machine-gun nest. The following morning, the squad was subjected to a barrage and was ordered to fall back. Ehlers had his squad cover the withdrawal of the whole platoon before then covering the withdrawal of his squad on his own, while wounded:

> I'm busy shooting at these three guys who are putting in the machine gun down there when I get hit in the back. It hit me in the back, went into my rib area, glanced off the rib, went out – made two holes: one where it went in, one where it came back – and went into my pack. It hit a bar of soap and went through my mother's picture there, and it came out my trench shovel in the back.[21]

Despite being wounded, Ehlers ran back while also carrying an injured rifleman to safety. However, in rescuing the rifleman he was unable to carry his own rifle – which he immediately and under continued fire doubled back to retrieve. After being treated in the field, he blankly refused to be evacuated, got up and continued to lead his squad deeper into Normandy. He was wounded twice more and eventually received a battlefield commission.

In 1955, Ehlers made an appearance in the film *The Long Gray Line* with the movie star Tyrone Power. (See more about Tyrone and his wife on page 182.) Ehlers died in 2014 at the age of 92.

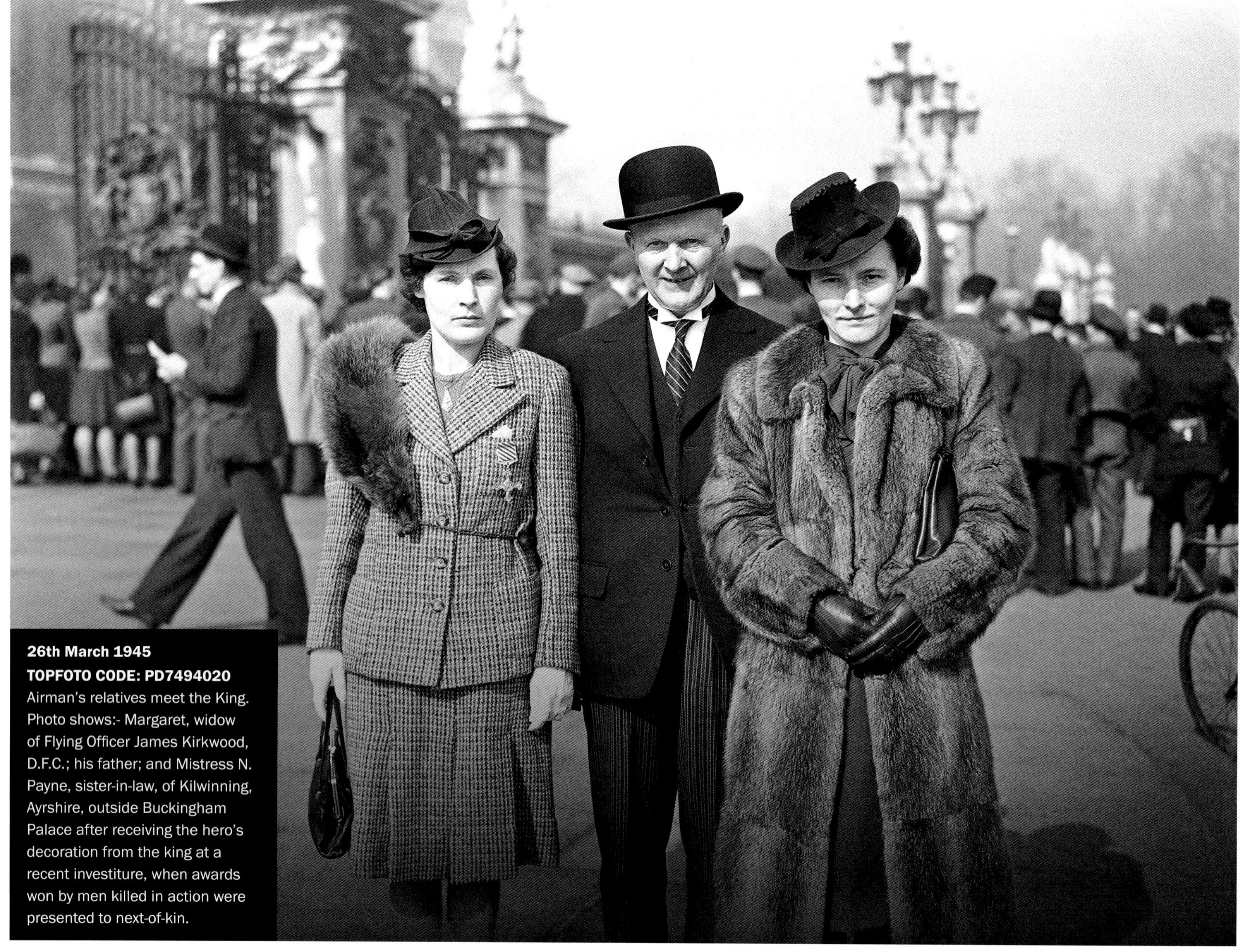

The night between 16 and 17 December 1943 is often referred to as 'the night of fog' or 'Black Thursday'. While the Battle of Berlin (read more about this on page 41) was raging and the Germans were causing heavy British casualties, the enemy that night was the British weather.

Flying Officer James Kirkwood was piloting Lancaster III JB219, along with his six-man crew, and took off from Bourn, Cambridgeshire, at 16.50. They successfully completed their bombing mission over Berlin, but returned to a dense and heavy fog hanging over most of south and east England, causing near-zero visibility.

Attempting to land at RAF Gransden Lodge, the plane sadly crashed in Hayley Wood in Cambridgeshire, not long after midnight. Twenty-eight-year-old James Kirkwood and his whole crew were killed instantaneously. A memorial stands today at the site of the crash.

Sources indicating the total losses for the raid vary greatly, although the men and planes lost to the weather were greater than those lost to the flak guns of Berlin. The estimates are that Bomber Command lost as many as seventy aircraft in total and that more than 300 aircrew were killed.

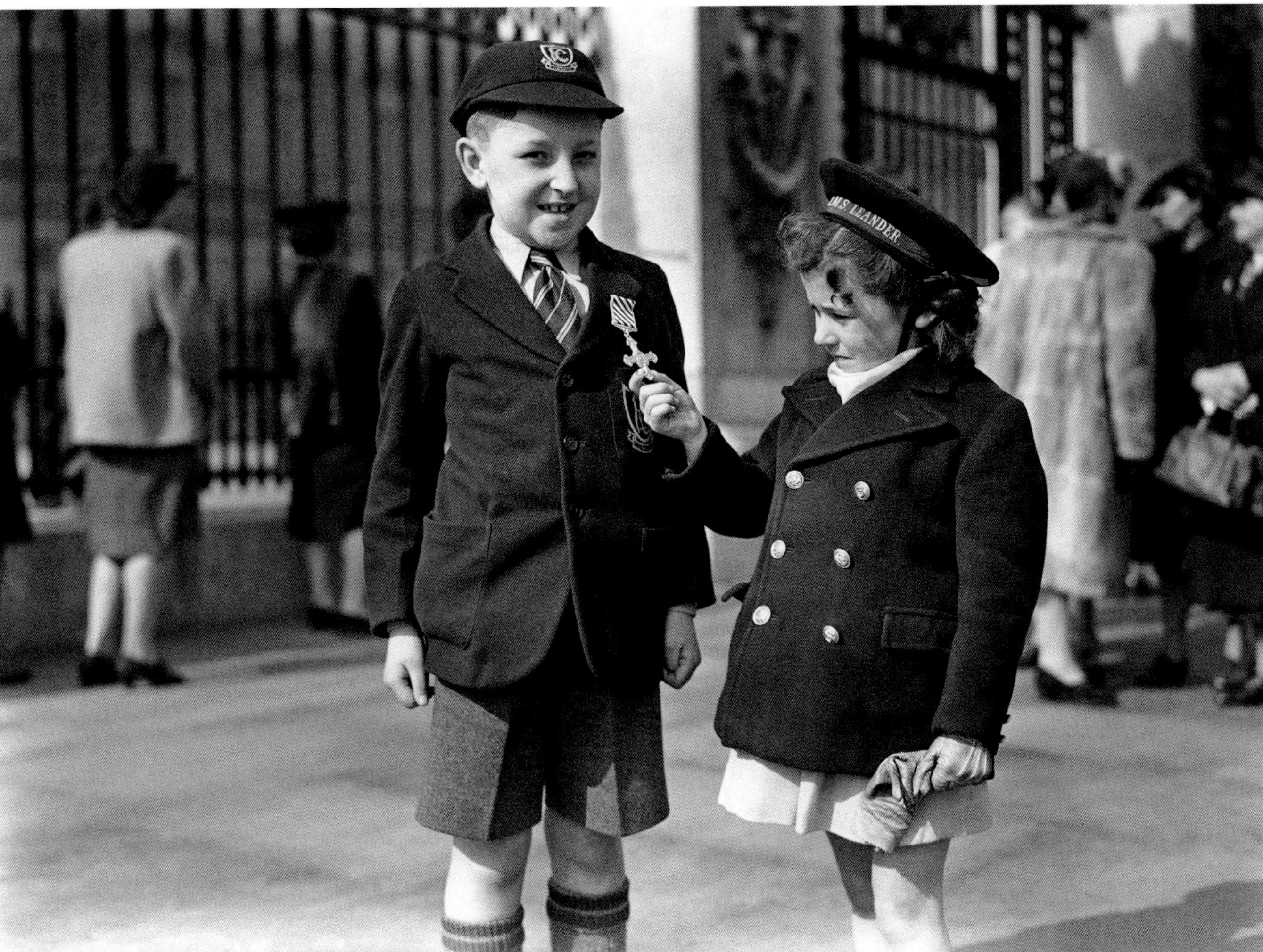

26th March 1945
TOPFOTO CODE:
PD7486007
Outside Buckingham Palace after recent investiture held by the King, eight-year-old William Hagon shows his cousin Jean Rees the D.F.C. won by his Pilot Officer father, who was killed in action.

William Henry Frederick George Hagon, also known as Biff, was a foreman engineer for the Landing Grounds Corporation. He joined the Royal Air Force Volunteer Reserve in 1942 and served as a rear gunner in 77 Squadron.

Hagon had returned safely from twenty-one successful missions when he participated in a major raid on Magdeburg on 21 January 1944. The crew took off from Elvington, North Yorkshire, at 19.51 in Halifax LL190. West of Magdeburg, they were attacked at 15,000ft by a fighter and went down, reported missing. A total of 648 aircraft took part in the attack, and fifty-seven of these aircraft never came back. It was a very high loss rate of 8.8 per cent, with the Halifax bombers in particular sustaining a horrifying loss rate of 15.6 per cent.

Hagon was posthumously awarded the DFC for a mission flown on 23 November 1943, one of 20,354 DFCs awarded during the war. He was the rear gunner in an attack on Kassel when two German fighters engaged the plane. Communicating great directions to his pilot, they managed to evade the enemy. Shortly after, another German fighter engaged them, but Hagon resolutely opened fire and downed the plane. The *London Gazette* No. 36258 from the same day states, 'This officer displayed great resolution and his alertness contributed materially to the success of the sortie.'

Present at the investiture was his wife Louisa Ellen Hagon, who had married William in 1933. On 31 March 1945, five days after the photo was taken, *Middlesex County Times* published a story about 8-year-old William Hagon and his mother. At this time Louisa expressed her hope that her husband might be alive as a POW in Germany and one day come home to meet their eight-and-a-half-month-old girl, Gloria, who he had never seen.

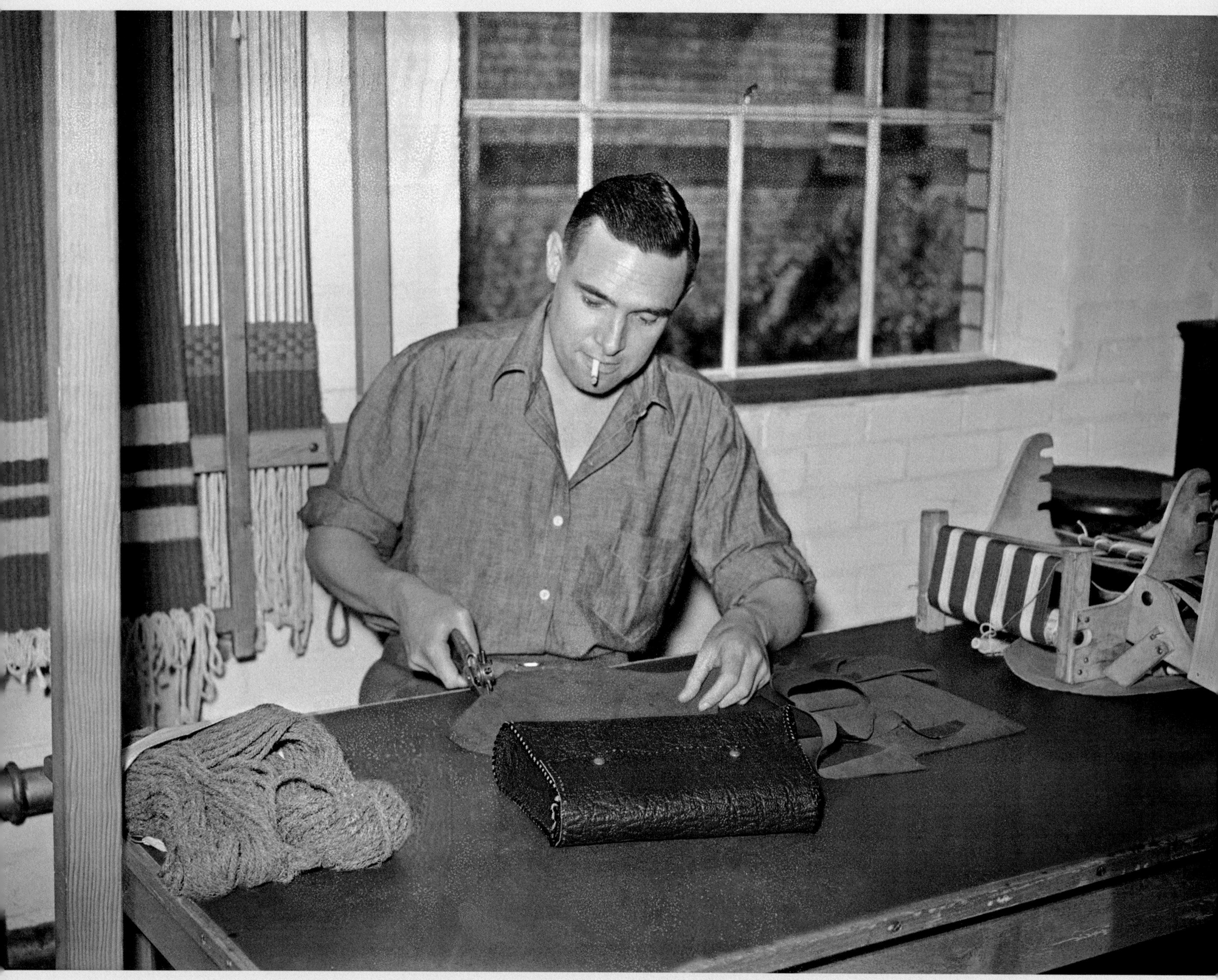

The Only British Survivor of the Nazi Camp Bergen-Belsen

The atrocities committed by the Nazi regime during the Second World War are arguably some of the most horrific war crimes in modern history. Many of the concentration camps were run under the SS practice *Vernichtung Durch Arbeit*, meaning 'extermination through labour'. The excruciating fifteen hours of daily hard physical labour, the brutal and random beatings by the overseers and the appallingly unhygienic conditions left little room for interpretation of the German Reich's intent. These were places you entered but were not supposed to leave alive. Bergen-Belsen was one of these Nazi concentration camps, and only one British man left that place alive – Harold Le Druillenec:

> No food, no water, sleep was impossible. We had to rise at 3.30 am. All my time here was spent lifting dead bodies into the mass graves. Jungle law reigned among the prisoners; at night you killed – or were killed; by day cannibalism was rampant.[22]

To understand Le Druillenec's story, one must begin with his sister Louisa Gould and the Russian pilot Feodor Polycarpovitch Burriy. Louisa was a shopkeeper on the island of Jersey and a member of the Channel Islands Resistance. Feodor crash-landed in 1941 and after escaping from a POW camp in 1942, Louisa sheltered him for eighteen months. In 1942, the Germans ordered all wireless sets owned by the civilian population of Jersey to be handed over, but Louisa kept hers and every night she and her many guests would listen in silence to the BBC news broadcast.

Despite efforts to conceal her actions, a neighbour's suspicions led to Louisa's eventual arrest in May 1944, though Feodor managed to escape. The informant also passed on the identities of her frequent guests to the Germans, among them Louisa's brother. It was never proven that Harold had ever listened to the radio, nor done anything else illegal, but that meant little. He was sentenced to five months' imprisonment for 'prohibited reception of wireless transmissions in company with other persons'.

The trial was completed on 22 June 1944, to the sounds of the battles ensuing in nearby Normandy. All parties were found guilty and sentenced. Louisa was sent to Ravensbrück Concentration Camp. Here she continued to teach the camp's inmates English, until she was executed in the gas chamber in 1945.

After Harold's conviction, an interim of fairly quick transfers followed. From St Malo Prison he went to Jacques-Cartier Prison, which housed many suspected French Resistance members, and then on to the third French prison at Fort Hatry in Belfort. On 1 September 1944, he arrived at Neuengamme Concentration Camp in Hamburg.

Neuengamme was one of the largest camps in the Nazi concentration camp system, with more than eighty-five sub-camps. More than 100,000 prisoners came through here during the war and the verified deaths were more than 42,900 individuals. Initially built to provide Hamburg with bricks (as Hamburg had been chosen to become one of five Führer cities in the 'New Reich'), it quickly grew and became the centre for mainly Russian POWs taken from the Eastern Front. It was a ruthless regime with daily beatings and arbitrary punishments. The guards and kapos (prisoners chosen by the SS to help run the camp) held supreme power with no repercussions nor accountability for the abuse, mistreatment and subsequent deaths that inevitably followed. Typhus, tuberculosis, malnutrition and dehydration were common, with no medication and no health professionals attending to the inmates. If you were taken to the 'hospital', chances were that instead of receiving medicine and care you would be experimented on, have a lethal injection or simply be led to the extermination bunkers to be gassed with Zyklon B. As an indication of the severity, the camp's first commander, Otto Thummel, was replaced after only two months for being 'too humane' to the prisoners.

Five days after arriving, Harold was sent on *arbeitskommando* (work party) in Wilhelmshaven. Here they were to build what was to become the Alter Banter Weg Concentration Camp, another sub-camp of Neuengamme. By this time Neuengamme had all but in name become an extermination camp. The inmates were in such poor physical and mental condition that few were able to actually perform any labour. Harold worked from 4.30 a.m. until 7 p.m. at night as a welder and stated about this detail:

> Banter Weg was a tough camp with torture and punishment the rule day and night. Means of putting inmates to death included beating, drowning, crucifixion, and hanging in various stances ... no-one escaped severe corporal punishment.[23]

On 5 April 1945, almost seven months later, Harold was finally sent to Bergen-Belsen concentration camp. He arrived after five days in a cattle wagon and was put in block 13 with 500 other people:

No food, no water – sleep was impossible. We had to rise at 3.30 am. All my time here was spent heaving dead bodies into the mass graves. Jungle law reigned among the prisoners; at night you killed or were killed; by day cannibalism was rampant.[24]

Later eyewitness statements told stories of how the kidneys, livers and hearts of the dead were devoured by the starving prisoners.

As the Allied forces tightened their grip on Germany, rather than giving up prisoners the Nazis kept moving them to still-occupied German territories, resulting in massive overpopulations and further deteriorating conditions for the inmates, already barely hanging on. Druillenec only spent ten days in Bergen-Belsen, but what he experienced there haunted him until his death. After finally being freed, Druillenec spent five months in the hospital. The following explains the condition of his body and mind:

His ailments included food poisoning with septi-cemia which led to a 'perturbing unbalance of mind'. He also had acute dysentery, fluid in the lungs, and various skin diseases including scabies and impetigo. Malnutrition meant that his weight was about six stone (38kg) at the time of his liberation. Longer-term, Le Druillenec was left with a weakened constitution, and his heart and lungs were affected (he suffered a coronary thrombosis in 1961). He also suffered a complete loss of memory of his pre-war life.[25]

Harold spent a further six months in Horton Emergency Hospital in rehabilitation (where the photo was taken). He testified in the Bergen-Belsen Trials in October 1945, interrupting his rehabilitation to do so, and in 1946 and 1947 he bravely gave further testimony in the trials of Neuengamme and Banter Weg. His story was so important that during the Christmas of 1945 he introduced the King's Speech and an interview about his experiences was broadcast by the BBC.

He returned to his pre-war profession as a teacher in 1949, but in the 1950s he suffered a mental breakdown. As one of only two British survivors of the Holocaust and the only British survivor of the Bergen-Belsen camp, he was given £1,835 (around £16,000 in today's money) as compensation for Nazi persecution.

Harold Le Druillenec passed away in 1985 at the age of 73. In 2008 a petition was made to call upon the British Prime Minister to change the laws in the UK so that under the British Honours System an award could be given to a person posthumously. This petition gained traction and in March 2009, MP Russell Brown secured 135 signatories.

On 9 March 2010, the UK government finally presented twenty-seven people with the new award named 'Hero of the Holocaust'. Twenty-five of these awards were presented posthumously, of which one each was bestowed upon Harold Le Druillenec and his sister Louisa Gould. Parts of this fascinating story have been made into a motion picture named *Another Mother's Son*, featuring Ronan Keating as Harold Le Druillenec.

The young Russian pilot Feodor Polycarpovitch Burriy survived. He returned for a reunion with the other survivors on Jersey in 1995, the fiftieth anniversary of the liberation, and died in 1998 at the age of 80.[26]

REFERENCES

1   A highly offensive term, but from a historical perspective it is important to show the intentionally derogatory propaganda used by the Allies during the Second World War.

2   Law Reports of Trials of War Criminals, United Nations War Crimes Commission, Vol. IX, 1949 – LOC.

3   Parts of this article are written with information provided courtesy of William H. Fullilove and Normandy1944.info.

4   Lieselotte Steveling: Lawyers in Münster. A contribution to the history of the Faculty of Law and Political Science at the Westfälische Wilhelms-University Münster/Westphalia (*Contributions to the History of Sociology*, 10) Lit, Münster, 1999, ISBN 3-8258-4084-0, p. 428.

5   Baron von der Heydte, *Daedalus Returned: Crete 1941* (Hutchinson, 1958).

6   Copy of full letter can be found here: www.worldwarmedia.com/tag/fallschirmjaeger/feed.

7   Fascinating further reading can be found at www.armouredcarriers.com.

8   US State Department www.2009-2017.state.gov/p/io/potusunga/207325.htm.

9   Ira Katznelson, *When Affirmative Action Was White: An Untold History of Racial Inequality in Twentieth-Century America* (W.W. Norton & Company, 2006).

10 Mistake in the original entry for the negative caption. The date is 6th Jan 1946 NOT 1945.

11 Eleanor Roosevelt, *My Day*, The Eleanor Roosevelt Papers Project.

12 Republished with permission from Telegraph Media Group Ltd.

13 Ibid.

14 Ibid.

15 Ibid.

16 Used by permission from the paradata.org.uk.

17 The National Archives, WO 373/3/407.

18 www.ibccdigitalarchive.lincoln.ac.uk/omeka/collections/document/10754.

19 Permission to use the quote granted by The National WWII Museum.

20 Ibid.

21 Ibid.

22 Harold Le Druillenec, testimony from War Crimes Belsen Trial, courtesy of Frank Falla Archives & Gilly Carr.

23 Harold Le Druillenec, testimony from War Crimes Belsen Trial, courtesy of Frank Falla Archives & Gilly Carr.

24 Ibid.

25 Courtesy of Frank Falla Archives & Gilly Carr.

26 Some information and quotes in this article are from the Frank Falla Archives (www.frankfallaarchive.org). Permission to use the information has been given by Gilly Carr, University of Cambridge.

BIBLIOGRAPHY AND FURTHER READING

The following works have been instrumental sources in the development of this book. For readers interested in exploring these subjects further, the suggested readings provide a range of articles, texts and recent research that expand upon the stories discussed in the chapters.

Chapter 1

www.bportlibrary.org/simon-lakes-submarines
www.britannica.com/technology/submarine-naval-vessel/Toward-diesel-electric-power
www.pigboats.com/index.php?title=Simon_Lake_non-Navy_Submarines
www.militarymatters.online/forgotten-aircraft/the-short-stirling-first-of-the-british-big-boys
www.planehistoria.com/the-short-stirling
www.key.aero/article/short-stirling-raf-service

www.walesonline.co.uk/news/wales-news/german-world-war-ii-fighter-8072752
www.iwm.org.uk/collections/item/object/205196920
www.asn.flightsafety.org/wikibase/227004
www.planehistoria.com/armin-faber
www.airandspace.si.edu/collection-objects/focke-wulf-fw-190-f-8r1/nasm_A19600318000

www.silverhawkauthor.com/post/warplanes-of-the-usa-vought-os2u-kingfisher
www.naval-encyclopedia.com/ww1/uk/hms-ark-royal-1914.php
www.naval-history.net/xGM-Chrono-04CV-Pegasus.htm

www.financialexpress.com/auto/car-news/a-brief-history-of-jeep/2510250
www.jeep.com/history.html
www.media.stellantisnorthamerica.com/newsrelease.do?id=22196
www.autoweek.com/car-life/a1849926/how-has-jeep-gotten-here-check-out-their-miraculous-75-year-story
www.ewillys.com
www.legendmag.co.uk/trademark-trouble

www.history.navy.mil/content/history/museums/nmusn/explore/photography/wwii/wwii-pacific/gilbert-marshall-islands-campaign/invasion-marshall-islands/invasion-kwajalein-atolls.html
www.history.com/topics/world-war-ii/battle-of-kwajalein
www.enroll.nationalww2museum.org/see-hear/collections/focus-on/d-day-kwajalein.html

www.nam.ac.uk/explore/auxiliary-territorial-service
www.bbc.co.uk/history/ww2peopleswar/timeline/factfiles/nonflash/a6650237.shtml
www.iwm.org.uk/history/the-vital-role-of-women-in-the-second-world-war
www.beta.nationalarchives.gov.uk/explore-the-collection/explore-by-time-period/second-world-war/women-and-the-second-world-war

www.beachesofnormandy.com/articles/The_Bazooka/?id=8da3c72260
www.warhistoryonline.com/war-articles/bob-burns-bazooka-name.html
www.historynet.com/how-a-world-war-i-jazz-playing-marine-gave-us-the-best-weapon-name-ever/?f#:~:text=A%20Sept.%203%2C%201919%20article%20from%20the%20New%20York%20Evening%20Telegram%20about%20the%20jazz%20instrument%20the%20%22bazooka.%22
www.bergflak.com/pshistory.html
www.tankmuseum.org/tank-nuts/tank-collection/m4-sherman

www.rafmuseum.org.uk/research/online-exhibitions/pilots-of-the-caribbean/across-the-commands/the-second-world-war-1939-to-1945-across-the-commands-part-3
www.uboat.net/allies/aircraft/raf_coastal.htm

Chapter 2

www.military.wikia.org/wiki/Operation_Crusader
www.worldhistory.org/Operation_Compass
www.warfarehistorynetwork.com/article/operation-compass-masterstroke-in-the-desert
www.iwm.org.uk/history/a-brief-history-of-the-eighth-army-and-the-desert-war
www.iwm.org.uk/history/a-short-guide-to-the-war-in-africa-during-the-second-world-war
www.iwm.org.uk/history/how-the-british-secured-a-victory-in-the-desert-during-the-second-world-war

www.history.army.mil/html/books/005/5-5/CMH_Pub_5-5.pdf
www.warfarehistorynetwork.com/article/operation-cartwheel-seizing-the-solomons-and-beyond
www.warhistoryonline.com/instant-articles/operation-cartwheel.html
www.historyhit.com/the-neutralisation-of-rabaul

www.armyaircorpsmuseum.org
www.384thbombgroup.com

www.airuniversity.af.edu/Portals/10/AUPress/Books/B_0099_DAVIS_BOMBING_AXIS_POWERS.pdf

www.iwm.org.uk/history/life-and-death-in-bomber-command

www.aad.archives.gov/aad/record-detail.jsp?dt=893&mtch=1&cat=all&tf=F&sc=24994,24995,24996,24998,24997,24993,24981,24983&bc=sl,fd&txt_24994=15323977&op_24994=0&nfo_24994=V,8,1900&txt_24995=dailey&op_24995=0&nfo_24995=V,24,1900&sort=24981%20desc&rpp=10&pg=1&rid=1146094

www.anesi.com/ussbs02.htm

www.aviation-safety.net/wikibase/220413

www.384thbombgroup.com/piwigo_384th_gallery/picture.php?/20940

www.history.navy.mil/research/library/online-reading-room/title-list-alphabetically/s/solomon-islands-campaign-i-the-landing-in-the-solomons.html

www.britannica.com/event/Battle-of-Guadalcanal

www.ww2classroom.org/system/files/essays/wip010_0.pdf

www.nationalww2museum.org/war/articles/solomon-islands-campaign-guadalcanal

www.iwm.org.uk/history/raf-bomber-command-during-the-second-world-war

www.rafbf.org/bomber-command-memorial/about-bomber-command

www.internationalbcc.co.uk/history/the-history-of-bomber-command

www.memorialflightclub.com/blog/bomber-command-battle-berlin

www.berlinexperiences.com/battle-of-berlin-november-22nd-1943

www.naval-history.net/xGM-Chrono-01BB-Anson.htm

www.uboat.net/allies/warships/ship/4073.html

www.world-war.co.uk/bb/anson.php

www.99bombgroup.org

www.americanairmuseum.com/archive/unit/99th-bomb-group

www.wingleader.co.uk/wp-content/uploads/2022/04/NACH-1944-Part2sample2.pdf

www.ibccdigitalarchive.lincoln.ac.uk/omeka/collections/document/17678

www.backtonormandy.org/the-history/air-force-operations/airplanes-allies-and-axis-lost/lancaster/78948-RAF61210.html

www.armyhistory.org/general-joseph-lawton-collins

www.nationalww2museum.org/war/articles/louisiana-lightning-joe-collins

www.armyupress.army.mil/Portals/7/combat-studies-institute/csi-books/WadeNo5.pdf

www.washingtonpost.com/archive/local/1987/09/13/gen-j-lawton-collins-dies/dcda8aea-766c-4532-8d39-87e71c75dfde

www.en.wikipedia.org/wiki/J._Lawton_Collins

www.theguardian.com/science/2021/apr/29/michael-collins-obituary

www.military-history.org/articles/operation-market-garden.htm

www.thekeep.eiu.edu/theses/1824

www.wearethemighty.com/mighty-tactical/operation-market-garden

www.businessinsider.com/why-wwii-operation-market-garden-failed-to-defeat-german-forces-2020-9

www.artuk.org/discover/stories/antony-beevor-on-eisenhowers-portrait-of-montgomery#

www.warhistoryonline.com/world-war-ii/hells-highway-101-airborne-part-1.html

www.web.archive.org/web/20160624044120/www.afhra.af.mil/shared/media/document/AFD-090602-016.pdf

Movie: *A Bridge Too Far*, 1977. Directed by: Richard Attenborough

Series: HBO *Band of Brothers*, 2001. Episode 4, 'Replacements'

www.guides.loc.gov/sino-japanese-war-1937-1945

www.arsof-history.org/articles/v2n1_end_run_galahad_page_1.html

www.cbi-theater.com/marauders/marauders.html

www.en.wikipedia.org/wiki/Merrill%27s_Marauders#Myitkyina_and_the_end

www.arsof-history.org/articles/v4n1_myitkyina_part_1_page_1.html

www.ww2db.com/battle_spec.php?battle_id=143

www.arsof-history.org/articles/v11n1_eiche_page_1_v1.html

www.warfarehistorynetwork.com/operation-eiche-benito-mussolini-the-gran-sasso-raid

www.blog.nationalmuseum.ch/en/2023/09/the-rescue-of-benito-mussolini-the-real-story-and-its-swiss-connection/

www.thecollector.com/who-was-otto-skorzeny-most-dangerous-man-in-europe

www.historyisnowmagazine.com/blog/2024/7/31/rescuing-mussolini-the-fallschirmjger-gran-sasso-raid

www.pacificbattleship.com

www.history.navy.mil/content/history/museums/nmusn/explore/photography/ships-us/ships-usn-i/uss-iowa-bb-61.html

www.oorlogsslachtoffers.nl/greif1944

www.codenames.info/operation/greif-iv

www.warfarehistorynetwork.com/2016/0¼9/otto-skorzeny-and-operation-grief

www.ihffilm.com/operation-greif-nazi-germany-trojan-horse-essay-by-blaine-taylor.html

www.allthatsinteresting.com/operation-greif

www.warfarehistorynetwork.com/2016/0¼9/otto-skorzeny-and-operation-grief

www.rarehistoricalphotos.com/german-commandos-captured-american-uniform-1944

www.elpais.com/cultura/2020-03-11/otto-skorzeny-y-lawrence-de-arabia-extrana-pareja.html

www.history.com/news/how-did-the-nazis-really-lose-world-war-ii

www.alchetron.com/Operation-Greif

www.express.co.uk/news/world/656824/Adolf-Hitler-favourite-bodyguard-turned-hitman-Mossad-Israel-Otto-Skorzeny

www.warfarehistorynetwork.com/article/operation-nordwind-the-other-battle-of-the-bulge

www.battleofthebulge.org/2013/12/24/the-maginot-line-and-operation-nordwind

Chapter 3

www.war-experience.org/events/the-1940-norway-campaign

www.warfarehistorynetwork.com/article/the-battles-of-narvik-the-norwegian-campaign

www.tandfonline.com/doi/abs/10.108%3585522.1965.10414365

www.svd.se/a/ee765b4c-b93a-38e7-88b0-8ee3ee5d0046/ny-bild-av-sverige-under-krigsaren

www.en.wikipedia.org/wiki/Swedish_iron-ore_industry_during_World_War_II#cite_note-3

www.en.natmus.dk/historical-knowledge/denmark/german-occupation-1940-1945/

http://rinnanbanden.no/?s=1940-41

www.snl.no/Gerhard_Flesch

www.historicalsites.se/lander/norge/trondheim-misjonshotellet

www.adressa.no/nyheter/trondheim/i/lVV1po/tinghusets-hemmelige-rom

http://efaidnbmnnnibpcajpcglclefindmkaj/www.duo.uio.no/bitstream/handle/10852/59800/Avhandling-IdarFlo.pdf

www.okkupasjonen.no/4540-2

www.snl.no/Sonderabteilung_Lola

www.nrk.no/trondelag/xl/70-ar-siden-henrettelsen-av-norges-mest-fryktede-nazist-1.13350333

www.snl.no/Henry_Rinnan

www.iwm.org.uk/history/the-blitz-around-britain

www.bbc.co.uk/teach/articles/z7dyxyc

www.britishheritage.com/history/buckingham-palace-bombing-wwii

www.royal.uk/80th-anniversary-bombing-buckingham-palace-during-blitz

www.iwm.org.uk/history/the-blitz-around-britain

www.bbc.co.uk/teach/articles/z7dyxyc

www.worldhistory.org/London_Blitz

www.spywriter.wordpress.com/201½0/30/ritzkrieg-of-wartime-london/www.theritzlondon.com/new-years-eve-palm-court

www.theculturetrip.com/europe/united-kingdom/england/london/articles/the-ritz-iconic-london-hotel-closes-its-doors-for-first-time-in-a-century

www.spectator.co.uk/article/the-ritz-in-the-blitz

http://magazine.theritzlondon.com/Best-of-British-How-the-Ritz-Became-an-Iconic-UK-Institution

www.independent.co.uk/arts-entertainment/books/features/titbits-from-the-ritz-in-the-blitz-6257706.html

www.metro.co.uk/2017/03/15/the-halcyon-5-surprising-facts-you-never-knew-about-luxury-hotels-in-the-1940s-6511328

www.spectator.co.uk/article/the-ritz-in-the-blitz

www.theguardian.com/travel/2011/oct/30/sex-politics-spying-londons-wartime-hotels

www.cntraveller.com/article/blitz-in-the-ritz

www.dailymail.co.uk/home/books/article-2057217/To-hell-Blitz--Ritz--WEST-END-FRONT-THE-WARTIME-SECRETS-OF-LONDONS-GRAND-HOTELS-BY-MATTHEW-SWEET.html

www.arkivet.no/en/history/during-the-war

www.blodveger.info/norway-under-german-occupation

www.arkivverket.no/en/using-the-archives/world-war-ii/norwegians-in-captivity

www.cryopolitics.com/2015/03/31/in-norway-a-railroad-of-dreams-and-nightmares-across-the-arctic-circle

www.apollon.uio.no/artikler/2018/1_nsb_krigsfanger.html

www.railwaysarchive.co.uk/docsummary.php?docID=1026

www.bbc.com/news/uk-england-cambridgeshire-48474718

www.bbc.com/news/articles/cg66k6vp709o

www.sohamgrammar.org.uk/EdenG-soham-rail-disaster.htm

www.soham.ccan.co.uk/content/catalogue_item/hero-of-soham-rail-disaster

www.ltmuseum.co.uk/collections/stories/war/deep-level-shelters

www.livinglondonhistory.com/a-look-inside-clapham-souths-deep-level-shelter

www.londonist.com/london/secret/where-to-see-london-s-secret-deep-level-shelters

www.straitstimes.com/world/europe/deep-beneath-london-one-time-bomb-shelters-will-become-a-tourist-attraction

www.ltmuseum.co.uk/whats-on/hidden-london/clapham-south

www.iwm.org.uk/history/the-terrifying-german-revenge-weapons-of-the-second-world-war

www.nationalarchives.gov.uk/education/resources/british-response-v1-and-v2

www.the-low-countries.com/article/75-years-ago-the-nazis-took-revenge-on-the-allies-with-the-v1-and-v2

www.nationalmuseum.af.mil/Visit/Museum-Exhibits/Fact-Sheets/Display/Article/196145/german-v-weapons-desperate-measures

Chapter 4

Courier-Mail (Brisbane, Qld: 1933–1954), Wednesday, 24 October 1951, p.2 – Article featuring the recollections of Winston Churchill

William Brinkley, 'The Ninety and Nine: A Novel About the United States Navy in World War II', 1 January 1966

www.trove.nla.gov.au/newspaper/article/50242927

www.dignitymemorial.com/obituaries/greenwich-ct/william-fullilove-11837313

www.abmc.gov/news-events/news/impact-operation-shingle-during-world-war-ii

www.normandy1944.info/stories/william-h-fullilove?highlight=WyJhbnppbyJd

www.britannica.com/technology/landing-ship-tank

www.uboat.net/allies/warships/ship/12321.html

www.navsource.org/archives/10/16/160062.htm

www.iwm.org.uk/history/anzio-the-invasion-that-almost-failed

www.montecassinotours.com/en/notizie/the-gustav-line-the-main-german-defensive-line/?sku=15

www.uk.forceswarrecords.com/subject/657810768/royal-red-cross-class-2-arrc

www.scarletfinders.co.uk/174.html

www.rcnarchive.rcn.org.uk/volumes/92/Volume%2092%20Page%203

www.parliament.uk/about/living-heritage/building/cultural-collections/medals/collection/royal-red-cross/history/

www.thenotforgotten.org

www.rnrmc.org.uk/not-forgotten-association

www.greatwar.co.uk/organizations/not-forgotten-association.htm

www.ppcli.com/the-regiment/colonel-in-chief/past-colonel-chief/countess-mountbatten-burma

www.museumstjohn.org.uk/edwina-mountbatten-viceroys-house

www.brownhistory.substack.com/p/nehru-and-edwina-an-unconventional

www.southampton.ac.uk/archives/mountbattendigitisationproject/mountbattendigitisationladymountbatten-diaries4.page

www.english-heritage.org.uk/visit/blue-plaques/louis-mountbatten

www.history.uscg.mil/Browse-by-Topic/Notable-People/All/Article/1895289/vice-admiral-roy-l-raney

(www.mca-marines.org/leatherneck/go-down-like-marines-the-ill-fated-voyage-of-ss-henry-r-mallory)

www.military.wikia.org/wiki/Friedrich_August_Freiherr_von_der_Heydte

www.worldwarmedia.com/2017/02/10/operation-stosser-kampfgruppe-von-der-heydte-in-the-ardennes-part-ii

www.worldwars.com/operation-stosser-last-parachute-drop-fallschirmjager

www.worldwarmedia.com/2017/02/09/operation-stosser-kampfgruppe-von-der-heydte-in-the-ardennes-part-i
www.warfarehistorynetwork.com/2016/09/12/battle-of-the-bulge-the-airborne-fallschirmjager
www.warhistoryonline.com/world-war-ii/von-der-heydte-german-paratrooper.html
www.history.howstuffworks.com/world-war-ii/the-battle-of-the-bulge-timeline.htm#pt15
www.nla.gov.au/nla.obj-542532919/view?sectionId=nla.obj-549707574&partId=nla.obj-542587471#page/n18/mode/1up

Friedrich August von der Heydte, *Modern Irregular Warfare in Defense Policy and as a Military Phenomenon*, New York, NY: New Benjamin Franklin House, 1986
www.onlinebooks.library.upenn.edu/webbin/book/lookupid?key=olbp19381

www.core.ac.uk/download/pdf/36737983.pdf
www.wlym.com/archive/pdf/iclc/modernwarfare.pdf
Baron von der Heydte, *Daedalus Returned: Crete 1941*, London: Hutchinson, 1958

www.wingleader.co.uk/wp-content/uploads/2022/04/NACH-1944-Part2sample2.pdf
www.iwm.org.uk/collections/item/object/205452336
www.nationalww2museum.org/war/articles/apocalypse-dresden-february-1945
www.warhistoryonline.com/world-war-ii/bombing-of-dresden-wwii.html
www.history.co.uk/article/was-the-destruction-of-dresden-an-allied-war-crime

Chapter 5

www.massimotessitori.altervista.org/sovietwarplanes/pages/sb/tapani/finnish/finnish-story.htm
www.iwm.org.uk/history/a-short-history-of-the-winter-war
www.rferl.org/a/finlands-winter-war-with-the-soviet-union/30280490.html
www.history.com/news/what-was-the-winter-war
www.finlandatwar.com/what-were-the-red-army-losses-during-the-winter-war

www.operobal.uel.br/internacional/2024/04/25/the-brazilian-way-in-world-war-ii
www.guides.loc.gov/brazil-us-relations/brazil-world-war-ii
www.uas7.org/en/blog/brief-history-germans-migration-brazil#:~:text=Most%20German%20immigrants%2C%20therefore%2C%20arrived,instability%20of%20the%20Weimar%20Republic
www.history.com/news/how-south-america-became-a-nazi-haven
www.agenciabrasil.ebc.com.br/en/direitos-humanos/noticia/2024-04/un-receives-report-alarming-rise-neo-nazi-groups-brazil

www.history.navy.mil/browse-by-topic/wars-conflicts-and-operations/world-war-ii/1942/operation-torch.html
www.britannica.com/event/North-Africa-campaigns/The-Allied-landings-in-North-Africa
www.combinedops.com/Torch.htm
www.abmc.gov/news-events/news/remembering-operation-torch-allied-forces-land-north-africa-during-world-war-ii
www.worldhistory.org/Operation_Torch
www.bmmhs.org/mers-el-kebir-sinking-the-french-fleet
www.economist.com/democracy-in-america/2017/11/09/remembering-operation-torch-on-its-75th-anniversary

www.armouredcarriers.com/uss-robin-hms-victorious
www.history.navy.mil/browse-by-topic/wars-conflicts-and-operations/world-war-ii/1943/beyond-guadalcanal/uss-robin.html
www.rmg.co.uk/collections/objects/rmgc-object-67507
www.commons.wikimedia.org/wiki/File:HMS_Victorious_(R38)_at_Noumea_in_1943.jpg
www.naval-history.net/xGM-Chrono-04CV-Victorious.htm

www.gotavapen.se/gota/artiklar/fs/new/stalingrd/stalingrad_eng.htm
www.marksimner.me.uk/hearts-of-steel-the-sword-of-stalingrad
www.dw.com/en/the-battle-of-stalingrad-a-decisive-turning-point-in-ww2/a-42344954
www.france24.com/en/europe/20220823-they-would-have-preferred-hell-the-battle-of-stalingrad-80-years-on
www.winstonchurchill.org/publications/churchill-bulletin/bulletin-186-nov-2023/sword-of-stalingrad
www.en.wikipedia.org/wiki/Sword_of_Stalingrad#cite_note-5

www.iwm.org.uk/history/the-big-three-and-the-tehran-conference
www.history.state.gov/milestones/1937-1945/tehran-conf
www.britannica.com/biography/Winston-Churchill
www.catherinegracekatz.com/player-cards/project-one-ge6tm
www.winstonchurchill.hillsdale.edu/brooke-wayward-daughter
www.winstonchurchill.org/publications/finest-hour/finest-hour-175/sarah-churchill-more-than-a-thread

www.archiveswest.orbiscascade.org/ark:80444/xv21093
www.newspapers.com/article/tyrone-daily-herald-1966-hugh-baillie-de/2654608/
www.timesmachine.nytimes.com/timesmachine/1966/03/02/79299479.html?pageNumber=41

www.militarymemorialmuseum.com/museum/Generals/Army_Generals/General_Mark_W_Clark_5693
www.montecassinobelvedere.fr/en/leading-figures-in-the-battle-of-belvedere/general-mark-w-clark-en

www.100thbattalion.org/history/battalion-history

www.archives.gov/milestone-documents/executive-order-9066
www.nationalww2museum.org/war/articles/japanese-american-100th-infantry-battalion
www.archives.gov/education/lessons/japanese-relocation
www.nps.gov/articles/historyinternment.htm
www.trumanlibrary.gov/education/presidential-inquiries/japanese-american-internment
www.nationalww2museum.org/war/articles/japanese-american-incarceration#:~:text=the%20United%20States.-,Following%20the%20Pearl%20Harbor%20attack%2C%20however%2C%20a%20wave%20of%20antiJapanese,for%20most%20of%20the%20war
www.congress.gov/bill/100th-congress/house-bill/442
www.bbc.com/news/world-us-canada-38362504

www.royalfamily.org/dinasty/hm-king-peter-ii-of-yugoslavia
www.exilegov.hypotheses.org/2430
www.oac.cdlib.org/findaid/ark:/13030/tf367n99b3/entire_text
www.chicagomag.com/city-life/january-2013/the-odd-life-and-curious-burial-place-of-king-peter-ii-yugoslavias-deposed-monarch
www.unofficialroyalty.com/king-peter-ii-of-yugoslavia

Chapter 6

www.en.natmus.dk/historical-knowledge/denmark/german-occupation-1940-1945
www.encyclopedia.ushmm.org/content/en/article/denmark
www.danmarkshistorien.dk/en/open-online-course/modules/module-7-the-world-war-era-1914-1945/6-the-occupation-1940-1945
www.eternalechoes.org/application/files/4216/1028/9111/the-danish-population-during-the-german-occupation-1940-45_en_eternal_echoes.pdf
www.history.com/news/wwii-danish-jews-survival-holocaust

www.nationalww2museum.org/war/articles/liberation-paris
www.smithsonianmag.com/history/during-world-war-ii-the-liberation-of-paris-saved-the-french-capital-from-destruction-180984943
www.history.com/this-day-in-history/paris-liberated
www.rfi.fr/en/france/20240825-france-marks-80th-anniversary-of-the-liberation-of-paris-from-nazi-occupation
www.frankenhuiscollection.com/is-paris-burning

www.archives-nationales-travail.culture.gouv.fr/Decouvrir/Dossiers-du-mois/Les-sources-sur-le-Service-du-travail-obligatoire-STO-aux-Archives-nationales-du-monde-du-travail
www.guides.loc.gov/french-resistance-world-war-two
www.smithsonianmag.com/history/vichy-government-france-world-war-ii-willingly-collaborated-nazis-180967160/
www.cheminsdememoire.gouv.fr/en/maquis-0

www.visitmaastricht.com/events-calendar/3569436851/north-caves-incl-the-vault-maastricht-underground
http://themuseumtimes.com/hidden-caves-st-pietersberg-maastricht-netherlands
www.theprovince.com/news/local-news/children-of-two-war-weary-men-who-saved-a-priceless-dutch-art-collection-from-nazis-meet-in-vancouver
www.erim.eur.nl/fileadmin/erim_content/documents/Jeroen_Euwe_-_The_Dutch_art_market_1940-1945.pdf
www.fokum-jams.org/index.php/jams/article/view/6/21

www.nytimes.com/2018/1⁄1/arts/design/in-a-netherlands-museum-director-the-nazis-found-an-ally.html
http://jennifersalderson.com/2017/1⁄15/restitution-of-nazi-looted-artwork-after-world-war-two-a-dutch-perspective
www.monumentsmenfoundation.org
www.theculturetrip.com/europe/the-netherlands/articles/what-are-the-jezuietenberg-tunnels-and-why-are-they-covered-in-art
www.jezuietenberg.eu
www.messynessychic.com/2016/12/22/why-are-there-underground-jesuit-caves-filled-with-egyptian-and-islamic-art
www.history.com/news/adolf-hitler-artist-paintings-vienna
www.khanacademy.org/humanities/art-1010/german-art-between-the-wars/nazi-visual-culture/a/art-in-nazi-germany
www.essentialvermeer.com/misc/van_meegeren.html
http://jennifersalderson.com/2017/1⁄15/restitution-of-nazi-looted-artwork-after-world-war-two-a-dutch-perspective

www.engelsbergideas.com/essays/how-the-nazis-weaponised-charlemagne
www.nationalww2museum.org/war/articles/xix-corps-breaks-through-siegfried-line
www.warfarehistorynetwork.com/article/bloodbath-in-aachen
www.themightyendeavor.com/battles/the-battle-of-aachen-56
www.warfarehistorynetwork.com/article/the-battle-of-aachen-breaking-down-the-door-to-europe-in-wwii
www.bbc.com/news/world-europe-41113605

www.standwheretheyfought.jimdofree.com/alsace-2011-2012-sites-of-the-alsace-campaign-in-1944-1945-then-and-now
www.battleofthebulge.org/2017/06/13/the-battle-of-the-colmar-pocket
www.codenames.info/operation/battle-of-the-colmar-pocket
www.warfarehistorynetwork.com/article/destruction-of-the-colmar-pocket

Chapter 7

www.theconversation.com/what-happened-to-german-prisoners-of-war-in-britain-after-hitlers-defeat-74859
www.nationalarchives.gov.uk/help-with-your-research/research-guides/prisoners-of-war-british-hands
www.pattertonpowcamp.co.uk/the-history/wwii-pow-camps-in-britain-an-overview
www.theguardian.com/news/datablog/2010/nov/08/prisoner-of-war-camps-uk
www.howitreallywas.typepad.com/how_it_really_was/2006/12/group_captives_.html

www.austerityfashion.wordpress.com/2016/01/04/drab-and-ill-fitting-or-black-market-gold-how-classism-infected-our-perception-of-the-demob-suit
www.bbc.co.uk/ahistoryoftheworld/objects/fUA_R4bBT2Shubxy-aj8Zg
www.blightymilitaria.com/en-GB/home-guard-and-home-front/original-ww2-british-army-raf-demob-suit/prod_10175
www.westminsterresearch.westminster.ac.uk/download/79e28484f2e302a43bc3874
9440859d308cdb562e39dc22927492cc00ba67826/165382/Demob%20suits_
author%20manuscript_VRE.pdf
www.stpcgor.org.uk/peal_ringer/264
www.belltrust.co.uk/nations-bells-fall-silent-for-the-first-time-since-wwii
www.ringbell.co.uk/info/WarBells.htm

www.bbc.co.uk/history/ww2peopleswar/stories/77/a1991577.shtml
www.belltron.com/en/campanology

www.2009-2017.state.gov/p/io/potusunga/207325.htm
www.whitehouse.gov/about-the-white-house/presidents/harry-s-truman
www.digitallibrary.un.org/record/1300969?ln=en&v=pdf

www.bbc.com/historyofthebbc/research/bbc-at-war/end-of-the-war
www.berlinexperiences.com/the-battle-of-berlin-may-2nd-1945-the-end-of-nazi-berlin
www.kb.dk/en/inspiration/liberation

www.iwm.org.uk/history/what-you-need-to-know-about-ve-day
www.nationalww2museum.org/war/topics/end-world-war-ii-1945
www.visit.archives.gov/whats-on/explore-exhibits/75th-anniversary-v-e-day-end-wwii-europe
www.bbc.co.uk/newsround/48201749
www.winstonchurchill.org/resources/speeches/1941-1945-war-leader/to-v-e-crowds

www.winstonchurchill.org/the-life-of-churchill/war-leader/resigns-as-prime-minister
www.blog.nationalarchives.gov.uk/beveridge-report-foundations-welfare-state

www.mylearning.org/stories/the-beveridge-report-making-the-welfare-state/1237
www.gov.uk/government/history/past-prime-ministers/clement-attlee
www.nuffieldtrust.org.uk/health-and-social-care-explained/the-history-of-the-nhs

www.nps.gov/articles/000/rationing-of-non-food-items-on-the-world-war-ii-home-front.htm
www.iwm.org.uk/history/what-you-need-to-know-about-rationing-in-the-second-world-war
www.historic-uk.com/CultureUK/Rationing-in-World-War-Two
www.history.ox.ac.uk/::ognode-637356::/files/download-resource-printable-pdf-11

www.nationalww2museum.org/war/articles/britain-moves-leftward-labour-party-and-july-1945-election
www.bbc.co.uk/bitesize/guides/zgmf2nb/revision/4
www.iwm.org.uk/history/how-winston-churchill-and-the-conservative-party-lost-the-1945-election
www.labour-party.org.uk/manifestos/1945/1945-labour-manifesto.shtml
www.nybooks.com/articles/2018/04/19/clement-atlee-mouse-that-roared

www.giuniversity.wordpress.com/shrivenham
www.historynet.com/the-most-contented-gis-in-europe-october-99-american-history-feature.htm
www.cranfield.ac.uk/study/life-on-campus/life-at-shrivenham
www.jstor.org/stable/381434?seq=1

www.archives.gov/milestone-documents/servicemens-readjustment-act
www.va.gov/education/about-gi-bill-benefits
www.historyandpolicy.org/policy-papers/papers/when-affirmative-action-was-white

www2.gwu.edu/~erpapers/myday/displaydoc.cfm?_y=1946&_f=md000228
www.whitehouse.gov/about-the-white-house/first-families/anna-eleanor-roosevelt
www.un.org/en/about-us/un-charter
www.journals.openedition.org/ejas/11920
www.erpapers.columbian.gwu.edu/postwar-europe-haunting-horror-1946
www.biography.com/history-culture/eleanor-roosevelt
www.raabcollection.com/harry-truman-autograph/harry-truman-appoints-eleanor-roosevelt-special-US-ambassador
www.womenshistory.org/education-resources/biographies/eleanor-roosevelt

www.scienceandmediamuseum.org.uk/objects-and-stories/post-war-homelessness
www.squattinglondon.wordpress.com/2017/07/18/the-1946-squatters
www.bbc.co.uk/bitesize/guides/zsd68mn/revision/5
www.fet.uwe.ac.uk/conweb/house_ages/council_housing/section5.htm
www.bristolideas.co.uk/projects/homes-for-heroes-100/housing-after-the-second-world-war
www.sure.sunderland.ac.uk/id/eprint/16447/4/John%20Temple%20-%20Slaying%20Squalor%20-%20Final%20-%20November%202022.pdf

Chapter 8

www.npg.org.uk/collections/search/person/mp53128/james-allan-mollison
www.thisdayinaviation.com/tag/james-allan-mollison-mbe
www.glasgowlive.co.uk/news/history/tragic-story-glasgows-flying-sweethearts-22241717
www.saam.org.au/history_group_docs/SAAM%20Events%20-%20MOLLISON%20Jim%20&%20JOHNSON%20Amy.pdf
www.e-voice.org.uk/pevenseyhistory/pevensey-people-2/1931-jim-mollison-the-flyin/
www.itv.com/news/meridian/2024-02-29/last-piece-of-famous-female-aviators-doomed-plane-sold-at-auction

James Jinks, Peter Hennessy, *The Silent Deep: The Royal Navy Submarine Service Since 1945*, London: Allen Lane, 2015
Andy Simpson, *Why Would Anyone Want to Swing a Cat*, London: Constable & Robinson, 2013
http://bea-bee.com/Family_History.htm
www.nmmc.co.uk/2024/06/guide-to-nautical-flags
www.telegraph.co.uk/news/obituaries/1459259/Vice-Admiral-Sir-John-Roxburgh.html
www.thetimes.com/article/vice-admiral-sir-john-roxburgh-9g6tphhrzcp
www.uboat.net/allies/commanders/2176.html
www.uboat.net/allies/warships/ship/3552.html

www.paradata.org.uk/people/rev-bernard-egan
www.linda-parker.co.uk/airborne-chaplains-of-the-second-world-war
www.paradata.org.uk/article/chaplains-arnhem
www.pegasusarchive.org/arnhem/bernard_egan.htm#:~:text=Captain%2FReverend%20Bernard%20Egan&text=Bernard%20Egan%20was%20a%20Roman,Army%20to%20earn%20his%20wings
www.media.library.ohio.edu/digital/collection/p15808coll15/id/5641
www.discovery.nationalarchives.gov.uk/details/r/D7348545
The National Archives of the UK – Reference WO 373/3/407

www.af.mil/About-Us/Biographies/Display/Article/105528/general-carl-a-spaatz
www.media.defense.gov/2010/Oct/12/2001330126/-1/-1/0/AFD-101012-035.pdf
www.americanairmuseum.com/archive/person/carl-andrew-spaatz
www.spaatz.org/the-awards/the-general-carl-a-spaatz-award
www.af.mil/About-Us/Biographies/Display/Article/107225/general-james-harold-doolittle
www.cmohs.org/recipients/james-h-doolittle
www.defense.gov/News/Feature-Stories/Story/Article/2998360/medal-of-honor-monday-army-air-corps-gen-jimmy-doolittle
www.history.com/topics/world-war-ii/james-h-doolittle
www.history.navy.mil/browse-by-topic/wars-conflicts-and-operations/world-war-ii/1942/halsey-doolittle-raid.html

www.imdb.com/name/nm0000061/bio
www.tyrone-power.com/biography_ty.html
www.en.wikipedia.org/wiki/Tyrone_Power
www.imdb.com/name/nm0030246
www.britannica.com/place/Hollywood-California
www.en.wikipedia.org/wiki/Annabella_(actress)
www.nationalww2museum.org/war/articles/world-war-ii-and-popular-culture

www.pacificwrecks.com/unit/usaaf/49fg/9fs.html
www.herocards.us/hero79
www.nationalww2museum.org/war/articles/richard-bong-medal-of-honor
www.wahf.org/hall-of-fame/richard-bong
www.militaryhallofhonor.com/honoree-record.php?id=72
www.afhistory.af.mil/FAQs/Fact-Sheets/Article/639628
www.apnews.com/article/richard-bong-marge-plane-new-guinea-expedition-76381a450191cc56dc96a88c6ad23daf
www.flyingmag.com/news/u-s-wwii-ace-richard-bongs-p-38-believed-found

www.ww2ondeadline.com/2021/06/06/covering-the-day-of-days
www.loc.gov/static/programs/national-recording-preservation-board/documents/DDayRadioBroadcastHicks.pdf
www.foxnews.com/science/d-day-discovery-reporters-famous-recording-found
http://ww2ondeadline.com/202%4/25/d-day-george-hicks-report-audio-nbc-blue-uss-ancon/

www.navyhistory.org.au/obituary-admiral-sir-victor-smith-ac-1913-1998
www.faaaa.asn.au/vat-smith-father-fleet-air-arm
www.navyhistory.org.au/admiral-sir-victor-smith-ac-kbe-cb-dsc
www.navy.gov.au/biography/admiral-sir-victor-alfred-trumper-smith

www.nationalww2museum.org/war/articles/ernie-pyle-world-war-ii
www.britannica.com/biography/Ernie-Pyle
www.nbcnews.com/id/wbna22980127
www.abqlibrary.org/whowaserniepyle
www.indianahistory.org/education/education-resources/educator-resources/famous-hoosiers/ernie-pyle

www.49squadron.co.uk/personnel_index/detail/Crabb_JL
www.heraldscotland.com/memorials/death-notices/death/30498497.john-louis-crabb
www.ibccdigitalarchive.lincoln.ac.uk/omeka/collections/document/10754
www.aircrewremembered.com
www.49squadron.co.uk/gallery_4
www.49squadron.co.uk/extras/turin

www.npg.org.uk/collections/search/person/mp07514/francis-owen-frank-salisbury
www.harpenden-history.org.uk/harpenden-history/people-2/artists/frank-o-salisbury/winston_s_churchill_and_frank_o_salisbury
www.artrenewal.org/artists/frank-o-salisbury/3319

www.nationalww2museum.org
www.cmohs.org
www.cmohs.org/recipients/walter-d-ehlers
www.nationalww2museum.org/war/articles/walter-david-ehlers-medal-of-honor
www.eisenhowerfoundation.net/ikessoldiers/walter-ehlers
www.pbs.org/kenburns/the-war/walter-ehlers

www.aircrewremembered.com/kirkwood-james-1.html
www.raf-pathfinders.com/crew-kirkwood
www.rafpathfinders.com/16-17-december-1943-the-night-of-the-fog/#:~:text=In%20total%2C%20Bomber%20Command%20suffered,later%20died%20of%20their%20injuries
www.cwgc.org/find-records/find-war-dead/casualty-details/2455678/james-kirkwood/

www.rafcommands.com/database/awards/details.php?qnum=146119&qname=KIRKWOOD

www.rafcommands.com/database/wardead/details.php?qnum=18473
National Archives UK – Air 27/656/1 and Air 27/656/2
www.discovery.nationalarchives.gov.uk/details/r/D8454143
www.discovery.nationalarchives.gov.uk/details/r/D8454144
www.cwgc.org/find-records/find-war-dead/casualty-details/2201396/william-henry-frederick-george-hagon/
www.thegazette.co.uk/London/issue/36196/data.pdf
www.losses.internationalbcc.co.uk/loss/211508
Article in *Middlesex County Times*, Saturday, 31 March 1945:
www.findagrave.com/memorial/18403571/william-henry-hagon#view-photo=302245778
www.thegazette.co.uk/London/issue/36258/supplement/5132/data.pdf

www.frankfallaarchive.org
www.theislandwiki.org/index.php/Louisa_Gould
www.theislandwiki.org/index.php/Harold_Le_Druillenec%27s_Belsen_trial_evidence
www.bbc.co.uk/archive/harold-osmond-le-druillenec/zdvghbk
www.itv.com/news/channel/2016-04-07/itv-news-uncovers-rare-interview-with-jerseyman-who-survived-german-concentration-camp
www.kingsbridge-today.co.uk/article.cfm?id=109345&headline=Salcombe%20man%20traces%20survivor%20of%20Bergen%20Belsen%20concentration%20camp§ionIs=news&searchyear=2017
www.bailiwickexpress.com/jsy/news/jersey-belsen-survivors-account-tells-mass-graves-and-cannibalism/#.XwwpvSgzY2x
www.bbc.com/news/world-europe-jersey-45104247
www.dailymail.co.uk/news/article-4322102/As-new-film-shows-price-paid-death.html
Dr Gilly Carr, Professor Paul Sanders, Dr Louise Willmot, *Protest, Defiance and Resistance in the Channel Islands*, London: Bloomsbury Academic, 2015
www.mirror.co.uk/tv/tv-news/bravery-real-life-heroes-who-10098814
www.historycollection.com/20-facts-about-the-nazi-occupation-of-the-uks-channel-islands/15
www.bbc.com/news/world-europe-jersey-39872771
www.jerseyeveningpost.com/news/2017/06/29/concentration-camp-survivors-body-to-be-returned-to-jersey
www.independent.co.uk/news/uk/home-news/cannibalism-rampant-at-nazi-concentration-camp-new-documents-reveal-a6960876.html
www.dailymail.co.uk/news/article-3516690/The-British-survivor-Belsen-concentration-camp-battle-rampant-cannibalism-torture-hands-Gestapo-harrowing-new-records-show.html
www.bbc.com/news/education-51538701
www.bbc.co.uk/programmes/p04hd4hm